Desk Reference on
AMERICAN
CRIMINAL JUSTICE

BOOKS IN THE DESK REFERENCE SERIES

CONGRESSIONAL QUARTERLY'S

Desk Reference on
AMERICAN
CRIMINAL
JUSTICE

PATRICIA G. BARNES

CQ PRESS

A Division of Congressional Quarterly Inc.
Washington, D.C.

CQ Press
A Division of Congressional Quarterly Inc.
1414 22nd St. N.W.
Washington, D.C. 20037

(202) 822-1475; (800) 638-1710

www.cqpress.com

Printed in the United States of America

∞ The paper used in this publication meets the minimum requirements of the American National Standard for Information Sciences—Permanence of Paper for Printed Library Materials, ANSI Z39.48-1992.

Library of Congress Cataloging-in-Publication Data

Barnes, Patricia G.
   CQ's desk reference on American criminal justice : over 500 answers to frequently
asked questions from law enforcement to corrections / Patricia G. Barnes.
      p.   cm.
   Includes bibliographical references and index.
   ISBN 1-56802-569-6 (cloth : alk. paper)
   1. Criminal justice, Administration of—United States. I. Title: Desk reference on American
criminal justice. II. Congressional Quarterly, inc. III. Title.

HV9950 B364 2001
364.973—dc21   00-045492

To Jeb.

May you always find justice.

CONTENTS

PREFACE

All Americans are touched, directly or indirectly, by the criminal justice system. Americans annually spend billions of dollars for taxes and insurance premiums in response to crime. This cost pales in comparison to the human cost of crime. Millions of Americans become crime victims, suffering emotional, physical, and financial trauma, and millions of Americans who commit crimes enter the criminal justice system, often leaving behind devastated families and communities. The number of people currently supervised by the United States correctional system exceeds the population of Massachusetts. Approximately two million people are in jails and prisons, and more than four million are on probation or parole. These numbers reflect a threefold increase in two decades. Even as crime declines, the system continues to grow.

Congressional Quarterly's *Desk Reference on American Criminal Justice* presents an accurate and up-to-date picture, in question-and-answer format, of the three basic institutions that make up the criminal justice system: courts, law enforcement, and corrections. Using information derived from hundreds of diverse sources, including government reports and scholarly publications, the book outlines the workings of the institutions that arrest, prosecute, sentence, imprison, and execute those who commit crimes. The *Desk Reference* is invaluable both as a reference tool and as a primer on this important topic.

Chronicling the history of the criminal justice system from America's founding to the present, the *Desk Reference* pauses at important milestones, such as the due process revolution of the 1960s and the war on drugs of the 1980s. The book provides both a comprehensive picture of the operations of the criminal justice system and a glimpse of the culture surrounding the courts, law enforcement, and corrections. Readers can discover, for example, which police department's officers refused to wear uniforms, why juvenile court was founded, and which prison warden was hanged.

Wary of big government after living under oppressive English rule, the Founders believed that criminal justice should largely be handled by the states. As a result, America's criminal justice system is among the most decentralized in the world, consisting of an array of institutions and bureaucracies at the federal, state, and local levels. The private sector also plays a role, most notably through the rise of private, for-profit prisons. The *Desk Reference* provides an invaluable guide through the criminal justice maze by identifying the major components of the system and the jurisdictional boundaries of courts, law enforcement agencies, and correctional institutions at the various levels of government.

The book begins by exploring the basic question, What is a crime? Every society claims the right to penalize citizens who inflict harm upon others. The criminal justice system balances the collective good against the rights of the individual, and the price an individual pays for violating society's laws may be the loss of freedom. The *Desk Reference* examines how the boundaries of acceptable behavior in American society are defined by focusing on the Bill of Rights, relevant U.S. Supreme Court decisions, and the ways in which states and the federal government address crime. Step by step, readers learn how crime is defined, classified, and measured. The *Desk Reference* documents fluctuations in America's crime rate and looks at the effects that drugs, guns, and other societal influences have on crime. It explores theories about what causes crime and how to curtail future crime, and it also reports on the victims of crime and the rise of the victims' rights movement.

The federal government's role in criminal justice has grown tremendously in recent decades, but criminal justice still remains largely a matter for the individual states. Each state criminal justice system developed independently. However, one thread binds the parts together—the U.S. Constitution. The U.S. Supreme Court has interpreted the Constitution to require that criminal defendants be accorded fair and equal treatment. The book examines landmark Court decisions pertaining to the fundamental rights of criminal defendants, from the point at which a law enforcement officer may stop and question a citizen, through prosecution, to the end result (which, typically, is conviction).

In the 1990s new sentencing policies, including laws that require juveniles to be tried as adults in adult court and felons to serve lengthier prison sentences, fueled an unprecedented expansion of prisons. The *Desk Reference* looks at these new policies, as well as at changes in court systems that address the problem of repeat criminal offenders, such as the creation of drug courts emphasizing treatment and rehabilitation. The book also examines the caseload of the federal and state criminal courts and shows what happens as cases make their way through the court system.

In the summer of 2000 newspaper headlines alternately excoriated the New York City police for being both too aggressive and too passive, in response to different circumstances. The *Desk Reference* examines the fine line that police tread as they implement different theories of policing and apply police procedures for using force. The book reviews the changing nature of law enforcement, how police departments operate, the perils of the job, and issues related to police corruption and oversight of police. In addition, it provides a comprehensive overview of federal and state law enforcement agencies, and it examines the role of campus and private police organizations in law enforcement.

The *Desk Reference* ends with a chapter examining the historical influences that have shaped America's prison system, how prisons today operate, the demographics of the prison population, and prison release policies. This chapter also describes the history of the nation's most drastic sanction—capital punishment—and the controversy surrounding its application.

The *Desk Reference* can be used in two ways. Readers seeking to obtain quick and convenient access to specific facts relating to the criminal justice system can look up their topic in the index or table of contents. To obtain a broad understanding of a topic or of the criminal justice system in general, readers can proceed through the book sequentially. Many answers are cross-referenced to alert the reader to additional relevant information. The appendix contains supplemental research materials, including the text of the U.S. Constitution, a glossary of common legal terms, a guide to reading a case citation, and contact information for various criminal justice agencies.

Thanks go to John R. McKivigan, for his support and advice as this volume took shape; to the talented folks at CQ Press, especially Christopher Anzalone, Patricia Gallagher, and Tom Roche, who made my sojourn into the byzantine world of crime and punishment a pleasant journey; and to Sharon Lamberton, for her graceful editing. Many thanks also to the helpful staff members at the Bureau of Justice Statistics of the U.S. Department of Justice and the National Center for State Courts; they provide reliable facts and figures in the area of criminal justice. Finally, thanks to my older sister, Kris Barnes-Veilleux, who many years ago helped me put back a black plastic spider on a rubber band that I desperately wanted to misappropriate from the shelves of a drugstore in Plattsburgh, New York.

Patricia G. Barnes

Desk Reference on

AMERICAN
CRIMINAL JUSTICE

THE CRIMINAL JUSTICE SYSTEM

IN GENERAL

Q **1. What is the criminal justice system?**

A The criminal justice system is less a system than a series of institutions and procedures that society has created to enforce accepted standards of conduct. Broadly speaking, the criminal justice system has three branches. Federal, state, and local governments operate independently to enforce criminal laws within their respective jurisdictions. Within each branch, the system typically consists of three subdivisions: law enforcement, courts, and corrections. State and local communities bear most of the responsibility for fighting crime, but the federal government plays a critical role by allocating federal dollars and resources toward nationwide priorities, such as drug abuse prevention.

The United States has no federal police force, per se. However, the U.S. Congress has authorized many agencies—including, most notably, the Federal Bureau of Investigation (FBI)—to enforce federal laws. These agencies refer cases to United States Attorneys Offices for prosecution in federal courts.

The federal court system includes the U.S. Supreme Court, twelve midlevel regional appellate courts (called U.S. Courts of Appeals) and the U.S. Court of Appeals for the Federal Circuit, several specialty courts, including the U.S. Court of Appeals for the Armed Forces, and ninety-four federal trial courts (called U.S. District Courts).

As the highest federal court and the highest court in the land, the U.S. Supreme Court is the final arbiter of the meaning of the U.S. Constitution. It is the only court that is specifically created by the U.S. Constitution.

Defendants who are convicted of federal crimes generally are either incarcerated in federal prisons, most of which are operated by the Federal Bureau of Prisons, or allowed to remain in the community under the supervision of the U.S. Probation Office. Crimes that have a distinct national or interstate aspect, such as treason or kidnapping and transporting across state lines, are exclusively the jurisdiction of the federal government. The vast majority of arrests, prosecutions, and incarcerations, however, take place on the state and local level. In 1998 14.6 million criminal cases were filed in state courts, compared to 58,000 in federal courts.

Every state but Hawaii has a state police force. State police officers or troopers patrol state highways and freeways. Other types of state law enforcement officers include fire marshals, fish and game wardens, and alcoholic beverage control officers.

Each state court system is unique, though all include trial courts that hear civil and criminal cases. All states have at least one high court or state court of last resort. Many states also have intermediate appellate courts that decide most appeals from the lower courts, leaving the state court of last resort free to decide the most important appeals. Most states also operate separate court and correctional systems for juveniles, or children and youths under the age of eighteen. Cases involving juveniles may be transferred to the adult court system, depending on the type of crime involved, the age of the juvenile, and other factors.

State correctional systems typically consist of a network of state prisons that are often bolstered by county and municipal jails. State prisons typically feature varying levels of security, from super-maximum to minimum security.

Many experts theorize that all crime is local—that crime trends reflect local conditions and affect local communities. Certainly, the vast majority of people come into contact with the criminal justice system at the local level.

Local police departments investigate most reported crimes. Authority for local law enforcement may be split between a municipal police department and a county sheriff's office. Sheriffs typically are responsible for protecting state courts and operating county jails.

Counties and municipalities also operate correctional systems that include jails and probation offices, sometimes including special facilities for juvenile offenders.

Although technically independent of one another, the federal, state, and local criminal justice systems are highly interconnected. For example, the federal and state governments have overlapping jurisdiction over certain crimes. Police and prosecutors may cooperate to investigate and prosecute crimes, may work independently, or may even compete with each other. Ideally, law enforcement officers, prosecutors, the judiciary, and correctional officers from both the federal and state systems work together to ensure the effective administration of justice.

Q 2. What type of criminal justice system was envisioned in the U.S. Constitution?

A When it was ratified on June 21, 1788, the U.S. Constitution established a general framework for the federal judicial system, including "one supreme Court and such inferior Courts as Congress may ordain from time to time." However, the Constitution said surprisingly little about the criminal justice system. Clearly, the Framers envisioned a system to be administered by the states. After experiencing the tyranny of the British criminal justice system, the Framers were loath to grant too much power to a new federal government. The Constitution grants all power to the states except that which it specifically delegates to the federal government. Furthermore, the Constitution divides federal power among the executive, legislative, and judicial branches, and includes checks and balances to prevent any one of these branches from dominating the others. The chief provisions of the Constitution relating to the criminal justice system are:

- Article I authorizes Congress "to provide for the Punishment of counterfeiting the securities and current Coin of the United States, [and] . . . to define and punish Piracies and Felonies committed on the high Seas, and Offenses against the Law of Nations"; to create "Tribunals inferior to the supreme Court." Article I also ensures the right of prisoners to challenge the legality of their imprisonment in the federal courts. The "Privilege of the Writ of *Habeas Corpus* [you shall have the body] shall not be suspended, unless when in cases of Rebellion or Invasion the public Safety may require it."
- Article III vests the judicial power of the United States in the U.S. Supreme Court and in inferior courts "as the Congress shall from time to time ordain and establish." It guarantees criminal defendants the right to a jury trial: "The Trial of all Crimes, except in Cases of Impeachment, shall be by Jury; and such Trial shall be held in the State where the said Crimes shall have been committed; but when not committed within any State, the Trial shall be at such Place or Places as the Congress may by Law have directed." Article III defines the crime of treason as levying war against the United States or "in adhering to their Enemies, giving them Aid and Comfort" and stipulates that no person shall be convicted of treason "unless on the Testimony of two Witnesses to the same overt Act, or on Confession in open Court."
- Article IV contains an extradition clause that ensures that a criminal may not flee from one state to another to escape prosecution: "any person charged in any State with Treason, Felony or other Crime, who shall flee from Justice and be found in another State, shall on Demand of the executive Authority of the State from which he fled, be delivered up, to be removed to the State having Jurisdiction of the Crime."
- Article VI establishes the U.S. Constitution as the supreme law of the land, binding the judges in every state.

See 312 From where do law enforcement officers derive their authority?

Q **3. What crimes are mentioned in the Constitution?**

A The U.S. Constitution specifically mentions only three categories of federal crimes. Article I gives Congress the power to punish counterfeiting of securities and currency and to punish piracies and felonies committed on the high seas. Article III gives Congress the power to declare the punishment of treason.

Q 4. What is the necessary and proper clause of the U.S. Constitution?

A The necessary and proper clause of the U.S. Constitution (Article I, Section 8, Clause 18) gives Congress the power to define and punish crimes whenever it is necessary and proper to do so to safeguard the goals of government and society.

Q 5. What is the significance of the Bill of Rights to criminal law?

A The Bill of Rights—the first ten amendments to the U.S. Constitution—protects the rights of individual citizens against abuses by the federal government. Ratified on December 15, 1791, the Bill of Rights has been called America's first code of criminal procedure.

Many freedoms considered fundamental to the American way of life are specified in the Bill of Rights. The Fourth Amendment protects citizens from unreasonable searches and seizures; the Fifth Amendment protects citizens against self-incrimination and double jeopardy; and the Sixth Amendment guarantees criminal defendants the right to assistance of counsel, to confront witnesses, to an impartial jury, and to a speedy and public trial. The Eighth Amendment protects citizens against cruel and unusual punishment or excessive fines.

Initially only the federal government was required to adhere to the Bill of Rights. However, the U.S. Supreme Court has ruled that most of the amendments that make up the Bill of Rights also apply to the states through the Fourteenth Amendment. Ratified in 1868, the Fourteenth Amendment prohibits states from depriving any person of life, liberty, or property without due process of law. Two guarantees have not been extended to apply to the states: the right not to be subject to excessive bail and the right to a grand jury indictment in felony cases.

See 152 May states deviate from requirements of the U.S. Constitution?

Q **6. What is a crime?**

A The word *crime* derives from the Latin *crimen*, which means fault or accusation. A crime is a public wrong. A crime is an act or a failure to act that violates a public law or statute and for which punishment may be imposed by government.

The concept of crime held by American colonists was influenced by the common law of England, which had emerged through custom or judicial rulings over many generations. English common law generally divided crimes into two categories: *Mala in se* crimes, which were inherently immoral or dangerous crimes, such as murder and rape, and *Mala prohibita* crimes, which were not naturally evil but were criminal because the law defined them as such. *Mala prohibita* crimes might include such things as regulatory violations or bigamy. After the American Revolution, state governments converted many of the familiar common law crimes into statutory offenses.

Today the U.S. Congress and state legislatures enact laws that define criminal behavior within their respective jurisdictions. The legislative branch, not the judiciary, is the dominant criminal law policymaker. However, laws are subject to interpretation by the courts and must not violate the U.S. Constitution or the constitution of the state in which they were enacted. Judges often use common law precedents from prior judicial rulings when they interpret laws.

Although the immediate victim of a crime is often an individual, a crime is considered an offense against the state and the public at large. A violent crime, for example, may threaten the peace and security of an entire community and leave many besides the immediate victim in fear for their lives.

Q **7. What is the difference between civil and criminal law?**

A Criminal law traditionally has been defined as public law that is enforced by the government on behalf of society for the protection of society. Civil law refers to the body of private law that pertains to civil relationships, such as citizenship, marriage, divorce, and certain contractual relationships.

Because a crime is an offense against the community and not just the victim, a criminal action is brought by the government. The government may proceed even if the prosecution is contrary to the wishes of the immediate victim. A defendant must be proven guilty beyond a reasonable doubt, which is the highest standard of proof contained in the U.S. justice system. This high standard reflects the severity of the possible sanctions faced by the defendant. America's Founders wanted to lessen the possibility of convicting an innocent person and to lessen the disparity between the government, which has enormous resources at its disposal, and the defendant, who may have few, if any, resources.

By contrast, civil law typically is enforced by individuals acting on their own behalf. In a civil lawsuit the moving party, or plaintiff, generally alleges a personal injury, such as negligence, or a breach of a contract. The court attempts to remedy the dispute by restoring the victim to his or her prior condition. The court may order the payment of money or direct a party to perform or refrain from performing a specific act. Because there is no threat of jail, the standard of proof is less than in a criminal proceeding. Typically plaintiffs must prove their claim only by a preponderance of the evidence—that is, by showing their case to be more believable than the defendant's.

When an action gives rise to both a criminal prosecution and a civil suit, the two proceedings are conducted independently of each other. For example, one-time football star O.J. Simpson was acquitted after a criminal trial for the 1994 murders of his ex-wife and her friend, but in later civil proceedings he was found liable for their wrongful deaths and ordered to pay a judgment of $33.5 million.

See 278 Are more civil or criminal cases filed in state courts?

Q 8. How does an act become criminal?

A A general legal principle, *nullum crimen sine lege,* attests that there can be no crime without a law. This principle appeals to the underlying theory that no person should be punished for conduct that was not prohibited at the time it was committed.

Criminal law in the United States originally derives from the English common law that was passed down over the centuries by custom and judicial precedent. Under the common law, cases were decided by reference to prior judicial decisions. Over the last two centuries the common law has been largely supplanted in the United States by laws enacted by the federal government or by state or local governments. Today an act becomes criminal when a legislative body enacts a law declaring it to be so.

Q 9. What is an *ex post facto* law?

A An *ex post facto* (after-the-fact) law retroactively alters an individual's rights. In the United States, criminal laws must be prospective, or forward-looking. Examples of ex post facto laws are laws that criminalize an act that was legal at the time it was committed; laws that increase the severity of a crime or enhance its punishment after-the-fact; laws that take away protections afforded a defendant at the time the act was committed; or laws that alter the amount of evidence required to convict the defendant. Ex post facto laws are prohibited by Article I, Section 9, of the U.S. Constitution. The prohibition against such laws was derived by the Framers from English common law.

Q **10. What rights are afforded to citizens by the Fourth Amendment to the U.S. Constitution?**

A The Fourth Amendment protects the basic freedom of Americans to be secure in their "persons, houses, papers, and effects, against unreasonable searches and seizures." This amendment prevents the government from making an arrest or searching someone's person or property without sufficient legal justification.

The U.S. Supreme Court has ruled that the Fourth Amendment indicates a preference that a search or seizure be conducted pursuant to a warrant. However, the Court has ruled that police may act without a warrant in certain circumstances, such as to prevent a criminal from fleeing or destroying evidence. The Fourth Amendment provides that "no Warrants shall issue, but on probable cause, supported by Oath or affirmation, and particularly describing the place to be searched, and the persons or things to be seized."

Police typically apply to a judge or a magistrate for a warrant. They must describe the places and persons to be searched and the things or persons to be seized. They also must file an affidavit or sworn statement that lists facts and circumstances that would lead a reasonable officer to believe that the places or persons to be searched will produce the items or persons named in the search warrant. Interpretation of the Fourth Amendment continues to lead to controversy, as the U.S. Supreme Court attempts to strike a balance between the rights of the accused, the need of police to investigate crime, and the broader right of society to be free from crime.

See 161 What is a warrant? 177 When does a citizen have a reasonable expectation of privacy? 178 When can law enforcement officers search a suspect or premises without a warrant?

Q **11. What rights are afforded defendants under the Fifth Amendment to the U.S. Constitution?**

A The Fifth Amendment to the U.S. Constitution limits the government's power to bring an individual to trial. It protects defendants from brutal tactics by police and prosecutors. It specifies the following rights:

- The right to have a serious criminal charge initiated by a grand jury, and not by police or prosecutors: "No person shall be held to answer for a capital, or otherwise infamous crime, unless on a presentment or indictment of a Grand Jury, except in cases arising in the land or naval forces, or in the Militia, when in actual service in time of War or public danger." The U.S. Supreme Court has ruled that this right applies to defendants facing felony charges in federal court, but the Court has not extended this right to defendants in state courts.

- Protection from multiple prosecutions for the same criminal conduct. No person shall "be subject for the same offence to be twice put in jeopardy of life or limb." This part of the Fifth Amendment is known as the double jeopardy clause.
- The privilege against self-incrimination. No person "shall be compelled in any criminal case to be a witness against himself."
- The right to due process of law. "No person shall be . . . deprived of life, liberty, or property without due process of law."

See 167 What is the significance of Miranda v. Arizona? *168 What are the Miranda warnings? 174 What happens if a suspect refuses to participate in a lineup or to give a blood or DNA sample? 175 What is the right to silence? 182 What entity formally charges an accused person with a crime? 216 What is a reasonable doubt? 225 Can a defendant ever be compelled to testify? 237 Can a crime be prosecuted more than once?*

Q 12. What rights are afforded defendants under the Sixth Amendment to the U.S. Constitution?

A The Sixth Amendment to the U.S. Constitution gives defendants important protections against false accusations and arbitrary acts of government. It provides defendants in all criminal prosecutions with the right to:

- a speedy and public trial;
- a trial by "an impartial jury of the State and district wherein the crime shall have been committed, which district shall have been previously ascertained by law";
- be "informed of the nature and cause of the accusation";
- be "confronted with the witnesses" against them;
- have "compulsory process for obtaining witnesses" in their favor; and
- "have the Assistance of Counsel" for their defense.

The right to a jury trial is widely considered to be a keystone of the American criminal justice system. However, this right is not absolute. This clause has always been interpreted in light of common law, which did not provide jury trials for petty offenses. The U.S. Supreme Court has ruled that defendants in all felony cases must be provided the right to a jury trial. However, the Court has declined to require states to provide the right to a jury trial to defendants who are facing misdemeanor charges that carry a penalty of potential imprisonment of less than six months, even if the defendant faces several charges having an aggregate possible sentence of more than six months in jail.

See 166 What is the significance of Gideon v. Wainwright? *168 What are the Miranda warnings? 170 Is the right to counsel unqualified? 171 When may a suspect invoke his or her right to counsel? 204 When is evidence admissible at trial? 217 What is the difference between a grand jury and a petit jury? 222 Must a jury be unanimous to convict a defendant of a crime? 223 Do defendants have a right to represent themselves at trial? 224 What is effective assistance of counsel?*

Q 13. Does the U.S. Constitution guarantee a jury of one's peers?

A The U.S. Constitution does not specifically mention the right to a jury of one's peers. However, the U.S. Supreme Court has found that this right is implied in the equal protection clause and in the Sixth Amendment of the U.S. Constitution. The notion of a jury of one's peers is traceable to 1215, when King John of England, seeking to placate rebellious barons, signed the Magna Carta and promised that "[n]o free man shall be taken or imprisoned . . . except by the lawful judgment of his peers or by the law of the land."

More than a century ago, the U.S. Supreme Court ruled in *Strauder v. West Virginia* (1879) that a state violated the equal protection clause when it put a black defendant on trial before a petit jury from which blacks were purposefully excluded. The Court invalidated a state statute that provided that only white men could serve as jurors.

According to the Court, "The very idea of a jury is a body . . . composed of the peers or equals of the person whose rights it is selected or summoned to determine; that is, of his neighbors, fellows, associates, persons having the same legal status in society as that which he holds." More recently, the Court has ruled that the Sixth Amendment right to a fair trial guarantees that a petit jury be selected from a pool of names representing a cross section of the community.

Since *Strauder* the Court has consistently refrained from imposing any requirement that a jury mirror the racial or ethnic diversity of a community, stating that it would be impossible to apply a concept of proportional representation to a petit jury in view of society's heterogeneous nature.

See 217 What is the difference between a grand jury and a petit jury?

Q 14. What rights are afforded defendants under the Eighth Amendment to the U.S. Constitution?

A The Eighth Amendment to the U.S. Constitution protects the presumption of innocence that is a cornerstone of the American criminal justice system. This amendment limits the government's ability to incarcerate individuals who have been arrested but not convicted of a crime. It also limits the type of punishments that the state can impose. The Eighth Amendment contains two important prohibitions:

- The government may not impose a requirement of excessive bail or excessive fines on criminal defendants.
- The government may not impose cruel and unusual punishments.

Bail is money or property pledged by a defendant to guarantee his or her appearance at trial. The U.S. Supreme Court has deemed excessive bail to be any amount higher than the amount reasonably calculated to ensure a defendant's appearance at trial. The U.S. Supreme Court has never explicitly ruled that the excessive bail prohibition applies to the states.

What constitutes cruel and unusual punishment is a topic of continuing debate. The U.S. Supreme Court has indicated that this clause in the Eighth Amendment generally protects against unusual methods of punishment but, except in death penalty cases, does not necessarily bar punishments that are cruel or disproportionate to the crime. The Court has declined to pronounce the death penalty to be cruel and unusual, stating that the Eighth Amendment's cruel and unusual punishments clause must be measured against evolving standards of decency.

See 189 What is bail? 540 What does the U.S. Constitution say about capital punishment?

Q 15. What is due process?

A Due process refers to the principle of treating all persons equally in accordance with the law. The due process clauses of the Fifth and Fourteenth amendments of the U.S. Constitution guarantee that fair procedures will be used when government acts to deny individuals life, liberty, or property.

The concept of due process is traceable to 1215, when England's King John signed the Magna Carta and promised that "[n]o free man shall be taken or imprisoned . . . except by the lawful judgment of his peers or by the law of the land." The Fifth Amendment provides that no person shall be deprived of life, liberty, or property without due process of law. This guarantee was intended to protect personal rights, property, and freedom from unreasonable and arbitrary restraint by the federal government. When adopted, the Fifth Amendment due process clause applied solely to the federal government and not to the states.

The Fourteenth Amendment to the U.S. Constitution, which was ratified in 1868, after the Civil War, prohibits states from depriving individuals of life, liberty, or property. The Fourteenth Amendment's due process clause was the vehicle used by the U.S. Supreme Court to extend many of the fundamental protections of the Bill of Rights to the states.

Due process generally protects people from governmental overreaching in the operation of both substantive and procedural law. Substantive due process refers to whether the law itself is unfair in that it offends society's notions of justice. This type of due process has been cited by the U.S. Supreme Court to protect certain fundamental rights of all citizens, such as the right to privacy. Procedural due process refers to the methods used to enforce legal rights. For example, the U.S. Supreme Court has ruled that procedural due process requires states to provide defendants with a speedy trial. Procedural due process is particularly important in criminal law because it limits the power of police, prosecutors, and the judiciary.

See 153 What was the due process revolution of the 1960s?

Q **16. What does the public believe is the most important part of the U.S. justice system?**

A In a 1999 nationwide survey of the general population by the American Bar Association, juries ranked as the most important feature of the United States justice system. More than two-thirds (69 percent) of respondents said that juries are the most important part of our justice system. More than three-quarters of those surveyed (78 percent) said that the jury system is the fairest way to determine guilt or innocence. The majority (80 percent) of respondents agreed or strongly agreed that, despite its problems, the American justice system still is the best in the world. The survey included 1,000 randomly selected respondents age eighteen and older.

See 217 What is the difference between a grand jury and a petit jury?

Q **17. What is the largest reward ever offered by the federal government for information leading to the arrest of a fugitive?**

A On November 4, 1998, the U.S. Department of State's Diplomatic Security Service, through its Counter-Terrorism Rewards Program, offered a reward of up to $5 million for information leading directly to the apprehension or conviction of Usama bin Laden, the leader of a terrorist organization known as Al-Qaeda (The Base). This reward represents the largest amount ever offered for a fugitive wanted by the federal government. On June 7, 1999, the Federal Bureau of Investigation put bin Laden on its "Ten Most Wanted Fugitives" list.

Bin Laden was charged in connection with the August 7, 1998, bombings of the U.S. Embassies in Nairobi, Kenya, and Dar es Salaam, Tanzania. These attacks resulted in the deaths of more than 200 people, including twelve American citizens, and the wounding of more than 4,000 individuals. Bin Laden was indicted by a federal grand jury on November 4, 1998, in the Southern District of New York, on charges of murder of U.S. nationals outside the United States, conspiracy to murder U.S. nationals outside the United States, and attacks on a federal facility resulting in death.

Officials said that a total of about $6 million has been paid out through the Counter-Terrorism Rewards Program in approximately twenty cases.

Q **18. How much confidence do Americans have in the criminal justice system?**

A Polling by the Gallup Organization, Inc., shows that 23 percent of Americans expressed "a great deal" or "quite a lot" of confidence in the criminal justice system in 1999. That percentage compares to 24 percent in 1998, 19 percent in 1997, 19 percent in 1996, 20 percent in 1995, 15 percent in 1994, and 17 percent in 1993. The criminal justice system ranks lower than most other major American institutions, including the military, clergy and organized religion, police, the U.S. Supreme Court, banks and banking, public schools, television news, newspapers, big business, Congress, and organized labor. The only institution ranking lower than the criminal justice system was the U.S. presidency.

CRIMES

Q **19. What are arguably the most notorious American crimes of the twentieth century?**

A The question of what makes a crime so heinous as to stand out in a century of crimes is, of course, subject to interpretation. Factors to consider include the severity of the impact on society and the victims and the degree of inhumanity involved in the event. Following are ten of the most notorious American crimes and criminals:

- On September 6, 1901, anarchist Leon Czolgosz shot President William McKinley in a receiving line at the Pan American Exposition in Buffalo, New York. McKinley died on September 14, 1901. Czolgosz was convicted after a brief trial and executed on October 29, 1901.
- On March 1, 1932, the twenty-month-old baby of America's most famed aviator, Charles Lindbergh Jr., was kidnapped from his nursery crib. Though Lindbergh

paid the $50,000 ransom, the child was found dead. Thousands of the marked bills that were used to pay the ransom were subsequently found in the modest New Jersey home of German-born Bruno Richard Hauptmann, a carpenter. Hauptmann was executed in 1935 for the crime. The trial was the first ever to be broadcast and attracted hundreds of reporters from around the world.

- On November 22, 1963, Communist sympathizer Lee Harvey Oswald fatally shot President John Fitzgerald Kennedy when Kennedy's motorcade passed the Texas School Book Depository Building in Dallas, Texas. Two days later, Oswald was shot and killed in a Dallas police station basement by nightclub operator Jack Ruby.

- On April 4, 1968, James Earl Ray fatally shot the Rev. Dr. Martin Luther King Jr. when King stepped out of a Memphis, Tennessee, hotel room to speak to aides waiting for him downstairs in the motel courtyard. The shooting prompted a wave of urban rioting across the nation. King, the 1964 Nobel Peace Prize winner, had advocated nonviolence throughout his life.

- Ted Bundy, a one-time law student and pornography addict, admitted to killing twenty-three women in ten states between 1973 and 1978 before he was apprehended and finally executed in Florida's electric chair in 1989. Bundy, who was both mobile and smart, defined a new breed of murderers called *serial killers*.

- On August 9, 1969, aspiring-musician-turned-cult-leader Charles Manson directed his counterculture "family" to commit a bizarre mass murder. Seven people were slashed and killed, including eight-months-pregnant actress Sharon Tate, the wife of movie director Roman Polanski. The word *PIG* was scrawled in blood on the front door. Manson claimed to take his cues from what he believed were hidden messages in Beatles songs, notably "Helter Skelter." Manson's death sentence was set aside in 1972 when the California Supreme Court ruled that the death penalty was unconstitutional.

- Richard Milhous Nixon, the thirty-seventh president of the United States, resigned in 1974 after conceding to some "wrong judgments" with respect to the break-in and bugging of the Democratic National Committee headquarters at the Watergate office complex and a plethora of crimes committed by government officials to cover up the break-in. Thus Nixon ended an unprecedented constitutional crisis that for months had ground to a virtual halt the work of government. Nixon subsequently received an unconditional pardon from his successor in office, Gerald Ford.

- On April 19, 1995, a 4,800-pound fertilizer bomb exploded and sent the nine-story Alfred P. Murrah Federal Building in Oklahoma City tumbling down. The bomb killed 169 people, including 19 children in a daycare center, and injured 600 more. The bombing, by two right-wing militia members, Timothy McVeigh and Terry Nichols, was the worst terrorist attack ever to occur on American soil.

- UNABOM (UNiversity and Airline BOMbing) was the code name for the Federal Bureau of Investigation's investigation into sixteen bombs that were mailed to various people over a seventeen-year period beginning in 1978. Three persons were killed and twenty-three people were injured. The bomber, Theodore Kaczynski, a Harvard University graduate and former mathematics professor at the University of California at Berkeley, was turned in to the police by his brother in 1996. Kaczynski was sentenced in 1998 to life in prison with no chance for parole.
- The nation was divided, mainly along racial lines, when popular African American ex-football player O.J. Simpson was acquitted in 1995 on criminal charges in the 1994 murders of his estranged wife, Nicole Brown Simpson, and her friend, Ronald Goldman, who were white. The jury deliberated for only a few hours despite a trail of evidence that seemed to lead inexorably to the defendant, including bloody shoe prints and DNA evidence found in Simpson's car. Simpson later was found liable for the wrongful deaths of Nicole Brown Simpson and Ronald Goldman in civil proceedings and ordered to pay a judgment of $33.5 million.

Q 20. What were the first crimes established by the U.S. Congress?

A The first Congress passed a general Crimes Act in 1790 that defined twenty-two crimes, including six crimes that carried the penalty of death by hanging by the neck until dead. Capital crimes included treason, murder on United States property, piracy and felony, accessories to piracy before the fact, forgery and counterfeiting, and rescue of a person convicted of a capital crime. The act forbade the use of the benefit of clergy in capital executions.

The following crimes were punishable by imprisonment, a fine, whipping, or time spent in a pillory: misprision [concealment] of treason (seven years, $1,000); rescue of a body ordered for dissection (one year, $100); misprision of murder or felony on United States property or on the high seas (three years, $500); manslaughter on United States property (three years, $1,000); accessories to piracy after the fact (three years, $500); confederacy to become pirates (three years, $1,000); maiming on United States property or on the high seas (seven years, $1,000); stealing or falsifying a record or process (seven years, $5,000, thirty-nine stripes); larceny on United States property or on the high seas (four times the value of property, thirty-nine stripes); receiving stolen goods (four times the value of the goods, thirty-nine stripes); perjury (three years, $800, one hour in the pillory); bribery of a judge (fine and imprisonment at the discretion of the judge); obstruction of process (one year, $300); rescue of a person before trial (one year, $500); suing an ambassador or foreign minister (three years, fine at discretion of the court); violation of safe conduct, or violence toward an ambassador or minister (three years, fine at the discretion of the court).

The Crimes Act guaranteed the accused a copy of the indictment and a list of the jury and witnesses, and provided that the accused should be allowed to make "his full defense by learned counsel either of his own choosing or assigned by the court."

Q 21. Are criminal laws and procedures the same in every state?

A No. Federal criminal laws must be applied uniformly throughout the nation, but state laws vary. Most criminal law is state law, and each state is free to enact its own criminal code. What is legal in one state may not be legal in another state. For example, Oregon is the only state to allow physician-assisted suicide. Punishments also vary from state to state. For example, some states have the death penalty, but others do not.

To prevent criminals from fleeing to neighboring states to avoid sanctions, states are required by Article IV of the U.S. Constitution to provide full faith and credit to the laws and judicial proceedings of other states. This means that states must cooperate with each other and honor a valid court order from another state, such as a warrant to arrest a citizen for a crime.

States are constrained by the U.S. Constitution in terms of the laws that they enact. Laws cannot violate the U.S. Constitution as it is interpreted by the U.S. Supreme Court. For example, a legislature cannot pass a bill of attainder (a law that punishes a named individual or easily ascertainable members of a group without a trial). Neither state legislatures nor the U.S. Congress can violate the rights guaranteed to all Americans by the U.S. Constitution.

Q 22. What happens if a criminal flees to another country?

A The president of the United States, with the advice and consent of the Senate, is authorized by the U.S. Constitution to make treaties with foreign countries. America has treaties with most countries governing the extradition of individuals who flee from one country to another country to avoid punishment for a crime.

Extradition treaties typically list offenses that warrant extradition, conditions that prevent extradition, and how requests are to be made. These treaties also contain a provisional arrest clause that allows for the immediate arrest of an accused person if it is likely the accused person will flee before the extradition request can be processed.

In addition to treaties, the general principle of comity requires one sovereignty to recognize the legislative, executive, or judicial acts of another as a matter of courtesy and respect unless to do so would be repugnant to its public policy or prejudicial to its interests or that of its citizens.

Q 23. What factors are necessary elements of a crime?

A A crime generally requires an *actus rea* (voluntary act) or a failure to act when the party has a legal duty to act. A crime also requires a *mens rea* (guilty mental state), the absence of a legally recognized defense, and a violation of a law.

The first element for criminal liability is the act. As Oliver Wendell Holmes stated in 1881, "There is no law against a man's intending to commit a murder the day after to-morrow. The law only deals with conduct." Conduct may be verbal (for example, treason, solicitation, or conspiracy) or physical (for example, homicide, assault, or robbery). Failure to act when one has a duty to do so also may give rise to criminal culpability, such as when one neglects a child. An individual is not liable for an act that is not voluntary, such as an act that results from a reflex, convulsion, or a bodily movement during unconsciousness or sleep.

The second major requirement for criminal liability is that the individual's state of mind must have been criminal when the crime was committed. *Actus non facit reum, nisi mens sit rea* means "There is no crime without a vicious will." An individual who takes another person's jacket believing it to be his or her own is not a thief.

A guilty mind is not always required for an act to qualify as a criminal act. Some conduct is criminal regardless of the actor's state of mind. Strict liability or absolute liability crimes, such as failing to file an income tax return or to register for selective service, speeding, or statutory rape, are examples of such crimes. Also, under some circumstances, employers and corporations can be held responsible for the acts of employees. An example of vicarious liability is price fixing or violating environmental laws.

Q 24. Can guilt attach before the commission of the crime?

A Yes. The law does not require that a defendant commit actual harm to be guilty of a crime. Even if the criminal act is not completed, the actor may be guilty of attempt, conspiracy, or solicitation.

An attempt generally requires a substantial step in furtherance of a crime by a person who intends to commit the crime. An attempt need not be successful. For example, a defendant may be guilty of attempted bank robbery if he or she goes to a bank to rob it but discovers the doors are locked because of a bank holiday. A defendant is guilty of attempt if he or she possessed the requisite criminal intent to commit the crime and acted in furtherance of that intent.

A conspiracy is an agreement by two or more persons to commit an unlawful act or to use unlawful means to accomplish an act that is not in itself unlawful. Criminals may conspire, for example, to commit a murder or to fix a bid for a government contract. With the exception of a serious felony, a conspiracy generally requires an overt act in furtherance of the agreement by one or more of the conspirators.

Criminal solicitation occurs when a defendant commands, encourages, or requests another person to engage in specific conduct that constitutes a crime, such as hiring someone to murder a spouse. Criminal solicitation involves a third party.

Q 25. How are crimes classified?

A Broadly speaking, crimes today are categorized as violent crimes, property crimes, or crimes against the public welfare. Violent crimes include murder and rape. Property crimes include burglary and theft. Crimes against the public welfare include public intoxication, illegal gambling, and prostitution.

Specifically, crimes are classified as felonies, misdemeanors, and violations. The difference generally falls in the seriousness of the offense and the extent of the punishment. The most serious crimes are felonies, which are punishable by imprisonment for a term of a year or more or death. Misdemeanors are criminal offenses that are punishable by a jail term not exceeding one year. Violations are crimes, such as traffic offenses, that are punishable by a fine or by a jail term not exceeding six months.

Treason falls into a separate category of crime. Treason is defined in Article III of the U.S. Constitution as levying war against the United States or adhering to or giving aid or comfort to its enemies.

See 127 What is a victimless crime?

Q 26. Is motive the same as intent?

A No. Motive is the reason or grounds for a person's behavior. Motive is not the same as criminal intent or *mens rea* (a guilty mind). Intent refers to the mental state that must be present to establish that a crime was committed. An individual with the requisite intent to commit a crime may have had a perfectly laudable motive. Such a case may exist, for example, when a mother steals food to feed her hungry children. The motive is benign, perhaps even admirable. Still, the mother is guilty of a theft.

Generally motive is immaterial to the matter of guilt, though several defenses may be asserted to avoid criminal culpability. For example, a person may claim that he or she acted in self-defense or out of necessity. In the latter situation, the person must show that his or her conduct was justified to avoid a harm to society that is greater than the harm caused by the person's conduct. A person may be justified in destroying another's property to stop the spread of a deadly fire (for example, by breaking into a house to find a telephone to call the fire department).

Q 27. What are specific and general intent crimes?

A For the purpose of determining culpability, the common law divided crimes into general or specific intent crimes, depending on the actor's mental state. However, this classification was not adopted in the Model Penal Code, a proposed code of criminal laws formulated by the American Law Institute in 1962 to serve as a model for reform by the states.

General intent refers to the intent to commit a physical act. The government must show that the person desired to commit the act that is the basis for the crime. A prosecutor does not have to prove that a person knew his or her conduct was unlawful, only that the person was generally aware that he or she was likely committing a criminal act. General intent crimes typically have included rape, battery, and involuntary manslaughter.

To prove a specific intent crime, the government must show that the person intended to commit the act that is the basis for the crime, and that the person possessed an additional specified level of knowledge or intent. A prosecutor must show that the person intended to produce the precise consequences of the crime. Specific intent crimes typically have included premeditated murder, solicitation, assault, larceny, forgery, false pretenses, and embezzlement.

Some crimes do not require that the government prove intent to obtain a conviction. Such crimes include strict liability crimes, such as speeding, and some common law morality offenses, including statutory rape. Crimes of negligence result from the unconscious creation of substantial and unjustifiable risk. For example, a person who throws a cigarette out a car window, precipitating a fire, might be guilty of negligence.

Q 28. What is the Model Penal Code?

A The Model Penal Code (MPC) is a highly influential code of criminal laws that was developed in 1962 by the American Law Institute to serve as a model for states seeking to improve their criminal laws and to help unify laws across the country. Most states have adopted all or part of the MPC, replacing a hodge-podge of sometimes-conflicting state and local laws.

The MPC has been credited with helping unify the nation's criminal laws and the administration of justice, but today the code is considered somewhat archaic. Under Section 213.1 of the MPC, for example, a defendant cannot be convicted of raping his wife because marriage is deemed to constitute a general waiver of the wife's right to say "no."

The American Law Institute (ALI) was established in 1923 "to promote the clarification and simplification of the law and its better adaptation to social needs, to secure the better administration of justice, and to encourage and carry on scholarly and scientific legal work." The ALI was created as a result of a 1922 study reporting that the two chief defects in American law were its uncertainty and its complexity. The ALI has drafted restatements and model codes of law on various topics that serve as models for states.

Incorporated as a perpetual society, the ALI has an elected membership of 3,000 judges, law professors and attorneys. Ex officio members include the following groups:

- The chief justice and associate justices of the U.S. Supreme Court
- The chief judges of each U.S. Court of Appeals
- The attorney general and solicitor general of the United States
- The chief judges of the highest court of each state
- Law school deans
- The presidents of the American Bar Association, each state bar association, and other prominent legal organizations

Q 29. What criminal mental states are specified in the Model Penal Code?

A According to the Model Penal Code (MPC), to be guilty of a crime a person must act purposely, knowingly, recklessly, or negligently, as the law requires, with respect to each of material elements of the offense.

These terms are defined as follows:

- *Purposely* means that it was the person's conscious object to engage in the conduct or to cause the result in question.
- *Knowingly* means that the person was aware that his or her conduct was practically certain to cause a particular result.
- *Recklessly* means that the person consciously disregarded a substantial and unjustifiable risk of harm and that the person's conduct constituted a gross deviation from the standard of conduct that a law-abiding person would observe in the same situation.

- *Negligently* means that the person failed to perceive a substantial and unjustifiable risk of harm in a way that involved a gross deviation from the standard of care that a reasonable person would observe in the same situation.

30. When does an individual become an accomplice to a crime?

An accomplice is someone who knowingly and voluntarily helps another person commit or conceal a crime. The law holds that all willing participants to a crime are accountable, whether or not they are present when the crime is committed. An accomplice is a person who abets a crime, or who encourages, orders, or helps another person to commit a crime. Classic examples of an accomplice are a person who plans the crime or who acts as the getaway driver. These individuals are subject to the same punishment as the person who executed the crime.

Another type of accomplice is an accessory after the fact. An accessory after the fact has no role in the crime before its commission, but might help conceal evidence of a crime or aid the principals in escaping detection. Accessories after the fact generally are treated as less culpable than the principals.

31. Are you criminally liable if you shoot at one person but hit someone else?

Yes. Under the doctrine of transferred intent, a person is liable if he or she intends the harm that is caused even if the injury occurs to a different victim or object. Incompetent marksmanship is not a legally recognized defense.

32. If you thought the white stuff in your possession was baby powder but it turns out to be cocaine, are you guilty of a crime?

A defendant may show that, as the result of a mistake, he or she lacked the requisite *mens rea* (guilty mental state) to commit a material element of the crime. Knowledge is typically a material element of the crime of possession of a controlled substance. However, a mistake must be not only honest but also reasonable. A defendant must convince the court that a reasonable person in the defendant's situation could have made the same mistake. This burden would be daunting if, for example, the defendant was childless, with a long history of drug convictions, and the "baby powder" was packaged in a parcel wrapped in brown paper.

Q 33. How does a case progress through the criminal justice system?

A Law enforcement agencies learn about crimes through reports by victims and other citizens, from tips by informants, by law enforcement officers' observations of crimes, or through investigative and intelligence work. When police determine that a serious crime has been committed, the police attempt to identify and apprehend one or more suspects and take them into custody.

A citation may be used to charge an offender for a minor offense, such as a traffic violation. Citations are paper forms that are given to the subject in lieu of arrest and booking. Citations constitute a legally enforceable order to appear in court on a specific date.

For more serious offenses, police typically present information about the case and the accused to a prosecutor, who decides whether to pursue the filing of formal charges with the court. The prosecutor may send the case to a grand jury, which is a panel of citizens that hears evidence against the accused. If the grand jury finds there is sufficient evidence to require the accused to undergo a trial, the panel issues an indictment. Alternatively, the prosecutor may file an *information,* a formal, written document in which the prosecutor accuses the defendant of a crime. Misdemeanor cases typically proceed by the issuance of an information.

After being arrested with a crime, the accused person is scheduled for an arraignment. The accused is informed of the charges, advised of his or her rights, and asked to enter a plea. The court may then set bail. (No bail is set for capital offenses.)

In non–grand jury cases, a preliminary hearing is held at which a judge or magistrate determines whether there is probable cause to believe the accused committed the crime. At this point, the vast majority of defendants enter into negotiations with the prosecutor to arrive at a plea bargain (an agreed-on outcome). Frequently the prosecutor agrees to drop some charges or to allow the defendant to plead guilty to a lesser charge.

In some cases, a defendant—usually a first-time, nonviolent offender with no criminal record—may be eligible for diversion from prosecution. If the defendant successfully completes an educational or treatment program, the charges against him or her may be dropped. Diversion programs may be available for drunk driving or domestic violence.

About 4 percent of all criminal defendants demand a trial, a formal proceeding presided over by a judge or magistrate to adjudicate a defendant's guilt or innocence.

Q **34. When was the nation's first war on crime?**

A The first war on crime followed the ratification of the Eighteenth Amendment to the U.S. Constitution in 1919, which made it illegal to manufacture, sell, or import intoxicating beverages into or from the United States. The 1920s are sometimes referred to as the *lawless years* because of gangsterism and public disregard for alcohol laws. In 1925 President Calvin Coolidge appointed the first National Crime Commission. A few years later, President Herbert Hoover campaigned successfully on a law-and-order platform. Americans reported in a national survey in the late 1920s that crime and disrespect for the law were the nation's number one problems. In 1934, with gangsters like John Dillinger evading capture by crossing state lines, Congress passed several federal crime laws that significantly enhanced federal jurisdiction over crime control. Until then, crime control had been considered a state and local concern.

Q **35. What may be the most violated federal law in U.S. history?**

A The Eighteenth Amendment to the U.S. Constitution, ratified in 1919, and the federal law that implemented it, the National Prohibition Enforcement Act (1920)—commonly known as the Volstead Act—made it a crime to sell alcoholic beverages. Thus began a thirteen-year period known as Prohibition, which, while perhaps not a complete failure, spurred the rise of organized crime in the United States and Canada. More importantly, Prohibition is blamed for widespread corruption of politicians and police, and for undermining respect for law and order by ordinary citizens who watched beer and liquor flow virtually unchecked into major cities. Gangsters smuggled illegal alcohol into the country from Canada and Mexico and became known as *bootleggers,* a term that referred to the practice of carrying liquor in the legs of tall boots. Some of the blame for Prohibition's failure has been attributed to the U.S. Congress, which never provided sufficient resources to enforce the law.

Records show that consumption of alcohol did decline during Prohibition. The annual per capita consumption of alcohol was 2.6 gallons during the period from 1906 to 1910 (before state dry laws were enacted). In 1934, when statistics were again available, the per capita figure was less than a gallon.

An estimated 300,000 people were convicted of violating federal prohibition laws before the Eighteenth Amendment was repealed in 1933.

Q **36. What percentage of violent crimes are reported to police?**

A Most crime goes undetected in the sense that it is either not discovered or not reported to the police. In the commission of some types of crime, such as drug- or vice-related crimes, all parties actively work to conceal the crime from police. Less than half of all violent crimes are reported to police. A 1999 federal study found that only 48 percent of violent crimes against adults and 28 percent of violent crimes against children ages twelve to seventeen are reported to police. Of crimes that involve weapons, 65 percent of crimes against adults and 48 percent of crimes against children are reported to police. Of crimes that result in injury, 65 percent of crimes with adult victims and 57 percent of crimes with child victims are reported to police.

Q **37. How is crime measured?**

A The U.S. Department of Justice measures crime in two ways. For its annual Uniform Crime Reports, the Federal Bureau of Investigation (FBI) collects statistics from law enforcement authorities across the country regarding select crimes that were reported to police. The Justice Department's Bureau of Justice Statistics conducts an annual telephone poll of a representative number of households nationwide as part of its National Crime Victimization Survey (NCVS). The NCVS includes data on nonfatal violent crimes, including both reported crimes and crimes that were not reported to police. Neither measure is complete, but together they give a broad picture of the extent of crime in the nation and help policymakers formulate crime policy.

Q **38. What is the Uniform Crime Reporting Program?**

A The Uniform Crime Reporting (UCR) Program is a crime statistics collection program operated by the Federal Bureau of Investigation (FBI). The UCR serves as the primary source of information about the magnitude and nature of crime in the United States. The UCR began in the 1920s, when the International Association of Chiefs of Police initiated a voluntary data collection effort to track national crime statistics. The FBI took over the job when the U.S. Congress subsequently authorized the FBI to serve as the national clearinghouse for statistical information on crime.

Since 1930 the FBI has tracked seven types of serious violent and property crimes: murder and non-negligent manslaughter, forcible rape, robbery, aggravated assault, burglary, larceny-theft, and motor vehicle theft. These crimes were chosen because they were deemed most likely to be reported to authorities and because they occur frequently enough to provide an adequate basis for comparison. Known collectively as the Crime Index, the data reflect monthly arrest counts that are voluntarily reported to the FBI by law enforcement agencies. An eighth type of crime, arson, was added to the index in 1979. The UCR Crime Index gauges fluctuations in the overall volume and rate of crime nationwide in a manner similar to the way the Dow Jones Industrial Average tracks economic growth.

Law enforcement agencies representing 96 percent of the U.S. population reported crime statistics to the FBI in 1998. The FBI publishes UCR findings in detail in an annual report, *Crime in the United States.*

In the 1980s the UCR began to enhance its data collection effort by moving from aggregate statistics toward a more comprehensive and detailed incident reporting system called the National Incident-Based Reporting System (NIBRS). Under this system the UCR analyzes detailed information about criminal incidents in twenty-two broad categories of offenses. They are arson, assault, bribery, burglary / breaking and entering, counterfeiting / forgery, destruction / damage / vandalism of property, drug / narcotic offenses, embezzlement, extortion / blackmail, fraud, gambling, homicide, kidnaping / abduction, larceny / theft, motor vehicle theft, pornography / obscene material, prostitution, robbery, forcible sex offenses, nonforcible sex offenses, stolen property offenses, and weapon law violations. At the end of 1998, law enforcement agencies reporting NIBRS data had jurisdiction over less than 10 percent of the U.S. population. Eventually the UCR program will convert to the NIBRS.

Q 39. What is the National Crime Victimization Survey?

A The National Crime Victimization Survey (NCVS) is a survey of nonfatal violent crimes that have occurred in a scientifically selected representative sample of households throughout the United States. The Bureau of Justice Statistics of the U.S. Department of Justice conducts an annual telephone poll of 100,000 persons in 49,000 households.

Begun in 1973, the poll is considered to be the primary source of information on the characteristics of criminal victimization and on the number and types of crimes not reported to law enforcement authorities.

The poll is designed to provide a detailed picture of the frequency and nature of the crimes of rape, sexual assault, personal robbery, aggravated and simple assault, household burglary, theft, and motor vehicle theft. It does not measure homicide or commercial crimes (such as burglaries of stores).

According to the NCVS, Americans aged twelve and older experienced about 28.8 million violent and property crimes during 1999, a decline of more than 10 percent from 1998 and the lowest rate since the survey began in 1973. The total includes 21.2 million property crimes, 7.4 million violent crimes, and 0.2 million personal thefts (pocket picking and purse snatching).

The NCVS is conducted in the same manner as a professional market survey. Members of the U.S. Bureau of the Census personally interview all members of households in the sample who are at least twelve years of age. Trend data are described as genuine only if there is at least a 90 percent certainty that the measured changes are not the result of sampling variation.

The Bureau of Justice Statistics publishes the NCVS poll results in an annual report, *Criminal Victimization in the United States.*

Q 40. What are the major differences between the Uniform Crime Reporting Program and the National Crime Victimization Survey?

A The two programs have different methodologies that sometimes yield different results. The Federal Bureau of Investigation's Uniform Crime Reporting (UCR) Program is intended to provide reliable criminal justice statistics for law enforcement administration, operation, and management. The Bureau of Justice Statistics' National Crime Victimization Survey (NCVS) was designed to complement the UCR and to provide previously unavailable information about crime victims, offenders, and crime, including crimes not reported to police. Major differences between the two programs include the following:

- The NCVS includes information about crimes both reported and not reported to police, while the UCR includes only reported crimes.
- The UCR counts crimes not covered by the NCVS, including homicide and arson, and crimes committed against all people and all businesses, organizations, governmental agencies, and so forth.
- The NCVS counts only crimes against persons age twelve and older.
- The UCR Crime Index does not include simple assaults and sexual assaults other than forcible rape. Also, the UCR measures the crime of rape against women only, while the NCVS measures it against both sexes.
- Because of methodology, the NCVS and UCR define some crimes differently. For example, the NCVS defines burglary as the entry or attempted entry of a residence by a person who had no right to be there. The UCR defines burglary as the unlawful entry or attempted entry of a structure to commit a felony or theft.

- The two programs use different bases to calculate the rate of property crime. The UCR rates these crimes per capita (number of crimes per 100,000 persons), and the NCVS rates these crimes per household (number of crimes per 1,000 households).

Q 41. How many serious crimes were reported in the United States in 1998?

A According to the Uniform Crime Report (UCR), 12,475,634 serious violent and property crimes occurred in the United States in 1998. Adjusted for population growth, this represented a decline of 6.4 percent from 1997. Across the board, 4,615 crimes occurred per 100,000 inhabitants of the nation in 1998.

The UCR Crime Index measures murder and non-negligent manslaughter, forcible rape, robbery, aggravated assault, burglary, larceny-theft, motor vehicle theft, and arson. Of the total Crime Index offenses, 12 percent involved violent crimes and 88 percent involved property crimes.

The 1,531,000 violent crimes that were reported in 1998 included 16,914 murders, 93,103 forcible rapes, 446,625 robberies, and 974,402 aggravated assaults. All violent crimes involve force or threat of force. Adjusted for population growth, the violent crime rate dropped 7.3 percent in 1998. There were 566 violent crimes per 100,000 inhabitants of the United States in 1998.

The almost 10,945,000 property crimes reported in 1998 included 2,329,950 burglaries, 7,373,886 larceny-thefts, 1,240,754 motor vehicle thefts, and at least 78,094 cases of arson. Adjusted for population growth, the property crime rate fell 6.2 percent in 1998. There were 4,049 property crimes per 100,000 inhabitants of the United States in 1998.

See 315 What percentage of crimes reported to police result in an arrest? Figure 1-1 Four Measures of Serious Violent Crime

Q 42. How often do crimes occur in the United States?

A In 1998 one property crime occurred every three seconds and one violent crime occurred every twenty-one seconds in the United States. With respect to violent crime, the Federal Bureau of Investigation (FBI) reports that in 1998 one murder occurred every thirty-one minutes; one forcible rape, every six minutes; one robbery, every minute; and one aggravated assault, every thirty-two seconds. With respect to property crime, the FBI reports that in 1998 one burglary occurred every fourteen seconds; one larceny-theft, every four seconds; and one motor vehicle theft, every twenty-five seconds.

Figure 1-1 Four Measures of Serious Violent Crime

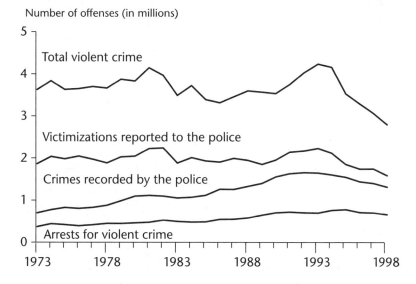

Number of offenses (in millions)

Note: The serious violent crimes included are rape, robbery, aggravated assault, and homicide. Because of changes made to the victimization survey, data prior to 1992 are adjusted to make them comparable to data collected under the redesigned methodology. Estimates for 1993–1998 are based on collection year, and earlier estimates are based on data year.

Source: Bureau of Justice Statistics, U.S. Department of Justice, http://www.ojp.usdoj.gov/bjs/glance/cv2.htm.

Q 43. What region of the country reports the highest levels of crime?

A Regionally, the South reported the highest overall crime rate in 1998: 5,223 offenses per 100,000 inhabitants. That rate compares to rates of 4,879 offenses per 100,000 inhabitants in the West, 4,379 in the Midwest, and 3,474 in the Northeast. With respect to violent crimes, regional numbers of incidents per 100,000 residents were as follows:

- South, 633
- West, 593
- Midwest, 498
- Northeast, 500

With respect to property crimes, regional numbers of incidents per 100,000 residents were as follows:

- South, 4,590
- West, 4,286
- Midwest, 3,881
- Northeast, 2,974

Q **44. How has the number of serious crimes changed over time?**

A The number of serious violent and property crimes reported to the Federal Bureau of Investigation's Uniform Crime Reporting (UCR) Program dropped in 1998 to its lowest point since 1985. From 1997 to 1998, the number fell 5.4 percent, including a 6.4 percent drop in violent crimes and a 5.3 percent drop in property crimes. The UCR Crime Index measures the crimes of murder and non-negligent manslaughter, forcible rape, robbery, aggravated assault, burglary, larceny-theft, and motor vehicle theft. (Because statistics on arson crimes were not collected as part of the Index until 1979, arson crimes are excluded from historical comparisons that include periods before 1979.) Following are the total offenses from 1960 through 1998 as measured by the UCR Crime Index:

Year	Total Number of Offenses	Year	Total Number of Offenses
1960	3,384,200	1975	11,292,400
1961	3,488,000	1976	11,349,700
1962	3,752,200	1977	10,984,500
1963	4,109,500	1978	11,209,000
1964	4,564,600	1979	12,249,500
1965	4,739,400	1980	13,406,300
1966	5,223,500	1981	13,423,800
1967	5,903,400	1982	12,974,400
1968	6,720,200	1983	12,108,600
1969	7,410,900	1984	11,881,800
1970	8,098,000	1985	12,431,400
1971	8,588,200	1986	13,211,900
1972	8,248,800	1987	13,508,700
1973	8,718,100	1988	13,923,100
1974	10,253,400	1989	14,251,400

Year	Total Number of Offenses	Year	Total Number of Offenses
1990	14,475,600	1995	13,862,700
1991	14,872,900	1996	13,493,900
1992	14,438,200	1997	13,194,600
1993	14,144,800	1998	12,475,600
1994	13,989,500		

See 50 What factors are commonly cited to explain the recent decline in the crime rate?

Q 45. How has the rate of serious crime changed over time?

A The rate of serious crime is measured by the number of offenses per 100,000 inhabitants. According to the Federal Bureau of Investigation's Uniform Crime Reports (UCR), the rate of serious violent and property crime fell in 1998 to its lowest point since 1973. From 1997 to 1998, the rate declined by 6.4 percent, including a 7.3 percent drop in violent crime and a 6.2 percent drop in property crime. The UCR Crime Index measures the crimes of murder and non-negligent manslaughter, forcible rape, robbery, aggravated assault, burglary, larceny-theft, and motor vehicle theft. (Because statistics on arson crimes were not collected as part of the Index until 1979, arson crimes are excluded from historical comparisons that include periods before 1979.) Following are offenses per 100,000 inhabitants from 1960 through 1998, as measured by the UCR Crime Index:

Year	Offenses per 100,000 inhabitants	Year	Offenses per 100,000 inhabitants
1960	1,887.2	1970	3,984.5
1961	1,906.1	1971	4,164.7
1962	2,019.8	1972	3,961.4
1963	2,180.3	1973	4,154.4
1964	2,388.1	1974	4,850.4
1965	2,449	1975	5,298.5
1966	2,670.6	1976	5,287.3
1967	2,989.7	1977	5,077.6
1968	3,370.2	1978	5,410.3
1969	3,680	1979	5,565.5

Year	Offenses per 100,000 inhabitants	Year	Offenses per 100,000 inhabitants
1980	5,950	1990	5,820.3
1981	5,858.2	1991	5,897.8
1982	5,603.6	1992	5,660.2
1983	5,175	1993	5,484.4
1984	5,031.3	1994	5,373.5
1985	5,207.1	1995	5,277.6
1986	5,480.4	1995	5,086
1987	5,550	1997	4,930
1988	5,664.2	1998	4,615.5
1989	5,741		

Q 46. What is the gender breakdown for arrests?

A Although males represent less than half of the U.S. population, they constitute 78 percent of the persons arrested in the United States in 1998. A total of 8,049,239 males were arrested in 1998, compared to 2,245,890 females. Of persons arrested for violent crimes and property crimes, 83 percent and 71 percent, respectively, were males.

According to the Federal Bureau of Investigation, 400,206 males were arrested for serious violent crimes in 1998, compared to 81,072 females. Violent crimes include murder, forcible rape, robbery, and aggravated assault. A total of 919,165 males were arrested for serious property crimes, compared to 373,660 females. Property crimes include burglary, larceny-theft, motor vehicle theft, and arson.

Men most frequently were arrested for drug abuse violations and driving under the influence of alcohol or drugs, which accounted for a combined 22 percent of all male arrests. Women most frequently were arrested for larceny-theft, which accounted for 15 percent of all female arrests.

See 93 For what serious crime are women arrested most often?

Q 47. What type of crime is a criminal least likely to get away with?

A A criminal is least likely to get away with a violent crime because crimes against people generally receive more intensive investigation by law enforcement agencies.

The Federal Bureau of Investigation reports that 21 percent of serious violent and property crimes (excluding arson) were solved in 1998. This includes 49 percent of violent crimes and 17 percent of property crimes (excluding arson). Of violent crimes, law enforcement authorities solved or cleared 69 percent of murders, 59 percent of aggravated assaults, 50 percent of forcible rapes, and 28 percent of robberies. Of property crimes, authorities cleared 19 percent of larceny-thefts and approximately 14 percent of both motor vehicle thefts and burglaries.

Crimes are solved—or cleared—when at least one person is arrested, charged with the commission of a crime, and turned over to the court for prosecution. A crime also may be cleared by exceptional means when elements beyond law enforcement's control preclude the placing of formal charges against the offender. For example, the death of the offender or the victim's refusal to cooperate after police have identified the offender would be exceptional means.

A criminal was most likely to be caught in the Northeast. The clearance rate for serious violent and property crimes was 24 percent in the Northeast, 22 percent in the South, 20 percent in the West, and 19 percent in the Midwest. Rural county law enforcement agencies cleared the highest percentage (23 percent) of reported crimes. Suburban county and city law enforcement agencies both cleared 21 percent of reported crimes.

See 35 What may be the most violated federal law in U.S. history?

Q 48. Is a murderer more or less likely to be caught today?

A Murderers are less likely to be caught today than they were in the past. In 1961 the homicide clearance rate was 94 percent, compared to 69 percent in 1998. Experts theorize that fewer murderers are being caught because there are more stranger-to-stranger and drug-related crimes, police resources are stretched thinner, and bystanders are less willing to cooperate in solving a crime.

A 1999 study by the Justice Research and Statistics Association showed that the following factors make it more likely that a homicide case will be solved:

- The victim was not a drug user or buyer.
- The victim had no criminal record.
- The victim was killed by the use of a rifle, knife, or personal weapon (hands or feet) rather than by a handgun.
- More than one detective was assigned to the case.
- The police arrived on the scene soon after the killing.
- The homicide occurred in a private location.
- The weather was not bad.
- At least one witness is available.

Q **49. What tends to be the most accurate single crime statistic?**

A Murder statistics tend to be the most accurate single crime statistics because virtually everyone agrees on the definition of murder, and because the crime is so serious that it has been carefully recorded by law enforcement agencies for many years. Long-term data show that the murder rate has increased from 4.6 per 100,000 population in 1950 to 6.3 per 100,000 population in 1998. In recent years, however, the number of murders has declined significantly, falling in 1998 to its lowest point in thirty-one years. According to Federal Bureau of Investigation statistics, annual murders nation-wide from 1990 through 1998 numbered as follows:

Year	Number of Murders	Year	Number of Murders
1990	23,440	1995	21,610
1991	24,700	1996	19,650
1992	23,760	1997	18,210
1993	24,530	1998	16,910
1994	23,330		

See 63 What is murder?

Q **50. What factors are commonly cited to explain the recent decline in the crime rate?**

A Many theories and viewpoints have been advanced to explain the declining crime rate. Criminologists have cited the following factors:

- Since 1993 the federal, state, and local governments have doubled the amount spent on law enforcement, litigation, judicial, and correctional activities.
- New get-tough sentencing laws and policies have sent a record number of violent and repeat offenders to prison for longer periods of time.
- Stricter gun control policies make it more difficult for fugitives, felons, and juveniles to obtain firearms.
- A booming economy has removed a financial incentive to commit crime.
- Since 1990 there has been a decline in the use of crack cocaine.
- More police are on the streets and police are using better police strategies, including effective antigang strategies and community policing (which emphasizes crime-fighting partnerships between police and citizen groups).

See 45 How has the rate of serious crimes changed over time? 109 What causes crime?

INCIDENCE OF VIOLENT CRIME

Q 51. What jurisdiction has the highest rate of violent crime?

A The District of Columbia has the highest violent crime rate in the nation. In 1997, there were 2,024 violent crimes per 100,000 population in the District of Columbia. Violent crimes include murder, non-negligent manslaughter, robbery, aggravated assault, and forcible rape. The rate in the District of Columbia is almost twice as high as that in the second highest jurisdiction, Florida.

For seventeen of the last eighteen years, Florida has recorded the highest overall crime rate and the highest violent crime rate of any state in the nation, with a reported violent crime occurring roughly every three minutes.

The states with the highest rates of violent crime per 100,000 population in 1997, ranked by descending number of incidents, were as follows:

- Florida, 1,023.6
- South Carolina, 990.3
- Illinois, 861.4
- Louisiana, 855.9
- New Mexico, 853.4
- Maryland, 846.6
- Nevada, 798.7
- California, 798.3
- Tennessee, 789.7

Q 52. What state has the lowest rate of violent crime?

A North Dakota had the lowest violent crime rate in 1997. Only 87.2 people out of every 100,000 residents of North Dakota were victims of a violent crime. Violent crimes include murder, non-negligent manslaughter, robbery, aggravated assault, and forcible rape. In 1997 the following states also had low rates of violent crime per 100,000 population:

- New Hampshire, 113.2
- Vermont, 119.7
- Maine, 120.8
- Montana, 132.1
- South Dakota, 197.4
- West Virginia, 218.7
- Wyoming, 255.2

- Idaho, 256.8
- Wisconsin, 270.6

Q 53. What are the safest cities in the country? The most dangerous?

A In 1999 Newton, Massachusetts, a city of 81,000 people outside Boston, was recognized as the safest city in the country by *City Crime Rankings,* a Lawrence, Kansas–based publication that analyzes crime statistics. The nation's most dangerous city was Detroit, Michigan. The ranking includes cities having populations of more than 75,000 that reported statistics to the Federal Bureau of Investigation's Uniform Crime Reporting (UCR) Program and is based on an analysis of six basic crime categories: murder, rape, robbery, aggravated assault, burglary, and motor vehicle theft. Newton, Massachusetts, had no murders and the third lowest burglary and robbery rates in the country in 1998. Other safe cities were, in order, Amherst, N.Y.; Mission Viejo, Calif.; Thousand Oaks, Calif.; and Greece, N.Y. Joining Detroit at the dangerous end of the crime scale were Atlanta, Ga.; Camden, N.J.; Baltimore, Md.; and St. Louis, Mo.

Q 54. What crime leads to the most arrests?

A Law enforcement agencies made 14.5 million arrests for all criminal infractions, excluding traffic violations, in 1998. Drug abuse and alcohol-related violations constitute the largest category of all arrests, close to 30 percent. Following are the numbers of arrests, by type of crime, in 1998, according to the Federal Bureau of Investigation (FBI):

- Drug abuse violations, 1,559,100
- Driving under the influence, 1,402,800
- Simple assaults, 1,338,000
- Larceny-theft, 1,307,100
- Drunkenness, 710,300
- Disorderly conduct, 696,100
- Liquor law violations, 630,400
- Aggravated assault, 506,630
- Fraud, 394,600
- Burglary, 330,700
- Vandalism, 300,200
- Weapons (carrying, possessing, and so on), 190,600
- Curfew and loitering violations, 187,800
- Runaways, 165,100

- Motor vehicle theft, 150,700
- Offenses against the family and children, 146,400
- Stolen property (buying, receiving, possessing), 137,900
- Robbery, 120,870
- Forgery and counterfeiting, 114,600
- Prostitution and commercialized vice, 94,000
- Sex offenses (except forcible rape and prostitution), 93,600
- Forcible rape, 31,070
- Vagrancy, 30,400
- Murder and non-negligent manslaughter, 17,450
- Arson, 17,200
- Embezzlement, 17,100
- Gambling, 12,800
- Suspicion, 5,200
- All other offenses, 3,824,100

The number of arrests is significant because it indicates the types of crime and their prevalence in the United States and the priorities of law enforcement authorities.

Q 55. What percentage of violent criminals had prior arrests?

A About two-thirds of all offenders arrested each year for a violent crime will have had at least one prior arrest, and 40 percent will have had at least five prior arrests. More than half of convicted sex offenders will be arrested for a new crime within three years of their release from prison. Authorities in the criminal justice system use the phrase "lack of accountability" to describe the problem of violent offenders who re-offend.

DRUG-RELATED CRIME

Q 56. What type of drug is involved in most drug abuse violations?

A Marijuana was involved in more federal drug abuse violations in 1998 than any other single drug, followed by powder cocaine and crack cocaine, respectively. Slightly more than 78 percent of drug abuse violations were for possession and 21.2 percent were for the sales and manufacture of illegal drugs. The breakdown is as follows:

- Possession of marijuana, 38.4 percent; of heroin or cocaine and their derivatives, 25.6 percent; of synthetic or manufactured drugs, 1.9 percent; and of other dangerous non-narcotic drugs, 12.9 percent.

- Sale and manufacture of heroin or cocaine and their derivatives, 11.2 percent; of marijuana, 5.4 percent; of synthetic or manufactured drugs, 1 percent; and of other dangerous non-narcotic drugs, 3.8 percent.

Q **57. What drug is most closely associated with violent crimes?**

A Alcohol is more closely associated with violent crimes than any other drug. The National Center on Addiction and Substance Abuse at Columbia University estimates that one-fifth of state prison inmates who are incarcerated for violent crimes were under the influence of alcohol when they committed their crimes, compared to 3 percent who were under the influence of cocaine or crack. Based on victim perceptions, from 1992 to 1995 some 2.7 million violent crimes occurred each year in which victims were certain that the offender had been drinking.

See 115 Does a link exist between drugs and crime?

Q **58. How has drug-control spending by the federal government changed over the years?**

A The national budget for drug control skyrocketed from 1981 to 1998. Following are national budget amounts for drug control (in millions of dollars, adjusted for inflation) from 1981 through 1998, according to analysis by Transactional Records Access Clearinghouse, a research center affiliated with Syracuse University:

Year	Drug Control Budget	Year	Drug Control Budget
1981	$2,747.0	1990	$12,170.7
1982	$2,903.4	1991	$13,113.7
1983	$3,268.4	1992	$13,837.2
1984	$3,707.3	1993	$13,729.3
1985	$4,167.1	1994	$13,401.2
1986	$4,284.8	1995	$14,172.9
1987	$6,876.3	1996	$13,977.0
1988	$6,486.7	1997	$15,267.4
1989	$8,759.5	1998	$16,097.3

Q 59. How does the federal government allocate its drug-control spending?

A According to the Office of National Drug Control Policy, which leads the federal drug control effort, 67.4 percent of 1999 federal drug spending was for programs aimed at reducing the supply of drugs, while 32.6 percent was directed toward programs aimed at reducing demand for drugs.

Q 60. What is the Office of National Drug Control Policy?

A The Office of National Drug Control Policy coordinates federal, state, and local efforts to control illegal drug abuse and to devise national strategies to carry out antidrug activities effectively.

The director of the office is a cabinet-level official who is commonly referred to as the country's *drug czar.* Appointed by the president with the advice and consent of the Senate, the director also advises the president regarding necessary changes in the organization, management, budgeting, and personnel allocation of federal agencies involved in drug enforcement activities.

The Office of National Drug Control Policy was established by the National Narcotics Leadership Act of 1988, effective January 29, 1989, later amended by the Violent Crime Control and Law Enforcement Act of 1994.

Q 61. Is there a war on drugs?

A Technically, no. In 1971 President Richard M. Nixon declared war on drugs, and in 1973 the federal Drug Enforcement Administration was established. In 1986 President Ronald Reagan declared a new war on drugs, calling drug trafficking an official threat to national security. Congress adopted several measures involving the military in antidrug efforts, and federal resources targeted criminal penalties and deterrence, with prevention and treatment receiving a lower priority. In 1989 President George Bush called drugs "the gravest threat facing our nation today" and established an Office of National Drug Control Policy.

By 1999, with no victory in sight, federal officials began backing away from the metaphor of a war on drugs. The then-director of the Office of National Drug Control Policy, General Barry R. McCaffrey, said the term *war on drugs* is inadequate to describe the nation's drug menace. A four-star Army general and decorated veteran of the Vietnam and Persian Gulf wars, McCaffrey stressed the complexity of the drug problem and the need for a multifaceted solution involving prevention, treatment, education, and law enforcement. "Dealing with the problem of illegal drug abuse is more akin to dealing with cancer [than war]," said McCaffrey.

Q 62. Is it a crime to be addicted to drugs?

A No. In the landmark case of *Robinson v. California* (1962), the U.S. Supreme Court invalidated a California law that made it a criminal offense for a person to "be addicted to the use of narcotics." The case involved Lawrence Robinson, who was convicted after a jury trial of violating the narcotics law despite his claim that alleged needle marks on his arm were the result of an allergic condition contracted during his military service. In a 6-2 decision, the Court likened the law to making it a criminal offense "to be mentally ill, or a leper, or to be afflicted with a venereal disease." States cannot punish persons merely because of their status of addiction, the Court said, noting that babies can be born addicted and that involuntary addiction can result from medical treatment. The Court found the law inflicted cruel and unusual punishment in violation of the Eighth and Fourteenth Amendments to the U.S. Constitution. This finding marked the first time that the Court held the Eighth Amendment's cruel and unusual punishment clause applicable to the states.

VIOLENT CRIME

Q 63. What is murder?

A Murder is defined as intentionally causing the death of another person without extreme provocation or legal justification or causing the death of another while committing or attempting to commit another crime. Murder includes non-negligent or voluntary manslaughter, which is intentionally and without legal justification causing the death of another when acting under extreme provocation.

In 1998 an estimated 16,914 persons were victims of murder or non-negligent manslaughter. This represents a 7.1 percent drop from 1997 and a 28 percent decline from 1994.

Of murder victims in 1998, 76 percent were male; 88 percent were age eighteen or older; and—of those for whom race was known—50 percent were white, while 48 percent were black. Fifty-one percent of victims knew their attacker. Sixty-five percent of all murder victims were killed with a firearm. Nine out of ten female murder victims were killed by males. Nine hundred and twenty persons under age thirteen were murdered.

See 47 What type of crime is a criminal least likely to get away with? 48 Is a murderer more or less likely to be caught today? 49 What tends to be the most accurate single crime statistic? 76 How has the rate of intimate partner homicide changed over time? 83 How has the arrest rate for juveniles charged with murder changed over time? 146 How much does personal crime cost society? 191 Does every defendant have a right to be released pending trial? 287 What type of criminal is least likely to enter a guilty plea? 307 Who is the youngest child to be tried and convicted as an adult for murder?

Q **64. How is murder classified?**

A Under the common law, all murders were considered capital (potential death-penalty) offenses. However, jurisdictions today typically divide murder into two broad categories, murder and manslaughter, depending on the perpetrator's *mens rea* (mental state). Many jurisdictions further divide these categories into different levels or grades of felonies, such as first- and second-degree murder and voluntary or involuntary manslaughter.

Killings that involve premeditation or deliberate thought and certain types of felony murder typically are classified as murder in the first degree. First-degree murder carries the most serious penalty and makes a defendant eligible for the death penalty in states that have a death penalty.

Second-degree murder involves gross negligence. The perpetrator must be aware of a serious and unwarranted risk to human life. Drunk drivers who kill generally are prosecuted for second-degree murder on the premise that their awareness of risk—or, technically, their lack of awareness—was affected by self-induced intoxication.

Felony murder occurs when a person intends to commit a felony that results in a death, even if the death was not intended. Felony murder would cover any death that occurs in the perpetration of, or attempt to perpetrate, an arson, escape, murder, kidnapping, treason, espionage, sabotage, aggravated sexual abuse or sexual abuse, burglary, or robbery.

Manslaughter is the unlawful killing of a human being without malice. Voluntary manslaughter is a killing that occurs as a result of a sudden quarrel or in the heat of passion. Voluntary manslaughter may include cases in which the perpetrator claims he or she was provoked or was attempting self-defense. Involuntary manslaughter is a killing that occurs in the commission of an unlawful act that does not amount to a felony or in the commission of a lawful act without due caution or circumspection, such as speeding in a motor vehicle.

Some states have created additional categories of manslaughter, including vehicular manslaughter (California) and causing or aiding a suicide (Pennsylvania).

Q **65. What constitutes sufficient provocation to qualify a killing as manslaughter rather than murder?**

A To demonstrate sufficient provocation, a person must show that he or she acted in the heat of passion or experienced extreme emotional disturbance at the time of the killing. Most courts say that the reason for the provocation should be sufficiently disturbing to inflame a reasonable third person. The classic example of provocation occurs when a spouse discovers his or her partner engaged in an intimate act with another person.

How much time elapses between the provocation and the killing is very important. Too much time cannot elapse, as a long period makes it unlikely that the defendant acted while still in the heat of passion. Sufficient provocation does not occur when a defendant, for example, walks away after the act of provocation and returns several hours later to kill the victim. Under the Model Penal Code, there can be no cooling-off period at all.

Q **66. Are murder victims more likely to have been murdered by an acquaintance or family member, or by a total stranger?**

A People are more likely to be murdered by friends or acquaintances than by strangers. The Federal Bureau of Investigation reports that 51 percent of murder victims in 1998 knew their assailants.

Q **67. What is the year-and-a-day rule?**

A Under the common law, a defendant could not be charged with murder or killing another unless the victim died within a year and a day of the defendant's act. This rule reflected the primitive state of medical care and the concern that many intervening factors could result in the death. In recent years many states have abandoned the so-called year-and-a-day rule, but it still applies in federal courts.

Q **68. In what city did the homicide rate more than quadruple from 1970 to 1995?**

A The homicide rate in New Orleans increased by 329 percent from 1970 to 1995. The situation became so desperate that one neighborhood held voodoo ceremonies imploring the spirits to do something about crime.

Q 69. What is robbery?

A Robbery is defined as the unlawful taking, by force or the threat of force, of property that is in the immediate possession of another.

In 1998 robberies accounted for losses estimated at nearly $446 million. That year 446,625 robbery offenses were reported to law enforcement authorities, a 10.4 percent decrease from 1997. Adjusting for population growth, 165.2 robberies took place per 100,000 inhabitants of the United States, a decline of 11.3 percent from 1997 and the lowest rate in twenty-nine years.

Almost half of all robberies occur on streets and highways, 24 percent occur in commercial and financial establishments, and 12 percent occur in residences. The Federal Bureau of Investigation reports that in 1998 only 28 percent of robberies were cleared by law enforcement agencies nationwide.

Q 70. What is aggravated assault?

A An aggravated assault is defined as intentionally and without legal justification causing serious bodily injury, with or without a deadly weapon, or using a deadly or dangerous weapon to threaten, attempt, or cause bodily injury, regardless of the degree of injury, if any. Aggravated assault includes attempted murder, aggravated battery, felonious assault, and assault with a deadly weapon. In 1998 sixty-four percent of all violent crimes were aggravated assaults, which makes it the most common violent crime.

According to the Federal Bureau of Investigation, 974,402 aggravated assaults took place in 1998, a 4.8 percent decrease from 1997. When adjusted for population growth, the rate of aggravated assault dropped 5.7 percent in 1998 to the lowest level in a decade. Nationwide, 360 aggravated assaults took place for every 100,000 people.

Of aggravated assaults in 1998, 27 percent were committed with personal weapons, including hands, fists, and feet. Firearms were used in 19 percent of aggravated assaults and knives or other cutting instruments were used in 18 percent of aggravated assaults.

Law enforcement agencies nationwide cleared or solved 59 percent of aggravated assault cases in 1998.

Q 71. What is forcible rape?

A The common law defined rape as forcible intercourse by a man with a woman who was not his wife. This definition persisted well into the twentieth century, despite the fact that it omitted the rapes of men and of married women by their spouses, and sharply limited the conduct that was held to constitute the crime.

In the past twenty years, all fifty states have revised their rape statutes. Most states have widened the scope of activity that constitutes rape and broadened the class of potential victims to include same-sex rape, acquaintance and date rape, and rape that occurs when a defendant induces intoxication of the victim. Today, rape typically includes forcible intercourse (vaginal, anal, or oral) with a female or male and forcible sodomy or penetration with a foreign object (sometimes called *deviate sexual assault*). Most states also have eliminated the traditional prosecutorial requirements that a third-party witness to the rape must be available or that the victim must demonstrate that she fought her rapist.

In 1976 Nebraska became the first state to abolish the so-called *marital rape exemption*. All states have now made spousal rape a crime under at least some circumstances.

The legacy of the past has not entirely disappeared. In its Uniform Crime Reports the Federal Bureau of Investigation (FBI) defines rape as the carnal knowledge of a female, forcibly and against her will. This definition excludes statutory rape and other sex offenses and undercounts the incidence of rape generally by omitting many victims, including all men.

The FBI reports that 93,103 women reported being forcibly raped to law enforcement authorities in 1998, a 3.2 percent decrease since 1997. Adjusting for population growth, 34.4 rapes occurred per 100,000 women in the country, a 4.2 percent decline from 1997 and the lowest rate in fifteen years. Half of the forcible rapes reported to law enforcement authorities in 1998 were cleared by an arrest or by exceptional means.

In a nationally representative survey of 8,000 men and 8,000 women conducted in 1998 by the National Institute of Justice and the Centers for Disease Control and Prevention, 18 percent of women said they had experienced a completed or attempted rape at some time in their lives, and 0.3 percent said they had experienced a completed or attempted rape in the previous twelve months. Of the women who reported being raped at some time in their lives, 22 percent were under age twelve and 32 percent were ages twelve to seventeen when they first were raped.

See 146 How much does personal crime cost society? 511 What is the extent of the problem of rape and coercive sex in correctional facilities?

Q 72. What crime is believed to be least reported to law enforcement agencies?

A Rape is believed to be the least reported crime based on discrepancies between the number of rapes reported to law enforcement agencies and the number revealed in interviews for the U.S. Department of Justice's annual National Crime Victimization Survey (NCVS) and other research studies.

Only 28 percent of all rapes and sexual assaults were reported to police in 1999, according to the NCVS. This number compares to 44 percent of all violent crimes and 34 percent of all property crimes.

One category of rape that is believed to be particularly underreported is rape by intimates. Experts theorize that either the victim does not know that marital rape and date rape are crimes or that the victim does not want to acknowledge the implications of her partner's behavior.

According to a 1998 survey of 8,000 men and 8,000 women by the National Institute of Justice and the Centers for Disease Control and Prevention, 25 percent of the women and 8 percent of the men said they had been raped or physically assaulted by a current or former spouse, cohabiting partner, or date. Physical assault was defined in the survey as behaviors that threaten, attempt, or actually inflict physical harm. The survey also found that women are significantly more likely than men are to be injured during an assault. Approximately one in three women who were injured during a rape or physical assault required medical care.

The NCVS disclosed that females in 1999 were victims of rape and sexual assault at 7.5 times the rate of males. During 1999, 3 females per 1000 were raped or sexually assaulted, compared to 0.4 males per 1000.

Q 73. What is statutory rape?

A Every state has a statute that establishes an age of consent for sexual intercourse—typically age sixteen—below which the law deems consent to be impossible. These laws commonly are known as *statutory rape laws*. Violators of these statutes are prosecuted for rape, sexual assault, or unlawful sexual intercourse. Sanctions typically include possible or mandatory prison or jail time, child support, and fines.

Traditionally, statutory rape has been a strict liability offense, which means that to obtain a conviction the state need only prove that the defendant committed the act. The state is not required to show that the defendant used force, fear, or fraud. The Model Penal Code, an influential code of criminal laws developed as a model for the states by the American Law Institute in 1962, allowed a defense based on reasonable mistake as to age.

In recent years, some states have adopted laws designed to encourage health care providers to report the crime and to target older offenders. In addition, some states have passed laws that avoid making consensual peer sex a crime.

DOMESTIC VIOLENCE

Q **74. What is domestic violence?**

A No universally accepted definition exists for domestic violence, also called family violence and intimate partner violence. Domestic violence includes a wide range of behaviors and is present along a spectrum of crimes, from intimidation to kidnapping and assault to rape and murder.

Legal definitions of domestic violence focus on physical or sexual assault or the threat of assault. Professionals in the fields of mental health and social work characterize domestic violence as a pattern of coercive control that is maintained by tactics such as physical violence, psychological abuse, sexual violence, and denial of resources.

Domestic violence rarely was acknowledged by the criminal justice system until the 1970s, when victims began filing lawsuits and winning damages against police who had failed to protect them from serious injury. The National Center for State Courts estimates the number of domestic violence cases filed in state courts increased by 178 percent from 1989 to 1998, to about 600,000 cases. By 1993 most states had passed laws allowing victims to obtain civil protection orders. Increasingly, police departments, prosecutors, and court systems are forming special domestic violence units to combat the problem, which is now acknowledged to be both a major crime and a major public health issue.

In 1994 Congress created new categories of federal crimes pertaining to interstate domestic violence and stalking. The federal government also created the Violence Against Women Office of the U.S. Department of Justice to, among other things, distribute grant money to the states to combat the problem.

Q **75. How prevalent is domestic violence?**

A The U.S. Department of Justice reports that domestic violence is the leading cause of injury to women in the United States. Women are at greater risk for becoming a victim of a violent crime in their own home than they are at any other place. During their lifetimes, an estimated 22 percent of all women will be physically assaulted by an intimate partner.

The National Crime Victimization Survey (NCVS), an annual federal survey of a representative sample of more than 100,000 Americans ages twelve and over, reported that women experienced an estimated 876,340 rape, sexual assault, robbery, aggravated assault, and simple assault victimizations at the hands of an intimate in 1998. This number decreased from 1.1 million such assaults in 1993. In both 1993 and 1998, men were victims of about 160,000 violent crimes by an intimate partner. Each year from 1993 to 1998, on average, 22 percent of all female victims of violence in the United States were attacked by an intimate partner, compared to 3 percent of all male violence victims. The NCVS tallies nonfatal violent crimes, both reported and unreported to law enforcement agencies, that victimized people ages twelve and older.

According to the Federal Bureau of Investigation (FBI), at least 27 percent of the victims of violent crimes reported to police in 1998 were related to one or more of their victimizers. The FBI defines family violence as a crime against a person or a robbery where the relationship of the victim to the offender is identified as "within family." The FBI's definition of family includes a spouse, child, grandparent, grandchild, in-law, stepparent, stepchild, stepbrother or stepsister, or other family member. It does not include a boyfriend, girlfriend, ex-spouse, ex-boyfriend or ex-girlfriend.

Of victims in 1998 who were identified as being related to their victimizers, the FBI reported that 42.7 percent were spouses or common law spouses. The next most frequent familial relationships were:

• Child, 9 percent
• Sibling, 8.4 percent
• Parent, 7.9 percent
• Other family member, 7.2 percent
• In-law, 2.4 percent
• Stepchild, 2.1 percent
• Stepparent, 1.4 percent
• Grandchild, 0.6 percent
• Grandparent, 0.4 percent
• Stepsibling, 0.4 percent

Family members who are both victims and offenders—for example, when in family disputes both the husband and wife have been charged with assault—accounted for 17.4 percent of the total.

The majority of offenses involving family members—94 percent—were assault offenses, including intimidation, simple assault, and aggravated assault. In order of prevalence, the breakdown was as follows:

• Simple assault, 72 percent
• Aggravated assault, 14.6 percent
• Intimidation, 7.3 percent
• Other offenses, 4.5 percent
• Forcible rape, 1.2 percent
• Murder, 0.2 percent
• Robbery, 0.1 percent

Q 76. How has the rate of intimate partner homicide changed over time?

A A significant decline in homicides by intimate partners has occurred in the past twenty-five years, particularly among male victims. The percentage of white and black females murdered by their intimate partners declined by 14 percent and 46 percent, respectively, whereas the percentage of white and black males murdered by their intimate partners declined by 55 percent and 77 percent, respectively. Some researchers have speculated that fewer men are being killed because women who are considering murder now avail themselves of alternatives, such as shelters, protection orders, and police arrest policies.

The FBI reports that 32 percent of the 3,419 women killed in the United States in 1998 died at the hands of a husband, a former husband, a boyfriend, or a former boyfriend. Many experts believe that the true figure is much higher, perhaps more than 50 percent. In comparison, 4 percent of 10,606 male homicide victims in 1998 were killed by current or former intimate partners.

Q 77. What does the Violence Against Women Office do?

A The U.S. Department of Justice's Violence Against Women Office administers the department's formula and discretionary grant programs authorized by the Violence Against Women Act of 1994. These programs help the nation's criminal justice system respond to the needs and concerns of women who have been or could be victimized by violence. The programs enhance delivery of services to women victimized by violence and work to strengthen outreach efforts to minorities and disabled women. The office provides technical assistance to state and tribal government officials in planning innovative and effective criminal justice responses to violent crimes committed against women.

JUVENILE CRIME

Q 78. What is the juvenile justice system?

A Every state has a separate juvenile justice system to address the needs of children and youths, who society perceives to be developmentally different from adults and more amenable to societal intervention. The juvenile justice system typically has a dual mission: it helps children who are the victims of abuse and neglect, and it processes the cases of children who break the law or engage in delinquent behavior. In the latter case, authorities attempt to balance the goal of rehabilitation with society's need for protection.

Many law enforcement agencies have specialized units that handle juvenile crime and delinquency. Close to 25 percent of juvenile cases are diverted from formal case processing by police, who release the children to parents or refer them to special programs.

The most prominent feature of the juvenile justice system is juvenile court. Although an American invention, juvenile court is based on a centuries-old doctrine from the chancery courts in England, *parens patriae*, which holds that the state or the sovereign is the ultimate parent of all infants. The goal of juvenile courts is both to protect society and rehabilitate the child.

Juveniles who are found to have committed an offense are declared to be delinquent. A judge may order a delinquent child to participate in a wide range of community-based or residential programs tailored for juveniles, from group homes to secure confinement in juvenile correctional centers and training schools. Many juvenile facilities are privately operated.

Faced with mounting public criticism regarding the effectiveness of juvenile courts, the U.S. Supreme Court in the 1960s began issuing a series of rulings that made juvenile courts more like adult criminal courts. The Court extended many due process rights to juveniles in juvenile court proceedings. However, the Court has continued to recognize certain fundamental differences between adult and juvenile courts.

In recent years all states have enacted new laws making their juvenile justice systems more punitive, emphasizing deterrence and the protection of society. Most states have made it easier to transfer juvenile offenders from the juvenile justice system to the adult criminal justice system. Many states have expanded sentencing options and reduced confidentiality protections for some juvenile offenders.

See 110 What factors are considered efficient predictors of youth violence? 111 Are changes in the rate of violent crime by juveniles tied to demographics? 293 What is juvenile court? 464 What is the juvenile correctional system?

Q 79. Who is a juvenile?

A A juvenile is a young person who has not yet reached the age at which he or she is treated as an adult for purposes of criminal law.

Federal and state statutes define which youth are under the original jurisdiction of the juvenile court. In the federal system a juvenile is a person who was below age eighteen at the time of the offense, arrest, or referral to court.

Seventeen is the oldest age for juvenile court jurisdiction in Alabama, Alaska, Arizona, Arkansas, California, Colorado, Delaware, the District of Columbia, Florida, Hawaii, Idaho, Indiana, Iowa, Kansas, Kentucky, Maine, Maryland, Minnesota, Mississippi, Montana, Nebraska, Nevada, New Jersey, New Mexico, North Dakota, Ohio,

Oklahoma, Oregon, Pennsylvania, Rhode Island, South Dakota, Tennessee, Utah, Vermont, Virginia, Washington, West Virginia and Wyoming. Fifteen is the oldest age for juvenile court jurisdiction in Connecticut, New York, and North Carolina and sixteen is the oldest age for juvenile court jurisdiction in Georgia, Illinois, Louisiana, Massachusetts, Michigan, Missouri, New Hampshire, South Carolina, Texas, and Wisconsin.

Four states have changed their age criteria since 1975. Alabama increased its upper age from fifteen to sixteen in 1976 and to seventeen in 1977; Wyoming reduced its upper age from eighteen to seventeen in 1993; and New Hampshire and Wisconsin both lowered the upper age from seventeen to sixteen in 1996.

Many jurisdictions have higher upper ages of juvenile court jurisdiction—typically age twenty-one—in status offense, abuse, neglect, or dependency matters. (A status offense is an offense that would not be a crime if it were committed by an adult—for example, truancy or running away.)

Q 80. Traditionally, at what age did a child become legally responsible for a crime?

A Under the common law, an "infant" below the age of reason (traditionally, age seven) was exempt from criminal prosecution and punishment because he or she was presumed to be incapable of criminal intent. A child between the ages of seven and fourteen was presumed to be incapable of committing a crime. Such a child could still be prosecuted, however, and if a prosecutor successfully rebutted the presumption, the child could be sentenced to prison or death. A youth over the age of fourteen did not receive the benefit of any presumption and was treated as an adult. Today some states have eliminated the conclusive presumption for all children and instead provide a rebuttable presumption for minors under a certain age, usually fourteen.

Q 81. What percentage of arrests involve juveniles?

A In 1998 law enforcement agencies in the United States made an estimated 2.6 million arrests of persons under age eighteen. According to the Federal Bureau of Investigation (FBI), juveniles accounted for 18 percent of all arrests and 17 percent of all violent crime arrests in 1998. The percentage of arrested juveniles in each age group was:

- Age seventeen: 4.7 percent
- Age sixteen: 4.2 percent
- Age fifteen: 3.5 percent
- Age thirteen to fourteen: 4.1 percent

- Age ten to twelve: 1.3 percent
- Under age ten: 0.3 percent

When only serious crimes are tallied, the percentage of juvenile arrests increases. Almost 29 percent of all persons arrested for crimes tracked in the FBI's Crime Index in 1998 were younger than age eighteen. These crimes include murder and non-negligent murder, forcible rape, robbery, aggravated assault, burglary, larceny-theft, motor vehicle theft, and arson. Of the 12.5 million serious crimes tallied in the FBI's Crime Index, the most common in 1998 was larceny-theft, which accounted for about 300,000 juvenile arrests. The next highest category, burglary, accounted for 81,894 juvenile arrests.

Q 82. How has the rate of juvenile crime changed over time?

A The most recent statistics show that, despite continuing growth in the juvenile population, juvenile crime is at its lowest level since 1987. Juvenile crime fell by 30 percent from 1994 to 1998. During that period, the number of juvenile arrests for murder declined by 48 percent. The rate of violent crime committed by juveniles in 1998 was 19 percent lower than in the peak year of 1994. Violent crime includes murder, forcible rape, robbery, and aggravated assault. The rate of juvenile property crime is at its lowest level in a generation. Juvenile property crime fell 14 percent from 1997 to 1998.

The Federal Bureau of Investigation reports that, in the past six years, the total numbers of offenses committed by children and youths under age eighteen were as follows:

Year	Offenses	Year	Offenses
1993	2,014,472	1996	2,103,658
1994	2,209,675	1997	1,969,408
1995	2,084,378	1998	1,855,002

This tally includes serious crimes, drug crimes, and less serious offenses, such as vandalism and curfew violations.

Despite these encouraging declines, the rate of juvenile crime remains higher than it was a few decades ago. The Office of Juvenile Justice and Delinquency Prevention reported in 1998 that the violent crime arrest rate for juveniles in 1996 was 60 percent higher than the 1980 rate for youth under age fifteen and 41 percent higher for youth ages fifteen and older. Property crime rates for youth under age fifteen had returned to 1980 levels, while rates for those ages fifteen and older had declined only slightly from 1991 peaks.

See 111 Are changes in the rate of violent crime by juveniles tied to demographics?

Q 83. How has the arrest rate for juveniles charged with murder changed over time?

A Perhaps the most disturbing juvenile crime trend in the past two decades was the skyrocketing homicide rate. From 1980 to 1993, the number of juveniles arrested for murder increased by more than 100 percent while the arrest rate of adults for murder remained essentially the same. The number of persons under age eighteen arrested for murder peaked in 1993 with 3,790 arrests. That number compares to 2,100 arrests in 1998. Despite an encouraging decline in juvenile murder arrests, the number remains above that of the early 1980s. Following are the number of juveniles arrested for murder each year from 1980 to 1998:

Year	Arrests	Year	Arrests
1980	1,860	1990	3,210
1981	1,960	1991	3,390
1982	1,860	1992	3,270
1983	1,510	1993	3,790
1984	1,300	1994	3,710
1985	1,520	1995	3,250
1986	1,670	1996	2,860
1987	1,830	1997	2,500
1988	2,370	1998	2,100
1989	2,740		

Research indicates that the juvenile homicide phenomenon was concentrated in certain states and cities and that the increase largely related to an increase in homicide by guns. One-third of all juvenile homicide arrests in 1994 were found to have taken place in four cities: Los Angeles, New York City, Detroit, and Chicago. These cities account for only 5.3 percent of juveniles nationwide. In 1993, 56 percent of all juvenile homicide arrests in the nation occurred in six states: Florida, Michigan, Illinois, New York, Texas, and California.

Q 84. What happens to juveniles after they are arrested?

A Approximately 25 percent of juveniles who are arrested and taken into custody by law enforcement officers are released, after receiving a warning, to parents, relatives or friends. The rest are referred to the next step in the juvenile justice system—either juvenile court or juvenile probation—or to adult court.

The Federal Bureau of Investigation reported in 1998 that 22 percent of arrests involving youth who were eligible in their state for processing in the juvenile justice system were handled within law enforcement agencies and then released. Sixty-nine percent were referred to juvenile court; 7 percent were referred directly to criminal court; and the others were referred to a welfare agency or to another police agency.

According to the Committee on the Judiciary of the U.S. House of Representatives, nearly 40 percent of violent juvenile offenders who come into contact with the justice system ultimately have their cases dismissed. Only 10 percent of violent juvenile offenders—those convicted of murder, rape, robbery, and assault—receive any sort of secure confinement.

Q 85. Are the criminal records of juveniles confidential?

A At one time, juvenile records were held to be strictly confidential. Today, forty-two states allow the names, and sometimes the pictures, of juveniles involved in delinquency proceedings to be released to the public, at least under some circumstances.

Q 86. What is the federal Office of Juvenile Justice and Delinquency Prevention?

A The Office of Juvenile Justice and Delinquency Prevention (OJJDP) is a division of the U.S. Department of Justice that serves as the primary federal agency for addressing the problems of juvenile crime and delinquency and missing and exploited children. It was created by Congress under the Juvenile Justice and Delinquency Prevention Act of 1974 in response to national concern about juvenile crime.

Among other things, the OJJDP provides funds directly to public and private non-profit agencies and individuals to foster new approaches to delinquency prevention and the improvement of the juvenile justice system. It also sponsors research about national trends in juvenile delinquency and drug use, serious juvenile crime, the causes of delinquency, prevention strategies, program evaluation, and improvement of the juvenile justice system.

The OJJDP also directs the Missing Children's Program, which was created in 1984 to provide federal leadership in ensuring that every practical step is taken to recover missing children, reunite them with their families, and prosecute abductors.

Q **87. Is property crime in the United States rising or falling?**

A As measured by the National Crime Victimization Survey (NCVS), property crime has been falling for the past twenty-five years, dropping by more than 60 percent since 1975. Property crime includes burglary, larceny, theft in general, and motor vehicle theft. The NCVS reports that in 1999 there were 198 property crimes per 1,000 households in the United States, a decline of 9 percent compared to 1998. The NCVS is an annual federal survey of a representative sample of more than 100,000 Americans ages twelve and over.

Experts attribute the decline in property crime to improved crime prevention, including more window and door alarms, better illumination in yards and driveways, better illumination inside homes when no one is present, more private security, gated communities, and the rise of automated teller machines (which has encouraged individuals to carry less cash). Also, more drug dealers are in prison, and thieves have turned to more lucrative crimes, such as robbery and Internet crime. According to one theory, more people stay home and watch videos, thus giving the nighttime burglar fewer opportunities.

See 146 How much does personal crime cost society?

Q **88. What is burglary?**

A Burglary is the unlawful entry with or without force or the attempted forcible entry of a fixed structure (residence or business) to commit a felony or theft. An estimated 2,329,950 burglaries took place nationwide in 1998, according to the Uniform Crime Reports. This number represents a decline of 5.3 percent from the prior year. When adjusted for population growth, the rate of burglaries declined by 6 percent to its lowest point in two decades.

In 1998 there were 862 burglaries per 100,000 inhabitants of the United States. Burglary victims experienced losses estimated at $3.1 billion. The average dollar loss per burglary was $1,299 for a residential offense and $1,432 for nonresidential offenses.

The highest rate of burglaries (43 percent) occurred in the most populous Southern states, followed by Western states (23 percent), Midwestern states (21 percent) and the Northeast (13 percent). Sixty-five percent of all burglaries in 1998 involved forcible entry, 28 percent involved unlawful entry without force, and the remaining 7 percent involved attempts at forcible entry.

Law enforcement authorities solved only 14 percent of all burglaries in 1998, a decrease of 5 percent from 1997.

Among reasons cited for the decline in burglaries are improvements in domestic and commercial security, an abundance of popular consumer items that has decreased demand for stolen goods, and other, more lucrative, crime opportunities, such as fraud and motor vehicle theft.

Q 89. Who commits more burglaries, adults or juveniles?

A Adults. Eighty-one percent of burglars apprehended by law enforcement authorities in 1998 were adults. The remaining 19 percent were juveniles under age eighteen. However, most burglars were young adults. Sixty-four percent of the adults arrested for burglaries in 1998 were under age twenty-five. Furthermore, 88 percent of burglary arrestees were male, 68 percent were white, and 29 percent were black.

Q 90. What is larceny-theft?

A The FBI defines larceny-theft as the unlawful taking, leading away, or taking away of property from the possession or constructive possession of another. No force, violence, or fraud is used. Larceny-theft includes such crimes as shoplifting, pickpocketing, purse-snatching, thefts from motor vehicles, and bicycle theft. It does not include embezzlement, confidence games, forgery, worthless checks, and motor vehicle theft itself.

Larceny-theft accounted for 59 percent of all crimes contained in the FBI's Crime Index in 1998, more than any other type of crime. In 1998 there were 7,373,886 crimes of larceny-theft in the United States, a 4.8 percent decline from 1997. When adjusted for population growth, 2,728.2 crimes of larceny theft took place per 100,000 inhabitants of the United States, a 5.7 percent decline and a twenty-year low.

Nationwide, larceny-theft cost its victims $4.8 billion in 1998. Although the crime is declining, the dollar value of the goods being stolen is rising. In 1998, the average value of property stolen by larceny-theft was $650, which is an increase of 11 percent from the 1997 value of $585. In addition, the number of persons arrested for larceny-theft fell by 9 percent compared to 1997.

Law enforcement authorities nationwide cleared or solved 19 percent of larceny-thefts in 1999. Police clear or solve a case when a person is arrested, charged with the commission of an offense, and turned over to the court for prosecution. A case also may be cleared if the offender dies or the victim refuses to cooperate with prosecution after the offender is identified by police.

Q **91. Are you more likely to be the victim of larceny-theft if you are an urban, suburban, or rural dweller?**

A You are most likely to be the victim of larceny-theft if you live in the suburbs. According to the Federal Bureau of Investigation, 3,435 crimes of larceny-theft occurred per 100,000 inhabitants in the suburbs; 2,911 such crimes occurred per 100,000 inhabitants in metropolitan areas; and 1,045 such crimes occurred per 100,000 inhabitants in rural counties.

Q **92. What is the most appealing target to a petty thief?**

A Of all larceny-thefts in 1998, 36.3 percent involved thefts from motor vehicles, including parts, accessories (such as radios or compact disc players), and contents (such as a briefcase left in plain sight). Following are the next most frequent larceny-thefts and their percentages of the total:

- Shoplifting, 14.8 percent
- Thefts from buildings, 13.4 percent
- Thefts of bicycles, 5.1 percent
- All others (including pocket-picking, purse-snatching, thefts from coin-operated machines, and other petty thefts), 30.4 percent

Q **93. For what serious crime are women arrested most often?**

A Seventy-two percent of women who were arrested for serious violent and property crimes listed on the FBI's Crime Index in 1998 were arrested for larceny-theft. Fifteen percent of all arrests of women, including both serious and petty crimes, were for larceny-theft. Thirty-five percent of all persons arrested for larceny-theft in 1998 were female.

More than half of the women arrested for larceny-theft were under the age of twenty-five. Forty-six percent of all women arrested for larceny-theft were under the age of twenty-one and 32 percent were under the age of eighteen. By race, 65 percent were white, 32 percent were black, and 3 percent were from all other races.

See 46 What is the gender breakdown for arrests?

Q 94. What is motor vehicle theft?

A Motor vehicle theft is the unlawful taking or attempted theft of a self-propelled road vehicle owned by another. This category of crime includes the theft of automobiles, trucks, snowmobiles, and motorcycles, but not the theft of boats, aircraft, or farm equipment (which is classified as larceny-theft). Typically motor vehicle theft includes receiving, possessing, stripping, transporting, and reselling stolen vehicles, and unauthorized use of a vehicle (joyriding).

According to the Federal Bureau of Investigation (FBI), 1,240,754 motor vehicle thefts occurred in 1998. This number represents a decrease of 8.4 percent from 1997 and is the lowest total for motor vehicle offenses since 1986. Adjusted for population growth, 459 vehicle thefts took place per 100,000 inhabitants of the United States, which is a decline of 9.3 percent from the 1997 figure.

The U.S. Justice Department estimates the value of motor vehicles stolen nationwide was more than $7 billion in 1997, or an average of $5,416 per vehicle.

Motor vehicle theft and burglary compete for the distinction of being the crime with the worst clearance rate among law enforcement officers nationwide. Law enforcement agencies reported a 14.2 percent motor vehicle theft clearance rate in 1998, compared to 13.6 percent for burglaries.

Of the 150,700 arrests for motor vehicle theft in 1998, FBI statistics show, 84 percent of those arrested were males, 67 percent were under the age of twenty-five, 58 percent were white, and 39 percent were black.

Q 95. From where is a car most likely to be stolen?

A Regionally, the highest motor vehicle theft rate was reported by Western states, which had 581 motor vehicle thefts per 100,000 inhabitants in 1998. This number compares to a rate of 470 in Southern states, 396 in the Midwest, and 373 in the Northeast.

Residents of metropolitan areas are more than twice as likely to be victims of motor vehicle thefts. Metropolitan areas experienced a rate of 533 motor vehicle thefts per 100,000 population in 1998, compared to rates of 223 thefts per 100,000 population in the suburbs and 129 thefts per 100,000 inhabitants in rural areas.

Q 96. What are the most frequently stolen motor vehicles?

A For several years, the Toyota Camry and Honda Accord have ranked as the most frequently stolen vehicles in the country. According to CCC Information Services, Inc., which tracks trends in theft and other vehicle damage claims for the insurance industry, nine of the top ten stolen vehicles in 1999 were models of Toyota Camry or Honda Accord. The other most-stolen vehicle was a Ford F-150 4X2 pickup truck. These rankings include cars that were never recovered or were stripped to the point that they were a total loss, and do not include temporary "joyride" thefts.

Q **97. What is the dollar value of property stolen in the United States?**

A The Federal Bureau of Investigation estimates that the total dollar value of property stolen in the United States through burglary, larceny-theft, and motor vehicle theft in 1998 was more than $15.4 billion. The average loss per offense was $1,407, which is slightly higher than the $1,314 average in 1997. Sixty-seven percent of property crimes involved larceny-theft in 1998, while burglaries accounted for 21 percent of property crimes and motor vehicle theft accounted for 12 percent.

DRIVING UNDER THE INFLUENCE

Q **98. What is impaired or drunk driving?**

A Every state has a driving under the influence (DUI) or driving while intoxicated (DWI) law that makes it a criminal offense to operate a motor vehicle while impaired or intoxicated by alcohol or other drugs. The offense is charged when there is evidence that the driver's behavior has been caused by the influence or impairment of alcohol or drugs.

Twenty-three states classify DUI as a felony offense. All but six states have adopted mandatory minimum sentences for drunk drivers, and twenty states require a short jail sentence for first-time offenders. All states have adopted zero-tolerance laws that make it illegal for drivers under age twenty-one to drive after consuming *any* alcohol.

Impairment laws allow a driver licensing agency to suspend or revoke a driver's license if the driver is found to have operated a motor vehicle at or above a specified blood- or breath-alcohol concentration. Thirty-five states and the District of Columbia have enacted vehicle impoundment or forfeiture laws for drunk drivers.

The National Highway Traffic Safety Administration (NHTSA) reports that the legal limit of intoxication set by most states is a blood alcohol concentration (BAC) of 0.10 grams per deciliter. Blood alcohol concentration is the amount of alcohol in an individual's body, measured by the weight of the alcohol in a volume of blood. Common methods of testing BAC include using a breath-testing device, which measures the alcohol level in the breath expelled from the lungs, and blood tests.

In 1998 President Clinton called for establishing a national standard making it illegal to operate a motor vehicle with a BAC of 0.08 grams per deciliter or higher anywhere in the country. Seventeen states and the District of Columbia had passed 0.08 BAC laws in 1999.

According to the NHTSA, 1.5 million drivers were arrested in 1997 for driving under the influence of alcohol or narcotics, which represents an arrest rate of 1 for every 122 licensed drivers in the United States.

The NHTSA defines a fatal traffic crash as being alcohol-related if either a driver or a nonoccupant (a pedestrian) had a BAC of 0.01 grams per deciliter or greater in a police-reported traffic crash. The NHTSA reports that 15,935 alcohol-related fatalities occurred in 1998. This number is equivalent to one alcohol-related fatality every thirty-three minutes. For each death, the NHTSA estimates that 19 persons are hospitalized and 300 have injuries requiring medical care. The NHTSA estimates that alcohol was involved in 39 percent of fatal crashes and in 7 percent of all crashes in 1998.

Intoxication rates for drivers in fatal crashes in 1998 were highest for motorcycle operators (31 percent) and lowest for drivers of large trucks (1 percent). The intoxication rate for drivers of light trucks (20 percent) was higher than that for passenger car drivers (18 percent).

In the case of drivers who are impaired by illegal drugs, a growing number of states are adopting laws that make it illegal to drive with any level of illicit drugs in the system.

See 146 How much does personal crime cost society?

Q 99. How has the number of fatalities caused by drunk drivers changed over time?

A The number of fatalities caused by drunk drivers has declined to an historic low. The 15,935 alcohol-related fatalities in 1998 (38.4 percent of total traffic fatalities for the year) is the lowest level of alcohol-related fatalities since the National Highway Traffic Safety Administration (NHTSA) began reporting these statistics in the 1970s. The number represents a 33 percent reduction from the figure for 1998, the peak year for alcohol-related traffic fatalities.

A major reason for this decline is believed to be the passage of laws setting the drinking age at twenty-one by all states and the District of Columbia. The NHTSA estimates that these laws have reduced traffic fatalities involving drivers ages eighteen to twenty by 13 percent and that they have saved an estimated 18,220 lives since 1975. An estimated 861 lives were saved by minimum drinking age laws in 1998 alone.

Another possible factor in the decline of alcohol-related fatalities is tougher prosecution of drunk drivers. According to the U.S. Department of Justice, the number of drunk drivers under correctional supervision (in prison or jail or on probation) nearly doubled between 1986 and 1997, despite the fact that the number of people arrested for driving while intoxicated (DWI) actually dropped 18 percent over the same time period. The blood alcohol concentration among jailed inmates at the time of their offense was an average of 0.24.

Q 100. What is MADD?

A Mothers Against Drunk Driving (MADD) is a national advocacy group that formed in California in 1980 after a thirteen-year-old girl, Cari Lightner, was killed by a hit-and-run drunk driver. The driver had been freed on bail two days earlier, following an arrest for another hit-and-run drunk-driving crash, and had three previous drunk-driving arrests and two convictions. MADD is widely credited for successfully lobbying to raise the national drinking age from eighteen to twenty-one years.

Q 101. How much do alcohol-related crashes cost society each year?

A A 1994 federal study estimated the direct costs of alcohol-related crashes at $45 billion a year, plus an additional $70.5 billion in lost qualify of life because of alcohol-related crashes.

See 146 How much does personal crime cost society?

OTHER CATEGORIES OF CRIME

Q 102. What is a hate crime?

A According to the Uniform Crime Report issues by the Federal Bureau of Investigation (FBI), a hate or bias crime is a criminal offense committed against a person, property, or society that is motivated, in whole or in part, by the offender's bias against a race, religion, disability, sexual orientation, ethnicity, or national origin. In selecting the victim, the perpetrator often wants to terrorize or intimidate the larger group to which the victim belongs.

In 1998, 7,755 hate crime incidents were reported to the FBI, including 4,321 motivated by racial bias, 1,390 by religious bias, 1,260 by sexual orientation bias, 754 by ethnicity or national origin bias, 25 by disability bias, and 5 by multiple biases.

The 7,755 incidents involved 9,235 separate offenses, 9,722 victims, and 7,489 known offenders.

Since the 1980s the federal government and forty-one states have adopted laws that increase the penalty for offenders who are convicted of hate crimes. In *Wisconsin v. Mitchell* (1993), the U.S. Supreme Court upheld such a law in Wisconsin. The Court said that hate crime offenders are punished more severely not because of their noxious beliefs but because of their conduct. The Court added that higher penalties for hate crimes are justified because these crimes are perceived to inflict greater individual and societal harm.

A recent example of a hate crime was the 1998 slaying of forty-nine-year-old James Byrd Jr. in Jasper, Texas, by white supremacists. Byrd was chained by the ankles to the back of a pick-up truck and dragged to death.

Q 103. Can you be the victim of a hate crime if you are white?

A Yes. This was the scenario in a landmark case, *Wisconsin v. Mitchell* (1993), in which the U.S. Supreme Court upheld a Wisconsin law that increased the penalty of those convicted of hate crimes.

On October 7, 1989, a group of young black men, including the defendant, Todd Mitchell, met in an apartment and discussed a scene from the film *Mississippi Burning* in which a young black boy who was praying was beaten by a white man. The group moved outside the apartment building and Mitchell said, "Do you all feel hyped up to move on some white people?" A young white boy approached the group on the opposite side of the street and Mitchell said, "You all want to —— somebody up? There goes a white boy; go get him." The group beat the boy so severely that he remained in a coma for four days. They also stole his tennis shoes. Mitchell was convicted of aggravated battery and his sentence was doubled under the state's penalty enhancement statute, from two years to four years.

Q 104. What is a lack-of-respect crime?

A In 1999 Louisiana Governor Mike Foster signed into law an act that requires students to address teachers as "ma'am" or "sir" or use the appropriate title of Mr., Mrs., Ms., or Mrs. The law, which is intended to foster respect in the classroom, does not include any provisions for punishment on violation. Each of Louisiana's sixty-six school systems may decide how to discipline students who fail to respond politely. However, no student may be expelled or suspended.

105. Is cursing a crime?

A It can be. A Michigan man was convicted by a jury in 1999 of using profanity in a public area where he should have known children might be present. Timothy Boomer—the "cursing canoeist"—violated a century-old state law prohibiting cursing in front of minors. A first-time canoeist, Boomer became annoyed when his rented canoe hit a rock and he fell into the river. At the same time, Michael and Tammy Smith were canoeing down the river with their two children. They attempted to cover their children's ears when Boomer engaged in his tirade. Boomer, who faced a possible 90-day jail sentence, was sentenced to perform four days of community service and ordered to pay a $75 fine. The court rejected Boomer's argument that the Michigan law was invalid because cursing is protected by free speech guarantees under the First Amendment of the U.S. Constitution. The judge did throw out a section of the law that prohibited the use of profane speech in front of women.

Q **106. What is organized crime?**

A Organized crime refers to self-perpetuating, structured, and disciplined associations of individuals who combine for financial gain, either wholly or in part, through illegal means. Their illegal enterprises include drug trafficking, gambling, loan-sharking, extortion, theft, arson, weapons trafficking, labor racketeering, pornography, prostitution, and money laundering. They often use extortion, graft, corruption, violence, or threat of violence to achieve their objectives. Historically, organized crime groups have a strong leader to whom group members and associates pay a percentage of their profits.

In the early 1900s large numbers of Irish, Jewish, Italian, and other immigrants arrived in the United States. Some of the new arrivals formed ethnic gangs and crime organizations. The most notorious organized crime group that began during this period is La Cosa Nostra, also called the Mafia, which is run by a network of *consiglieres,* capos, soldiers, and associates. In 1950 Congress's Special Committee to Investigate Organized Crime in Interstate Commerce warned that Mafia organizations had risen to prominence through bootlegging, rackets, gambling, and violence.

In recent years federal authorities have successfully prosecuted high-ranking Mafia leaders, seriously weakening the organization. However, organized crime is in no danger of disappearing. Increasingly, the United States is prey to international organized crime groups from Russia, China, Latin America, and other places. Organized crime now includes international money laundering, drug trafficking, gambling, illegal immigration, arms dealing, murder-for-hire, theft, extortion, and infiltration of legitimate businesses.

See 35 What may be the most violated federal law in U.S. history? 361 Who were the Untouchables? 374 "Who said, "Income tax law is a lot of bunk"?

Q 107. What is white-collar crime?

A The Federal Bureau of Investigation (FBI) defines white-collar crime as illegal acts that are characterized by fraud, concealment, or a violation of trust and that do not depend on the application or threat of physical force or violence. Violators seek to obtain money, property, or services, to avoid the payment or loss of money or services, or to secure a personal, political, or business advantage. White-collar crime includes economic crimes, such as wire and mail fraud; financial institution crimes, including check fraud and embezzlement; and government fraud and corruption by public officials.

No accurate tally exists of the number of white-collar crimes that are committed each year in the United States. Definitions vary regarding what constitutes white-collar crime. Also, these crimes are difficult to investigate and prosecute, and they are becoming increasingly so with economic globalization. Nevertheless, authorities agree that white-collar crime drains billions from public and private coffers and wreaks untold havoc on American institutions and citizens. The cost of white-collar crime in the United States has been estimated to be three times that of organized crime. The U.S. General Accounting Office estimates, for example, that fraud and abuse consumed roughly 10 percent ($100 billion) of the $1 trillion expenditures for the nation's health care in 1995.

In the private sector, the Association of Certified Fraud Examiners (ACFE) estimated in 1999 that employees, managers, and owner-executives in the United States misappropriated more than $400 billion a year from their organizations. Occupational fraud and abuse ranges from pilferage to sophisticated investment swindles. Common violations include asset misappropriation, corruption, false statements, false overtime, petty theft and pilferage, use of company property for personal benefit, and payroll and sick-time abuses.

The ACFE estimates that losses caused by occupational fraud amount to at least $9 per employee day or 6 percent of the annual revenue of the employing organizations, excluding indirect costs such as the loss of productivity from the firing of abusive employees and the expense of government intervention.

The ACFE reported that 58 percent of reported fraud and abuse cases in its study were committed by nonmanagerial employees, 30 percent by managers, and 12 percent by owner-executives. For employees, the median loss was $60,000. For managers, the median loss was $250,000. For owner-executives, the median loss was $1 million. The median loss per case caused by males was about $185,000; by females, about $48,000.

 108. Who was the top corporate criminal of the 1990s?

 According to the *Corporate Crime Reporter*, a legal publication based in the District of Columbia, the top corporate criminal of the decade was Swiss pharmaceutical giant F. Hoffmann–La Roche Ltd., which in 1999 pleaded guilty in the District of Columbia to leading an international conspiracy to suppress and eliminate competition in the vitamin industry. The corporation agreed to pay a record $500 million fine, which will go into a fund to benefit the victims of crime.

Two top Hoffmann–La Roche executives, both Swiss residents, entered guilty pleas in connection with the conspiracy. Dr. Kuno Sommer, former director of worldwide marketing for Hoffman–La Roche's Vitamins and Fine Chemicals Division, was sentenced on July 23, 1999, to a four-month prison term and fined $100,000. Dr. Roland Brönnimann, former president of the Vitamins and Fine Chemicals Division of Hoffmann–La Roche, agreed to serve a five-month jail sentence and pay a $150,000 fine.

The corporation was prosecuted by the U.S. Department of Justice's Antitrust Division, which collected fines for criminal violations of antitrust laws in excess of $955 million in 1999. That number compares to about $17 million in fines collected by the division in 1987.

CAUSES OF CRIME

 109. What causes crime?

 In the eighteenth century German physician and anatomist Franz Joseph Gall advanced the "scientific" explanation that skull structure determines criminal proclivities. Italian criminologist Cesare Lombroso believed that criminals are born with certain recognizable hereditary physical traits, particularly skull and body types. French political philosopher Montesquieu said criminal behavior is related to natural, physical environmental factors, such as the climate.

Modern experts have posited that crime is caused by poverty and unemployment, the breakdown of the family unit and societal institutions, genetics, biology, drugs, easy access to guns, and leniency in the criminal justice system. Former Federal Bureau of Investigation (FBI) Director J. Edgar Hoover, who led the nation's premier crime-fighting agency for three decades, believed lack of religious training was the root of crime.

Some theories about the causes of crime seem contradictory. In the 1960s Democratic President Lyndon Baines Johnson insisted that social reforms, such as his war on poverty, would eliminate the root causes of criminal behavior. In the 1980s Republican President Ronald Reagan complained that welfare kept the poor from gaining affluence, destroyed families, and contributed to the rising crime rate. Reagan advocated a punitive, get-tough approach to crime.

Most causation theories boil down to one of two underlying premises: that the criminal chooses or is born to a life of crime or that environmental factors propel the criminal into a life of crime.

Modern research points to a cycle of crime and violence. Children who are victims of or witness violent crime are at an increased risk for delinquency, adult criminality, and violent behavior. Being abused or neglected as a child increases the likelihood of arrest as a juvenile by 53 percent and of arrest for a violent crime as an adult by 38 percent. Research shows that, on average, abused and neglected children begin committing crimes at younger ages, commit nearly twice as many offenses as nonabused children, and are arrested more frequently. Abuse also places children at significant risk for substance abuse, mental illness, and suicide.

In a 1999 national poll of American attitudes toward violence by Louis Harris and Associates, Inc., respondents said that the following factors "contribute a lot" to violence in America:

- Lack of adult supervision of children, 90 percent
- Easy availability of handguns, 65 percent
- Television, 58 percent
- Movies, 57 percent
- Video games, 47 percent
- Television news, 39 percent

See 395 What crime prevention methods work best?

Q 110. What factors are considered efficient predictors of youth violence?

A After a two-year study the Office of Juvenile Justice and Delinquency Prevention (OJJDP) reported in April 2000 that the following factors might predict future youth violence:

- Individual factors, such as pregnancy and delivery complications, low resting heart rate, internalizing disorders, hyperactivity, aggressiveness, early initiation of violent behavior, involvement in other forms of antisocial behavior, and beliefs and attitudes favorable to deviant or antisocial behavior

- Family factors, such as parental criminality, child mistreatment, poor family management practices, low levels of parental involvement, poor family bonding and family conflict, parental attitudes favorable to substance abuse and violence, and parent-child separation
- School factors, such as academic failure, low bonding to school, truancy, dropping out of school, and frequent school transitions
- Peer-related factors, such as delinquent siblings and peers and gang membership
- Community and neighborhood factors, such as poverty, community disorganization, availability of drugs and firearms, neighborhood adults involved in crime, and exposure to violence and racial prejudice.

The most reliable predictor of subsequent violence or serious delinquency is the commission of a juvenile offense by ages six to eleven, even if the offense did not involve violence. The strongest predictors for youth ages twelve to fourteen were lack of social ties and involvement with antisocial youth. The OJJDP report represents the conclusions of twenty-two researchers who were brought together to analyze data on the development of serious violent juvenile offenders.

Q 111. Are changes in the rate of violent crime by juveniles tied to demographics?

A The number of juveniles is expected to increase to 77.6 million by 2020, with greater percentage increases among minorities living in inner cities. Some experts are predicting a new juvenile crime wave as a result of the juvenile population increase.

Other experts maintain that demography is not destiny. The juvenile population topped 69.9 million in 1968, a level not exceeded until 1998, when the juvenile population reached 72.8 million. Yet juvenile crime in the 1960s did not approach the level and intensity of the late 1980s and early 1990s, when guns and drugs fueled gang wars in the inner cities and the juvenile murder arrest rate doubled.

According to the U.S. Department of Justice's Office of Juvenile Justice and Delinquency Prevention (OJJDP): "It is clear . . . that the Nation is not doomed to high levels of juvenile violence simply because the juvenile population will increase." The OJJDP predicts that social and policy changes will have more effect on juvenile violent crime and arrest trends than will population changes.

See 79 Who is a juvenile? 82 How has the rate of juvenile crime changed over time?

Q 112. Did legalizing abortion lower the crime rate?

A After analyzing the declining U.S. crime rate, two scholars concluded that the legalization of abortion in 1973 might account for as much as half of the overall crime reduction from 1991 to 1997. Steven Levitt, a University of Chicago economist, and John Donohue III, a Stanford University law school professor, said that people who would have been at risk to commit crimes during the peak crime years of young adulthood—unwanted offspring of poor, teenage, and minority women—were aborted at disproportionately high rates more than two decades ago. The authors concluded that women who chose abortion were those at greatest risk for bearing children who would have been most likely to commit crimes as young adults. The study also relied on research of long-term studies of women living in various European countries where government approval to have an abortion was required. These studies showed that children born because their mothers' requests for abortion were denied were substantially more likely to be involved in crime and have poorer lives.

Q 113. How does the economy affect the crime rate?

A The connection between the economy and the crime rate is unclear. An economic theory of deterrence posits that the business cycle influences the crime rate. As the economy worsens, criminals have fewer opportunities to earn legitimate income and more incentive to commit crimes. At the same time, however, fewer opportunities present themselves for crime. For example, unemployment creates a financial motive to sell cocaine, but fewer buyers may be able to purchase it. In recent years, experts have noted, unprecedented increases in the U.S. crime rate occurred during periods of economic boom. An indirect connection may exist between the economy and the crime rate. Much of the unprecedented increase in juvenile crime in the 1980s was blamed on guns and the illegal drug trade, which disproportionately affected disadvantaged urban neighborhoods.

Q 114. Does a link exist between violence in the media and actual violence?

A During the 1950s rock 'n' roll music and youth rebellion movies such as *The Blackboard Jungle* were blamed for inciting crime. Today many experts say that a steady bombardment of highly sensationalized crime and violence on television and in video games, popular music, and the Internet contributes to crime. The theory is that *entertainment violence* desensitizes consumers and helps blur the line between fantasy and reality, especially for the most disturbed and psychologically vulnerable young people.

Numerous studies have found a connection between entertainment content and behavior. The National Television Violence Study, a three-year study that was the largest study of media content ever undertaken, found that viewing television violence is a factor in the learning of aggression and has a negative impact on children. The UCLA Television Violence Monitoring Report of the UCLA Center for Communication Policy concluded in 1995 that evidence "strongly suggests that there is a link between violence on television and that in the real world."

The entertainment industry implicitly acknowledged that violent materials are inappropriate for young people by adopting ratings systems for movies, television, and music lyrics. Successful new industries have arisen in recent years reflecting parental concern about entertainment violence, including the development of browsers and filters that help parents to shut out unwanted programming.

See 139 What is the mean-world syndrome?

Q 115. Does a link exist between drugs and crime?

A A clear link has been established between crime, drug use, and drug trafficking. Studies over the past decade show that between one-half and three-quarters of adult individuals arrested and charged with crimes had drugs in their systems when arrested. The rate for juveniles ranged from 40 percent to 69 percent.

The Federal Bureau of Investigation reports that, of the 15,289 homicides that occurred in 1997 in which circumstances of the crime were known, 5.1 percent were narcotics related. Murders that occur during a narcotics felony, such as drug trafficking or manufacturing, are considered drug related.

Various federal surveys show that addicts commit crimes to get money to buy illegal drugs. A 1997 survey found that 19 percent of state prisoners and 16 percent of federal inmates said they committed their most recent offense to obtain money for drugs. A 1996 profile of jail inmates found that, overall, 16 percent of convicted jail inmates said they had committed their offenses to get money for drugs. Of convicted property and drug offenders, about one in four had committed their crimes to get money for drugs.

Some criminologists attribute the juvenile crime wave of the mid-1980s to a deadly mix of drugs, guns, and juveniles.

See 56 What type of drug is involved in most drug abuse violations? 57 What drug is most closely associated with violent crimes? 61 Is there a war on drugs? 62 Is it a crime to be addicted to drugs? 148 What generates more revenue, the sale of illegal drugs or the pharmaceutical industry? 520 Do substance abuse treatment programs cut recidivism among inmates?

Q 116. What percentage of high school students have consumed an illegal substance?

A A federal study showed that 54 percent of U.S. high school seniors in 1997 had used an illegal drug at least once, as had more than 29 percent of eighth graders. Among adolescents ages twelve to seventeen, the average ages of first use of marijuana, cocaine, and heroin were 13.7, 14.7, and 14.4 years, respectively. Youth tobacco smoking rates were higher than at any time in the past seventeen years. Two-thirds of U.S. high school students had tried cigarettes and more than one-third currently smoked.

The study, by the Office of National Drug Control Policy and the Department of Health and Human Services, also found that more than 80 percent of U.S. high school students had tried alcohol. In 1997 more than 31 percent of twelfth graders, 25 percent of tenth graders, and 14 percent of eighth graders claimed to have consumed five or more alcoholic drinks in the preceding two weeks. Among twelve- to seventeen-year-olds who exhibited no other problem behaviors, those who used marijuana, alcohol, or cigarettes in the past month were seventeen times more likely to consume illegal drugs such as cocaine, heroin, or LSD than those who had not used these drugs.

Q 117. Does a link exist between mental illness and crime?

A Evidence is growing of a link between mental illness and crime. The proportion of prisoners who are mentally ill is estimated to be five times that found in the general population.

A 1999 study by the U.S. Department of Justice found that approximately 16 percent of state prison inmates, 7 percent of federal prison inmates, and 16 percent of prisoners in local jails were mentally ill. At midyear 1998 a total of 283,800 mentally ill offenders were being held in the nation's state and federal prisons and local jails, and an additional 547,800 mentally ill people were on probation in the community.

Compared to other inmates and probationers, mentally ill prisoners and probationers reported higher rates of prior physical or sexual abuse and higher rates of drug and alcohol abuse by at least one parent or guardian while they were growing up.

See 515 How many prisoners are mentally ill?

Q 118. Does a link exist between handguns and crime?

A A clear link exists between the availability of handguns and crime. In fact, access to handguns is thought to be a major reason that the United States has led the industrialized world in homicide rates for as long as records have been kept. The Federal

Bureau of Investigation (FBI) reports that 65 percent of all murder victims were killed with a firearm in 1998.

In 1998 adults were more likely to be killed with a firearm (68 percent) than were juveniles (48 percent). However, of murdered juveniles ages thirteen or older, 77 percent were killed with a firearm, compared to 16 percent of murdered juveniles under age thirteen. According to the Office of Juvenile Justice and Delinquency Prevention, teenage boys are more likely to die from gunshot wounds than from all natural causes combined. The National Crime Victimization Survey reports that offenders used a weapon in 25 percent of all violent offenses in 1998.

Alfred Blumstein, director of the National Consortium on Violence Research, advances the *diffusion hypothesis* to explain the sharp increase in juvenile crime that occurred in the 1980s. According to Blumstein, as new crack entrepreneurs were setting up business, taking over turf previously dominated by others, they recruited young people as sellers and middle managers. These low-level dealers needed guns to defend themselves, and the guns, once in the hands of impulsive adolescents, quickly diffused into the youth culture. Suddenly, garden-variety adolescent squabbles over girlfriends and valued clothing were being settled by gunfire. Between 1985 and 1992, both the homicide rate for persons age eighteen and younger and the number of gun-related juvenile homicides doubled. Only by getting guns out of the hands of youths, says Blumstein, will the nation lower the incidence of violent crime committed by juveniles.

See 147 Which amount is higher, the annual cost of treating gunshot victims or the annual amount that Americans spend on guns?

Q **119. What percentage of male tenth and eleventh graders carry or possess a firearm?**

A A federal survey found that 29 percent of male tenth and eleventh graders from fifty-three high schools nationwide carried or possessed at least one firearm in 1996. Of these young people, 6 percent carried a gun outside the home. Fifty percent of the juveniles believed they could obtain firearms relatively easily. Family and friends were the primary sources of guns. Most of the juveniles said the primary reason for carrying or possessing firearms was protection, not criminal activity or status enhancement. The Youth Handgun Safety Act, passed as part of the 1994 Crime Act, generally prohibits juveniles age eighteen and under from possessing handguns.

Q 120. What does the Second Amendment right to bear arms mean?

A The Second Amendment to the U.S. Constitution states: "A well regulated Militia, being necessary to the security of a free State, the right of the people to keep and bear Arms shall not be infringed."

Debate continues about whether America's Founders intended the Second Amendment to provide every citizen with the right to carry any type of firearm. Gun-control advocates argue that the Founders adopted a right to bear arms to secure the protection of the country. They note that the Second Amendment itself is prefaced by a statement regarding the necessity of securing a free state through a well-regulated militia. In any case, they argue, the Founders' original intent was based on conditions that existed in 1791 and should not dictate a response to the modern-day threat posed by gun violence.

Gun-control opponents argue that the Senate, in the process of adopting the Bill of Rights, rejected an amendment to the Second Amendment that would have limited the keeping and bearing of arms to doing so "for the common defense." They say that this means the Founders intended the right to bear arms to be an individual right.

The U.S. Supreme Court has sided with those who take the position that the Second Amendment does not establish an individual right to possess firearms. In *United States v. Cruikshank* (1875), the Court held that the right "of bearing arms for a lawful purpose" is "not a right granted by the Constitution." More recently, in *United States v. Miller* (1939), the Court said that the Second Amendment obviously was adopted "to assure the continuation and render possible the effectiveness" of the militia and "must be interpreted and applied with that end in view."

Q 121. What is the Brady Handgun Violence Prevention Act?

A On November 30, 1993, the U.S. Congress enacted the Brady Handgun Violence Prevention Act, which amended the Gun Control Act of 1968. The first major piece of federal legislation enacted to combat gun violence in America, the Gun Control Act of 1968 passed in the wake of the shootings of presidential hopeful Robert Kennedy and civil rights leader Dr. Martin Luther King Jr. Among other things, the Gun Control Act of 1968 outlawed certain types of so-called gangster weapons.

The 1993 Brady law, named after James Brady, a press secretary to President Ronald Reagan who was wounded during the attempt on Reagan's life by John Hinckley Jr. in 1981, imposed as an interim measure a five-day waiting period before a licensed importer, manufacturer, or dealer could sell, deliver, or transfer a handgun to an unlicensed individual.

The Brady law prevented an estimated 312,000 felons, fugitives, stalkers, and other prohibited purchasers from legally buying firearms from 1993 to November 30, 1998, when the interim provisions of the new law expired and the permanent provisions took effect.

The permanent provisions of the Brady law call for an "instant background check" system. The Federal Bureau of Investigation (FBI) has established a National Instant Criminal Background Check System (NICS) in Clarksburg, West Virginia, to perform background checks of all purchasers of firearms from federally licensed dealers. Federal firearms licensees, including pawnbrokers, must initiate a criminal background check through NICS before transferring a firearm to an unlicensed individual. The NICS may take up to three business days to notify the firearms licensee whether receipt of a firearm by the prospective purchaser would be in violation of the law.

The permanent provisions of the Brady law prevented 62,189 people with criminal records from purchasing firearms in 1999. According to the FBI, more than 12 million prospective gun sales will be reviewed in 2001.

The FBI administers the NICS system and conducts the background checks but the Bureau of Alcohol, Tobacco and Firearms (ATF) is responsible for enforcing the provisions of law. The ATF regulates and inspects federal firearms licensees and investigates criminal violations of the Brady law.

EFFECTS OF CRIME

Q 122. Who is a crime victim?

A The definition of a crime victim is far from unanimous. The federal government and the states have adopted legislation pertaining to the establishment and protection of the rights of crime victims, but definitions vary as to who is a victim. The definition is important because it determines eligibility for important rights, such as who must be notified and allowed to attend or participate in judicial proceedings related to a crime and who is eligible for restitution from the perpetrator.

A proposed 1996 amendment to the U.S. Constitution would extend victims' rights to each "individual who is a victim of a crime for which the defendant can be imprisoned for a period longer than one year or any other crime that involves violence." The Judicial Conference of the United States, the chief policy-making body of the federal judiciary, criticized this definition as too sweeping. The conference noted that in 1996 the amendment would have affected 34,000 felonies filed in federal courts and 1.7 million felonies filed in state courts, plus an undetermined number of millions of misdemeanors involving violence. While the proposed constitutional amendment included no definition of the term *victim*, the Judicial Conference noted that accompanying proposed federal legislation defined a victim as any person who has "suffered direct physical, emotional, or pecuniary harm as a result of the commission of a crime." The conference complained that this definition could overwhelm courts by extending victims' rights to, for example, every resident of a large metropolitan area where an environmental crime occurred, such as a toxic discharge into the air or water. The conference has expressed its preference for federal legislation guaranteeing victims' rights rather than a constitutional amendment.

Q 123. How many Americans are victims of crime each year?

A In 1999 there were 28.8 million criminal victimizations of Americans ages twelve and older, according to the National Crime Victimization Survey (NCVS), an annual federal survey of a representative national sample of more than 100,000 Americans. The number of criminal victimizations in 1999 was the lowest recorded since 1973, when approximately 44 million victimizations occurred.

The survey results include both reported crimes and unreported crimes. In 1999 victims reported fewer than half of all violent crimes (44 percent) and about a third of property crimes (34 percent) to the police.

Overall, some 21.2 million property crimes (burglary, motor vehicle theft, and household theft), 7.4 million violent crimes (rape or sexual assault, robbery, aggravated assault, and simple assault), and 0.2 million personal thefts (pocket picking and purse snatching) occurred in 1999.

Between 1993 and 1999 the rate of violent crime fell 34 percent, from 50 to 33 crimes per 1,000 persons ages twelve or older. Property crime decreased by almost 40 percent and personal theft rates decreased by 61 percent during the same period.

In a 1999 survey commissioned by the National Association of Police Organizations (NAPO), half of 800 registered voters polled reported that they or a close family member had been a victim of a crime. NAPO is a coalition of police unions and associations.

See 315 What percentage of crimes reported to police result in an arrest?

Q 124. What are victims' rights?

A The U.S. victims' rights movement first appeared in the 1960s, after Great Britain, New Zealand, and other nations enacted the first victim compensation programs. California created the first state crime victimization fund in 1965 and enacted the nation's first law permitting crime victims to deliver impact statements at sentencings in 1978.

The 1980s saw an explosion of concern for crime victims. In 1982, the Presidential Task Force on Victims of Crime called the American criminal justice system "appallingly out of balance" and made sixty-four recommendations to improve victims' rights. That year the U.S. Congress passed the Victim and Witness Protection Act, which offered protection for crime victims and witnesses. In 1984 Congress passed the Victims of Crime Act, which established a fund to provide financial assistance to state governments to compensate and assist victims of crime.

In 1990 Congress passed the first federal bill of rights for crime victims, the Victims' Rights and Restitution Act. This law requires federal law enforcement officers to use their best efforts to ensure that victims are treated with fairness, reasonably protected from the accused, and notified of all court proceedings. Furthermore, the law entitles federal crime victims to be present at all public court proceedings unless the court determines otherwise, to restitution, and to receive information about the offender's conviction, sentencing, imprisonment, and release.

Today, the federal government and every state has a law that guarantees crime victims the right to participate in the criminal justice process. Every state allows courts to consider victim impact information at sentencing and at least half of the states expressly require the courts to consider that information. Forty-one states allow victims to make an oral statement during a sentencing hearing. Most states give victims the right to notice of and the right to attend events and proceedings associated with the crime.

Despite this progress, officials estimate that only a small fraction of the nation's estimated 31 million crime victims receives services such as emergency financial assistance, crisis and mental health counseling, shelter, and information and advocacy within the criminal and juvenile justice system.

In 1996 President Bill Clinton called for an amendment to the U.S. Constitution to protect the rights of crime victims. One proposed amendment under consideration by the U.S. Congress would give victims the right to reasonable notice of, and the right not to be excluded from, any public proceedings relating to the crime; the right to be heard, if present; and the right to submit a statement at all such proceedings to determine a conditional release from custody, an acceptance of a negotiated plea, or a sentence.

Q **125. How many states have passed constitutional amendments to ensure that victims have rights in criminal proceedings?**

A Twenty-nine states had amended their constitutions to include protection for crime victims as of February 2000, according to the U.S. Department of Justice Office for Victims of Crime.

Q **126. What is the significance of *Payne v. Tennessee*?**

A In a rare reversal, the U.S. Supreme Court ruled in *Payne v. Tennessee* (1991) that the grandmother of a young boy who had witnessed the murder of his mother and sister could testify at the killer's sentencing about how the boy continued to cry out for his dead family members. Chief Justice William H. Rehnquist argued that "victim impact evidence is simply another form or method of informing the sentencing authority about the specific harm caused by the crime." In earlier rulings, the Court had barred the use of victim impact statements in cases involving the death penalty on the grounds that the emotional pleas could lead to an arbitrary imposition of capital punishment. Opponents of victim impact statements argue that victim impact statements result in sentences that are overly influenced by the status or worth of the victim.

Q **127. What is a victimless crime?**

A Some crimes appear to have no victims. The parties voluntarily consent to engage in a criminal act and may actively seek to avoid the attention of law enforcement officers. Such victimless crimes may include drug abuse, prostitution, obscenity, euthanasia, suicide, dueling, and sodomy.

Some social commentators argue that no such thing as a victimless crime is possible because these illegal transactions victimize society at large. A crack house, for example, can quickly destroy a residential neighborhood. Research indicates that violent pornography desensitizes viewers to violence against women. So-called victimless crimes may ultimately force society to spend billions annually for medical care, crime control, and prisons.

See 57 What drug is most closely associated with violent crimes? 114 Does a link exist between violence in the media and actual violence? 115 Does a link exist between drugs and crime?

Q 128. What percentage of Americans lock their doors?

A By far, most Americans lock their doors. A poll conducted by the National Opinion Research Center at the University of Chicago in 1997–1998 found that 94.3 percent of Americans had locked their doors during the past year to protect themselves from crime. Other crime prevention measures taken included the following:

- Acted more aware or cautious, 78.9 percent
- Stayed in at night, 36.1 percent
- Kept a gun in the house, 32.8 percent
- Kept a dog, 29.9 percent
- Joined or participated in a neighborhood watch program, 21.2 percent
- Used a home burglary or security system, 19.5 percent
- Carried mace or some other self-protection chemical, 18.6 percent
- Obtained self-defense training or education, 17.8 percent
- Carried a gun while away from home, 11 percent

Q 129. Who is most likely to be victimized by a violent crime?

A Young black males are the demographic group most vulnerable to violent crime. According to the National Crime Victimization Survey (NCVS), an annual federal survey of a representative national sample of more than 100,000 Americans ages twelve and older:

- Persons ages sixteen to nineteen were most likely to experience a violent crime in 1999.
- Forty-two violent victimizations occurred per 1,000 blacks in 1999, compared to 32 victimizations per 1,000 whites and 25 victimizations per 1,000 persons of other races.
- Thirty-seven victimizations occurred per 1,000 males in 1998, compared to 29 victimizations per 1,000 females.
- Urban residents experienced higher rates of violent victimization in 1999 than residents of suburban and rural areas.

Q 130. How many Americans will be victims of violent crime at least once in their lifetimes?

A One often-quoted statistic is that five out of six Americans will be victims of a completed or attempted violent crime at least once in their lives. U.S. Justice Department officials say that this number, derived from a 1987 federal study, remains the most recent estimate.

Q 131. What percentage of Americans are afraid to walk alone at night in their own neighborhoods?

A In a poll conducted in 1998 by the Roper Center for Public Opinion Research, University of Connecticut, 41 percent of Americans said they were afraid to walk alone at night in their own neighborhoods, while 57 percent said they were not afraid. Women, blacks, and older people are most fearful. Fifty-two percent of women said they were afraid, compared to 26 percent of men. Half of the blacks polled expressed fear, compared to 36 percent of whites. The most fearful age group consisted of people fifty years and older, 43 percent of whom said they were afraid to walk alone at night in their own neighborhoods. Interestingly, 46 percent of Democrats expressed fear, compared to 36 percent of Republicans and 40 percent of independents.

Q 132. Are children safer in school or out of school?

A Despite several highly publicized incidents of school violence in recent years, children are safer at school than they are outside of school. A joint study conducted in 1998 by the U.S. Department of Education and the U.S. Department of Justice found that children ages twelve to eighteen were at least two-and a-half times more likely to be victims of serious violent crime while away from school than while at school. The only crime for which youth faced greater risk while in school was theft. The study examined data over a twenty-year period and found no change in the percentage of high school seniors who had been injured by violence. Other studies indicate that school violence has declined along with the juvenile crime rate.

Concern about school safety escalated after the April 1999 shooting of thirteen high school students and a teacher at a high school in Littleton, Colorado. Some researchers have suggested that the nation is experiencing a false panic because of increased media attention on school violence. Other researchers contend that schools have been unacceptably violent all along.

According to the U.S. Department of Education, 10 percent of public schools reported at least one incident of serious violent crime in 1996–1997; 47 percent reported at least one incident of less serious or nonviolent crime; and 43 percent reported no crimes to police. The U.S. Department of Justice estimated that 8 out of every 1,000 students would be the victims of violent crime in 1997.

Q **133. How many children are victims of abuse each year?**

A Officials estimate that nearly 3 million children were the subjects in 2 million reports of abuse in 1996—an increase of 161 percent since 1980. One possible reason for the increase is greater willingness to report suspected child abuse and less societal tolerance for such abuse.

According to a 1997 study funded by the National Institute of Justice, an estimated 1 million violent crimes involving child victims are reported to police annually; another 1.1 million cases of child abuse are substantiated by child protection agencies annually; and in their lifetimes, roughly 1.8 million of adolescents ages twelve to seventeen will be victims of a serious sexual assault, 3.9 million adolescent children will be victims of a serious physical assault, and almost 9 million will witness serious violence.

The Office of Juvenile Justice and Delinquency Prevention reports that one-third of murdered juveniles were under age six; females are at greatest risk of being murdered in their first year of life and at age twenty-three; and children under age twelve are the victims in one-third of all sexual assaults reported to police.

Q **134. What percentage of violent crimes against juveniles are reported to police?**

A Twenty-eight percent of violent crimes against children ages twelve to seventeen are reported to police, according to a 1999 study by the U.S. Department of Justice's Office of Juvenile Justice and Delinquency Prevention. This compares to 48 percent of violent crimes against adults. A major factor in the under-reporting of crimes against juveniles is that 16 percent of crimes against children are reported to authorities other than police, such as school authorities. Also, many parents believe that nonsexual assaults on children are not crimes but are, instead, youthful fights or scuffles. Some parents also fear that reporting the crime may lead to reprisals from criminals.

Q **135. What kind of person violently victimizes a child?**

A A 1991 survey of state prisoners who had committed violent crimes against children found that the vast majority are older white males. Specifically, the survey found:

- Ninety-seven percent of child victimizers are male and 75 percent of their victims are female.
- Nearly 70 percent of child victimizers are white.
- Thirty-one percent of violent child-victimizers report being physically or sexually abused themselves as children, compared to an average of 17.1 percent of all adults.

Child victimizers tended to be older than adult victimizers. More than 45 percent of violent inmates arrested were in their fifties, and fewer than 14 percent were in their twenties.

- Nearly two-thirds of child victimizers were married, compared to 40 percent of adult victimizers.

- Child victimizers almost always know their victims. Fewer than 10 percent of inmates serving time for the rape or sexual assault of a child reported that the victim was a stranger to them.

- The average prison sentence term for violent offenders with child victims was eleven years, which is shorter than the average received by violent offenders with adult victims.

Q 136. What is the Office for Victims of Crime?

A The Office for Victims of Crime (OVC) is the U.S. Department of Justice's chief advocate for crime victims and their families. The OVC carries out the mandates of the Victims of Crime Act of 1984; monitors compliance with the provisions regarding assistance for federal crime victims of the Victim and Witness Protection Act of 1982; and implements the recommendations of the President's Task Force on Victims of Crime and the Attorney General's Task Force on Family Violence.

A major activity of the OVC is administering a Crime Victims Fund that was created in the U.S. Treasury by the Victims of Crime Act of 1984 to provide federal financial assistance to state governments to compensate and assist victims of crime. Monies in the fund come from fines and penalties assessed on convicted federal defendants. The OVC awards grants to states to compensate crime victims for expenses, such as medical costs, resulting from their victimization. Grants also are awarded to states to support state and local programs that provide direct assistance to crime victims and their families. Priority for victim assistance funds is given to programs serving victims of sexual assault, spouse abuse, and child abuse. A small portion of the Crime Victims Fund is available to support services for victims of federal crimes.

Deposits into the fund have increased from an initial $77 million in fiscal year 1987 to $363 million in fiscal year 1998. In total, the fund has received more than $2 billion since its inception to support thousands of crime victim programs throughout the United States.

Each year, the OVC sponsors National Crime Victims' Rights Week to increase public awareness of crime victims' special needs and to honor those who work on behalf of victims.

137. Are African Americans disproportionately affected by crime?

A African Americans are overrepresented both as victims and as perpetrators of crime, compared to their numbers in the population. They have been more likely than whites to be victims of violent crime. Forty-two violent victimizations occurred per 1,000 blacks in 1998, compared to thirty-two victimizations per 1,000 whites. Black households also experienced property crime at a higher rate than white households (249 versus 190 crimes per 1,000 households).

Blacks represented 12 percent of the U.S. adult population in 1996 but 44 percent of all convicted felons. Minorities are incarcerated at a higher rate than are whites. Overall, black men and women were at least 7 times more likely than whites and 2.5 times more likely than Hispanics to have been in prison or jail on June 30, 1999.

Statistics like these lead some experts to theorize that crime is largely an intraracial phenomenon rather than an interracial one. This theory implies that ethnic groups, including minorities, are more likely to commit crimes within their own communities. In fact, more than 80 percent of homicides where the race of the killer is known are either white-on-white or black-on-black killings.

Some experts also blame racism in the criminal justice system for the high numbers of blacks in jail and prison. According to a 1998 study, blacks account for fewer than half of arrests for violent crimes but just over half of the convictions and approximately 60 percent of the prison admissions. Civil rights advocates say that minorities are subject to disparate treatment at arrest, bail, charging, plea bargaining, trial, sentencing, and every other stage of the criminal process.

More than half of black Americans in a 1995 Gallup poll said that the justice system was biased against them, and two-thirds said that police racism against blacks is common nationwide.

The racial disparity in arrests and convictions is particularly apparent with respect to young males. In 1998 the racial composition of the juvenile population of the United States was 79 percent white, 15 percent black, and 5 percent other races, with most Hispanics classified as white. Yet 42 percent of juvenile arrests for violent crimes involved black youths, compared to 55 percent that involved white youths. Almost half of all juveniles arrested for murder were black.

In 1999 federal officials estimated that nearly 30 percent of black males in their twenties and early thirties were in jail, in prison, on probation, or on parole.

An often-cited 1990 study found that homicide was the leading cause of death among black males ages fifteen to twenty-four. At that time, 25 percent of black males ages twenty to twenty-nine were in prison, on parole, or on probation, whereas only 4 percent were enrolled in college.

See 129 Who is most likely to be victimized by a violent crime? 299 Who is most likely to be detained by juvenile authorities? 390 What police beating incident exposed the shortcomings of military-style policing? 463 Who is more likely to be incarcerated— African Americans, whites, or Hispanics? 558 Is the death penalty discriminatory?

Q 138. Are rich people or poor people more likely to be victimized by crime?

A Poor people are more likely to be victimized by violent crime. In 1998 people earning less than $7,500 were twice as likely to be the victims of a violent crime as people earning in excess of $35,000 per year.

According to the National Crime Victimization Survey (NCVS), households in 1999 with incomes of less than $75,000 suffered the highest rates of rape/sexual assault, robbery, aggravated assault, simple assault, and personal theft. The NCVS is an annual survey of a representative sample of Americans ages twelve and older.

Q 139. What is the mean-world syndrome?

A Many Americans today feel more vulnerable to crime and victimization than ever before, despite the fact that the crime rate has been declining for years. This feeling reflects a phenomenon labeled the *mean-world syndrome*. Research has shown that viewers who watch television more than three hours a day are more likely than viewers who watch two hours or less to feel at high risk of victimization from violence, to perceive their neighborhoods as unsafe, and to regard the world as "mean and gloomy." Thus, elderly residents of gated apartment communities in Florida tremble at the thought of leaving their apartments even though their actual risk of crime is remote, and parents worry about sending their children to school even though children are actually safer in school than elsewhere. According to the Rocky Mountain Media Watch, the proportion of media time devoted to crime, disaster, war, and terrorism averaged roughly 40 percent in 1998.

See 114 Does a link exist between violence in the media and actual violence?

SPENDING ON CRIME AND COST OF CRIME

Q 140. How much does the government spend on the criminal justice system?

A The federal government predicts the amount of resources devoted to the administration of justice in the United States by the federal, state, and local governments will reach $175 billion in 2001. This represents a 79 percent increase over the 1993 level of $98 billion.

Data released by the U.S. Department of Justice in November 1999 show that federal, state, and local governments spent a combined total of $112,868,000,000 in 1995 on direct and intergovernmental expenditures for criminal justice. The U.S. Bureau of the Census, using slightly different definitions, calculates that total direct expenditures on criminal justice by local, state, and federal governments in fiscal year 1995 amounted to $119,304,000,000.

Q 141. What percentage of all government spending is devoted to preventing crime and punishing criminals?

A The U.S. Bureau of the Census estimates that 4.4 cents of every dollar in government spending goes to justice activities. Of the 4.4 cents, 1.8 cents went for police; 1.7 cents, for corrections; and 0.9 cents, for judicial and legal services. The Census Bureau calculates that total direct expenditures on criminal justice by local, state, and federal governments in fiscal year 1995 amounted to $119,304,000,000. Of all of the federal dollars spent by the U.S. government in 1995, the Bureau calculates that criminal justice represented just a small percentage. The federal government spent 37.9 percent of all federal dollars in 1995 on social insurance, 22.2 percent on national defense and international relations, and 15.8 percent on debt interest.

Q 142. For what does government spend more—police, courts, or corrections?

A The single largest annual criminal justice expenditure is for police protection. The U.S. Justice Department reports that in 1995 the nation spent $48.6 billion for police protection, $39.8 billion for corrections (including jails, prisons, probation, and parole), and $24.5 billion for the combined activities of courts, prosecution, legal services, and public defense.

143. How has spending on the justice system changed over time?

A The following statistics from the U.S. Department of Justice present the annual total direct expenditures for justice-related activities by federal, state, and local governments from 1982 through 1996:

Year	Total Direct Expenditures (in $ millions)	Year	Total Direct Expenditures (in $ millions)
1982	$35,842	1990	$79,434
1983	$39,680	1991	$87,567
1984	$43,943	1992	$93,777
1985	$48,563	1993	$97,542
1986	$53,500	1994	$103,471
1987	$58,871	1995	$112,868
1988	$65,231	1996	$120,194
1989	$70,949		

An analysis of spending on the justice system from 1982 to 1995 shows that direct spending on the justice system increased by almost 215 percent during the thirteen-year period. The sharpest increase in spending was at the federal level, where spending rose from $4.3 billion in 1982 to $16.7 billion in 1995, an increase of almost 292 percent. In comparison, state spending increased by 251 percent and local spending by 181 percent.

Direct expenditures include salaries, wages, fees, supplies, capital outlays, and all other expenditures except those classified as intergovernmental. Intergovernmental expenditures consist of payments from one government to another for grants-in-aid, shared revenues, payments in lieu of taxes, and services performed by one government for another on a reimbursable or cost-sharing basis.

144. What level of government (local, state, or federal) spends the most on criminal justice activities?

A According to the latest statistics from the U.S. Justice Department, local government spends the most on criminal justice. In 1996 the total direct expenditure by local government on the justice system was $62.8 billion, whereas states spent $39.9 billion and the federal government spent $17.5 billion.

The U.S. Bureau of the Census estimates that local governments also devote the highest percentage of their budgets to criminal justice activities. In 1995 local governments devoted 7.9 percent of their total spending to criminal justice, compared to 7.4 percent spent by state governments and 1.1 percent by the federal government.

Q 145. How much do individuals and private organizations spend to prevent crime?

A In 1993 individuals and private organizations spent $65 billion on alarms, private guards, security systems, and the like.

Q 146. How much does personal crime cost society?

A In a 1996 study the federal government estimated that personal crime in America cost crime victims $105 billion annually in medical costs, lost earnings, and public program costs related to victim assistance. When pain, suffering, and lost quality of life were figured in, the total cost topped $450 billion, of which $426 billion was attributed to violent crime (including arson and drunk driving) and $24 billion to property crime. This comes out to approximately $1,800 per U.S. resident.

Following are the crimes that cause the highest losses:

- Rape and sexual assault (excluding child abuse), $127 billion
- Fatal crime, $93 billion
- Other assault or attempted assault, $93 billion
- Child abuse, $56 billion
- Drunk driving, $41 billion
- Robbery or attempted robbery, $11 billion
- Larceny or attempted larceny, $9 billion
- Burglary or attempted burglary, $9 billion
- Motor vehicle theft or attempted theft, $7 billion
- Arson, $5 billion

The total cost of crime equals approximately 5 percent of the U.S. gross domestic product (GDP).

See 97 What is the dollar value of property stolen in the United States? 101 How much do alcohol-related crashes cost society each year?

Q 147. Which amount is higher, the annual cost of treating gunshot victims or the annual amount that Americans spend on guns?

A According to a 1999 study published in the Journal of the American Medical Association, the cost is about the same. Each year, the nation spends some $2.3 billion treating gunshot victims, an amount that matches what Americans annually spend on guns. The study found that the government paid $1.1 billion of the total cost of treating gunshot victims, mostly through Medicaid and Medicare payments. Private insurers covered 18 percent of the cost and victims picked up 19 percent.

See 118 Does a link exist between handguns and crime? 120 What does the Second Amendment right to bear arms mean?

Q 148. What generates more revenue, the sale of illegal drugs or the pharmaceutical industry?

A The United Nations International Drug Control Program estimates that the illegal drug trade generates retail sales of about $400,000 million a year, nearly double the sales of the global pharmaceutical industry. At least $200,000 million of drug money is laundered every year. The International Monetary Fund (IMF) estimates that earnings from drug trafficking account for about 2 percent of the global economy. More than 150 nations meeting at a special session of the UN General Assembly in 1998 called for the establishment and strengthening of national money laundering legislation by 2003.

See 115 Does a link exist between drugs and crime?

Q 149. How much does crime cost the insurance industry?

A A 1996 federal study found that insurers pay out approximately $45 billion annually because of crime, which translates to $265 per American adult.

The amounts paid by insurers by type of crime or attempted crime involved are as follows:

- Drunk driving, $25.1 billion
- Motor vehicle theft or attempted theft, $3.6 billion
- Burglary or attempted burglary, $3.5 billion
- Assault or attempted assault (other than rape), $3.3 billion
- Arson, $2.4 billion
- Larceny or attempted larceny, $2.1 billion
- Rape (omitting sex abuse), $1.7 billion
- Murder, $1.2 billion
- Child abuse (other than sex abuse), $0.8 billion
- Child sex abuse, $0.6 billion

Types of insurance used to pay crime-related bills and the amounts paid are as follows:

- Auto, $23.5 billion
- Health, $11 billion
- Homeowners' fire and theft, $7.9 billion
- Workers' compensation, $1 billion
- Life, $1.5 billion

These figures exclude an estimated $12 billion in medical payments that insurers do not pay directly but may absorb due to cost shifting and long-term disability insurance.

Q **150. Are justice costs rising faster than the costs of other government functions?**

A No. The per capita expenditure for justice activities (including civil and criminal justice activities) across all levels of government in 1995 constant dollars was $429.56. This represents a 57 percent increase over 1985 and compares to a 78 percent increase in spending for education, 139 percent for public welfare, 88 percent for healthcare, and 3 percent for national defense and international relations. From 1985 to 1995, the per capita cost of corrections rose 99 percent, judicial and legal costs rose 56 percent, and police protection rose 35 percent.

CRIMINAL PROCEDURE

IN GENERAL

Q 151. What is criminal procedure?

A In the United States, criminal procedure governs how criminal laws are enforced and how justice is dispensed.

The federal government and the various states adopt their own laws pertaining to criminal procedure within their respective jurisdictions. All such laws, however, must comport with the U.S. Constitution as it is interpreted by the U.S. Supreme Court. Since the 1960s the Court has issued many landmark rulings pertaining to criminal procedure. Among other things, the Court effectively ended coerced confessions and required states to provide counsel to indigent defendants facing imprisonment.

Criminal procedure also derives from state constitutions, federal and state statutes, court decisions, and rules adopted by the highest court within the respective jurisdiction. It also includes policy and administrative rules adopted by various agencies within the criminal justice system.

Criminal procedure affects the entire spectrum of the criminal justice system, from the point at which a law enforcement officer focuses on a suspect to a criminal defendant's final appeal. Ultimately, criminal procedure balances the state's interest in speedy and efficient justice with the accused's rights to equal protection and due process of law in accordance with the Fifth Amendment and the Fourteenth Amendment to the U.S. Constitution.

At each step along the road to justice, someone employed by the criminal justice system exercises discretion. Police decide whether to make an arrest; prosecutors decide which charges to bring; judges make critical rulings about the evidence or testimony; and juries weigh the facts. Criminal procedure limits the discretion exercised by these officials and helps to ensure the fair and uniform treatment of criminal defendants.

The Framers of the U.S. Constitution were skeptical about the power of big government. They required the state, which has far more resources than any individual defendant, to surmount a heavy burden of proof to convict a defendant. The rules of criminal procedure help to keep the scales of justice in balance.

Q 152. May states deviate from requirements of the U.S. Constitution?

A The U.S. Constitution, as interpreted by the U.S. Supreme Court, sets forth the minimum amount of protection that must be accorded to criminal defendants. However, states can be more protective of an accused's rights. For example, a state may adopt stricter requirements with respect to unreasonable searches and seizures by police. States also may decline to exercise the full extent of their authority. For example, a dozen states have no death penalty.

Q 153. What was the due process revolution of the 1960s?

A In the 1960s the U.S. Supreme Court issued a flurry of decisions that significantly expanded the rights of criminal suspects in police custody. Most of these decisions were issued by the Court under the leadership of a former California prosecutor, Earl Warren, who was chief justice from 1953 to 1969.

The first ten amendments to the U.S. Constitution (the Bill of Rights) were enacted as limitations on the federal government. The Fourteenth Amendment, ratified in 1868, provided that no state could deprive any person of "life, liberty, and property, without due process of law." The Warren Court interpreted the Fourteenth Amendment to require that states abide by most of the provisions of the Bill of Rights. Important decisions affecting the rights of defendants include:

- *Mapp v. Ohio* (1961). The Court said that that evidence obtained by police in an illegal search could not be used at trial in state or federal courts.
- *Gideon v. Wainwright* (1963). The Court guaranteed that an attorney would be provided to indigent defendants facing serious charges.
- *Malloy v. Hogan* (1964). The Court held that states must observe the Fifth Amendment privilege against self-incrimination.
- *Miranda v. Arizona* (1966). The Court expanded the right against self-incrimination by requiring police to inform defendants of their right to remain silent, of the fact that their words may be used against them, and of their right to retain counsel.
- *Duncan v. Louisiana* (1968). The Court said that the Sixth Amendment required states to provide jury trials in serious state criminal cases.

Criticism over rising crime prompted the Court to revisit issues raised in some of these cases after Warren's retirement. The Court, under Chief Justice Warren E. Burger in the 1970s and Chief Justice William H. Rehnquist in the 1980s, narrowed some of the Warren Court's more controversial rulings. In *United States v. Leon et al.* (1984), for example, the Court restored some of the power that it had taken away from police in *Mapp* when it ruled that illegally obtained evidence could be used at trial if police had acted in "good faith" and were unaware that their actions were in violation of the U.S. Constitution. At the same time, subsequent Courts also broadened some of the Warren Court's rulings. For example, in *Argersinger v. Hamlin* (1972), and *Scott v. Illinois* (1979), the Burger Court extended the right to counsel to misdemeanor cases where a term of imprisonment is imposed.

See 15 What is due process? 166 What is the significance of Gideon v. Wainwright? *167 What is the significance of* Miranda v. Arizona?

ARREST

Q 154. What is an arrest?

A An arrest occurs when police take an individual who is suspected of criminal activity into custody or detain the person in connection with a criminal charge.

Police do not have to physically restrain a person or say that the person is under arrest. In *Florida v. Royer* (1983), the U.S. Supreme Court ruled that police may approach people on the street or in another public place and ask them if they are willing to answer questions. However, the Court said, a *seizure* occurs when a reasonable person does not believe that he or she is free to leave. This might occur, for example, if police block the individual's path or take the individual's car keys.

Unlike a simple stop, which may be justified by reasonable suspicion, police must have probable cause to make an arrest.

See Figure 2-1 Arrests for Federal Offenses.

Q 155. Can police detain a citizen for no apparent reason?

A No. In *Terry v. Ohio* (1968), the U.S. Supreme Court ruled that police may stop and investigate unusual or suspicious behavior when an officer reasonably believes that an individual is engaged in criminal activity. However, a fine line exists between no apparent reason and behavior that justifies a stop. The Court said that such cases

Figure 2-1 Arrests for Federal Offenses

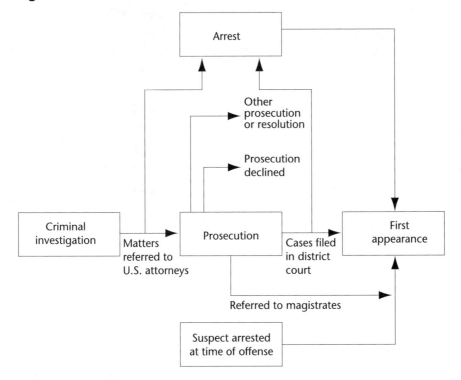

Source: Department of Justice, Bureau of Justice Statistics Publication NCJ180258, *Compendium of Federal Justice Statistics, 1998* (Washington, D.C.: U.S. Government Printing Office, May 2000), 12.

must be viewed in terms of their full circumstances to determine whether the stop was justified.

On January 12, 2000, in a 5–4 decision, the Court gave police broad authority to stop and question people who run at the sight of an officer. In *Illinois v. Wardlow* (2000), the Court said that such flight may indicate that a crime is being committed and therefore can help justify a police stop. The case involved a Chicago man who was stopped by police because he was standing in front of a building in a high-crime area and ran when police spotted him. Until *Wardlow* state and lower federal court rulings showed wide disagreement as to whether running at the sight of police creates sufficient suspicion to justify a stop.

156. What is a *stop and frisk*?

A In *Terry v. Ohio* (1968), the U.S. Supreme Court ruled that police can stop and frisk someone in a public place without a warrant if the officers reasonably believe that the person may be armed and dangerous, has committed a crime, or is about to commit a crime. The Court said that police may stop someone whose unusual conduct leads the officer to reasonably conclude that "criminal activity may be afoot." The officer may then make a reasonable inquiry about the person's behavior and conduct a superficial examination of the person's body surface or outer clothing to discover weapons or contraband. If in the course of the pat-down the officer detects an object that might be a weapon, the officer may reach inside and take the object without violating that person's Fourth Amendment right to be free from unreasonable search and seizure. Police may seize a weapon that is unlawfully possessed.

In *Florida v. J.L.* (2000), the U.S. Supreme Court ruled that an anonymous tip that a person is carrying a gun is not sufficient cause to justify a police officer's stopping and frisking that person.

See 10 What rights are afforded to citizens by the Fourth Amendment to the U.S. Constitution?

Q 157. What is probable cause?

A The term *probable cause* connotes the minimum amount of evidence that is necessary to encroach on a citizen's constitutional right to be free from search and seizure.

As the term implies, probable cause deals with probabilities. In *Brinegar v. United States* (1949), the U.S. Supreme Court said that probable cause exists where the facts and circumstances within the arresting officer's knowledge are trustworthy and sufficient to warrant a person of reasonable caution to believe that a crime was or is being committed.

Probable cause is more than a reasonable suspicion but less than the standard required to convict a defendant (proof beyond a reasonable doubt).

Probable cause is based on what the officer knew before the arrest or search, not on any information that may later have come to light. If the court finds a lack of probable cause, an arrest can be invalidated as improper and evidence that resulted from the search may be excluded at trial.

158. When can a law enforcement officer make an arrest?

A A law enforcement officer generally can make an arrest for any crime that is committed in the presence of the officer or, in the case of a felony, when an officer has knowledge that a felony was committed and probable cause to believe that a specific suspect committed the crime. Police also can make an arrest under the authority of an arrest warrant, which is a written order issued by a court. Ultimately, the U.S. Constitution requires police to have probable cause to make an arrest.

Q **159. Can police rely on an informant to make an arrest?**

A Yes. In *Draper v. United States* (1959), the U.S. Supreme Court ruled that police may act on information provided by a reliable informant if the information is sufficiently accurate to lead the officers directly to the suspect. In *Illinois v. Gates* (1983), the Court said that whether an informant's information is reliable enough to establish probable cause depends on the "totality of the circumstances." The Court said that a neutral magistrate may consider whether the informant gave police sufficient facts to indicate that a crime was being committed and whether police verified these facts.

Q **160. What is racial profiling?**

A Minority communities call racial profiling "driving while black or brown." The practice involves law enforcement officials targeting an individual as being a potential criminal on the basis of his or her race.

Critics say the practice of racial profiling escalated as a result of the federal war on drugs. According to the American Civil Liberties Union, the U.S. Drug Enforcement Administration's "Operation Pipeline" trained 27,000 law enforcement officials to use racial profiling to spot drug couriers on highways.

In June 1999 President Bill Clinton called racial profiling by police a "morally indefensible, deeply corrosive practice" and issued an executive order requiring federal law enforcement officials to collect data on the race and gender of the people they stop to question or arrest. President Clinton expressed concern that racial profiling erodes the confidence of minorities in law enforcement authorities.

Q **161. What is a warrant?**

A A warrant is a document issued by a judge or magistrate commanding that law enforcement officers make an arrest or conduct a search and seizure. The Fourth

Amendment to the U.S. Constitution states that warrants may be issued only upon probable cause, supported by oath or affirmation, and must particularly describe the place to be searched and the persons or things to be seized.

To obtain a warrant, police must file a written complaint with the court that contains the name or a description of the accused or the objects sought, supported by affidavits describing the offense and its surrounding circumstances. The court must determine whether probable cause exists to believe that a crime was committed and that the suspect is the probable offender or that the objects sought will be found in the place to be searched.

An arrest warrant that is given directly to a police officer by a judge is called a bench warrant.

See 10 What rights are afforded to citizens by the Fourth Amendment to the U.S. Constitution?

Q 162. Under what circumstances must police obtain an arrest warrant?

A Unless the suspect consents or an emergency exists, police must have an arrest warrant to arrest a suspect at the suspect's home or at the home of a third party. In *Payton v. New York* (1980), the U.S. Supreme Court held that the Fourth Amendment "has drawn a firm line at the entrance to the house. Absent exigent circumstances, that threshold may not reasonably be crossed without a warrant." According to the Court, the Fourth Amendment prohibits police from making a warrantless and nonconsensual entry into a suspect's home to make a routine felony arrest. The *Payton* holding subsequently was extended to require police to obtain an arrest warrant to arrest a suspect at the home of a third party.

Q 163. What is the likelihood that a felony arrest will lead to a felony conviction?

A According to the U.S. Department of Justice, there was a 71 percent likelihood that a felony arrest would lead to a felony conviction in 1996. That figure compares to a 65 percent likelihood in 1992 and 48 percent in 1988.

Q 164. What is a statute of limitations?

A A statute of limitations is a period of time specified by the legislature within which a civil action or a criminal charge can be made or an appeal can be filed.

With respect to a crime, the clock typically begins to run when the violation is committed. If authorities bring a charge after the time period has elapsed, an accused may raise the statute of limitations as a defense and seek dismissal of the charge.

Statutes of limitations in criminal law are intended to encourage prompt investigation and prosecution of crimes, to prevent the deterioration of valuable evidence, and to protect defendants from being convicted based on stale evidence. The statutes ultimately protect society from crime by promoting accurate results at trial and the efficient use of the prosecutor's resources.

With the exception of murder, virtually all crimes have statutes of limitations. Under federal law, "Except as otherwise expressly provided by law, no person shall be prosecuted, tried, or punished for any offense, not capital, unless the indictment is found or the information is instituted within five years next after such offense shall have been committed." The Model Penal Code, a proposed code of criminal laws developed as a model for the states by the American Law Institute, established time limitations of six years for a serious felony, three years for any other felony, two years for a misdemeanor, and six months for a petty misdemeanor.

A statute of limitations may be suspended for several reasons, such as when a defendant has fled the jurisdiction or concealed the crime through fraud.

Q **165. If a police officer refuses to make an arrest, can a citizen make the arrest instead?**

A State statutes typically grant any person the power to make a citizen's arrest for certain categories of crime committed in their presence or within their view. This right is most often exercised by private security guards, police officers who are outside their jurisdiction, and by so-called bail enforcement agents, popularly known as bounty hunters, who track down fugitives.

Bounty hunters typically are independent contractors who work for a fee. Bounty hunters may be employed by bail bondsmen, private individuals, or firms that lend bail money to defendants who are awaiting trial. If a defendant skips his or her court appearance—as roughly one in seven clients do—the bounty hunter can earn 10 percent of the bail amount by apprehending and returning the fugitive.

The Supreme Court recognized the common law rights of bail bondsmen and their agents in 1872. In *Taylor v. Taintor* (1872), the Court said that bail bondsmen may arrest persons for whom they have undertaken bail at any time during the existence of their relationship without resort to any new judicial process. According to the Court, the bail bondsman may pursue a defendant "into another State; may arrest him on the Sabbath; and, if necessary, may break and enter his house for that purpose."

Q 166. What is the significance of *Gideon v. Wainwright*?

A Earl Gideon, who was indigent, was charged with a felony in Florida after allegedly breaking into a pool hall. Under Florida law, only defendants facing the death penalty had a right to appointed counsel. Gideon represented himself at trial and was convicted and sentenced to five years in state prison.

In *Gideon v. Wainwright* (1963), the U.S. Supreme Court said that the right to counsel is a fundamental right that is essential to a fair trial. The Court held that the Fourteenth Amendment's due process clause requires states to provide counsel to indigent defendants in felony trials. This ruling later was extended to virtually all defendants who face a possible prison term. According to the *Gideon* Court, "That government hires lawyers to prosecute and defendants who have the money hire lawyers to defend are the strongest indications of the widespread belief that lawyers in criminal courts are necessities, not luxuries. . . . From the very beginning, our state and national constitutions and laws have laid great emphasis on procedural and substantive safeguards designed to assure fair trials before impartial tribunals in which every defendant stands equal before the law. This noble ideal cannot be realized if the poor man charged with crime has to face his accusers without a lawyer to assist him."

As if to demonstrate the Court's point, Gideon was retried and acquitted by a jury in his second trial, during which he was represented by court-appointed counsel.

See 153 What was the due process revolution of the 1960s?

Q 167. What is the significance of *Miranda v. Arizona*?

A At one point in American history, forced confessions were commonplace. Police used brutal techniques, including beatings that were known as the *third degree.* This began to change in the 1960s when the U.S. Supreme Court, under the leadership of Chief Justice Earl Warren, issued a series of rulings expanding constitutional protections afforded to criminal defendants and extending them to state as well as federal criminal defendants. In the most famous of these cases, *Miranda v. Arizona* (1966), the Court ruled that the Fifth Amendment prohibition against self-incrimination applies to an individual who is in police custody or "deprived of his freedom of action in any significant way."

Ernesto Miranda had confessed to kidnapping and rape after he was questioned by police in a small interrogation room for two hours without ever being told he had a Sixth Amendment right to the assistance of counsel. The confession was admitted into evidence at a state court trial over Miranda's objection, and he was convicted.

In a 5–4 decision, the Court said that police must, before questioning suspects who are in police custody, inform them of their constitutional right to remain silent and to have the assistance of counsel. The purpose of the Miranda warnings, the Court said, is "to make the individual more acutely aware that he is faced with a phase of the adversary system—that he is not in the presence of persons acting solely in his interest." The Court reversed Miranda's conviction.

The Miranda decision provoked a storm of criticism and remains controversial today.

See 153 What was the due process revolution of the 1960s?

Q 168. What are the Miranda warnings?

A In *Miranda v. Arizona* (1966), the U.S. Supreme Court required law enforcement authorities, before beginning questioning, to warn suspects who are in police custody of their "right to remain silent, that anything they say can be used against them in a court of law, that they have the right to the presence of an attorney, and that if they cannot afford an attorney one will be appointed for them before any questioning if they so desire." Interrogation must cease if a suspect requests counsel or wants to remain silent. Suspects may waive their Miranda rights, but the prosecution bears a heavy burden of showing that the waiver was made voluntarily, knowingly, and intelligently.

Q 169. Must a law enforcement officer always give the Miranda warning before questioning?

A No. A Miranda warning applies only to "custodial" questioning. It does not apply if a person is not in police custody or "otherwise deprived of freedom of action in any significant way." Thus the Miranda warning may not apply in a conversation between a suspect and an undercover police officer or government informant; if police do not ask the suspect any questions; when the person volunteers information before the police have asked a question; or when a suspect gives a statement privately to a friend or acquaintance (as long as the government did not orchestrate the situation). In *New York v. Quarles* (1984), the U.S. Supreme Court also carved out a public safety exception that allows police to dispense with the Miranda warnings in an emergency when their safety or the public's safety is at risk.

Q 170. Is the right to counsel unqualified?

A Yes. The Sixth Amendment to the U.S. Constitution provides that "in all criminal prosecutions, the accused shall enjoy the right to have the assistance of counsel for his defense." In *Chandler v. Fretag* (1954), the U.S. Supreme Court ruled that the right of a defendant to be represented by privately retained counsel is unqualified.

However, not all defendants have the ability to hire counsel, and the government is not required to provide court-appointed counsel to all indigent criminal defendants at all stages of a criminal proceeding.

The Court first recognized the constitutional right of an indigent defendant to the assistance of court-appointed counsel in a capital case in 1932. The Court has since interpreted the Sixth Amendment to require the government to appoint counsel for indigent defendants when the defendant is charged with a felony and faces a jail term. In *Argersinger v. Hamlin* (1972), the Court extended the right to counsel to indigent defendants in misdemeanor prosecutions who face a jail sentence. The Court subsequently ruled in *Scott v. Illinois* (1979) that the U.S. Constitution does not require a state trial court to appoint counsel for a criminal defendant who is charged with an offense for which imprisonment on conviction is authorized if imprisonment is not actually imposed. In other words, if the state fails to appoint counsel when an indigent defendant is entitled to counsel, the defendant cannot be forced to serve a prison term upon conviction.

The Court also has ruled that indigent defendants have a right to appointed counsel when they appeal their criminal convictions. However, indigent defendants have no right to appointed counsel for discretionary second-level appeals, including most appeals to the state or federal supreme courts.

See 12 What rights are afforded defendants under the Sixth Amendment to the U.S. Constitution?

Q 171. When may a suspect invoke his or her right to counsel?

A In *Miranda v. Arizona* (1966), the U.S. Supreme Court ruled that the right to counsel attaches as soon as there is "custodial interrogation" or the suspect is "otherwise deprived of freedom of action in any significant way."

The right to counsel exists at all critical stages of the prosecution, including pre-trial confrontation procedures (police lineups), the defendant's initial appearance in court if bail is set or the defendant is required to enter a plea, the trial, sentencing, and the first level of appeal.

To ascertain when the right to counsel arises, the court determines the point at which the suspect entered police custody. Questioning that takes place at a police station is not automatically considered custodial interrogation giving rise to the suspect's right to counsel. Most questioning by police outside of the police station is not considered custodial interrogation, including the general questioning of persons at the scene of a crime. However, custodial interrogation may occur whenever a suspect reasonably believes that he or she is not free to leave the custody of police, so it could conceivably take place anywhere, including a suspect's home, the side of a road, and so forth.

Q 172. Can police continue to question a subject after he or she requests a lawyer?

A In some circumstances, police may continue to question a suspect who has invoked his or her right to counsel. The U.S. Supreme Court has ruled that police may further question a suspect who has asked to see a lawyer if the suspect reinitiates conversation with police before the lawyer's arrival or if the suspect fails to unequivocally and assertively invoke his or her right to counsel. In *Davis v. United States* (1994), the Court held that police were not required to cease questioning a suspect who speculated, "Maybe I should talk to a lawyer." Also, invoking the right to counsel with respect to one arrest may not be applicable to another. In *McNeil v. Wisconsin* (1991), the Court concluded that the Sixth Amendment right to counsel is "offense-specific." A suspect in police custody who requested counsel at an initial appearance at a judicial proceeding was found to have invoked his Sixth Amendment right to counsel only as to the charged offense. Police were not precluded from interrogating the suspect on unrelated, uncharged offenses.

Q 173. What are a show-up, a lineup, and a photo array?

A A show-up occurs when a suspect who matches the description given by a witness is apprehended near the scene of the crime and is returned to the scene for possible identification by the witness. A lineup involves lining up physically similar people, one of whom is the suspect, in front of a witness at the police station for possible identification. A third type of police identification procedure involves the use of a photo array in which witnesses are presented with police "mug shots" of people whom police consider possible suspects and asked to identify the perpetrator of the crime.

Q 174. What happens if a suspect refuses to participate in a lineup or to give a blood or DNA sample?

A The Fifth Amendment to the U.S. Constitution protects suspects against compulsion of testimonial or communicative disclosures, such as factual assertions or confessions. It does not protect suspects who are asked to stand or walk in a police lineup, to speak prescribed words, to model particular clothing, or to give samples of handwriting, fingerprints, blood, or even the genetic material deoxyribonucleic acid (DNA). Suspects who refuse these requests may be held in contempt of court and jailed. Furthermore, their refusal may be used against them in a court of law.

In *Schmerber v. California* (1966), the U.S. Supreme Court acknowledged that a coerced blood test infringes on the "inviolability of the human personality" and the "requirement that the State procure the evidence against an accused 'by its own independent labors.' " However, the Court said that the Fifth Amendment privilege against self-incrimination bars the state only from compelling testimonial evidence. Because a blood test is physical, or *real* evidence, the Court said, it is not protected by the privilege against self-incrimination.

The Court subsequently held that a state may require a suspected drunk driver to submit to a blood-alcohol test. In *South Dakota v. Neville* (1983), the Court said that the driver's refusal could be admitted into evidence at his or her trial and used as evidence of guilt. "A refusal to take such a test, after a police officer has lawfully requested it, is not an act coerced by the officer, and thus is not protected by the privilege against self-incrimination," said the Court.

According to the U.S. Department of Justice, every state has passed laws requiring anyone convicted of a felony sex offense to provide appropriate state law enforcement officials with a DNA sample for analysis.

See 211 What is DNA?

Q 175. What is the right to silence?

A The right to silence stems from the Fifth Amendment privilege against self-incrimination. It means that a suspect may refuse to answer police questions and that this refusal cannot be held against the suspect. The right to silence is a pillar of the presumption of innocence.

In *Griffin v. California* (1956), the U.S. Supreme Court ruled that a judge or a prosecutor may not tell a jury that a defendant's failure to testify as to a matter which the defendant could reasonably be expected to deny or explain is an indicator of guilt. The Court said that such comments effectively invalidate a defendant's privilege against self-incrimination by holding the defendant's refusal to testify against him or her. According to the Court, "What the jury may infer, given no help from the court, is one thing. What it may infer when the court solemnizes the silence of the accused into evidence against him is quite another."

See 11 What rights are afforded defendants under the Fifth Amendment to the U.S. Constitution?

Q 176. What is entrapment?

A Entrapment occurs when an undercover agent induces a suspect who would not otherwise have done so to perform a criminal act.

In *Jacobson v. United States* (1992), the U.S. Supreme Court ruled that, in its zeal to enforce the law, the government "may not originate a criminal design, implant in an innocent person's mind the disposition to commit a criminal act, and then induce commission of the crime so that the Government may prosecute."

In *Jacobson* the government set up a sting operation in which it solicited suspected pedophiles to purchase child pornography through the mails. After two and a half years on the government's mailing list, Keith Jacobson, a fifty-six-year-old farmer, ordered a magazine depicting young boys engaged in sexual activity. The Court reversed Jacobson's conviction after finding prosecutors had failed to adduce evidence to support the jury's verdict that Jacobson was predisposed, independent of the government's acts and beyond a reasonable doubt, to violate the law by receiving child pornography through the mails.

Q 177. When does a citizen have a reasonable expectation of privacy?

A The Fourth Amendment to the U.S. Constitution protects people from unreasonable searches and seizures. The U.S. Supreme Court has ruled that a search is unreasonable if it intrudes on a person's reasonable expectation of privacy. Absent exigent circumstances, police must obtain a warrant to conduct a search that violates a person's reasonable expectation of privacy. The test for whether a person's expectation of privacy is reasonable is whether the individual expected privacy and whether that expectation was reasonable as judged from the perspective of an objective third party. Individuals always have a reasonable expectation of privacy in their homes, but they also may have a reasonable expectation of privacy outside their homes. For example, in *Katz v. United States* (1967), the U.S. Supreme Court ruled that an individual making telephone calls from a public phone booth had a reasonable expectation of privacy.

See 10 What rights are afforded to citizens by the Fourth Amendment to the U.S. Constitution?

Q **178. When can law enforcement officers search a suspect or premises without a warrant?**

A Most arrests and searches are warrantless. Circumstances in which law enforcement officers may conduct a search or seizure without a warrant include the following:

- Police can conduct searches under exigent circumstances, or when there is insufficient time to obtain a warrant because a suspect might flee or destroy the evidence to be searched.
- Police may seize unconcealed evidence that is in plain view if the officer is at the location legally doing police work. This is called the *plain view doctrine.*
- Police may search a container within an automobile without a warrant if they have probable cause to believe that it holds contraband or evidence.
- Police can search a person's discarded garbage left on or at the side of a public street.
- Police can conduct routine inventory searches of cars they impound because the expectation of privacy in one's automobile is deemed to be significantly less than that relating to one's home or office.
- Individuals can waive their Fourth Amendment rights and consent to a search or seizure that would otherwise be unconstitutional.
- A person sharing a room with the suspect may allow police to search the room.
- For their protection, police can search a suspect incident to a custodial arrest. An object that comes into view during a search incident to an arrest may be seized without a warrant.
- Police can conduct searches and seizures at national borders to prevent smuggling.

See 10 What rights are afforded to citizens by the Fourth Amendment to the U.S. Constitution?

Q **179. What is the exclusionary rule?**

A Freemont Weeks was convicted of illegal use of the mails based in part on papers taken from his home by police who had no search warrant. In *Weeks v. United States* (1914), the U.S. Supreme Court overturned Weeks's conviction on the grounds that "if letters and private documents can thus be seized and held and used in evidence against a citizen accused of an offense, the protection of the Fourth Amendment declaring his right to be secure against such searches and seizures is of no value." This rule came to be known as the *exclusionary rule.*

The Court extended the exclusionary rule to the states in *Mapp v. Ohio* (1961). That case involved unlawful entry and search and seizure by police that resulted in the conviction of Dollree Mapp for having "certain lewd and lascivious books, pictures, and photographs" in her possession. The Court ruled that the due process clause of the Fourteenth Amendment made the Fourth Amendment's guarantee of a right to privacy applicable to the states. The requirement that evidence be obtained legally may seem to benefit a guilty party, the Court wrote, but "tolerance of shortcut methods in law enforcement impairs its enduring effectiveness."

Since *Mapp*, the Court has adopted many exceptions to the exclusionary rule. In *Nix v. Williams* (1984), the Court ruled that evidence improperly obtained from a suspect still may be admissible in court if police establish that the evidence would have been discovered anyway. In *United States v. Leon et al.* (1984), the Court held that evidence obtained unconstitutionally would be admissible if police had acted in good faith or in the belief that their actions were within the confines of the Fourth Amendment.

Q 180. What is the fruit of the poisonous tree?

A Evidence that is illegally obtained by police cannot be used as a stepping stone to gain other evidence. Such derivative evidence is considered fruit of the poisonous tree and, with some exceptions, is inadmissible in court. The doctrine does not apply if the evidence in question came from two independent sources, only one of which was illegal. This is the independent source exception to the fruit-of-the-poisonous-tree doctrine.

Q 181. What is forensic science?

A Forensic science is the application of scientific methods in criminal cases to obtain, analyze, and explain physical evidence in a court of law. The role of forensics in criminal investigation has increased dramatically in recent years, especially with the advent of genetic fingerprinting. According to the American Academy of Forensic Sciences (AAFS), forensic sciences include a broad range of disciplines. Forensic scientists work for criminalistics laboratories, medical examiner or coroner offices, and toxicology laboratories. Most states use a combination of state, county, and municipal laboratories to provide law enforcement agencies with forensic services, including

DNA testing and the analysis of biological evidence collected from crime scenes. Forensic science–related disciplines include the following:

- *Criminalistics:* the analysis, comparison, identification, and interpretation of physical evidence, such as fingerprints, semen, hair, clothing fibers, and firearms;
- *Forensic pathology:* the performance of autopsies to determine the cause and manner of a person's death (natural, accidental, suicide, homicide, or undetermined);
- *Forensic odontology:* a branch of dentistry dealing with the collection, evaluation, and proper handling of dental evidence;
- *Forensic psychiatry:* a subspecialty of psychiatry in which scientific and clinical expertise is applied to legal issues;
- *Forensic anthropology:* the application of anthropological techniques to identify a body or skeleton found by police and individuals who are killed in disasters such as plane crashes, explosions, fires, or other tragedies that result in the loss of life and mutilation of bodies;
- *Forensic toxicology:* the interpretation of analytical, clinical, and environmental data as it applies to law and medicine.

A forensic odontologist might examine bite marks to identify a suspect or look at oral-facial structure to determine how an injury occurred. A forensic psychiatrist might be called on to evaluate a patient's competence to stand trial or whether a defendant was legally insane when he or she committed a crime. A forensic toxicologist might help determine the cause of death in a chemical or drug-related case.

Other forensic science–related disciplines include engineering sciences, accounting, jurisprudence, questioned documents, polygraph examination, medicine and nursing, mental health services, photography, computer image enhancement, social work, and speech analysis.

The AAFS, which is based in Colorado Springs, Colorado, met for the first time in 1948.

PROSECUTION

Q 182. What entity formally charges an accused person with a crime?

A After an arrest, the law enforcement authority typically presents information about the case and the accused to the jurisdiction's prosecuting authority. The prosecutor reviews the prior record of the arrestee and all of the circumstances of the offense. The prosecutor has great discretion in deciding whether to prosecute some or all of the charges indicated by the arresting officer, pursue different charges, or whether to proceed at all.

An accused person is formally charged with a crime either by a prosecutor, who files a criminal information with the court, or by a grand jury, which files an indictment. In state courts a prosecutor typically files a criminal information. This document informs the defendant of the exact offense and when and against whom the offense allegedly occurred. In cases that are particularly serious or controversial, the prosecutor may opt to seek a grand jury indictment.

All felony prosecutions in federal court must begin with a grand jury indictment pursuant to the Fifth Amendment unless the defendant waives his or her right to a grand jury indictment.

A grand jury is a panel of twelve to twenty-three citizens appointed by the court to decide whether the prosecutor has amassed sufficient evidence to require the accused to stand trial for a criminal offense. In its day-to-day operations the grand jury normally operates outside the presence of a presiding judge. It operates under the direction—but not the control—of a prosecutor, who may present evidence that would be inadmissible at a trial. The grand jury deliberates in total secrecy.

If the grand jury finds sufficient evidence to hold the defendant over for trial, it files a true bill of indictment with the court. An indictment is a written statement that charges the commission of an offense and is presented by the grand jury to a court. If a grand jury finds insufficient evidence, it returns a *no bill.*

Most states retain the option of using a grand jury, but few states require its use to begin felony proceedings.

After charges are filed against a defendant, the prosecutor may drop the charges with the filing of a notice of *nolle prosequi* (to be unwilling to pursue). The prosecutor may *nol-pros* a case at any time after charges are brought, provided that a plea was not entered and a verdict was not returned. This is essentially an admission that the prosecutor does not (yet) have sufficient evidence to pursue the case.

See 11 What rights are afforded defendants under the Fifth Amendment to the U.S. Constitution? Also see Figure 2-2 Prosecution of a Federal Offense.

Q 183. Does a prosecutor have to present both sides to a grand jury?

A No. In *Williams v. United States* (1972), the U.S. Supreme Court ruled that prosecutors have no obligation to disclose to the grand jury evidence that detracts from the government's case. Such a requirement, said the Court, would transform the historic role of the grand jury from an accusatory body that sits to assess whether there is

Figure 2-2 Prosecution of a Federal Offense

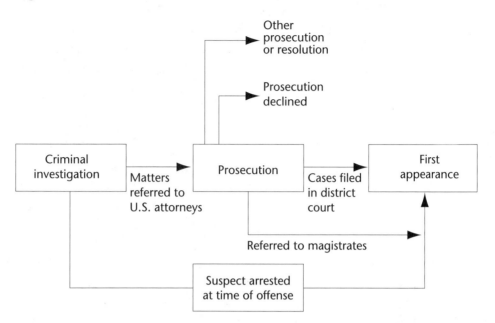

Source: Department of Justice, Bureau of Justice Statistics Publication NCJ180258, *Compendium of Federal Justice Statistics, 1998* (Washington, D.C.: U.S. Government Printing Office, May 2000), 20.

adequate basis for bringing a criminal charge into an adjudicatory body that sits to determine guilt or innocence. Traditionally, the grand jury hears only the prosecutor's side of a case, and the prosecutor is allowed to present evidence that would not be admitted at trial. The grand jury indicts 99 percent of the time, prompting critics of the grand jury system to characterize the body as a rubber stamp for the prosecutor. As a result of these concerns, many jurisdictions have abolished grand juries.

See 217 What is the difference between a grand jury and a petit jury?

Q **184. What occurs during booking?**

A Booking is the process by which the offender's arrest becomes part of the official public record. Police enter the offender's arrest into a chronological arrest log or an arrest register, and the arresting officer files an arrest report and prepares a statement of charges against the offender. In addition, police take and record personal information about the arrestee, including name, address, birth date, sex, and race as well as personal identifying characteristics such as eye and hair color, weight, and scars or tattoos. If the arrest is for a felony or serious misdemeanor, the arrestee is fingerprinted. Several sets of fingerprints are made, including one for the arresting agency's files, one for the statewide criminal record repository and, for some cases, a set for the Federal Bureau of Investigation (FBI). The arresting authority checks local, state, and sometimes FBI records to ascertain the arrestee's criminal history and determine whether the subject has pending cases that may affect processing on the current charge.

Q 185. When is the defendant entitled to see a judge or magistrate?

A After the defendant has been arrested and booked, the defendant is entitled to make an initial appearance before the nearest judge or magistrate without unnecessary delay. At this initial appearance the judge or magistrate informs the suspect of his or her rights, appoints counsel if needed for an indigent defendant, and—except in death-penalty or capital cases—sets bail.

In the case of *Riverside County, California v. McLaughlin* (1991), the U.S. Supreme Court issued a forty-eight hour rule. This rule requires that a defendant be taken before a judge or magistrate within forty-eight hours of his or her arrest.

If the defendant's initial appearance is delayed beyond the required forty-eight hours, the state must demonstrate that extraordinary or emergency circumstances caused the delay.

Before *Riverside*, the Court held that defendants were entitled to appear before a judge or magistrate promptly after their arrest. However, the Court failed to define the term *promptly*. In *Riverside* the Court said that ordinarily a delay of up to two days between booking and the defendant's appearance could be considered prompt. This rule serves as a general guideline for police and prosecutors but is not hard and fast. A defendant may still argue that a delay of forty-eight hours was unreasonable, and prosecutors may argue that delays beyond forty-eight hours were unavoidable.

Q 186. What is a preliminary hearing?

A A preliminary hearing, also known as a probable cause hearing, is an adversary proceeding before a judge or magistrate to determine whether sufficient evidence against the defendant exists to proceed with a trial. A preliminary hearing is held when a defendant was arrested via a prosecutor's information.

The hearing is the equivalent of a mini-trial in which the defendant has a right to be represented by counsel, to cross-examine witnesses, and to challenge evidence offered by the prosecutor. The judge must be satisfied beyond a reasonable doubt that a crime was committed and that probable cause exists that the defendant committed the crime. If the judge finds that the case should proceed, the judge will bind over the defendant for trial. The judge can dismiss some or all of the charges, make or change a pretrial release decision, and increase or decrease the defendant's bail.

The preliminary hearing typically is conducted not later than ten days after the defendant's initial appearance in court if the defendant is in custody and no later than twenty days later if the defendant is not in custody. Defendants may—and often do—waive the preliminary hearing.

Q 187. What is an arraignment?

A An arraignment is a court proceeding at which a defendant is asked to enter a plea. In some jurisdictions and under some circumstances, the defendant's initial appearance may be combined with the arraignment.

Typically a judge or magistrate reads the criminal offense set forth in the prosecutor's information or the grand jury indictment, provides a copy of the complaint to the defendant, advises the defendant of his or her rights, and asks the defendant to enter a plea to the charge(s). The court also may set, raise, or lower bail. A defendant generally can request a waiver of the formal arraignment if he or she files a written plea of not guilty.

The defendant has a right to be represented by an attorney. The court generally will allow the defendant additional time to obtain counsel if he or she has not already done so. If a defendant is indigent and counsel has not already been appointed, the court will appoint a public defender or a private attorney at state expense to represent the defendant.

If a defendant refuses to enter a plea, the court may enter a plea of not guilty.

Before accepting a guilty plea, the court must inform the defendant of the nature of the charge to which the plea is offered, the mandatory minimum penalty provided by law, if any, and the maximum possible penalty provided by law.

In some cases, if a defendant who is charged with a misdemeanor enters a guilty plea, the court may immediately sentence the defendant. If a defendant who is charged with a felony enters a guilty plea, the judge typically schedules a future court date for sentencing. For defendants who plead not guilty, the court may schedule pretrial proceedings and the trial.

A defendant may be arraigned more than once if the criminal charge(s) are altered or if additional charges are added.

Q **188. How may a defendant plead?**

A A defendant generally has three choices. He or she may plead guilty, *nolo contendere* (the accused waives his or her right to a trial and accepts the penalty without admitting guilt), or not guilty. If the accused pleads not guilty, a trial is scheduled.

If the accused enters a guilty or *nolo contendere* plea, the judge or magistrate must determine if the plea was made knowingly and voluntarily and whether the defendant understood the nature of the charges or the consequences of the plea. If the plea is accepted, the defendant may be sentenced immediately or a sentencing date will be scheduled. For serious crimes, the judge typically defers sentencing and orders probation officials to prepare a presentence report so that the judge can make a fully informed sentencing decision.

A presentence report generally includes information about a defendant's prior criminal activity. The federal government and most states have passed laws that require or permit the court to consider an arrested person's criminal history when making pre- and post-trial release decisions.

Q **189. What is bail?**

A Bail is a sum of money that an accused person promises to pay as a condition of release from the custody of law enforcement officers. The purpose of bail is to ensure that the defendant reappears when scheduled in court. It must be paid if the defendant defaults or fails to appear in court. Bail generally is set at a defendant's initial appearance in court, within forty-eight hours of his or her arrest.

Frequently, a defendant will enter into an agreement with a bail bondsman, who promises to pay the full amount of bail on behalf of the defendant if the defendant fails to appear in court. The defendant pays the bail bondsman a fee in exchange for this surety bond.

If a defendant is released and fails to appear for arraignment or trial, the court typically issues an arrest warrant for the defendant's arrest and the bail bond is either revoked or changed.

The court also may release a defendant on his or her own recognizance before the trial without imposing any bail or financial conditions. In this case, the court determines that the defendant poses little flight risk or threat to the community and accepts the defendant's promise to appear in court to answer the charges against him or her.

See 14 What rights are afforded defendants under the Eighth Amendment to the U.S. Constitution? 165 If a police officer refuses to make an arrest, can a citizen make the arrest instead?

Q 190. What are preventive detention laws?

A The federal government and at least thirty states have passed preventive detention laws that allow judges to deny bail to suspects with prior records of violence or non-appearance for trial. Critics charge that preventive detention violates the presumption of innocence and deprives citizens of liberty without due process of law. However, in *United States v. Salerno* (1987), the U.S. Supreme Court ruled that preventive detention is not punishment but a means to achieve the legitimate goal of preventing danger to the community. As such, the Court said that preventive detention is "a potential solution to a pressing social problem."

Q 191. Does every defendant have a right to be released pending trial?

A No. The Eighth Amendment to the U.S. Constitution states that "excessive bail shall not be required." It does not guarantee the right to pretrial release. Bail is denied in capital or death penalty cases and, depending on the law in the jurisdiction, may be denied at the court's discretion when a defendant poses a risk to the community. Indigent defendants who are entitled to be released on bail but who cannot afford bail generally are kept in a local jail or lockup until the date of their trial.

See Figure 2-3 Pretrial Release

Q 192. What percentage of felony defendants are released before trial?

A According to a U.S. Department of Justice study released in 1994, roughly 63 percent of all felony defendants are released on bond or otherwise before court disposition. Most of the rest are detained until the disposition of their cases because they lack the money to pay the bail amounts to secure their release. Six percent of all felony defendants were denied bail, with defendants charged with murder (40 percent) the most likely to be denied bail. Following are the percentages of state court defendants, listed by crime, who were released during the 1992 study period:

- Assault, 68 percent
- Burglary, 51 percent
- Drug trafficking, 66 percent
- Felony driving offenses, 73 percent
- Murder, 24 percent
- Rape, 48 percent
- Robbery, 50 percent

Figure 2-3 Pretrial Release

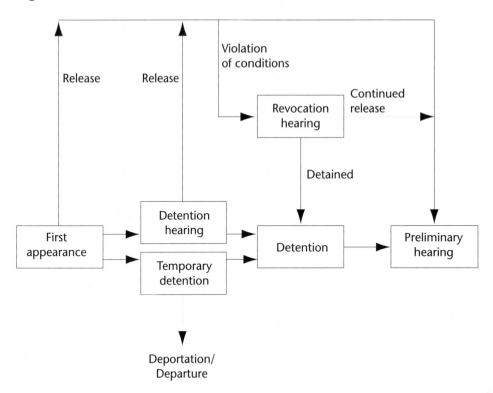

Source: Department of Justice, Bureau of Justice Statistics Publication NCJ180258, *Compendium of Federal Justice Statistics, 1998* (Washington, D.C.: U.S. Government Printing Office, May 2000), 20.

- Theft, 67 percent
- Weapons offenses, 71 percent

193. How does the court decide what bail is appropriate?

No universally accepted system exists for setting bail. Typically each jurisdiction adopts general guidelines that establish a recommended bail amount for a particular offense. The bail amount for a defendant charged with murder might exceed $100,000, while the bail for a weapons offense might be less than $5,000. Judges may depart from these guidelines depending on a host of other factors particular to the individual case, such as the heinousness of the crime and the need to protect the community, the type of evidence gathered by police, the defendant's prior criminal record, the defendant's flight risk and immigration status, and the defendant's character in the community. Another factor that may influence the amount of bail set by a judge in a case is whether the community in question has overcrowded jails.

Q 194. What percentage of criminals fail to appear for trial?

A About one in twelve felony defendants released by state courts absconded before their trials and were still missing a year later, according to a Department of Justice study released in 1994.

Q 195. What methods of case disposition are available to a court?

A The primary methods of case disposition available to the court are:

- The court may accept a plea of guilty or *nolo contendere* (without admitting or denying guilt, the defendant indicates that he or she will not contest the charges) and proceed to sentencing.
- The court may order a trial, after which a defendant is acquitted or convicted of some or all of the charges pending against him or her.
- The court may dismiss the charges against the defendant or enter a judgment of *nolle prosequi* (no further prosecution).
- The court may place the defendant on probation without verdict. During the probationary period, the defendant must comply with specific restrictions or conditions. If the defendant is successful, the charges are dismissed. If not, a trial is scheduled or, if the defendant previously entered a guilty plea, the court may enter a judgment of conviction and proceed to sentencing.
- The court may indefinitely postpone the case. This usually occurs pursuant to a plea agreement in which the defendant agrees that he or she will have no contact with law enforcement for a specific period of time. If the defendant is successful, the case is dismissed. If not, a trial is resumed.

Q 196. What is a plea bargain?

A A plea bargain occurs when the prosecutor and the defendant, who is generally represented by defense counsel, negotiate an agreement to conclude the case. Usually the prosecutor agrees to make concessions or to seek concessions in exchange for the defendant's agreement to enter a guilty plea and give up numerous rights, including the right to require the government to prove its case beyond a reasonable doubt, the right to cross-examine witnesses, the right to present a defense, and the right to have a jury determine guilt or innocence.

The several types of plea bargains include:

- *Charge bargaining:* The prosecutor agrees to reduce the charges against the defendant, minimizing potential prison time for the defendant.
- *Sentence bargaining:* The prosecutor agrees to recommend that the judge impose a lighter sentence or may recommend the defendant be placed in a counseling or drug rehabilitation program.
- *Count bargaining:* If a defendant is charged with more than one count, the prosecutor agrees to drop certain counts, minimizing potential prison time for the defendant.

Plea bargaining is believed to be an American invention that arose in Boston, Massachusetts, in the 1830s as part of a campaign by the city's elite to promote order and assure political stability. Plea bargaining enabled local judges to handle episodes of social unrest, including labor strikes, expeditiously. By the end of the nineteenth century, most cases in criminal courts throughout the nation were being resolved through this process.

In modern times plea bargaining has come under attack. Law-and-order advocates complain that defendants get off too easy. Civil libertarians complain that prosecutors coerce defendants into accepting plea bargains by holding numerous charges carrying long prison sentences over their heads. A study group appointed by President Richard Milhous Nixon called in 1973 for the abolition of plea bargaining. Some jurisdictions have barred plea bargaining under some circumstances, such as for certain crimes or after a grand jury indictment was issued in the case.

Critics say that the passage of federal sentencing guidelines in 1987 increased federal prosecutors' power in the sentencing process. The guidelines require prosecutors to base their charges on a defendant's actual conduct, while judges must calculate sentences according to complex formulas set by the U.S. Sentencing Commission. Judges have only limited authority to make downward departures from the guideline-calculated sentence.

See 271 What percentage of federal criminal defendants plead guilty? 286 How are most criminal cases disposed of in state courts?

Q 197. What percentage of convictions result from guilty pleas?

A Most criminal cases end with guilty pleas, mostly as a result of plea bargains.

Nationwide, the National Center for State Courts reports, 63.4 percent of criminal cases were disposed of by guilty pleas in 1998. In 18.4 percent of cases the court or the prosecutor dismissed the charges, and 14.5 percent of cases were resolved without a trial by other means. Trials were conducted in approximately 4 percent of cases.

The U.S. Sentencing Commission reports that the percentage of guilty pleas filed in federal courts grew from 1989 to 1996. The year and percentage of federal cases that ended in guilty pleas were:

Year	Guilty Pleas	Year	Guilty Pleas
1989	88.1 percent	1993	88.5 percent
1990	87.7 percent	1994	90.5 percent
1991	85.4 percent	1995	91.9 percent
1992	87.0 percent	1996	91.7 percent

Q 198. What type of felony case is most likely to go to trial?

A Murder cases (35 percent) were the most likely to be adjudicated by trial in 1996. According to the U.S. Department of Justice, 77 percent of all trials resulted in guilty verdicts, including 86 percent of murder trials.

Q 199. Is a defendant who is convicted at trial more likely to go to prison than one who pleads guilty?

A Yes. Numerous studies show that defendants who plead guilty generally receive lighter sentences than those convicted after trial.

In federal courts, 86 percent of offenders who were convicted after a trial in 1997 received prison sentences, compared to 69 percent of offenders who were convicted by guilty plea.

According to the U.S. Department of Justice, 38 percent of felons who pleaded guilty in state courts in 1996 received a prison sentence, compared to 76 percent of felons convicted by a jury and 49 percent of those convicted by a judge. Prison sentences were longer for felons convicted by a jury trial (12.5 years) than for felons who pleaded guilty (4.5 years) or who were convicted at trial by a judge (5 years, 10 months).

Q 200. Must judges accept a guilty plea?

A No. A criminal defendant does not have an absolute right to plead guilty. The U.S. Constitution provides criminal defendants with a privilege against self-incrimination, a right to a jury trial, and a right to confront one's accusers. To safeguard these rights, the Court must ensure that defendants who seek to enter a guilty plea are aware of their rights and are giving them up voluntarily. Federal rules of criminal procedure—and similar rules adopted by the individual states—require that before accepting a guilty plea, a judge must be satisfied that a factual basis exists for the plea.

In *Brady v. United States* (1970), the U.S. Supreme Court ruled that judges must reject guilty pleas that are induced by threats or promises to discontinue improper harassment; misrepresentation, including unfilled or unfulfillable promises; or bribes or promises that are by their nature improper.

Typically judges ask a series of questions of a defendant who seeks to enter a guilty plea. The judge may ask whether the defendant's plea was voluntary and ask the defendant to reveal the terms of a plea bargain, if any. The judge also asks if the defendant understands the nature of the charge against him or her; asks if the defendant appreciates that pleading guilty means waiving important constitutional rights; inquires whether the defendant understands that he or she will now be sentenced by the court; and informs the defendant of the extent of the possible sanction in the case.

Q **201. Can a judge accept a guilty plea if a defendant maintains his or her innocence?**

A Yes. A judge may accept a guilty plea even if the defendant maintains his or her innocence, provided that the judge finds that a factual basis exists for the plea and that it was made voluntarily and knowingly. This type of plea is called an Alford Plea. In *North Carolina v. Alford* (1970), the Supreme Court ruled that a defendant who said he was innocent of murder may enter a guilty plea to avoid the imposition of the death penalty. In *Alford* the defendant pleaded guilty to second-degree murder and was sentenced to thirty years in prison. According to the Court, "while most pleas of guilty consist of both a waiver of trial and an express admission of guilt, the latter element is not a constitutional requisite to the imposition of criminal penalty. An individual accused of crime may voluntarily, knowingly, and understandingly consent to the imposition of a prison sentence even if he is unwilling or unable to admit his participation in the acts constituting the crime."

Q **202. What percentage of felony cases ultimately are dismissed?**

A According to a 1996 study by the National Center for State Courts' Court Statistics Project, on average, about 11 percent of felony cases in seventeen major urban court systems end through dismissal of the charges.

EVIDENCE

Q 203. What is evidence?

A Evidence is proof presented at trial that tends to confirm or deny a fact of consequence to the outcome of the case. Evidence falls into two broad categories: testimonial evidence and physical (or real) evidence.

Testimonial evidence refers to the testimony of witnesses and includes direct evidence and circumstantial or indirect evidence. Direct evidence is evidence that was witnessed by the person giving testimony and is offered to establish the fact in question. Circumstantial (or indirect) evidence is evidence that, even if believed, does not establish the truth of the fact in question but instead supports the likelihood of the fact. Indirect evidence might include, for example, fingerprints or a personal object of the defendant's left at the crime scene.

Physical evidence includes physical items, such as weapons, stolen property and fingerprints, that are presented to the court in the form of exhibits. Physical evidence is grouped into several subcategories, including:

- *Impression evidence:* Objects or materials that retain the characteristics of other objects that have been physically pressed against them;
- *Trace evidence:* Physical evidence that results from the transfer of small quantities of materials (such as hair, textile fibers, paint chips, glass fragments, and gunshot residue particles);
- *Transient evidence:* Evidence that by its very nature or the conditions at the scene will lose its evidentiary value if not preserved and protected (for example, blood in the rain).

Q 204. When is evidence admissible at trial?

A To be admissible, evidence must be relevant, which means it must tend to prove or disprove a fact in question. For example, a prosecutor generally cannot introduce evidence of a suspect's prior arrest for a distant unrelated crime to show guilt of the current offense. Evidence also must be reliable. Although many exceptions exist, the court generally will not admit hearsay, which is testimony by a witness about a statement made by someone else. The primary reason for excluding hearsay is that the defendant cannot exercise his or her Sixth Amendment right to confront or cross-examine the person who made the original statement. Evidence also must be material or probative, nonprejudicial, and obtained legally. To determine whether evidence is admissible, judges interpret rules of evidence that are adopted by the court system or the legislature having jurisdiction over the case.

See 12 What rights are afforded defendants under the Sixth Amendment to the U.S. Constitution?

Q 205. What are the rules of evidence?

A In 1961 Chief Justice Earl Warren appointed a Special Committee on Evidence to study the desirability and feasibility of a uniform code of evidence for federal courts that would unify existing evidence doctrines. This study ultimately yielded the Federal Rules of Evidence, which were approved by the U.S. Congress and took effect in 1975. The rules govern whether evidence may be introduced at a trial and how and when the evidence may be presented. The rules are designed to ensure uniformity in the treatment of evidentiary issues in federal court.

The rules change periodically. The Judicial Conference of the United States is the chief policy-making body of the federal court system. The conference, chaired by the Chief Justice of the U.S. Supreme Court, recommends proposed rule changes to the full Court. If the Court agrees with the proposed changes the Court sends them on to the U.S. Congress, which has seven months to enact legislation to change the rule changes. If Congress does not act, the changes become law.

See 249 Do the rules of evidence apply in sentencing proceedings? 536 Do parolees have the same rights as criminal defendants?

Q 206. What is the chain of custody?

A Law enforcement authorities and prosecutors use a process called the *chain of custody* to maintain and document the chronological history of evidence. The chain of custody is compromised if at any time before the conclusion of a case, evidence that has been collected by the police cannot be accounted for. If the chain of custody is compromised, the defendant may attack the authenticity and validity of the evidence, claiming it was switched or contaminated.

Typically the chain of custody is set forth in documents that include the name or initials of the individual collecting the evidence, each person or entity subsequently having custody of it, dates the items were collected or transferred, the agency and case number, the victim's or suspect's name, and a brief description of the item. The handling of physical evidence is one of the most important aspects of a criminal investigation.

207. How did the use of fingerprints to identify criminals begin?

The ancient Assyrians and Chinese used the first recorded fingerprints for identification purposes in conjunction with the signing of legal documents. However, not until the nineteenth century were fingerprints used to identify criminals.

In the 1880s British scientist Sir Francis Galton developed an elementary system for classifying fingerprints by grouping patterns into arches, loops and whorls. Galton's system served as the basis for a fingerprint classification system developed by Sir Edward R. Henry, who later became chief commissioner of the London metropolitan police. Officially introduced at Scotland Yard in 1901, the Galton-Henry system of fingerprint classification became the basis for the department's criminal-identification records.

In the United States, the International Association of Chiefs of Police (IACP) established the first national-scale fingerprint identification system in Chicago in 1896. In 1924 the U.S. Congress directed the FBI to create an identification division to acquire and use fingerprint information. The division started out with 800,000 fingerprints, including those collected by the IACP and fingerprints taken by the Federal Bureau of Investigation (FBI) from prisoners at the federal penitentiary at Leavenworth, Kansas.

A truly efficient national fingerprint database remained elusive until 1967, when the President's Commission on Law Enforcement and Administration of Justice concluded that the nation's criminal justice system was too antiquated to mount an effective response to the growing crime problem. The commission called for stepped-up federal efforts to create a fingerprint-based national criminal history information system. In response, the FBI began the National Crime Information Center to implement a nationwide computerized criminal history record system as a cooperative state and federal venture. Congress also created the Law Enforcement Assistance Administration (LEAA) in 1969 to provide funding to states to establish individual computerized criminal records repositories.

By the 1970s most states had developed statewide computer systems that allowed individual law enforcement agencies to store and match fingerprints in an automated database.

In 1999 the FBI launched the Automated Fingerprint Identification System, which allows federal, state, and local criminal justice agencies to electronically transmit fingerprint information. Fingerprint impressions are scanned into a computer and converted to a digital format that is matched against digital codes assigned to other fingerprints. The recognition points of a fingerprint recovered at a crime scene can be compared instantaneously with the millions of fingerprints stored in a computer's memory.

Today national and state criminal justice automated fingerprint identification systems contain the records of more than 50 million individuals. Authorities rely on fingerprint records to identify and track offenders, make trial and pretrial release decisions, and make decisions about correctional supervision and release of offenders. Fingerprints also make possible missing-child and sex-offender registries. Noncriminal uses of fingerprints include background checks for employment, licensing and security clearances, determining eligibility to purchase firearms, and helping to assure that unsuitable persons are not given positions of trust involving children, the elderly, and the disabled.

See 318 Who is the father of modern professional policing in America?

Q **208. What is the Interstate Identification Index?**

A The Interstate Identification Index is a national fingerprint database system operated by the Identification Division of the Federal Bureau of Investigation (FBI) in cooperation with more than twenty-five participating states. The Interstate Identification Index provides access to the fingerprint-based criminal history records of 25 million individuals and enables police to conduct nationwide computer searches of identification records of persons arrested for felonies or serious misdemeanors under state or federal law.

The FBI receives an average of 50,000 fingerprint submissions every day. Half of those submissions are criminal fingerprints, including about 5,000 first-time arrests. The rest of the submissions are civil.

Q **209. What is ballistics?**

A Ballistics is the science of the propulsion, flight, and impact of projectiles. Since the 1900s police have used ballistics technology, or microphotography, to analyze the relationship between bullets used in a crime and weapons found at a crime scene.

Ballistics refers to the motion of the projectile and whether the spent bullet carries any distinguishing marks, or signatures, that were etched on it when the bullet was fired from a specific gun.

The U.S. Department of Justice is in the process of creating a National Integrated Ballistic Information Network. This network will be the first national computerized database and will enable police to link shell casings and bullets used in violent crimes across the nation. Eventually, authorities say, the system will able to identify the individual fingerprint left by virtually every gun that has been used in a violent crime.

The U.S. Justice Department's Bureau of Alcohol, Tobacco, and Firearms (ATF) and Federal Bureau of Investigation (FBI) each began ballistic imaging technology programs in the early 1990s. They agreed in 1999 to merge their separate programs into a jointly managed program with a unified computer system.

Their joint memorandum of agreement called for the FBI to be responsible for establishing a nationwide network based on a secure, high-speed communications vehicle and for the development and deployment of ancillary databases to support firearms examiners. The ATF was assigned responsibility for Crime Gun Operations such as hardware, software, training, security, maintenance, database maintenance, and so forth.

Q 210. Do polygraph machines work?

A Polygraph results are not admissible as evidence at trial in most jurisdictions because the scientific theory on which polygraphs are based is not generally accepted in the scientific community. However, polygraphs are a valuable tool for law enforcement agencies and help weed out suspects in criminal investigations.

Proponents claim that polygraphs have accuracy rates of from 75 percent to 95 percent, but opponents say the polygraph's success rate is little better than chance, because innocent people become nervous when hooked up to the machine and savvy crooks learn to think other thoughts to fool the machine.

The Chinese are said to have used doctors at trials 4,000 years ago to measure the heartbeats of defendants to ascertain whether they were telling the truth. The modern-day polygraph dates to the 1920s, when a professor at Fordham University, William Marston, published an article stating that telling lies affects a person's blood pressure. Marston's article inspired August Vollmer, the police chief of Berkeley, California, to introduce the first lie detector, a machine based on a primitive blood pressure cuff. By 1926 the lie detector machine measured blood pressure, pulse, breathing rate, and perspiration.

A polygraph machine records the physiological reactions of a human subject who answers questions posed by a polygraph operator. The polygraph instrument consists of a central unit that records on chart paper measurements transmitted from a cardiograph or blood pressure cuff that monitors changes in blood pressure and heart rate; a pneumograph, which monitors respiratory activity in the abdominal and thoracic areas of the body; and a galvanograph, which measures sweating or skin conductivity. By comparing the responses to several different questions, the operator attempts to detect a pattern of emotion that serves as the basis for making a conclusion about the subject's sincerity.

Other methods police use to detect lying include voice-stress analysis, a somewhat controversial device designed to analyze a person's voice to detect deception, and kinetic interviewing, which is the "science" of reading body language. Kinetic interviewing is based on the premise that the manner in which a person gestures or moves when answering questions can indicate deception.

See 318 Who is the father of modern professional policing in America?

Q 211. What is DNA?

A Deoxyribonucleic acid, or DNA, was first discovered by the German biochemist Friedrich Miescher in 1869. DNA is the basic genetic material found in all living cells and the fundamental building block for a person's entire genetic makeup. Each person's DNA is distinctive, providing a blueprint that determines eye and hair color, height and bone structure, and so forth.

Police use DNA "fingerprinting" to identify physical evidence (such as blood, semen, or hair) as belonging to a suspect. Even a minute sample of DNA allows investigators to identify a criminal with virtual certainty, to connect suspects to crimes, and to exonerate wrongly convicted defendants. A genetic profile of an individual can be obtained from saliva left on an envelope or a shaft of hair found on a victim's clothing. In 1996, the National Academy of Sciences announced there was no longer any reason to question the reliability of DNA evidence.

DNA evidence was first introduced into criminal court proceedings in the United States in the late 1980s. Today, every state allows the introduction of this kind of evidence, either by statute or by court rule. Every state also has passed legislation permitting the testing of different categories of convicted offenders to support a national database under construction by the federal government.

In 1994 Congress passed the DNA Identification Act, which authorized the FBI to establish a national index of DNA identification records of convicted criminals, analyses of DNA samples recovered from crime scenes, and samples recovered from unidentified human remains. Almost half of the states sent samples to the FBI's Combined DNA Index System in 1999.

Some civil libertarians argue that the government should not stockpile DNA information because the information is subject to misuse. DNA includes data such as markers for up to 4,000 diseases. Critics argue that by forcibly collecting genetic samples from criminals, the government violates the Fourth Amendment to the U.S. Constitution, which protects citizens against unreasonable search and seizure. In 1998 U.S. Attorney Janet Reno established the National Commission on the Future of DNA Evidence to suggest guidelines for the justice system's use of DNA technology.

According to the U.S. Department of Justice, all fifty states have passed laws requiring anyone convicted of a felony sex offense to provide appropriate state law enforcement officials with a DNA sample for analysis.

See 174 What happens if a suspect refuses to participate in a lineup or to give a blood or DNA sample?

Q 212. Is DNA evidence foolproof?

A No. While scientifically compelling, DNA evidence is not guaranteed to win a conviction. The significance of DNA evidence is subject to challenge. A defendant can allege that police misinterpreted the results, planted the evidence, that the sample is contaminated, or that it is not dispositive of guilt. A defendant in a rape case can, for example, still present a valid defense of consent.

On October 3, 1995, a jury declared former football star O.J. Simpson to be not guilty of fatally stabbing his former wife, Nicole Brown Simpson, and her friend, Ronald Goldman, despite DNA evidence that linked Simpson to the crime scene. Prosecutors demonstrated that blood with DNA matching Simpson's was found at Brown's house and that blood spots in Simpson's car and at Simpson's house contained DNA matching Nicole Simpson's and Goldman's. Simpson's "dream-team" defense team argued that the DNA evidence was tainted by laboratory contamination and alleged that it may have been planted by racist police officers.

See 236 What is jury nullification?

Q 213. How reliable is eyewitness testimony?

A Eyewitness testimony was considered very reliable until the 1990s, when more than fifty defendants who had been convicted in part on the testimony of eyewitnesses were exonerated based on DNA evidence. DNA evidence showed that it was highly unlikely or impossible for these defendants to have committed the crimes for which they had been convicted.

Increasingly, courts allow defense attorneys to present expert testimony questioning the reliability of eyewitness identifications. In the past, the only way a defense attorney could challenge an eyewitness identification was to discredit the witness during cross-examination. Many factors affect eyewitness identifications, including race, stress, lighting, a witness's focus on a weapon rather than a suspect, the length of time the witness saw the suspect, and the time between the crime and the identification. Despite these complicating factors, eyewitness testimony often carries great weight with jurors.

Q **214. Must a prosecutor apprise the defense about favorable evidence?**

A Yes. The government must disclose to the defense at or before the trial certain prior statements of its trial witnesses and material that can be used to attack or impeach the witness.

In *Jencks v. United States* (1957), the U.S. Supreme Court ruled that the prosecutor's primary duty is to assure that justice is done. The Court said that this duty requires the government to give the defendant relevant reports and statements of government witnesses that pertain to their evidence at trial. According to the Court, justice requires no less.

Federal law requires the government to disclose to the defense all statements made by a government witness that relate to the subject matters about which the witness has testified after the witness has completed direct examination.

In *Brady v. Maryland* (1963), the Court held that suppression by the prosecution of evidence favorable to an accused who has requested it violates due process if the evidence is material either to guilt or to punishment, irrespective of the good faith or bad faith of the prosecution. To be material, the evidence must have a reasonable probability of affecting the result of the proceeding. The Court subsequently said that disclosure is required even if no request has been made by the accused.

TRIAL

Q **215. What is a criminal trial?**

A A criminal trial is a proceeding before a judge or magistrate in a court of law that requires a prosecutor to produce evidence proving beyond a reasonable doubt that the defendant committed the crime with which he or she is charged. The decision as to the defendant's guilt or innocence is made by a jury or, at the request of the defendant, the judge. In the latter case, the proceeding is called a bench trial. America's Founders thought that the right to a jury trial in criminal cases was so important that they included it in both Article III of the U.S. Constitution and the Sixth Amendment. The Founders believed that an impartial jury would protect citizens from abuses of state power.

See Figure 2-4 Adjudication.

Figure 2-4 Adjudication

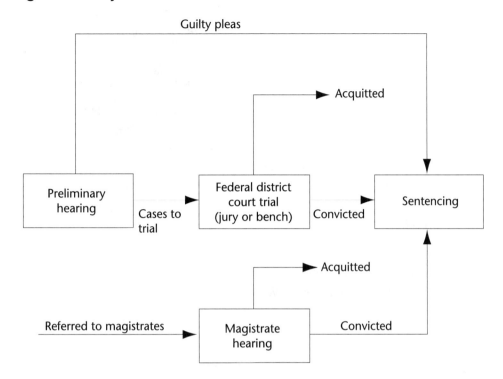

Source: Department of Justice, Bureau of Justice Statistics Publication NCJ180258, *Compendium of Federal Justice Statistics, 1998* (Washington, D.C.: U.S. Government Printing Office, May 2000), 50.

Q 216. What is a reasonable doubt?

A The state must prove a defendant's guilt beyond a reasonable doubt. This requirement means that a juror must be fully satisfied that the defendant is guilty, after drawing reasonable, logical inferences from proven facts and without resorting to speculation or conjecture. A reasonable doubt has been defined as a doubt that would cause a prudent person to hesitate before acting in a matter of importance to him- or herself. A juror is not required to be 100 percent convinced in order to vote to convict but should not be swayed by a mere whim. A doubt must be substantial and based on reason and common sense.

In the case *In re Winship* (1970), the U.S. Supreme Court ruled that the reasonable doubt standard is required by the due process clause of the U.S. Constitution. According to the Court, the reasonable doubt standard "is a prime instrument for reducing the risk of convictions resting on factual error . . . [A] society that values the good name and freedom of every individual should not condemn a man for commission of a crime when there is reasonable doubt about his guilt."

Q 217. What is the difference between a grand jury and a petit jury?

A A grand jury is a panel numbering from twelve to twenty-four citizens who are appointed by the court to determine whether sufficient evidence exists to charge a defendant with a crime. A petit jury is a trial jury. It typically consists of twelve jurors who are selected by the prosecutor and defense attorney, under the supervision of the court, to hear evidence at a trial and determine whether the defendant is guilty or not guilty of the crime charged. Both panels comprise ordinary citizens who are chosen at random from lists of official government records, usually voter registration lists, tax rolls, telephone directories, and driver's license lists.

See 12 What rights are afforded defendants under the Sixth Amendment to the U.S. Constitution? 16 What does the public believe is the most important part of the U.S. justice system?

Q 218. What percentage of criminal cases go to trial?

A About 4 percent of all criminal cases went to trial in 1996, with rates ranging from a low of 1.3 percent in Vermont to a high of 9.3 percent in Arkansas. Jury trials accounted for about two-thirds of all trials.

Q 219. What is a speedy trial?

A The Sixth Amendment of the U.S. Constitution guarantees all criminal defendants the right to a speedy trial. The federal Speedy Trial Act (1974) specifies that a criminal trial must be held within seventy days of the defendant's information or indictment, or within seventy days from the date when the defendant appeared before a judicial officer of the court in which the charge is pending, whichever last occurred. The Speedy Trial Act recognizes several bases to postpone trial, including plea negotiations. Unless the defendant consents in writing, the earliest that a trial can begin under the act is thirty days from the first court appearance of the defendant or counsel acting on behalf of the defendant. The act also stipulates that no more than thirty days may pass between arrest and indictment and no more than ten days may pass between indictment and arraignment.

Q **220. What is *voir dire*?**

A *Voir dire* (speak the truth) is the process by which jurors are selected in a civil or criminal case. The judge and/or the attorneys question potential jurors in open court about their competency to serve on the panel.

Attorneys can file an unlimited number of challenges for cause to strike jurors from the panel. The attorney must satisfy the judge that the prospective juror is unfit to serve because, for example, the candidate demonstrated bias, could not understand English, or was mentally incompetent.

Attorneys also are allowed a limited number of peremptory challenges to strike jurors from the panel without stating a cause. Attorneys may file peremptory challenges for any reason except for an illegal reason, such as race discrimination. The Federal Jury Selection and Service Act prohibits exclusion of potential jurors based on race, color, religion, sex, national origin, or economic status.

Depending on the jurisdiction and the seriousness of the crime, an attorney is entitled to between five and ten peremptory challenges for felony trials and between ten and twenty for capital trials. An attorney who uses up all of his or her peremptory challenges must accept all of the remaining potential jurors, unless there is justification to challenge the juror for cause.

Q **221. When were women first allowed to serve on juries?**

A In March 1870 the first mixed petit jury in America was impaneled in Laramie, Wyoming, to preside over a murder trial. The experiment followed the passage of women's suffrage in Wyoming and occurred during a period of concern over disorder in the territory. All-male juries had repeatedly refused to convict persons being prosecuted for a wide variety of public-order offenses. The judge who presided over the first mixed jury expressed the hope that women, by serving on juries, would "aid in suppressing the dens of infamy which curse the country." One observer noted that the presence of women on juries prompted lawyers to take their heels off the table and to "quit whistling and expectorating." The six women and six men on the jury voted to convict the defendant.

Q **222. Must a jury be unanimous to convict a defendant of a crime?**

A The U.S. Constitution contains no explicit requirement that a jury verdict be unanimous. Nevertheless, the federal government and most states require unanimity for jury verdicts in criminal cases. However, the U.S. Supreme Court in

1972 permitted nonunanimous verdicts in criminal trials with votes of 10–2 in Oregon and 9–3 in Louisiana. The Court ruled that nonunanimous verdicts are not, by themselves, evidence of reasonable doubt concerning guilt. Oregon, Louisiana, and Puerto Rico allow nonunanimous verdicts in trials that involve felonies, with the exception of the death penalty. Oklahoma allows nonunanimous verdicts in trials involving misdemeanors.

Q 223. Do defendants have a right to represent themselves at trial?

A Yes. Criminal defendants have a Sixth Amendment right to represent themselves at trial. However, this right does not extend to appellate proceedings.

In *Faretta v. California* (1975), the U.S. Supreme Court ruled that a defendant's right to counsel under the Sixth Amendment implies that criminal defendants have a right to forgo the assistance of counsel.

The Court recognized the possibility that a defendant may be concerned about the risk of disloyalty of a court-appointed counselor. Also, the Court noted that the Sixth Amendment provides a right of assistance of counsel. To require a defendant to accept the services of a lawyer would make the lawyer a master rather than an assistant.

The *Faretta* Court said that a trial court must assure itself that a defendant is aware of the dangers and disadvantages of self-representation and that the defendant is making a knowing waiver of counsel.

The Court said that the defendant's rights are not violated if a trial judge appoints standby counsel, even over the defendant's objection, to relieve the judge of the need to explain and enforce basic rules of courtroom protocol or to assist defendants in overcoming routine procedural obstacles. However, *pro se* defendants must be able to preserve actual control over the case they choose to present to the jury and standby counsel cannot destroy the jury's perception that the defendant is in charge.

The right to self-representation was incorporated into the Judiciary Act of 1789, which was enacted by the First Congress and signed by President Washington. The act provided that "in all the courts of the United States, the parties may plead and manage their own causes personally or by the assistance of . . . counsel."

The Court has ruled that right to self-representation does not extend to appeals because a defendant has no right under the U.S. Constitution to file a criminal appeal.

See 12 What rights are afforded defendants under the Sixth Amendment to the U.S. Constitution?

Q 224. What is effective assistance of counsel?

A The right to counsel means the right to effective assistance of counsel. The U.S. Supreme Court has set forth a two-pronged standard to determine whether an attorney's performance is so defective that it denies the defendant his or her Sixth Amendment right to counsel. In *Strickland v. Washington* (1984), the Court said that the defendant must prove the attorney's performance fell below an objective standard of reasonableness. The reviewing court must indulge a "strong presumption that counsel's conduct falls within the wide range of reasonable professional assistance." The defendant must then show that the attorney's deficient performance prejudiced the defense. Prejudice is demonstrated by proving that a reasonable probability exists that, but for counsel's unprofessional errors, the result of the proceeding would have been different. Thus, it is not enough to show that a lawyer was, for example, drunk throughout the trial. The defendant also must show the lawyer's drunkenness caused the jury to return a different verdict than it would have otherwise.

See 12 What rights are afforded defendants under the Sixth Amendment to the U.S. Constitution?

Q 225. Can a defendant ever be compelled to testify?

A Defendants who invoke their Fifth Amendment privilege against self-incrimination generally cannot be compelled to testify against themselves. However, the government can compel testimony from a defendant who asserts the privilege in certain circumstances.

The government may grant immunity from prosecutorial use of any compelled inculpatory testimony in subsequent criminal proceedings, or any evidence derived directly or indirectly from the testimony. This type of immunity is called *use immunity*.

In *Kastigar v. United States* (1972), the U.S. Supreme Court ruled that a witness who was granted immunity may still be prosecuted but that the government must prove that the evidence it proposes to use is derived from a legitimate source wholly independent of the defendant's compelled testimony. Furthermore, the government cannot use the compelled testimony as a starting point to investigate the witness.

It also is a well-established rule that a witness, in a single proceeding, may not testify voluntarily about a subject and then invoke the privilege against self-incrimination when questioned about the details. A defendant who opens the door by testifying about a matter waives the privilege against self-incrimination as to that matter. The justification for this rule is that a witness may not pick and choose what aspects of a particular subject to discuss without casting doubt on the statements' trustworthiness and diminishing the factual inquiry's integrity.

See 11 What rights are afforded defendants under the Fifth Amendment to the U.S. Constitution?

Q 226. Do prosecutors always bear the burden of proof?

A Yes. The prosecutor must prove each element of a crime beyond a reasonable doubt. However, once the prosecution has met this burden, a defendant may be required to prove an affirmative defense, such as self-defense, defense of others, protection of property, necessity, duress, infancy, entrapment, or, in some states, insanity. When this occurs, the defendant is said to bear not the burden of proof but the burden of production.

See 231 Who bears the burden of proving insanity? 235 Under what circumstances does society consider a defendant's criminal acts to be justified?

Q 227. Under what circumstances are defendants excused for their crimes?

A The law recognizes many circumstances that mitigate or eliminate criminal responsibility for a crime. These defenses include:

- *Insanity:* States use different legal tests to ascertain whether a defendant was insane or incapable of forming the intent to commit a crime because of a mental disease or defect.
- *Intoxication:* Generally this defense is valid only if the intoxication was involuntary, such as in the case of an adverse drug interaction. Voluntary intoxication may be a defense for a crime that requires specific intent.
- *Diminished capacity:* In some jurisdictions, diminished mental capacity, including mental retardation, is a defense to a crime that requires specific intent.
- *Infancy:* Traditionally, children under age fourteen were presumed to be incapable of forming the intent necessary to commit a crime.
- *Entrapment:* A defendant may be excused if the government unfairly induced him or her to commit the crime.
- *Duress or coercion:* This defense is appropriate if the defendant was compelled to commit a crime by another person's use of force or threat of death or serious bodily injury.

Q 228. When is a defendant competent to stand trial?

A The U.S. Supreme Court has ruled that a state may presume that a defendant is competent to stand trial and require the defendant to prove otherwise by a preponderance of the evidence. (A preponderance of the evidence is sufficient evidence to show that it is more likely than not that the defendant is incompetent to stand trial.) The federal government and most states use this standard.

In *Dusky v. United States* (1960), the Court said that a defendant may not be put to trial unless he "has sufficient present ability to consult with his lawyer with a reasonable degree of rational understanding . . . [and] a rational as well as factual understanding of the proceedings against him."

The criminal trial of an incompetent defendant violates the defendant's constitutional right to due process. Competency is essential to the defendant's right to a fair trial, including the right to effective assistance of counsel; the rights to summon, confront, and cross-examine witnesses; and the right to testify on one's own behalf or to remain silent without penalty for doing so.

Q 229. What is criminal insanity?

A Criminal insanity is a legal standard, not a medical conclusion. States use several tests to determine whether a criminal was legally insane at the time of a crime and therefore lacked the intent necessary to be found guilty of the crime. These tests include:

- *M'Naghten test:* At the time of the offense, "a defect of reason produced by a disease of the mind" caused the person to "not know the nature of the act" or to "not know right from wrong."
- *Irresistible impulse test:* A loss of control caused by a mental disease or defect destroyed the defendant's power to choose right from wrong.
- *Durham Rule:* A defendant is not guilty of a crime because he or she was "suffering from a disease or defective mental condition at the time of the act and there was a causal connection between the condition and the act."
- *Model Penal Code standard:* "A person is not responsible for criminal conduct if at the time of such conduct, as a result of mental disease or defect, he lacks substantial capacity either to appreciate the criminality (wrongfulness) of his conduct or to conform his conduct to the requirements of law."

The federal government adopted the M'Naghten test after John Hinckley Jr. was found not to be criminally responsible in the 1981 shootings of President Ronald Reagan, Press Secretary James Brady, and a Washington, D.C., police officer. Hinckley was driven by an obsession to get the attention of actress Jodie Foster.

The Hinckley case also prompted a dozen states to adopt new laws that provide for a "guilty but mentally ill" verdict. In these states, a defendant who is found to be mentally ill is held to be criminally liable for the crime. The court may order the defendant to receive psychiatric treatment. When the inmate recovers from the mental illness, he or she is transferred to prison to serve out the rest of the sentence imposed at trial.

Q 230. Does every state permit an insanity defense?

A No. Three states—Utah, Montana, and Idaho—abolished the insanity defense in the wake of public outcry after John Hinckley Jr. was found by a jury to be not guilty by reason of insanity in the 1981 shootings of President Ronald Reagan, Press Secretary James Brady, and a Washington, D.C., police officer. Many defendants in these states who previously would have asserted an insanity defense now are ruled incompetent to stand trial and are committed directly to a state hospital, bypassing the question of an insanity defense.

Q 231. Who bears the burden of proving insanity?

A The defendant must raise the insanity defense. After that, the federal government and most states require the defendant to prove insanity by clear and convincing evidence. However, some states require the prosecution to *disprove* insanity beyond a reasonable doubt.

Q 232. Who was Daniel M'Naghten?

A Daniel M'Naghten admitted that he traveled to London on April 25, 1843, to shoot Prime Minister Sir Robert Peel but, by mistake, instead fatally shot Peel's secretary, Edward Drummond. M'Naghten pleaded and was adjudged not guilty on the grounds that he was laboring under a morbid delusion and did not know he had performed a wicked act.

M'Naghten's case led to adoption of the following rule in many U.S. jurisdictions: "[T]o establish a defense on the ground of insanity, it must be clearly proved that, at the time of the committing of the act, the party accused was labouring under such a defect of reason, from disease of the mind, as not to know the nature and quality of the act he was doing; or, if he did know it, that he did not know he was doing what was wrong."

Q **233. What was the first successful use of the insanity defense in America?**

A In 1859 the insanity defense was successfully used when New York Representative Daniel Edgar Sickles was found not guilty by reason of insanity after killing Philip Barton Key, the son of the composer of the national anthem, Francis Scott Key. Sickles said he became deranged on discovering that Philip Key was having an affair with Sickles's wife. After the trial, Sickles became a major general in the Union Army, lost a leg in the Battle of Gettysburg, and reportedly had an affair with Queen Isabella II of Spain.

Q **234. How often is the insanity defense successful?**

A National studies show that fewer than 1 percent of defendants charged with felonies use the insanity defense. Of these, fewer than 25 percent are found not guilty by reason of insanity.

Furthermore, defendants who are found not guilty by reason of insanity are not automatically freed. In most states a special hearing is conducted to evaluate whether defendants who are found not guilty by reason of insanity require psychiatric hospitalization. Other states automatically hospitalize these defendants.

Some states limit a defendant's term of commitment to the maximum prison term for the crime. Other states allow for indefinite commitment until the individual is deemed to be no longer dangerous to others, meaning that defendants who are found not guilty by reason of insanity can be incarcerated for longer time periods than if they had been convicted of the crime.

Q **235. Under what circumstances does society consider a defendant's criminal acts to be justified?**

A Justification defenses include the following:

- *Self-defense:* People are justified in using reasonable force to protect themselves from the threat of an immediate and unlawful threat. In many jurisdictions, an individual must retreat before using deadly force.
- *Defense of others:* In many jurisdictions, individuals can use force if they reasonably believe such force is necessary to defend a third person from imminent unlawful attack.
- *Protection of property:* Reasonable force—short of deadly force—may be used under some circumstances to defend property.
- *Necessity:* Under some circumstances, a person facing an imminent physical threat may commit a crime if it is the lesser of two evils and if no legal alternative is

apparent. For example, a starving person may be considered justified in having stolen food if there truly was no alternative.

Q 236. What is jury nullification?

A Jury nullification occurs when a jury considers extralegal factors, such as racial bias or political activism, when deciding a case and acquits an obviously guilty defendant to achieve the larger goal of justice or to send a message expressing the jury's displeasure with a law or the criminal justice system. Although a rare event, jury nullification has a long history in the United States. In one famous 1735 case, John Peter Zenger was acquitted for violating a law that prohibited publishing materials critical of the British government. More recently, until recent decades, Southern juries frequently acquitted whites accused of crimes against African Americans. In 1995 the acquittal of black football star O.J. Simpson in the face of powerful evidence of guilt on a charge of murdering his ex-wife and her friend, both white, renewed debate about jury nullification.

See 212 Is DNA evidence foolproof? Also see Figure 2-5 Sentencing.

Q 237. Can a crime be prosecuted more than once?

A The answer is yes, though it rarely happens. The Fifth Amendment's double jeopardy clause guarantees that no person shall be "subject for the same offence to be twice put in jeopardy of life or limb." This guarantee means that the government cannot launch successive criminal proceedings against a defendant for the same crime. According to Justice Hugo Black:

> the State with all its resources and power should not be allowed to make repeated attempts to convict an individual for an alleged offense, thereby subjecting him to embarrassment, expense and ordeal and compelling him to live in a continuing state of anxiety and insecurity, as well as enhancing the possibility that even though innocent he may be found guilty.

The U.S. Supreme Court has ruled, however, that the double jeopardy clause does not prohibit two separate prosecutions for conduct that violates two separate sovereigns. Therefore, a defendant could be prosecuted (and punished) separately for the same crime by the state and the federal government, the federal government and an Indian tribe, and so forth.

Q 238. Can a prosecutor appeal a defendant's acquittal?

A No. An acquittal is final and no government appeal is possible under the Fifth Amendment double jeopardy clause. In *United States v. Scott* (1978), quoting *Green v. United States* (1957), the U.S. Supreme Court said, "To permit a second trial after an acquittal, however mistaken the acquittal may have been, would present an unacceptably high risk that the Government, with its vastly superior resources, might wear down the defendant so that 'even though innocent he may be found guilty.' "

SENTENCING

Q 239. What sentencing models do states use?

A Thirty years ago, every state used an indeterminate sentencing model that allowed judges to exercise broad discretion in sentencing. Today many jurisdictions have adopted determinate sentencing, which requires that an offender be imprisoned for a specific period of time, generally with time off for good behavior.

Indeterminate sentencing allows the court to impose a period of incarceration having a minimum and a maximum term. Judges typically review cases on a case-by-case basis and make an individual decision about the offender. The goal of indeterminate sentencing is to encourage prisoners to rehabilitate themselves. A parole authority determines, within the confines of the range stipulated by the court, when the offender is eligible for release.

Indeterminate sentencing came under a two-pronged attack in the 1970s, leading to erosion of public confidence in the system. Civil rights activists charged that racial bias led to stark disparities in sentencing for similar crimes. Law-and-order advocates complained that criminals were treated too leniently and served only a fraction of their sentences. In the mid-1970s Maine and California became the first states to reject core features of indeterminate sentencing, such as probation for all prisoners and parole release.

By 1996 fourteen states and the federal government had adopted determinate sentencing models, which require fixed prison terms that can be reduced by good-time or earned-time credits. Many states have established sentencing commissions that create ranges of sentences for given offenses and offender characteristics. Sentencing guidelines may be mandatory or presumptive. Typically judges can revise a sentence upward or downward from the guidelines if they cite their reasons for doing so.

Figure 2-5 Sentencing

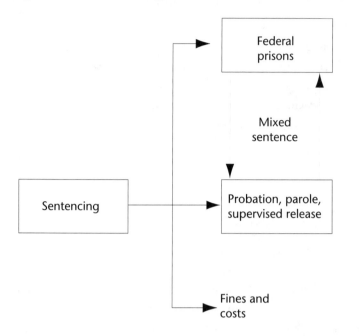

Source: Department of Justice, Bureau of Justice Statistics Publication NCJ180258, *Compendium of Federal Justice Statistics, 1998* (Washington, D.C.: U.S. Government Printing Office, May 2000), 20.

One of the primary benefits of sentencing guidelines is that they offer policymakers a way to establish sentencing priorities, to control prison populations, and to avoid prison overcrowding.

Many states are experimenting with new approaches to sentencing. For example, some states have created drug courts and domestic violence courts that effectively divert defendants from the criminal justice system if they participate in court-approved therapeutic programs.

See 484 What is good time?

Q 240. What are sentencing guidelines?

A About fifteen years ago the U.S. Congress set in motion a process for establishing uniformity in sentencing in the ninety-four federal districts throughout the United States. The goal was to ensure that defendants in federal courts who commit similar crimes receive similar punishments no matter where they are sentenced. Today the federal government and many states have established sentencing commissions that are charged with establishing sentencing guidelines within their respective jurisdictions. These panels typically comprise judges, prosecutors, corrections officials, and members of the public. Sentencing guidelines may be voluntary, serving merely to advise the sentencing authority, or they may be mandatory. Generally courts may deviate from sentencing guidelines if they find that certain enumerated aggravating or mitigating factors exist.

Q 241. What are mandatory sentencing laws?

A All states have adopted mandatory sentencing laws that stipulate some minimum period of incarceration for certain types of offenses. Mandatory sentencing laws often target violent and repeat criminals. These laws tend to reduce judicial discretion and emphasize retribution and deterrence.

By 1997 the federal government and twenty-three states had adopted so-called *three-strikes laws* requiring judges to sentence offenders with three serious felony convictions to long prison terms.

See 528 How many prisoners are released each year?

Q 242. What are intermediate sanctions?

A Intermediate sanctions refer to a variety of sentences that are less severe than incarceration in a prison or jail but that are more restrictive than traditional probation. Intermediate sanctions include fines, restitution, community service, work release, weekend sentences, day reporting centers, residential community corrections, electronic monitoring, drug and alcohol treatment, house arrest, intensive probation supervision, boot camps, and forfeiture. Every state uses some type of intermediate sanction.

Intermediate sanctions typically are cheaper than prison, which costs about $20,000 a year. Intermediate sanctions may be as effective as prison or even more so for certain types of offenders, including low-risk, nonviolent offenders who have a stake in the community. Intermediate sanctions also offer jurisdictions a way to reduce prison overcrowding.

Since the 1970s some judges have used controversial shame punishments that are reminiscent of the pillories and stocks of colonial America. One offender, for example, was required to wear a sandwich-board-type sign around his neck in public with lettering on both sides stating, "I am a convicted thief." In another case a drunk driver was required to place an article in the local newspaper describing his crime. These types of punishments often are challenged—sometimes successfully—as an abuse of judicial discretion.

Q 243. Does the judge always choose the sentence?

A No. The jury sets the sentence for noncapital cases in Arkansas, Missouri, Texas, and Virginia, though the judge can alter the sentence in each of these states except Texas. In Indiana and Kentucky the jury recommends a sentence, which is set by the judge.

In most states that have a death penalty, the jury sets the sentence. In a few of these states, the jury recommends a sentence to the judge.

A prosecutor who brings a capital case often charges one or more special circumstances that the jury must find to be true in order to sentence the defendant to death. These special circumstances, which are defined by state statute, may include especially heinous crimes, multiple murders, or crimes that involved a bomb. The jury typically first determines guilt and then decides, in a separate sentencing hearing, whether the defendant should be put to death or serve a sentence of life in prison.

Q 244. What factors influence judicial discretion in sentencing?

A The U.S. Department of Justice reported in 1999 that judicial discretion in sentencing appears to be influenced mainly by the judges' predictions of whether the offender will commit future crime, the perceived importance of rehabilitation for the offender, the seriousness of the charge, the offender's criminal record, the number of counts in the conviction, and the recommendation of the probation officer. The type of sentence imposed also appears to be influenced by the age of the offender and whether the felony was a property crime or a violent crime. The judge's assessment of these factors determines whether the judge selects a noncustodial sentence, jail, youth facility, or prison.

Q 245. What is a three-strikes law?

A Three-strikes laws are sentencing enhancement laws that target habitual serious offenders. Such a law may be geared to a particular type of offender, such as persons convicted of violent crimes, sex offenses, or crimes in which firearms were used. Three-strikes laws often are mandatory, which means the judge has no discretion but must impose the enhanced penalty.

If convicted, the offender typically is required to serve many years in prison above the normal sentence imposed for his or her current offense. In several states, felons found guilty of a third serious crime may be sentenced to an additional twenty years in prison, while offenders convicted of a violent crime may receive a sentence of life in prison without the possibility of parole.

Washington state passed the first three-strikes law in 1993. Since then at least a dozen more states have adopted three-strikes laws and many more have legislation pending. Many legislators see the three-strikes laws as a way of dealing with persistent, dangerous criminals, the proverbial three-time losers. Opponents of three-strikes laws say these laws result in draconian sentences for nonviolent offenders accused of relatively petty crimes, discourage plea bargains, clog the courts, and overburden the corrections system.

See 248 Do tougher prison sentences deter crime?

Q 246. What is Megan's law?

A Megan's law refers to a type of law that requires prosecutors to notify the public when sex offenders—usually those who are classified as a moderate or high risk—move into a community. Megan Kanka, a seven-year-old New Jersey girl, was killed in 1994 by a convicted child molester who kidnapped her from her home after moving into her neighborhood. The killing prompted national outrage. Since then every state has adopted some type of sex offender notification law. The New Jersey law requires a judge to approve carefully written notification plans for each case that map out which people on which blocks should be informed. For sex offenders who are considered low risk, only the police must be notified.

Q 247. What is truth in sentencing?

A Truth-in-sentencing laws require offenders—generally violent offenders—to serve most of the sentences imposed in their cases. The U.S. Department of Justice's Truth-in-Sentencing grant program provides funding to states that require violent offenders to serve at least 85 percent of their sentences. More than half of the states and the District of Columbia met the grant program criteria in 1998. Indiana, Maryland, Nebraska, and Texas require offenders to serve 50 percent of their minimum sentences; Arkansas requires 70 percent; Colorado and Massachusetts, 75 percent; and Idaho, Nevada, and New Hampshire, 100 percent.

Q 248. Do tougher prison sentences deter crime?

A Confinement in prison or jail deters crime in the sense that the inmate is incapacitated, but it makes no difference in terms of recidivism as measured by new arrests and charges. This was the conclusion reached by the U.S. Department of Justice (DOJ) in 1999 based on a twenty-year federal study of almost a thousand felony offenders in New Jersey. The research indicates the following factors have no deterrent effect on crime: extending the length of the maximum sentence, imposing jail with probation, and the imposition of fines and restitution. According to the DOJ report, research "offers little support, aside from incapacitation, for increased use of confinement, emphasis on longer terms, or more acceptance of specific deterrence as a crime control strategy."

More than half of the offenders in the study were rearrested in the first five years after they were sentenced. The 962 offenders were arrested 5.3 times on an average in the twenty years after sentencing. Thirty percent of the offenders had no arrests in the twenty years after sentencing.

Q 249. Do the rules of evidence apply in sentencing proceedings?

A No. A judge or magistrate may consider material at a sentencing hearing that would be inadmissible at a criminal trial. For example, a defendant's prior criminal activity may be considered prejudicial and irrelevant at trial but is routinely considered by the court at sentencing. Typically the court reviews a presentence report prepared by probation or other designated officials. These reports include details about the circumstances of the crime, including any aggravating or mitigating circumstances, and the defendant's prior history of criminal behavior. A court also may allow the victim or a victim's relatives to submit a statement or be heard at the hearing.

See 205 What are the rules of evidence?

Q 250. Who was Judge Lynch?

A Judge Lynch was the inspiration for the term *lynch law*. Judge Lynch is reputed to have been a Virginia planter and justice of the peace, Charles Lynch (1736–1796), who ordered extralegal punishment for Tory acts during the American Revolution.

Lynching is a form of mob violence. Lynch law is a form of vigilante violence in which a mob injures or executes a person who is accused of some offense without first providing the victim with a trial or due process of law. In some cases, lynching victims have been snatched from jail.

In the South during the Reconstruction era, mobs seeking to restore white supremacist political rule lynched hundreds of African Americans and white Republicans. Victims of lynching often were hung from a tree or mutilated to terrify others with similar characteristics or sentiments.

From 1882 to 1968, a total of 4,743 lynchings were recorded. The greatest number, 3,446, were lynchings of black men and women. The highest number of recorded lynchings occurred in Mississippi, where 539 blacks and 42 whites were murdered. The most lynchings recorded in any one year was 230, in 1892. Many more unreported lynchings are thought to have occurred.

The federal and state response to the problem of lynching was ineffective, at best. The South Carolina constitution of 1895 contained a clause pertaining to lynching which provided damages of "not less than two thousand dollars" assessed against the *county* in which the lynching took place. An anti-lynching statute passed in the U.S. House of Representatives on three occasions in the early 1900s but failed in the Senate as a result of real or threatened filibusters by southern Democrats and northern conservative Republicans. The first major federal legislation to address the problem of lynching was the 1968 Civil Rights Act, which provided for federal intervention if a person is injured while seeking to exercise his or her constitutional rights.

Q 251. Can any authority override a conviction or sentence imposed by the judiciary?

A The power to pardon is believed to date back to ancient times, when the supreme monarch alone had the power to punish or forgive. Today the U.S. President and the chief executive officers of most states have clemency powers that essentially override the judiciary's authority to impose a criminal conviction and sentence. In a handful of states, clemency authority is delegated to a pardons board.

Article II, Section 2, of the U.S. Constitution vests the president of the United States with "power to grant reprieves and pardons for offenses against the United States, except in cases of impeachment."

The U.S. Supreme Court has declared the president's pardoning power to be unlimited (with the exception of treason) and not subject to legislative control. According to the Court, the president may, among other things, remit fines and forfeitures, pardon criminal contempt of court, award conditional pardon, and commute sentences (even against the wishes of the individuals involved).

Typically the president's clemency authority takes several forms, including the following:

- Pardons for criminals who have been convicted of a federal offense after the completion of their sentences
- Commutation of sentences or reduction in the period of incarceration that an inmate must serve
- Remittance of fines

A pardon allows offenders to simply walk away from jail as if they had never been tried and sentenced.

The Office of the U.S. Pardon Attorney in the U.S. Department of Justice receives and reviews all petitions for executive clemency, initiates the necessary investigations, and prepares a recommendation for approval by the deputy attorney general, who submits it to the president.

Q **252. How many acts of presidential clemency are sought and granted annually?**

A Following are the number of applications received and pardons commuted or granted from 1980 through 1999:

Year	Clemency Petitions	Commutations Granted	Pardons Granted
1980	523	11	155
1981	547	7	76
1982	462	3	83
1983	447	2	91
1984	447	5	37
1985	407	3	32
1986	362	0	55
1987	410	0	23
1988	384	0	38
1989	373	1	41
1990	354	0	0
1991	318	0	29
1992	379	0	0
1993	868	2	36
1994	808	0	0

Year	Clemency Petitions	Commutations Granted	Pardons Granted
1995	612	3	53
1996	512	0	0
1997	685	0	0
1998	608	0	21
1999	1009	14	34

A commutation is a reduction of sentence and may include remission of fines.

Q 253. Which president used the clemency power the most? The least?

A The Warren Harding administration granted an average of 419 acts of clemency per fiscal year, the highest average number. The George Bush administration granted fifteen clemency actions per year, the lowest average number. One study found that the seventeen U.S. presidents from William McKinley to George Bush were responsible for or had authorized about 20,000 acts of executive clemency, including 13,593 pardons, 5,223 commutations, and 1,083 remissions of fines.

Q 254. Does receiving a pardon mean having to say you're sorry?

A A prisoner generally is not required to make a statement or expression of remorse to qualify for a pardon or a commutation of sentence. According to the Office of the Pardon Attorney, however, such a statement is an important consideration when assessing a petitioner's application. Nevertheless, with respect to highly publicized pardons, apologies are rare.

President Andrew Johnson pardoned former Confederate leader Jefferson Davis in 1868 despite the fact that Davis did not request or even want a pardon. Davis was charged with complicity in the assassination of President Abraham Lincoln. Davis told the 1884 Mississippi legislature, "repentance must precede the right of pardon, and I have not repented."

President Gerald Ford gave a blanket pardon to his predecessor, Richard Milhous Nixon, without requiring Nixon to apologize for the break-in of Democratic national headquarters at the Watergate complex or the elaborate coverup that ultimately forced Nixon to resign from office in 1974 to avoid impeachment proceedings. Ford had earlier told congressional confirmation committees that "the American people would not stand for a [Nixon] pardon" and that he did not intend to grant one.

In 1999 President Bill Clinton was criticized when he commuted the sentences of thirteen Puerto Rican nationalists who were imprisoned for a variety of terrorist acts committed in the early 1970s and 1980s. Clinton demanded that the prisoners renounce violence but did not require them to apologize. Most of the prisoners were members of a militant Puerto Rican independence group believed to have been responsible for scores of bombings. Clinton's grant of leniency also was criticized as being influenced by the political ambitions of his wife, Hillary Rodham Clinton, who was running for the office of U.S. Senate from New York, home to 1.3 million residents of Puerto Rican descent.

APPEAL

Q 255. What is an appeal?

A An appeal is a petition asking a higher court to review a judgment or decision of a lower court. An appeal generally is based on a claim that the judge who presided over the defendant's trial made an error that deprived the defendant of his or her right to a fair trial or that the law forbidding the conduct that resulted in the defendant's criminal prosecution was unconstitutional.

The appellant is the party who appeals a losing decision to a higher court or from one court or jurisdiction to another; the appellee is the party who won the lower court decision and against whom the appeal is taken. In criminal cases, the burden of proof shifts from the government to the defendant in an appeal. Thus, the appellant must prove that his or her rights were violated and that the conviction must be overturned.

An appeal begins when the appellant files a notice of appeal within the time limitations established by the court, usually thirty days from the date of judgment. The appellate judge normally accepts as true any facts admitted into the trial court record and does not accept new evidence. The appellant and the appellee file written briefs or arguments that set forth their respective positions. They also may be allowed to make oral arguments explaining their position.

If an appellate court decides that a mistake was made that changed the outcome of the case, the court may direct the lower court to conduct a new trial. A judge also may find that the error had no effect on the outcome of the case and thus requires no remedy.

See 274 Where may a federal trial court decision be appealed? 291 Where may state trial court decisions and judgments be appealed? 472 Have inmates always been able to file lawsuits challenging their imprisonment? Also see Figure 2-6 Appeals.

Figure 2-6 Appeals

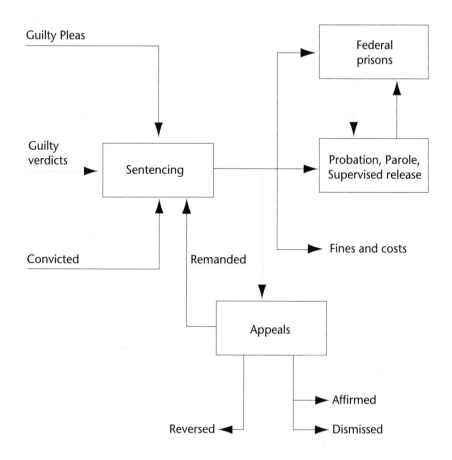

Source: Department of Justice, Bureau of Justice Statistics Publication NCJ180258, *Compendium of Federal Justice Statistics, 1998* (Washington, D.C.: U.S. Government Printing Office, May 2000), 74.

Q 256. What are the most common grounds for appeal in a criminal case?

A Perhaps the most common grounds for an appeal are trial court error, ineffective assistance of counsel, and incorrect sentencing. Other common grounds for appeal are improper jury instructions, admission of inadmissible evidence, and misapplication of the law.

Q 257. What is harmless error?

A All states and the federal government have adopted rules that prohibit appellate courts from reversing convictions based on harmless error, or error that did not affect "substantial rights" of the accused. These rules block setting aside convictions for small errors or defects that have little, if any, likelihood of having changed the result of the trial.

In *Chapman et al. v. California* (1967), the U.S. Supreme Court held that an error that violates a defendant's constitutional rights may be deemed harmless if it is unimportant or insignificant. However, the Court said, when an error involves a constitutional right the state must prove beyond a reasonable doubt that the error was harmless.

The Court indicated that in some circumstances an error can never be deemed harmless and requires automatic reversal of the defendant's conviction. Such circumstances include cases of coerced confessions and denial of right to counsel.

In *Chapman* the Court found that the defendant's right to silence was violated when a prosecutor repeatedly commented on the accused's failure to testify. In ordering a new trial, the Court said, "Such a machine-gun repetition of a denial of constitutional rights, designed and calculated to make petitioners' version of the evidence worthless, can no more be considered harmless than the introduction against a defendant of a coerced confession."

Q 258. Does every defendant have a right to file an appeal?

A The U.S. Constitution does not require appellate review of criminal convictions. However, virtually all jurisdictions allow criminal defendants to file at least one appeal of right and all states with the death penalty automatically provide for an appeal of a death sentence. The U.S. Supreme Court has ruled that where a right of appeal exists it cannot be conditioned on the defendant's financial status and the state must appoint counsel to represent indigent defendants.

In *Griffin v. Illinois* (1956), the Court held that where an Illinois law conditioned appellate review on the availability of a stenographic transcript of trial proceedings, the state must make a transcript available to indigent defendants without charge. "There can be no equal justice where the kind of trial a man gets depends on the amount of money he has," said the Court.

A A writ of *habeas corpus* (you shall have the body) is a petition that prisoners file with a federal appellate court challenging a conviction or a sentence imposed in state court on constitutional grounds after normal state appeals are exhausted. Such petitions typically allege that police, prosecutors, defense counsel, or the trial court deprived the prisoners of their constitutional rights. Where petitions are found to be meritorious, federal judges can order that prisoners be released from custody, that their sentences be reduced, or that their cases be remanded for retrial or resentencing.

A writ of *habeas corpus* is not the equivalent of an appeal because it can only be filed by a prisoner and must involve a constitutional claim.

Article I, Section 9, of the U.S. Constitution forbids the suspension of *habeas corpus* except in cases involving rebellion or invasion that threaten the public safety. However, reacting to a sharp increase in such petitions in recent years, the U.S. Congress has placed sharp limits on the right to *habeas corpus* review.

The Antiterrorism and Effective Death Penalty Act of 1996 placed a one-year statute of limitations on the filing of petitions for writ of *habeas corpus* and limited the filing of motions attacking a sentence under the statute's purview. The one-year statute of limitations begins to run at the latest of four triggering events:

- the date on which the judgment of conviction becomes final;
- the date on which the impediment to making a motion created by governmental action in violation of the Constitution or laws of the United States is removed, if the movant was prevented from making a motion by such governmental action;
- the date on which the right asserted was initially recognized by the Supreme Court, if that right has been newly recognized by the Supreme Court and was made retroactively applicable; or
- the date on which the facts supporting the claim or claims presented could have been discovered through the exercise of due diligence.

See 472 Have inmates always been able to file lawsuits challenging their imprisonment?

III
COURTS

IN GENERAL

Q **260. What is the federal criminal court system?**

A Article III of the U.S. Constitution created a Supreme Court of the United States and allows Congress to create such lower courts as it deems necessary. Congress has created a series of midlevel appellate courts, specialty courts, and trial courts. All federal courts have limited jurisdiction. They can decide only cases that they are specifically authorized to consider by the U.S. Constitution or the U.S. Congress.

At the pinnacle of the system is the U.S. Supreme Court, which is the ultimate arbiter of the meaning of the Constitution. Many of the fundamental rights granted to all criminal defendants, such as the right to counsel for indigent defendants charged with serious crimes and freedom from forced confessions, stem from Supreme Court decisions interpreting the Bill of Rights.

The Court has two kinds of jurisdiction: original (this means the Court can act as a trial court) and appellate (the Court can review the decisions made by a lower court). The Court's original jurisdiction is extremely limited and includes cases that affect foreign diplomats and cases in which a state is a party (usually disputes between two states).

In most cases the Court acts as an appellate court. It considers appeals from lower federal courts and from state supreme courts when the case involves an important question of federal law. The Court does not engage in fact-finding but determines whether the lower court erred or misapplied the law to the facts of a case.

In addition to the Supreme Court, the federal court system consists of:

- *U.S. courts of appeals.* Congress has divided the United States into twelve geographical regions, each with a federal court of appeals. These midlevel appellate courts hear virtually all appeals of decisions and judgments from federal trial courts within their respective circuits. The Court of Appeals for the Federal Circuit also has nationwide jurisdiction over appeals in certain types of cases, such as trade and patent law cases.

- *Specialized courts.* These courts and their jurisdictions include the U.S. Court of Appeals for the Armed Forces, which hears appeals arising from trials by court-martial in the United States Army, Navy, Air Force, Marine Corps, and Coast Guard; U.S. Court of Federal Claims, which hears cases against the federal government for monetary damages; U.S. Court of International Trade, which hears cases involving international trade and customs duties; U.S. Court of Appeals for Veterans Claims, which hears cases involving veterans' and survivors' benefits; and U.S. Tax Court, which hears cases involving underpayment of federal income, gift, and estate taxes.
- *U.S. district courts.* Congress has divided the United States into ninety-four judicial districts, including at least one district in each state. Each district has a district court. These are general trial courts.

The federal judiciary includes nine U.S. Supreme Court justices and about 1,500 federal judges and magistrate judges. Federal judges are appointed by the president of the United States with the consent of the U.S. Senate to serve for life during "good behavior." Magistrate judges are appointed to eight-year terms by district judges in the federal judicial district in which they serve.

Q 261. What is the state criminal court system?

A State court systems process the vast majority of criminal cases in the United States. No single prototype exists for a state court system. Each state developed its court system independently in accordance with the U.S. Constitution and the laws of the state, and each system has unique elements. However, basic similarities exist among state court systems.

All states have a court of last resort, usually called the *supreme court,* which has final jurisdiction over appeals emanating from lower state courts. Two states, Texas and Oklahoma, have two courts of last resort, which hear criminal and civil matters, respectively. State courts of last resort have from five to nine judges who typically meet *en banc,* or all together, to decide cases.

Thirty-nine states and Puerto Rico also have intermediate (midlevel) appellate courts that hear most criminal appeals in their respective jurisdictions, subject to review by the state court of last resort. These courts were created to free the state's highest court to handle the most pressing matters. Rather than with the full court sitting together, these courts undertake review through panels of three or more judges.

Every state has a court of general jurisdiction, where trials are conducted in cases involving felonies and serious misdemeanors. About 2,500 general jurisdiction courts exist in the United States. These courts are usually divided into circuits, or districts, that include one or more counties. They are called by various names, including *superior court, district court,* and *court of common pleas.* State courts of general jurisdiction also may exercise some form of limited appellate jurisdiction over decisions and judgments from state courts of limited jurisdiction.

The lowest-level court in most state court systems is a court of limited jurisdiction, which handles cases involving criminal misdemeanors and preliminary hearings. Forty-four states and Puerto Rico have courts of limited jurisdiction. Their jurisdiction typically follows the boundaries of a local governmental unit, such as a county, city, or town. Magistrate judges and judges typically accept guilty pleas from defendants in misdemeanor cases and then impose sentences. They also bind over felony defendants for trial in a court of general jurisdiction. Almost 14,000 courts of limited jurisdiction exist in the United States.

Courts of limited jurisdiction are called by many names, including *municipal court* and *magistrates' court.*

Most states also have created specialty courts that process cases involving a single subject matter, such as drugs or domestic violence. Most of these specialty courts are subunits of either a court of general jurisdiction or a court of limited jurisdiction.

In the interests of efficiency, in recent years more than a dozen jurisdictions have consolidated their general and limited jurisdiction courts into a single court system that has jurisdiction over all cases and procedures. Jurisdictions that have adopted some type of unified court system include California, Illinois, Massachusetts, Missouri, Oregon, Puerto Rico, Minnesota, Wisconsin, Iowa, Connecticut, Kansas, the District of Columbia, North Dakota, Idaho, South Dakota, and Utah.

About 29,000 trial judges and quasi-judicial officers served in state trial courts in 1998. Judges are selected by various methods, including election, appointment, or a combination of the two. A magistrate's authority is defined by state law or the chief judge of the district in which the magistrate serves. A magistrate's criminal caseload typically is limited to simple misdemeanors or preliminary hearings.

See Figure 3-1 State Court Structure Prototype.

Figure 3-1 State Court Structure Prototype

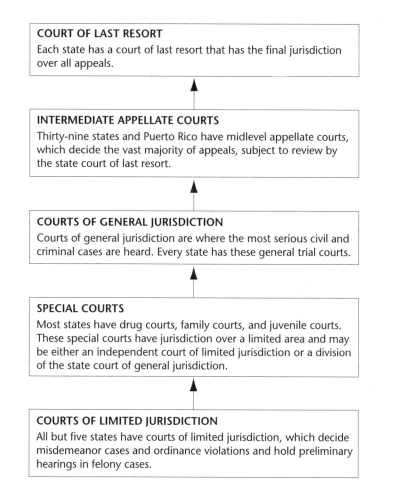

COURT OF LAST RESORT
Each state has a court of last resort that has the final jurisdiction over all appeals.

INTERMEDIATE APPELLATE COURTS
Thirty-nine states and Puerto Rico have midlevel appellate courts, which decide the vast majority of appeals, subject to review by the state court of last resort.

COURTS OF GENERAL JURISDICTION
Courts of general jurisdiction are where the most serious civil and criminal cases are heard. Every state has these general trial courts.

SPECIAL COURTS
Most states have drug courts, family courts, and juvenile courts. These special courts have jurisdiction over a limited area and may be either an independent court of limited jurisdiction or a division of the state court of general jurisdiction.

COURTS OF LIMITED JURISDICTION
All but five states have courts of limited jurisdiction, which decide misdemeanor cases and ordinance violations and hold preliminary hearings in felony cases.

 262. Are more criminal cases filed in state or federal courts?

The vast majority of all criminal cases are filed in state courts. A record number of 14.6 million criminal cases were filed in state courts in 1998, the latest year for which state court statistics are available. This number compares to 58,000 criminal cases filed in federal courts in the same year.

Q **263. What is the major difference between the federal and state court systems?**

A The major difference between the federal and state court systems relates to jurisdiction (the court's authority to rule on a case). Jurisdiction is a legal concept that refers to a court's lawful authority to exercise its judicial powers over individuals, certain subject matters, and specific geographic areas. State courts have jurisdiction over the vast majority of criminal cases.

Federal courts are courts of limited jurisdiction. They cannot hear a case unless they are specifically authorized to do so by the U.S. Constitution or the U.S. Congress. The Constitution specifically authorizes federal courts to hear cases involving the counterfeiting of securities and currency, piracies and felonies committed on the high seas, and treason.

Over the years Congress has greatly expanded the jurisdiction of federal courts by passing new laws creating federal crimes that have a national or interstate dimension, such as laws pertaining to arson, stalking, hate crimes, firearms offenses, and domestic drug trafficking. Many of these federal crimes overlap with existing state crimes, creating concurrent jurisdiction between the federal court and state courts. However, even with the so-called federalization of criminal law, federal prosecutions make up less than 5 percent of all criminal prosecutions.

Q **264. How much does the nation spend annually on courts?**

A The latest statistics from the U.S. Department of Justice show that in 1995 the nation spent $25.4 billion on the combined activities of courts, prosecution, legal services, and public defense. That compares to $48.6 billion for police protection and $39.8 billion for corrections, including jails, prisons, probation, and parole.

Q **265. How much of every dollar of government spending goes to courts?**

A The U.S. Department of Justice reports that less than a penny—about 0.9 percent—of every government dollar spent nationwide in 1995 went for judicial and legal services. That figure compares to 1.8 percent for police protection and 1.7 percent for corrections. Judicial and legal services include all civil and criminal courts and activities associated with courts, including law libraries, grand and petit juries, and court reporters. Judicial and legal services also include the activities of the offices of federal and state prosecutors.

Q **266. How many criminal cases are filed in federal court each year?**

A The Administrative Office of the U.S. Courts reports that 59,923 criminal cases were filed in U.S. district courts in 1999, a 3.9 percent increase over 1998, when 57,691 criminal cases were filed. The number of defendants in 1999 rose about 2 percent, to 80,822. The current levels of criminal cases and defendant filings are higher than in any year since 1933, when the Eighteenth Amendment (Prohibition) was repealed. The growth in cases and filings in recent years has been attributed to increased filings of drug and immigration law cases.

Q **267. How has the federal criminal caseload changed over time?**

A From 1982 to 1999 the federal criminal caseload increased by more than 75 percent. The largest increase was in felony filings, the most serious crimes handled by the criminal justice system, which almost doubled. According to the Administrative Office of the U.S. Courts, following are the year and number of criminal misdemeanor and felony cases filed in U.S. district courts since 1982:

Year	Cases Filed	Year	Cases Filed
1982	32,682	1991	47,123
1983	35,872	1992	48,366
1984	36,845	1993	46,786
1985	39,500	1994	45,484
1986	41,490	1995	45,788
1987	43,292	1996	47,889
1988	43,607	1997	50,363
1989	45,792	1998	57,691
1990	46,568	1999	59,923

Q **268. What kinds of cases make up the bulk of the federal criminal caseload?**

A Drugs, fraud, and immigration filings accounted for 60 percent of all criminal cases filed in federal courts in 1999.

Drug cases represented 30 percent of the total federal criminal caseload. There were 17,483 drug filings in 1999, a 7 percent increase over 1998 and a 52 percent increase over 1995.

Immigration cases accounted for 18 percent of the federal criminal docket in 1999. There were 10,641 immigration cases filed in 1999, a 14 percent increase over 1998 and a 169 percent increase over 1995.

Much of the increase in drug and immigration cases was attributed to increased federal resources along the nation's southwestern border. In recent years the U.S. Immigration and Naturalization Service has more than doubled the number of border patrol agents stationed along the border with Mexico.

Fraud cases accounted for 13 percent of federal criminal cases in 1999. There were 7,654 fraud cases filed in federal court in 1999, a 2 percent drop from 1998. Following are the types and numbers of fraud cases filed:

- False claims and statements, 1,600
- Lending institution, 1,244
- Postal, 1,065
- Income tax, 645
- Social Security, 542
- Passport, 301
- Nationality laws, 267
- Securities and exchange, 56
- False personation, 25
- Veterans, 3
- Other, 1,906

Following are the numbers for other types of federal cases filed in 1999:

- Larceny and theft, 3,514
- Violations of federal statutes (food and drug, civil rights, antitrust, and so on), 2,241
- Embezzlement, 1,315
- Robbery, 1,295
- Forgery and counterfeiting, 1,292
- Sex offenses, 893
- Assault, 529
- Homicides, 383
- Auto theft, 189
- Burglary and breaking and entering, 72
- Liquor, internal revenue, and taxation, 3
- Miscellaneous general offenses, 11,747

Q **269. What does a U.S. attorney do?**

A A U.S. attorney is the chief federal prosecutor in his or her respective federal judicial district. U.S. attorneys are appointed by the president of the United States with the approval of the U.S. Senate, and serve under the direction of the attorney general. A U.S. attorney typically serves the length of the term of the appointing president.

U.S. attorneys decide whether to prosecute defendants who are investigated by various federal law enforcement agencies, such as the Federal Bureau of Investigation, the U.S. Customs Service, and the Drug Enforcement Administration. They have wide latitude to set priorities within their districts and to determine how federal resources are allocated there.

There are ninety-three U.S. attorneys stationed throughout the United States, Puerto Rico, the Virgin Islands, Guam, and the Northern Mariana Islands. One U.S. attorney is assigned to each federal judicial district, with the exception of Guam and the Northern Mariana Islands, where a single U.S. attorney serves both districts.

The U.S. attorney may conduct trial work before the court, or, in larger districts, may primarily supervise a staff of assistant U.S. attorneys.

In 1998 U.S. attorneys initiated investigations involving 115,692 suspects for possible violations of federal law. Almost one-third of the persons investigated were suspected of drug violations. A total of 77,236 defendants were prosecuted; 60,958 offenders were convicted, and 42,405 offenders were sentenced to prison.

In addition to prosecuting criminal cases brought by the federal government, U.S. attorneys prosecute and defend civil cases in which the United States is a party and collect debts owed the federal government that administrative agencies have been unable to collect.

Q **270. What percentage of federal criminal defendants are convicted? What percentage of defendants are acquitted?**

A Eighty-eight percent of all federal criminal defendants whose cases closed in the year ending September 30, 1999—64,815 defendants—were convicted. Of those defendants who were convicted, 3,189 defendants were convicted after a trial. Of all defendants who were convicted, about 70 percent went to prison—up from 60 percent in 1990.

Twelve percent of all such federal criminal defendants—8,666 defendants—were not convicted. Of these, 1,017 defendants were acquitted after their trials and 7,649 had the charges against them dismissed.

Q 271. What percentage of federal criminal defendants plead guilty?

A Eighty-four percent of federal criminal defendants whose cases closed in the year ending September 30, 1999—61,239 defendants—pleaded guilty. Three-hundred eighty-seven defendants entered pleas of *nolo contendere* (no contest), and 3,189 defendants were convicted after their trials.

Q 272. How many federal criminal trials are held each year?

A Some 4,206 (about 6 percent) of federal criminal defendants whose cases closed in the year ending September 30, 1999, chose to have their cases decided by a trial. Jury trials were held for 3,166 defendants, of whom 2,702 were convicted and 464 were acquitted. Bench trials (also called *court trials*) were held for 1,040 defendants, of whom 487 were convicted and 553 were acquitted.

Q 273. How long do federal criminal trials typically last?

A In 1999 the median case disposition time for criminal defendants in federal court was 5.9 months. That time compares to a median of 5.6 months in 1998.

Q 274. Where may a federal trial court decision be appealed?

A A defendant who is convicted in a U.S. district court is entitled to file an appeal with the U.S. court of appeals in the region where the trial court is located. In 1999 federal courts of appeals handled 54,693 appeals, including 10,231 criminal appeals, a 1.7 percent increase from the prior year. Death-penalty appeals typically are filed directly with the court of last resort in the jurisdiction.

In 1891 Congress created regional appellate courts to relieve the U.S. Supreme Court of the burden of considering all appeals in cases decided by federal trial courts and to free the Court to hear the cases that it deems to be most important to the nation. A panel of three or more judges typically reviews the lower court record of a case and written arguments or briefs filed by the parties. The panel also may hear oral arguments.

A defendant who loses in the U.S. court of appeals can file a petition with the U.S. Supreme Court asking it to review the case. However, the Supreme Court typically does not have to grant review. The Court considers only about 1 percent of the approximately 8,000 cases on its docket each year. In recent years, the Court has issued from 75 to 100 opinions per year. The Court generally agrees to hear an appeal if it involves important questions of federal law or if there is a disagreement among federal courts of appeals. Federal death-penalty appeals are filed directly with the U.S. Supreme Court.

See 255 What is an appeal? 259 What is a writ of habeas corpus?

MILITARY AND TRIBAL COURTS

Q **275. What are military courts?**

A Congress has assigned jurisdiction to military courts to prosecute cases involving military discipline and crimes by military personnel. The Uniform Code of Military Justice contains the substantive and procedural laws that govern the military justice system. Military crimes include offenses that would not be criminal for civilians, such as dereliction of duty and failure to obey orders.

A convening authority, generally a military commander, convenes a court-martial by ordering that charges previously preferred against an accused service member will be tried by a specified court-martial.

According to the code, a general court-martial is the highest trial court in the military justice system. This court has the power to issue any authorized punishment, including life in prison and death. The general court-martial typically is where the most serious crimes are adjudicated, such as treason and murder. A military judge and at least five jurors who are members of the armed forces normally conduct a general court-martial. If convicted, the accused may file an appeal with the U.S. Court of Appeals for the Armed Forces, which consists of five judges who are appointed by the U.S. president and confirmed by the Senate to fifteen-year terms.

A special court-martial is an intermediate-level court. It is conducted by a military judge and at least three jurors who are military personnel or—at the request of the accused—by a military judge acting alone. The maximum sentences that can be imposed by a special court-martial are confinement for six months, forfeiture of two-thirds pay for six months, reduction to the lowest enlisted grade, and in some cases, a bad-conduct discharge.

A summary court-martial is a military trial by one commissioned officer who need not be a lawyer. The maximum punishment that can be imposed by a summary court-martial depends on the rank of the accused. Punishments are limited to confinement for one month, forfeiture of two-thirds pay for one month, and reduction in grade. No counsel is furnished to the prosecution or defense. If an objection to trial by summary court-martial is made by an accused, a trial may be ordered by special or general court-martial as may be appropriate.

Investigations of serious offenses involving military personnel, such as murder, rape, indecent assault, drugs, or larceny, generally are conducted by a military criminal investigative agency, such as the Army's Criminal Investigation Command. For less serious offenses, the authority rests with military or security police investigators.

According to the Uniform Code of Military Justice, "When it can be avoided, no member of an armed force may be tried by a court-martial by any member of which is junior to him in rank or grade."

In 1999, about 1,000 U.S. Army personnel were tried in military courts, including 26 officers and 985 enlisted personnel. About 92 percent of these cases resulted in conviction.

Q 276. What are tribal courts?

A More than 500 Native American tribes have tribal courts that adjudicate misdemeanor cases and strictly tribal offenses involving Indians who commit crimes on Indian land.

Native American tribes are sovereign nations but legally are considered *domestic dependent nations* of the United States. As such, the federal government has concurrent jurisdiction with tribal courts over criminal matters. Federal law grants the FBI authority to investigate major crimes on Indian land, such as homicide and child abuse. The U.S. Attorney's Office prosecutes these crimes in U.S. district court. A handful of states, including California and Alaska, exercise exclusive jurisdiction over state crimes committed on Indian reservations.

The U.S. Congress has delegated the primary responsibility for law enforcement on Indian reservations to the U.S. Department of the Interior's Bureau of Indian Affairs (BIA). The BIA operates about 50 law enforcement programs on Indian lands and monitors an additional 150 programs that are contracted for or operated by Indian tribes. The BIA also operates an Indian Police Academy.

The U.S. Supreme Court has sharply circumscribed the jurisdiction of tribal courts. In *Oliphant v. Suquamish Indian Tribe* (1978), the Court ruled that tribal courts cannot try to prosecute non-Indians because they do not sufficiently guard individual rights that are considered fundamental to Americans under the federal and state constitutions. The Court also has ruled that the Fifth Amendment double jeopardy clause does not bar the federal government from prosecuting an Indian defendant who has already been prosecuted in a tribal court because these cases involve two separate sovereigns. Thus, the federal government could still prosecute a defendant who has been acquitted by a tribal court, and vice versa.

In addition to tribal courts and law enforcement agencies, many tribes operate detention facilities. Under the Indian Civil Rights Act of 1968, tribal courts may not impose sentences requiring incarceration of any person for more than one year for any offense. Moreover, any person has the right to seek a writ of *habeas corpus* in federal court to test the legality of his or her detention by any tribal court.

STATE COURTS

Q 277. How many state courts are there?

A There are 16,288 state courts. This number includes 2,500 state courts of general jurisdiction and 13,788 state courts of limited jurisdiction.

State courts of general jurisdiction are the highest trial courts in a state and the forum for the most serious criminal cases. Filings in general jurisdiction courts accounted for 26 percent of state court caseloads in 1998. State courts of general jurisdiction are called by various names, including district, superior, and circuit court.

State courts of limited jurisdiction generally hear a narrow range of matters, sometimes just one particular type of case. Their criminal caseload may be limited to misdemeanor filings and ordinance violation cases and to holding preliminary hearings in felony cases. Filings in limited jurisdiction courts accounted for 74 percent of state court caseloads in 1998. Courts of limited jurisdiction are called by various names, including:

- Municipal courts
- Magistrate courts
- District courts
- Police courts
- County courts
- City courts
- Justice of the peace courts
- Courts of common pleas

State courts of general jurisdiction often exercise appellate review over dispositions rendered in state courts of limited jurisdiction.

Q **278. Are more civil or criminal cases filed in state courts?**

A More civil cases than criminal cases are filed in state courts. According to the National Center for State Courts, the breakdown of the caseload of state courts in 1998 was:

Type of Case	Number of Filings
Criminal	14,623,330
Civil	15,416,649
Domestic	5,023,831
Juvenile	2,097,025
Traffic	54,325,712
Total	91,486,547

Q **279. How have criminal caseloads changed in state courts over time?**

A The criminal caseload in state courts increased by almost 50 percent from 1984 to 1998, when it reached a high of 14,623,330 cases. According to the Administrative Office of State Courts, factors that influenced the caseload increase include population growth, a trend in state legislatures to criminalize more behaviors, and differences in prosecutorial charging procedures.

The largest increase occurred in felony filings, which rose by more than 80 percent. Felonies are the most serious crimes handled by the criminal justice system and include violent, property, and drug crimes punishable by incarceration of one year or more. There were 1.93 million felony filings in 1998. Following are the years and numbers, according to the National Center for State Courts, of all criminal cases filed in state courts from 1984 through 1998:

Year	Criminal Cases Filed	Year	Criminal Cases Filed
1984	9,769,414	1992	12,889,305
1985	10,165,406	1993	12,662,878
1986	10,718,247	1994	13,081,088
1987	11,171,382	1995	13,485,615
1988	11,691,329	1996	13,802,959
1989	12,182,596	1997	14,136,752
1990	12,679,774	1998	14,623,330
1991	12,595,542		

See 7 What is the difference between civil and criminal law?

Q 280. What types of cases are heard in state courts of general jurisdiction?

A State courts of general jurisdiction, or state trial courts, handle the most serious criminal cases. According to the National Center for State Courts (NCSC), in 1998 their caseload composition was:

- Felonies, 73 percent
- Misdemeanors,15 percent
- Drunk driving, 4 percent*
- Other (appeals, extradition, and so forth), 8 percent

Q 281. What types of cases are heard in state courts of limited jurisdiction?

A Most Americans come into contact with the judicial system through state courts of limited jurisdiction, which handle lesser criminal offenses. According to the National Center for State Courts (NCSC), their caseload in 1998 was:

- Misdemeanors, 89 percent
- Drunk driving, 9 percent*
- Felonies, 1 percent
- Other, 1 percent

Most of the misdemeanor cases heard in state courts of limited jurisdiction involve traffic offenses, including driving while under the influence of drugs or alcohol.

Q 282. Who prosecutes cases in state court?

A Every state court jurisdiction has a chief prosecutor, commonly known as the district attorney, county attorney, commonwealth's attorney, or state's attorney. The chief prosecutor is the equivalent of the U.S. attorney on the federal level. Prosecutors generally decide what crimes and suspects to prosecute and whether to negotiate a plea bargain with a defendant or to marshal the state's resources and take the case to trial.

State law determines the number of chief prosecutors in a state and whether they are elected or appointed. More than 95 percent of the nation's approximately 2,300 chief prosecutors are elected locally.

In large jurisdictions the chief prosecutor serves primarily as an administrator, setting policy and supervising a staff of prosecuting attorneys. In small jurisdictions, chief prosecutors may conduct trial work and also maintain a private practice.

---

*The NCSC categorizes cases involving drunk driving separately because these cases are often handled differently than other felonies and misdemeanors.

A 1996 national survey by the U.S. Department of Justice found that three-fourths of all state court prosecutors' offices employed a full-time prosecutor. Nationwide, prosecutors' offices employed approximately 71,000 prosecutors, paralegals, investigators, victims' advocates, and support staff, and had a median annual budget of $254,000. Half of all prosecutors' offices closed or concluded 250 or more felony cases with a conviction rate of 89 percent.

See 269 What does a U.S. Attorney do?

Q 283. What cases tend to be most difficult to prosecute?

A The National Institute of Justice reports that about 92 percent of prosecutors surveyed in 1995 said that child abuse cases, including molestation, create the most serious workload problems in their offices because they are difficult and time-consuming to prosecute. Ranking a close second was domestic violence, because many victims have second thoughts about cooperating with the prosecution.

Q 284. How do courts fulfill their mandate to provide legal counsel to the poor?

A The U.S. Supreme Court has ruled that the right to counsel under the Sixth Amendment of the U.S. Constitution requires that the federal and state governments provide legal counsel to indigent defendants who are charged with serious crimes. In *Gideon v. Wainwright* (1963), Justice Hugo L. Black observed that "lawyers in criminal courts are necessities, not luxuries."

Federal judicial districts provide indigent representation through a panel of private attorneys or through federal public or community defender offices. There are sixty-four federal public defender organizations. A total of 104,928 appointments of counsel were made in 1999 for indigent defendants in federal criminal proceedings.

States fulfill their mandate to provide counsel to indigent defendants in various ways. Sometimes a combination of methods will be used within a single jurisdiction. Some states operate public defender programs with full-time or part-time staff. Other states use an assigned counsel system in which private counsel is appointed from a roster to represent the poor for a fee. Depending on the jurisdiction, a judge or an administrator makes the appointment. Finally, some states use contract attorney systems in which the government contracts with private attorneys, bar associations, or law firms to provide services for a specified dollar amount.

A 1996 study by the U.S. Department of Justice found that about three-fourths of state prison inmates and about half of federal prison inmates received publicly provided legal counsel for the offense for which they were serving time.

Indigent defense services suffer from chronic underfunding relative to other components of the criminal justice system, largely as a result of political hostility to poor people who are facing criminal charges.

Q 285. Does wealth affect the quality of justice?

A Most Americans say that money talks in a courtroom. In a 1999 survey by the National Center for State Courts, 80 percent of a nationally representative sample of 1,826 respondents said that wealthy people receive better treatment in the courts. Most Americans also felt that it was not economical to go to court. Only one-third of respondents agreed with the statement that it is affordable to bring a case to court, whereas 68 percent disagreed and 38 percent strongly disagreed.

Q 286. How are most criminal cases disposed of in state courts?

A Most criminal cases in state courts end when the defendant enters a guilty plea, often after having entered into a plea bargain with the prosecutor. Of the 96.3 percent of cases that were disposed of in 1998 by means other than a trial, 63.4 percent were disposed of by guilty pleas, 18.4 percent were dismissed (either by the prosecutor or the court), and 14.5 percent were disposed of by various other means.

See 196 What is a plea bargain?

Q 287. What type of criminal is least likely to enter a guilty plea?

A Defendants who are charged with murder or manslaughter are least likely to enter a guilty plea and are most likely to demand a trial.

Defendants who are charged with serious violent crimes are the most likely to seek a trial. These defendants face higher sanctions than do other defendants and have the most to lose if convicted. Also, prosecutors may be less willing to negotiate a plea with these defendants.

The U.S. Department of Justice reports that about 83 percent of felons who were convicted of a violent crime in 1996 entered guilty pleas. That figure compares to 94 percent of felons who were convicted of property offenses and 92 percent of felons who were convicted of drug offenses. Only 54 percent of felons who were convicted of murder or manslaughter in 1996 had entered guilty pleas.

Of all defendants, those most likely to enter a guilty plea were felons convicted of fraud or forgery. Ninety-four percent of felons who were convicted of these offenses in 1996 had entered guilty pleas.

Q 288. How many cases go to trial in state court?

A Almost 2.1 million trials took place in state courts in 1998. This number represents 3.7 percent of all criminal cases that were disposed of that year. The state with the lowest percentage of trials was Vermont, where 1.1 percent of cases came to trial. The state with the highest percentage of trials was Wyoming, where 13.1 percent of cases came to trial. A major factor in the trial rate is whether plea-bargaining is encouraged or discouraged within the jurisdiction.

Q 289. How many jury trials versus bench trials are held in criminal cases in state courts?

A About 55 percent of all defendants who demand a trial request a jury trial. Of the 3.7 percent of criminal cases that came to trial in 1998, 2.1 percent were disposed of by jury trial and 1.6 percent were disposed of by bench trial. A judge determines guilt or innocence in a bench trial.

Q 290. What is the profile of a convicted felon?

A According to the U.S. Department of Justice:

- Males make up 48 percent of the adult population and 84 percent of convicted felons.
- Whites make up 84 percent of the adult population and 54 percent of convicted felons.
- Blacks make up 12 percent of the adult population and 44 percent of convicted felons.
- Persons in their twenties make up 19 percent of the U.S. population and 41 percent of convicted felons.

Q 291. Where may state trial court decisions and judgments be appealed?

A Every state allows a defendant to appeal a felony conviction, and it is estimated that about one-third of all defendants do so. In order to appeal, a defendant must allege grounds, such as trial court error, ineffective assistance of counsel, or an error in sentencing.

Thirty-nine states and Puerto Rico have midlevel appellate courts that hear most first appeals in non-death-penalty cases in their respective jurisdictions. These courts were created to free the state court of last resort to handle cases of statewide significance. Typically, these courts work in panels of three or more judges.

In jurisdictions that lack midlevel appellate courts, criminal appeals are filed directly with the state court of last resort. These mostly small jurisdictions are the District of Columbia, West Virginia, Nevada, Vermont, Montana, Wyoming, Delaware, New Hampshire, Rhode Island, Maine, South Dakota, and North Dakota. Courts of last resort generally sit *en banc,* or with the full court present.

In 1998 the total number of appellate filings in state courts was 297,285, an increase of 1 percent over 1997. This number represents a tiny fraction of the 14.6 million criminal filings in state courts in 1998. The number of criminal appeals filed with appellate courts has increased by 35 percent since 1986.

A defendant who loses an appeal filed with an intermediate appellate court may petition the state court of last resort to review the matter. However, these courts typically are not obligated to hear the appeal.

Defendants who have exhausted all proper state court remedies may file a petition or a writ of certiorari asking the U.S. Supreme Court to review their claims. The Court may consider appeals from the highest court of any state provided that the case involves an important question of federal law. The Court agrees to consider less than 1 percent of such requests.

Of those defendants who appeal their convictions, an estimated 20 percent have their convictions reversed. However, many of these defendants are retried and ultimately re-convicted.

See 255 What is an appeal?

Q 292. Do Americans trust the courts in their community?

A In a 1999 survey by the National Center for State Courts, a nationally representative sample of 1,826 respondents rated the courts in their communities sixth out of eight major American institutions in terms of trust and confidence. From high to low, the institutions ranked as follows:

- Medical profession
- Local police
- U.S. Supreme Court
- Office of the governor
- Public schools
- Courts in your community
- State legislature
- Media

Following are the percentages of respondents and the degree of trust or confidence they expressed in state courts:

- A great deal, 23.2 percent
- Some, 52.2 percent
- Only a little, 16.9 percent
- None, 7.7 percent

Almost 70 percent of African American respondents thought their community was treated somewhat worse or far worse than whites or Hispanics, and 40 percent of whites and Hispanics agreed.

JUVENILE COURT

Q 293. What is juvenile court?

A Juvenile courts handle criminal matters involving juveniles and protect juveniles from abuse and neglect. Juvenile courts have jurisdiction over juveniles who are at or below the maximum age established by the state legislature for juvenile court jurisdiction, typically eighteen years.

In three states—Connecticut, New York, and North Carolina—defendants age sixteen and older are excluded from the juvenile court system and automatically sent to adult courts. In ten other states defendants age seventeen and older are excluded from the juvenile system and sent directly to adult court. In the remaining thirty-seven states and the District of Columbia, all persons age eighteen and older are processed as adult offenders. Juvenile courts typically have jurisdiction over the following areas:

- *Delinquent acts:* acts committed by a juvenile that would also be criminal if committed by an adult
- *Status offenses:* behavior that is an offense only when committed by a juvenile but not by an adult (such as running way from home, being beyond the control of parents or guardians, and truancy)
- *Dependency offenses:* actions on the part of parents or guardians involving the neglect or inadequate care of minors (such as abandonment, desertion, abuse or cruel treatment, absence, or physical or mental incapacity of the parents)

Q 294. When was the first juvenile court established?

A During the nineteenth century, children who were liable for criminal acts were imprisoned, and there are records of children being hanged as late as 1708. Recognition of the need for special treatment of juvenile offenders emerged from the nineteenth-century reformatory movement, which sought to establish training institutions for young offenders as an alternative to confinement in adult prisons.

The first juvenile court was the Cook County Juvenile Court, established in Chicago, Illinois, on July 1, 1899. Although a uniquely American invention, juvenile court is premised on a centuries-old doctrine from the chancery courts in England. This doctrine, *parens patriae*, holds that the state or the sovereign is the ultimate parent of all infants.

The Cook County Juvenile Court was promoted by child advocate Lucy Flower, social worker Jane Addams (founder of Chicago's Hull House, one of the first neighborhood social welfare agencies), and Julia Lathrop, who became the first director of the U.S. Children's Bureau, a federal agency established in 1912 to oversee national standards of child welfare. These activists enlisted the aid of Chicago women's clubs, the Chicago Bar Association, and the Catholic Visitation and Aid Society.

The Cook County Juvenile Court took children out of the adult criminal system, which was seen as unnecessarily harsh and regressive toward children. The court's mission was to serve the best interests of the child by offering protection and rehabilitation. Less formal than adult criminal courts, the juvenile court dispensed with many due-process protections afforded to adult criminal defendants. Outcomes were individually tailored and ranged from warnings to probation supervision or training school confinement. Chicago's juvenile court initially had jurisdiction only over juveniles charged with petty criminal offenses.

While the Chicago juvenile court was being established, a juvenile court also was taking shape in Denver, Colorado. Pioneered by Judge Ben B. Lindsey, who has been called the father of juvenile court, the Denver court was considered more socially progressive than the Chicago court. Legal procedure and language were all but eliminated, and the judge sat at eye level with the children.

By 1925, all but two states had juvenile courts.

See 78 What is the juvenile justice system? 79 Who is a juvenile?

Q 295. How many juveniles are processed in juvenile court each year?

A Juvenile filings in state courts reached a record high of nearly 2.1 million in 1998, a 3 percent increase over the number of filings in 1997. Sixty-five percent of juvenile cases were for some type of delinquent act, and 17 percent involved status offenses or incidents of misconduct that would be noncriminal if committed by an adult (truancy, runaways, and so forth). Seventeen percent of cases involved child victimization, including child abuse.

Q 296. What is the caseload composition of juvenile court?

A According to a 1999 report by the Office of Juvenile Justice and Delinquency Prevention (OJJDP), property offenses make up the single largest category of delinquency cases. Following are the numbers of offenses by type, as analyzed by the OJJDP from the estimated 1,757,600 delinquency cases handled by juvenile courts in 1996:

Category of Offense	Includes
Property offenses, 874,000	Larceny-theft, 421,600
	Burglary, 141,100
	Vandalism, 119,800
	Trespassing, 65,000
	Motor vehicle theft, 51,600
	Stolen property, 32,900
	Arson, 8,900
	Other, 33,400
Offenses against persons, 381,500	Simple assaults, 216,600
	Aggravated assaults, 89,900
	Robbery, 37,300
	Forcible rape, 6,900
	Other violent sex offenses, 8,900
	Homicide, 2,400
	Other, 19,400
Public order offenses, 325,400	Obstruction of justice, 125,800
	Disorderly conduct, 90,200
	Weapons offenses, 41,200
	Nonviolent sex offenses, 10,600
	Liquor law violations, 10,300
	Other, 47,300
Drug law violations, 176,300	

Note: Sub-categories may not add to the total for each category due to rounding.

Most juvenile status-offense cases involve liquor-law violations. Status offenses are crimes only if committed by juveniles. Juvenile courts formally processed about 162,000 status-offense cases in 1996. This total breaks down as follows:

- Liquor law violations, 44,800
- Truancy, 39,300
- Runaways, 25,800
- Ungovernability (being beyond the control of parents or guardians), 20,100
- Other (such as curfew violations, smoking tobacco, and violations of a valid court order), 32,000

Q 297. What happens to juveniles in juvenile court?

A Juveniles can enter the juvenile court system through referral by law enforcement officers, school officials, social services agencies, neighbors, and parents. In practice, however, most delinquency cases—86 percent in 1996—are referred to courts by law enforcement agencies.

An administrator, called a court intake officer, or a prosecutor typically determines whether sufficient evidence exists to warrant filing a petition asking a judge to hold an adjudicatory hearing, which would determine whether the juvenile is responsible for a delinquent act or a status offense. In most states, the judge may hold the hearing, waive jurisdiction and transfer the case to an adult criminal court, or refer the juvenile to an alternative program, such as a drug-treatment, counseling, educational, or recreational program.

Judges granted petitions to adjudicate 58 percent of the 1,757,600 delinquency cases filed in 1996, and about 1 percent of cases were waived to adult court. Of the remaining cases, 60 percent were dismissed, 20 percent resulted in voluntary probation, 18 percent involved other sanctions, and 2 percent resulted in voluntary out-of-home placement at a court-approved program or facility. Fifty-eight percent of juveniles who underwent an adjudicatory hearing in 1996 were found to be delinquent.

An adjudicatory hearing is markedly different from a trial in an adult court. Juveniles have no right to a jury trial, and—to shield the juvenile from adverse publicity—proceedings in juvenile court generally are closed to the public. However, the standard of proof in juvenile proceedings is the same as in adult court.

If a juvenile is found to be responsible for his or her actions, the judge holds a disposition hearing to determine the appropriate sanction, generally after reviewing a predisposition report prepared by the probation department. The judge typically has more discretion than does a judge in adult court. A juvenile may be committed to a

Figure 3-2 How Cases Flow through the Juvenile Justice System

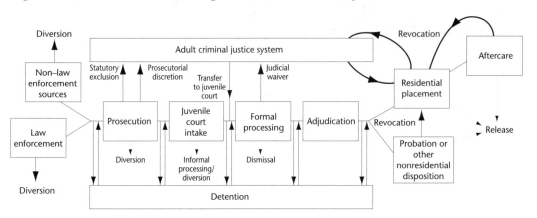

Source: Office of Juvenile Justice and Delinquency Prevention, U.S. Department of Justice.

secure institution; placed in a group home, foster home, or other residential facility; placed on probation; referred to an outside agency, day treatment or mental health program; fined; or ordered to do community service or to make restitution.

See Figure 3-2 How Cases Flow through the Juvenile Justice System.

Q 298. When may a juvenile be placed in secure detention?

A Juveniles may be placed in a secure juvenile detention facility at any point during the processing of their cases in juvenile court. States require a hearing be held, usually within twenty-four to forty-eight hours of the referral placement, to allow a judge to review the decision to detain the youth. Detention generally is ordered if juvenile court authorities believe a youth is a threat to the community, will be at risk if returned to the community, or may fail to appear at an upcoming hearing or for sentencing. A youth also may be detained for diagnostic testing.

In *Schall v. Martin* (1984), the U.S. Supreme Court upheld preventive detention in juvenile cases. The Court said that preventive detention is not intended to punish a juvenile and serves a legitimate state objective by protecting the juvenile and society from pretrial crime. The Court said that enough procedures exist to protect juveniles from wrongful deprivation of liberty, including notice, a statement of the facts and reasons for detention, and a probable cause hearing within a short time.

According to a 1999 report by the Office of Juvenile Justice and Delinquency Prevention, delinquents who are charged with property offenses are the most likely to be detained. Following are the most serious offenses for which juveniles were detained in 1996:

- Property offenses, 39 percent
- Crimes against persons, 27 percent
- Public order offenses, 21 percent
- Drug law violations, 12 percent

Q 299. Who is most likely to be detained by juvenile authorities?

A Even after controlling for type of offense, black juveniles are more than twice as likely as white juveniles to be detained in a secure facility, according to a 1999 report by the Office of Juvenile Justice and Delinquency Prevention (OJJDP). The OJJDP generally cited a "widespread disparity in juvenile case processing" within the juvenile justice system. In 1997, the OJJDP reported, minorities represented about one-third of the juvenile population nationwide but two-thirds of the population of offenders incarcerated in secure juvenile facilities. The OJJDP suggested that a possible explanation for the disparity was that minority youth were discriminated against at early stages of their case processing, such as when the decision was made to make an arrest and prosecute the offender. The OJJDP announced that it was making the elimination of "disproportionate minority confinement" a priority issue.

An earlier (1995) report by the U.S. Department of Justice suggested that "processing decisions" at all stages of state and local juvenile justice systems were not racially neutral. The report recommended developing educational initiatives aimed at juvenile justice agencies and developing specific programs designed to address differences in the ways that minority youth are processed in the juvenile justice system.

See 137 Are African Americans disproportionately affected by crime?

Q 300. What is the significance of *In re Gault*?

A In the landmark case *In re Gault* (1967), the U.S. Supreme Court agreed that the constitutional guarantee of due process applies via the Fourteenth Amendment to state proceedings in which juveniles are charged as delinquents and face possible incarceration in an institute of confinement. Gerald Francis Gault, age fifteen, was declared to be a juvenile delinquent by the Juvenile Court of Gila County, Arizona, after it was determined that he and another boy had made an obscene telephone call to a neighbor. Gault previously had been placed on probation. After a hearing, the judge committed Gault to the State Industrial School until he reached age twenty-one. The Supreme Court declared that the procedures used in Gault's case violated the requirements of the U.S. Constitution. The Court noted that were Gault an adult, he would have been subject only to a fine of from $5 to $50, adding, "Under our Constitution, the condition of being a boy does not justify a kangaroo court." In its decision the Court said that a juvenile has the right to:

- adequate written notice informing the juvenile and his or her parents or guardian "of the specific issues that they must meet" sufficiently in advance of the hearing to permit preparation;
- representation by counsel and, if the juvenile or his or her family is unable to afford counsel, the appointment of counsel to represent the child;
- freedom from self-incrimination, meaning that an admission by the juvenile may not be used against him or her unless clear and unequivocal evidence exists that the admission was made with knowledge that the juvenile was not obliged to speak and would not be penalized for remaining silent; and
- confrontation and sworn testimony of witnesses available for cross-examination.

See 15 What is due process?

Q 301. Why don't juveniles have a right to trial by jury?

A In *McKeiver v. Pennsylvania* (1971), the U.S. Supreme Court ruled 6–3 that a jury is not required in juvenile court because a "fully adversary proceeding" would "put an effective end" to the positive aspects of juvenile courts: "fairness . . . concern . . . sympathy and . . . paternal attention." Most states do not provide juries in juvenile courts.

As of 1996, four states—Alaska, Massachusetts, Michigan, and West Virginia—gave juvenile delinquents the unqualified right to a trial by jury in juvenile court. Thirteen states—Arkansas, Colorado, Idaho, Illinois, Kansas, Minnesota, Montana, New Mexico, Oklahoma, Rhode Island, Texas, Virginia, and Wyoming—gave juvenile delinquents the right to a trial by jury under at least some circumstances.

Q 302. Have juvenile court filings declined with the juvenile arrest rate?

A No. Juvenile filings in state courts reached a historic high of nearly 2.1 million in 1998. Meanwhile, the Federal Bureau of Investigation reports that juvenile arrests declined by 30 percent from 1994 to 1998. One reason for the incongruity between court filings and the arrest rate may be that fewer juvenile complaints are being informally resolved. In 1996 only 44 percent of juvenile delinquency cases were handled informally, compared to 53 percent in 1987.

Q 303. What is the most common method of disposition in delinquency cases?

A Probation. In 1996 judges ordered probation in 54 percent of cases of juveniles who were adjudged to be delinquent. Twenty-eight percent were placed in out-of-home residential facilities; 13 percent were subjected to other sanctions, including restitution or fine; and 4 percent were released. A total of 306,900 delinquent juveniles were placed on formal probation in 1996, an increase of 58 percent from 1987.

Probation often is used for low-risk, first-time offenders or as an alternative to institutional confinement for more serious offenders. The offender may remain in the community and continue to go to school or to work, but must comply with conditions established by the court. Typically the juvenile must meet regularly with a probation supervisor, adhere to a strict curfew, and complete a period of community service. Violation of these conditions may result in revocation of probation and resentencing by the court.

Residential placement includes placement at a training school, camp, ranch, or drug treatment facility, or private placement in a facility or group home.

Q 304. How many juvenile cases are transferred to adult criminal court each year?

A According to a 1999 report by the U.S. Department of Justice, about 10,000 delinquency cases that were formally handled by the juvenile court system (1 percent of such cases) were waived to criminal court in 1996. Juveniles tried in adult court face adult sentences of up to life in prison, whereas sentences in juvenile court typically last only until the offender reaches age twenty-five.

The number of juvenile cases waived to adult court skyrocketed by 73 percent between 1987 and 1998, then declined by 15 percent between 1994 and 1996. However, a reversal of the downward trend is anticipated in the future.

In reaction to drug-gang violence and a series of highly publicized school shootings, more than thirty states have changed their laws since 1992 to prosecute more juveniles in adult criminal courts. These laws increase the number of offenses that qualify for transfer and lower the age at which juveniles may be transferred. They also designate certain offenses for which juveniles are automatically transferred or establish a presumption that a juvenile should be transferred and give prosecutors the authority to decide.

Q 305. For what types of crimes are juveniles sent to adult court?

A According to a 1999 report by the U.S. Department of Justice, 43 percent of cases waived from the juvenile court system to the criminal court system in 1996 involved offenses against persons; 37 percent involved property offenses; 14 percent involved drugs; and 6 percent involved public order offenses. Waived cases generally involved male juveniles ages sixteen or older who were charged with a serious offense, had lengthy prior records, or who were considered to be unreceptive to treatment in the juvenile justice system.

Q 306. What mechanisms do states use to transfer juvenile cases to adult court?

A States use the following mechanisms to transfer juvenile cases to adult court:

- *Judicial waiver.* Juvenile court judges may waive jurisdiction over a case and transfer it to criminal court in all states except Nebraska, New Mexico, and New York. The waiver and transfer may be based on the judge's own judgment, in response to a prosecutor's request, or in some states at the request of juveniles or their parents.
- *Concurrent jurisdiction statute.* Criminal and juvenile courts share original jurisdiction for some cases. These statutes give prosecutors the discretion to file certain juvenile cases in either court. In 1997 ten states and the District of Columbia had concurrent jurisdiction statutes.
- *Statutory or legislative exclusion.* Legislatures may adopt state statutes that exclude certain juvenile offenders from juvenile court jurisdiction. These excluded cases originate in criminal court rather than juvenile court. In 1997 twenty-eight states and the District of Columbia excluded selected offenses from juvenile court jurisdiction. The most common excluded offenses were capital murder, murder of other types, and serious crimes against persons. Several states excluded juveniles charged with felonies if they had prior adjudications or convictions. However, twenty-two states allowed the criminal court, usually on a motion from the prosecutor, to transfer excluded cases back to the juvenile court for adjudication or disposition.
- *Presumptive waiver.* Juvenile offenders may be waived to criminal court unless they can prove that they are amenable to juvenile rehabilitation. This provision shifts the burden of proof from the prosecutor to the juvenile. About a dozen states had enacted presumptive waiver provisions as of 1995.

In the federal system, juveniles may be adjudicated as adults if the offense charged was a violent felony or drug trafficking or importation and if the offense was committed after the juvenile's fifteenth birthday. If the juvenile possessed a firearm during a violent offense, the juvenile may be adjudicated as an adult if the offense was committed after the juvenile's thirteenth birthday.

Before proceeding against a juvenile in federal court, the U.S. attorney must certify to the court a substantial federal interest in the case and at least one of the following conditions:

- The state does not have or refuses to assume jurisdiction.
- The state with jurisdiction does not have adequate programs or services for juvenile offenders.
- The offense charged is a violent felony, a drug-trafficking or importation offense, or a firearm offense.

Q 307. Who is the youngest child to be tried and convicted as an adult for murder?

A Nathaniel Abraham is believed to be the youngest child in U.S. history to be tried and convicted as an adult for murder. In 1997 Abraham was charged with first-degree murder by Michigan authorities. He was convicted in November 1999 of murder in the second-degree.

At age eleven, Abraham had fired a stolen .22-caliber rifle from behind some trees on a steep hillside and killed eighteen-year-old Ronnie Greene Jr., a complete stranger who had walked out of a convenience store about 200 feet away. Abraham allegedly had fired the same gun at a neighbor, and missed, shortly before going to the hillside. Abraham said he was shooting at the trees and didn't mean to kill Greene, but prosecutors introduced evidence that Abraham had bragged to a girl at his school of his intention to kill someone.

Michigan had adopted one of the toughest juvenile justice laws in the nation in 1996. Prosecutors are allowed to obtain judicial approval to try any juvenile as an adult, no matter how young. Previously, Michigan youths ages seventeen or older were tried as adults and juveniles as young as age fourteen could be tried as adults with a judge's permission.

Q 308. Are juveniles likely to receive more lenient sentences in criminal courts than adults receive?

A No. The Office of Juvenile Justice and Delinquency Prevention reported in 1999 that juveniles who were convicted of felony murder in criminal court in 1994 received longer sentences than did their adult counterparts. In 1994 the average maximum prison sentence imposed on transferred juveniles convicted of felony murder was twenty-three years and eleven months, two years and five months longer than the average maximum prison sentence for adults convicted of felony murder.

OTHER COURTS

Q 309. What is a drug court?

A Drug courts are courts that offer a multidisciplinary, treatment-oriented approach to nonviolent offenders who have substance-abuse problems, as an alternative to the traditional, punitive response of incarceration.

The first drug court was created in Dade County, Florida, in 1989. Since then, the federal government has encouraged all states to establish drug courts. The U.S. Department of Justice's Drug Court Program Office was formed pursuant to Title V of the Violent Crime Control and Law Enforcement Act of 1994 to support the development and implementation of effective Drug Court programming at the state, local, and tribal level.

Drug courts work closely with agencies and organizations involved in recovery. Continuing judicial supervision of an offender is linked with mandatory periodic substance-abuse testing and substance-abuse treatment. Sanctions are forthcoming for failure to comply with program requirements.

The number of drug courts has skyrocketed in recent years as drug courts report significant cost savings for the justice system, especially in the use of jail space and probation services. Drug courts also help the court system target chronic recidivists as well as first offenders. In 1998, 327 drug courts were in operation in forty-three states, the District of Columbia, Puerto Rico, Guam, and two federal jurisdictions, including more than fifteen Native American tribal courts.

The U.S. Department of Justice reported in 2000 that drug courts that emphasize treatment, services, and sanctions reduce drug use and later recidivism more effectively than drug courts that rely on simple drug testing and judicial monitoring. Researchers estimated the value of the arrest reductions resulting from the model drug court program in Washington, D.C., approached $1.5 million, including reduced costs to victims and the criminal justice system.

Q 310. What is a reentry court?

A Reentry courts use the power of judicial authority to help integrate a released offender back into the community.

In 1999 almost 585,000 felons were released from prisons and jails. The U.S. Department of Justice estimates that 62 percent of these felons will be charged with new crimes and 41 percent will be incarcerated again within three years.

Reentry courts are designed to reduce recidivism by linking offenders with supportive agencies and community organizations and by helping offenders find new housing, jobs, or job training. Modeled after drug courts, reentry courts allow authorities to closely monitor returning prisoners and to implement a series of graduated sanctions for violations of court-imposed release conditions. In early 2000 nine states had or were developing reentry court programs: California, Colorado, Delaware, Florida, Iowa, Kentucky, New York, Ohio, and West Virginia.

IV
LAW ENFORCEMENT

IN GENERAL

Q 311. What is the origin of the word *police*?

A The Latin word *politia* (civil administration) derives from the Greek word *polis* (city). The word originally referred to the civil administration of a city. The French first applied the word *police* to the administration of public order in the early eighteenth century.

Q 312. From where do law enforcement officers derive their authority?

A Federal, state, and local law enforcement officers derive their authority from constitutions and legislative enactments. Ultimately, police derive their power from the people, who elect the legislators who pass laws governing conduct that is deemed unacceptable to society and deserving of sanction.

A longstanding national debate continues about the federal government's role in criminal law and law enforcement. The U.S. Constitution says that any power that is not specifically delegated to the federal government belongs to the states. With the exception of a couple of federal crimes, the Constitution is virtually silent about criminal law. However, the commerce clause in the Constitution grants Congress general powers to regulate activities affecting interstate commerce. Congress has used the commerce clause to create hundreds of new federal crimes, from prohibitions against child labor to hate crimes.

In *Lopez v. United States* (1995), the U.S. Supreme Court voted 5–4 to strike down a 1995 law making it a federal crime to possess a gun near a school. Congress passed the law after finding that gun violence had an adverse affect on classroom learning, which posed a substantial threat to trade and interstate commerce. The *Lopez* majority said the law is a criminal statute that has nothing to do with commerce or any sort of economic activity. The majority opinion stressed that Congress's power to regulate interstate commerce does not confer on it any general police powers over the nation.

See 2 What type of criminal justice system was envisioned in the U.S. Constitution?

Q 313. How many law enforcement agencies exist?

A The United States system of law enforcement may be the most decentralized in the world. America's Founders rejected the concept of a national police force and left the primary responsibility for law enforcement to state and local governments. As a result, state, county, and municipal governments and the federal government operate almost 20,000 separate public law enforcement agencies in the United States. In addition to agencies that are constituted exclusively for law enforcement purposes, myriad special police forces report to agencies that operate universities, bridges, tunnels, parks, airports, and so forth.

The more than 18,000 state and local law enforcement agencies in the United States include 13,540 local police departments, 3,088 sheriffs' departments, 49 state police departments, 1,332 special police departments, and 751 Texas constable agencies. The latest statistics show that, as of June 1997, local police departments employed an estimated 420,000 sworn personnel with arrest powers, and sheriffs' departments employed about 175,000 sworn personnel.

Some thirty federal agencies each employ at least 100 full-time law enforcement officers with arrest powers and firearms authorization. Of these federal agencies, sixteen employ 500 or more officers. Eighteen federal agencies employ fewer than 100 officers. The federal government employs about 74,500 full-time law enforcement officers with arrest powers and firearms authorization.

Q 314. How many arrests are made annually by law enforcement officers?

A Law enforcement agencies nationwide made an estimated 14.5 million arrests for all criminal infractions, excluding traffic violations, in 1998. The arrest rate was 5,534 arrests per 100,000 inhabitants of the United States.

Contrary to popular perception, the rate of crime is dropping. The total number of arrests for all offenses, excluding traffic violations, decreased by 1 percent from 1997 to 1998. Arrests for serious crimes declined by 7 percent, including a 5 percent drop in serious violent crimes and an 8 percent drop in serious property crimes. Despite these recent declines, however, overall arrests have increased by 7 percent from 1989 to 1998.

See 54 What crime leads to the most arrests?

Q 315. What percentage of crimes reported to police result in an arrest?

A Fewer than 25 percent of the crimes that are reported to police result in an arrest. According to the Federal Bureau of Investigation (FBI), 21 percent of crimes were cleared by arrest in 1998. This number includes 49 percent of violent crimes and 17 percent of property crimes.

An offense typically is cleared when at least one person is arrested, charged with the commission of the offense, and turned over to the court for prosecution. A crime also may be cleared by exceptional means when elements beyond law enforcement's control preclude the placing of formal charges against a defendant, such as suicide, the victim's refusal to cooperate with the prosecution after the offender was identified, or the denial of extradition of a defendant who has fled to a different jurisdiction.

See 41 How many serious crimes were reported in the United States in 1998?

Q 316. How were laws enforced in colonial America?

A Colonial Americans adopted variations of the law enforcement models of their European homelands, such as the night watch, constabulary, and sheriff. The articles of incorporation of colonial villages such as Boston, Charles Town, New York, and Philadelphia included provisions for a constable-and-watch system.

The first night watch was established in Boston on April 12, 1631. Initially a military guard, the group changed to a citizen watch in 1636. Every able-bodied man was required to serve in the night watch or to hire a substitute.

The constable was elected by town freeholders and served as the chief colonial law enforcement officer during the early eighteenth century. The constable charged fees for his services. He supervised the night watch, a delegation of citizens appointed, drafted, or hired to keep watch over the community at night and to protect it from crime and external threats. In New York City, the constable was authorized to "whip or punish" individuals who shirked their night watch duty "unless they can get another person to do it." Many night watchmen actually were paid substitutes for volunteers and were drawn from society's unemployables.

In many rural communities the colonial governor or town leader appointed a constable or a sheriff to maintain order. The term *sheriff* derives from the older term *shire reeve,* the title of the officer responsible for keeping the peace in England around 700 A.D. The reeves protected the shires, or estates, of the kings. Sheriffs often were not paid a salary but instead received a fee for each arrest they made.

In Southern colonies, where planters sought to control large populations of slaves and indentured servants, slave patrols served as rural police, captured runaway slaves, and sought to prevent a possible slave insurrection. Initially part of the colonial militias, the patrols later were staffed by volunteers appointed by townspeople. The first slave patrol was established in South Carolina in 1704 to "prevent all caballings amongst Negroes, by dispersing of them when drumming or playing, and to search all Negro houses for arms or other offensive weapons."

Another method of law enforcement in the eighteenth century was vigilantism, wherein mobs enforced written and unwritten laws. The first American vigilantes were the South Carolina Regulators, who appeared in 1767 to patrol the backcountry of South Carolina in the wake of the Cherokee War of 1760–1761. Initially, the Regulators battled outlaws who were terrorizing respectable settlers. Later, they targeted what they called *lower people,* including vagrants and prostitutes, who fell short of their moral standards. Eventually citizens came to feel the Regulators had gone too far, and courts were established in the region. Hundreds of vigilante groups also appeared throughout the West, particularly in Texas, exacting swift and terrible retribution for criminal acts in the absence of any formal legal authority.

All of these informal arrangements became less workable as America's population grew and its borders expanded.

See 20 What were the first crimes established by the U.S. Congress? 444 How did the colonists punish criminals?

Q 317. What model of policing was adopted in America?

A Policing has evolved over thousands of years. For example, under the emperor Augustus, Rome was divided into fourteen *regiones* (wards) and subdivided into *vici* (precincts). The precincts were overseen by *vicomagistri* who were responsible for fire and police protection. However, early American police forces were directly modeled after the Metropolitan Police of London, England, formed in 1829 by British Statesman Sir Robert Peel.

Peel declared that the basic mission for which police exist is to prevent crime and disorder. However, he said, police must secure the public's approval and cooperation. The London model of policing emphasized uniformed, unarmed, and highly visible officers who patrolled the streets of London on foot. Command passed through a centralized, quasi-military administration. The administration typically included a sergeant who supervised a squad of nine constables, or *Bobbies* (named after Peel), who were directed to prevent crime through their presence and persuasion. By contrast, the continental mode of policing, such as that used in France, relied on armed secret police and paid informers.

Americans eschewed some aspects of the London model. Americans retained local, rather than national, control over police. As a result, critics say that American police were more susceptible to influence and corruption by local politicians. In the nineteenth century many police departments effectively served as the enforcement arm of the political party in power.

Also unlike their English counterparts, American police initially opposed the wearing of uniforms as unmanly. And while London Bobbies carried only a wooden *billy club,* or truncheon, many American law enforcement officers were at least tacitly permitted to carry firearms.

Q 318. Who is the father of modern professional policing in the United States?

A August Vollmer (1876–1955), a former police chief in Berkeley, California, and the first professor of police administration in the United States, is considered the father of modern professional policing in the United States. The son of German immigrants, Vollmer was appointed in 1905 to head Berkeley's six-person police department. Vollmer was an ardent supporter of higher education for police and in 1908 began a formal training school for his deputies that was the first to educate officers in scientific methods of crime detection. He pioneered the use of bicycle patrols in 1911, motorcycle patrols in 1912, automobile patrols in 1913, and police radio cars in 1921. He was the first to use a lie detector machine in police work, established an innovative classification system for fingerprinting and handwriting samples, and devised one of the first centralized police records systems. Vollmer was president of the International Association of Chiefs of Police in 1922 and, through it, created the Uniform Crime Reports, which became an important indicator of the level of crime in America. He also supervised the preparation of the first national study of law enforcement in the United States, the Report on Police for the Wickersham Commission. Vollmer exposed many unconstitutional police practices to public scrutiny, especially the practice of detectives using the third degree in questioning suspects. He reorganized police departments in Los Angeles, San Diego, Minneapolis, Detroit, Kansas City, Dallas, Portland, and Chicago. Though he lacked a college degree, Vollmer wrote or co-wrote several books on policing and became the first professor of police administration in the United States at the University of Chicago.

See 210 Do polygraph machines work?

Q **319. What city formed the first full-time police force in America?**

A Boston, Massachusetts, formed the first organized police force in 1835. The force consisted of eight paid officers who worked during the daytime and who also were charged with maintaining public health. However, New York City established the first true American police department in 1845. The New York City force employed 800 salaried full-time officers and supervisors who were charged with providing twenty-four-hour protection. Patterned after the Metropolitan Police Department of London, England, the force replaced a hodge-podge of constables, dock masters, and various inspectors.

The new force of "Day and Night Police" patrolled the city investigating crimes and performing essential services, such as lighting the city's gas lamps at night and occasionally sweeping the streets. Each officer carried a copper, star-shaped identification badge. The mayor appointed police officers from among a group of men nominated by local aldermen. Each ward in the city had its own station house, to which one captain and one assistant captain were assigned. To provide overall supervision the mayor appointed a chief of police, who served a one-year term.

Other cities quickly followed New York's lead, including Chicago (1851), New Orleans (1852), Cincinnati (1852), Philadelphia (1854), Boston (1854), St. Louis (1855), Newark (1857), and Baltimore (1857). By the end of the nineteenth century every major city and every state had formed law enforcement agencies.

Q **320. What police department refused to wear uniforms?**

A New York City police refused to wear uniforms until 1853, eight years after the department was formed. Police and the general public had opposed the wearing of uniforms by police as militaristic, undemocratic, and unmanly. At the time, New York City police carried only copper, star-shaped badges for identification. Police were reluctant to do even that, claiming that the badges deprived them of anonymity, detracted from their ability to catch crooks, and made them walking targets. Finally, the city's police commission refused to reappoint any police officer who would not wear a uniform. The commissioners felt the visibility of uniforms encouraged officers to stay on the job and out of local bars.

Q **321. What is the origin of the word *cop*?**

A Several theories exist about the derivation of the term *cop* as it applies to police officers. Cop may refer to the copper buttons worn on early police uniforms, or to early copper police badges. The word may be an acronym for the terms *constabulary on patrol* or *constable on patrol*. Some linguists believe the term comes from the verb *to cop*, which means *to catch*.

Q 322. Why are police uniforms blue?

A Police departments were organized along military lines, with officers, titles, and uniforms. Some historians speculate that the color blue was chosen for police uniforms because that was the color of uniforms worn by Union troops during the Civil War.

Q 323. Does a link exist between civilian police and the military?

A In the decade after the Civil War, the military provided civilian law enforcement in military districts created out of the former Confederacy. Eventually local opposition, fueled by military excesses, led the U.S. Congress to enact the Posse Comitatus Act of 1878. The act prohibits using the military for civilian law enforcement except where expressly authorized by law.

The historic separation between civilian police and the military has eroded in recent years, largely because of the nation's crisis with illegal drugs.

In 1981 Congress passed the Military Cooperation with Law Enforcement Officials Act to encourage the military to supply intelligence, equipment, and training to civilian police to fight the war on drugs. In 1989 President George Bush established regional joint task forces within the Defense Department to coordinate the activities of the military and police forces in the drug war. In 1994 the Defense Department and Justice Department signed a Memorandum of Understanding encouraging the military to transfer wartime technology, such as grenade launchers and armored personnel carriers, to local police departments.

Perhaps the clearest example of the militarization of police departments is the formation of Special Weapons and Tactics (SWAT) teams by virtually every large police department. SWAT teams often have a rigid military structure, with a commander, tactical team leader, scout, sniper, and so forth. Members wear military gear, including combat boots and helmets, and use military equipment and weapons.

The term *posse comitatus* (force of the county) comes from the ancient English practice of the shire (or sheriff) assembling a force of able-bodied private citizens to help maintain public order. In the American West, local sheriffs often called on townspeople to form a *posse* to pursue a fleeing fugitive or to help quell a disturbance.

Q 324. How confident in police are Americans generally?

A Relatively speaking, police are held in high esteem by Americans. A 1998 survey by the Gallup Organization found that 58 percent of Americans expressed either a great deal of confidence or quite a bit of confidence in police. Thirty percent said that they had some confidence in police, 10 percent reported very little confidence, and 1 percent said that they had no confidence in police. Two institutions ranked higher than police in terms of the percentage of Americans expressing a great deal of or quite a bit of confidence: the military, at 64 percent, and the clergy or organized religion, at 59 percent.

Q 325. What private police force helped industrialists battle organized labor?

A The Pinkerton National Detective Agency, the first nationwide investigative agency, became anathema to organized labor after the famous Homestead Strike near Pittsburgh, Pennsylvania, in 1892.

In the 1860s Pennsylvania passed a statute giving powerful private interests, such as the railroads and steel mills, the power to employ their own private police forces. Industrialist Andrew Carnegie hired the Pinkerton agency to break the Homestead Strike against the Carnegie Steel Company. Workers represented by the nation's most powerful trade union, the Amalgamated Association of Iron, Steel, and Tin Workers, had gone on strike and refused to leave the plant after they were locked out and discharged when they refused to accept stepped-up production demands.

Ten thousand strikers met 300 Pinkerton guards as they arrived by barge at Homestead on July 6, 1892. After a full-scale shootout, the Pinkertons surrendered and were forced to run a gauntlet through the crowd. Nine strikers and seven Pinkerton guards were killed, and scores were wounded.

Six days later Pennsylvania Governor William Stone sent 8,000 militia members to reopen the steel mill and protect strikebreakers, thus crippling the union. Sympathy for the striking workers waned after anarchist Alexander Berkman shot Carnegie's plant manager, Henry Clay Frick, on July 23, 1892. Carnegie had succeeded in instituting longer hours and lowering wages for the workers at the plant.

The Pinkerton agency was begun in 1850 by Chicago attorney E. H. Rucker and Allan Pinkerton, a Scottish immigrant who was Chicago's first police detective. The term *private eye* probably stems from the agency's logo, "The Eye That Never Sleeps," and its trademark, an open eye.

Before the Civil War, Pinkerton's agency tracked desperadoes like Jesse James and performed cross-jurisdictional detective work. Pinkerton and his men were active on behalf of the Union during the Civil War, where they gathered intelligence on Southern spies and slipped behind Confederate lines to gather information. After the war the agency provided agents to "ride shotgun" on stagecoaches in the West and worked for companies involved in labor disputes.

During the last years of his life, Allan Pinkerton wrote sixteen detective novels based on his exploits as a detective.

Q **326. What was the Code of the West?**

A In the absence of any formal law and order, an unofficial code of conduct arose on America's western frontier in the mid- to late-1800s. This code held that it was a man's responsibility to protect his family and honor. If a man did not offer to fight when threatened or wronged, he was considered cowardly. The Code of the West led to much senseless violence, particularly in cattle and mining towns where young men congregated and had little to do but drink.

Between 1877 and 1883, forty-five shootings occurred in Borlic, California, a small town in the heart of the mining region that became known as "shooter's town." Twenty-nine men died, though only one man was convicted of murder.

The West's most prolific gunman reputedly was John Wesley Hardin, who killed more than twenty men in gun duels and ambushes in Texas between 1868 and 1877. Hardin reportedly fired a shot through the wall of his hotel room to silence a snoring neighbor. Hardin was fatally shot in the back of the head while standing at the bar of the Acme Saloon on August 19, 1895. The shooter, John Selman Sr., an El Paso policeman who was feuding with Hardin, subsequently was acquitted of murder.

Perhaps the West's most famous lawman was Wyatt Earp, a gambler and gunslinger who served as a local assistant marshal of Dodge City, Kansas, from 1878 to 1879. Earp, two of his brothers, and gunman Doc Holliday resolved a celebrated feud with the Ike Clanton gang in a gunfight at the O.K. Corral in Tombstone, Arizona, on October 26, 1881. Three members of the Clanton gang were killed in the gunfight.

Q **327. Did any U.S. presidents previously work as law enforcement officers?**

A In 1884–1885 a young rancher, Theodore Roosevelt, helped organize an association of stockmen to represent law and order and to apprehend cattle thieves in the prairies of the Dakota Bad Lands.

Later, Roosevelt would lead the New York City police department as president of the city's police commission from 1895 to 1897. During his tenure Roosevelt, a

Republican, attempted to depoliticize the department and instituted many progressive policies that affected not only New York but also the nation. At the time, the department was marked by widespread corruption and dominated by political spoils. Roosevelt introduced merit-based hiring and management and the general concept of police professionalization. He vowed that he would pay no heed to the political or religious affiliations of anyone seeking appointments, adding, "I shall act solely with a view to the well-being of the city and of the interests of the service, and shall take account only of the efficiency, honesty, and records of the men." Roosevelt also is credited with establishing one of the first police academies in the country. Roosevelt required his officers to make semiannual trips to the revolver range, where they were instructed to "dry fire" their revolvers as practice and then to fire ten shots at bull's-eye targets.

The Federal Bureau of Identification, the predecessor to the Federal Bureau of Investigation, was founded in 1908 during Roosevelt's U.S. presidential administration.

Q 328. Who was the first female police officer?

A The first female police officer is thought to have been Alice Stebbins Wells, who was hired by the Los Angeles Police Department on September 13, 1910. Wells had circulated a petition urging the admission of women to the police force that was signed by 100 noted Los Angeles residents and several civic organizations, including the Women's Christian Temperance Union. Wells was given a badge—but no uniform or baton—and was assigned to patrol places of public amusement, including the parks on Sunday. Announcing her appointment, a *Los Angeles Times* article stated, "The first woman policeman, if such an anomaly is possible, in Los Angeles, will be Mrs. Alice Stebbins Wells." A former student of religion, Wells believed the police department was "the strategic point at which virtue can meet vice, strength can meet weakness, and guide them into preventive and redemptive channels."

By 1925 some 145 U.S. police departments had hired female police officers. They typically performed clerical duties, worked with juveniles and women prisoners, and handled missing persons cases.

A few women, known as *matrons,* were hired by police departments beginning in the 1870s to oversee lost children, women's lodging rooms, and women prisoners. These positions sometimes were funded by social welfare organizations rather than by the city, suggesting the matrons' status as social workers rather than law enforcement officers.

Women's clubs and the Women's Christian Temperance Union lobbied to hire women in police departments. The first matron was reportedly hired in 1878 in

Portland, Maine, after a woman physician happened into a courtroom and became disturbed by the treatment of women prisoners. By 1890 matrons were employed by police departments in thirty-six cities.

Q 329. What was the earliest record-keeping system used by American police?

A Until the advent of the computer, most American police departments relied on the police blotter. The blotter was a chronological listing of daily events in a department or a subdivision of a department. Traditionally, the blotter listed the name, age, and sex of each person arrested, along with a listing of the charges in each case.

Around the time of the Civil War, detective Allan Pinkerton (founder of the famed Pinkerton National Detective Agency) devised one of the first criminal history record-keeping systems to track individual career criminals. Pinkerton also called for the establishment of a national record-keeping system.

The International Association of Chiefs of Police developed the first national criminal identification system in 1896 in Chicago, Illinois. In 1924 Congress directed the Federal Bureau of Investigation (FBI) to launch an identification division to acquire and use fingerprint information for criminal identification and other purposes.

Frenchman Alfonse Bertillon is credited with developing the first systematic criminal identification system in the mid nineteenth century. Bertillon's system required police to take exact measurements of a criminal's physical features, including any abnormalities, and record them in a register alongside the criminal's photograph and name.

Q 330. How did the District of Columbia Metropolitan Police blotter record the assassination of President Abraham Lincoln?

A The following entry was made in the District of Columbia Metropolitan Police blotter at 11:00 P.M. on April 14, 1865: "At this hour the melancholy intelligence of the assassination of Mr. Lincoln, President of the U.S., at Ford's Theater was brought to this office, and information obtained from the following persons goes to show that the assassin is a man named J. Wilks [sic] Booth." Lincoln was shot as he sat in Ford's Theater watching a comedy. Booth escaped but was tracked by the Union cavalry to Virginia, where—refusing to surrender—he was trapped in a burning barn and shot.

Q **331. What is a rap sheet?**

A A rap sheet is a record of an individual's criminal history. Each state operates a central repository for records that contain the criminal histories of offenders within their respective jurisdictions. These records include an offender's fingerprints and case-processing information contributed by law enforcement agencies, prosecutors, courts, and corrections agencies throughout the state. The information on a rap sheet allows police to make identifications and to link prior arrest and conviction records to persons who use false names. The Federal Bureau of Investigation (FBI) maintains a telecommunications system that enables federal, state, and local criminal justice agencies to conduct nationwide criminal record searches.

Rap sheets are distributed to criminal justice personnel and to some noncriminal justice agencies that are authorized by state law to use the records for such purposes as employment screening and occupational licensing.

Criminal history information contained on a rap sheet includes current and past arrests or other formal criminal charges, and the disposition of these arrests or formal charges. Where court action led to conviction, the record reflects the sentence and, if a jail or prison term was imposed, information about the correctional facility.

Identification information contained on a rap sheet includes a subject's fingerprints, name, address, birth date, Social Security number, sex, race, and physical characteristics, such as hair and eye color, weight, scars, or tattoos. The rap sheet also may include a subject's place of employment, automobile registration, and other relevant information.

Q **332. What is the leading duty-related cause of death for law enforcement officers?**

A Accidents. Seventy-eight law enforcement officers who lost their lives in the line of duty in 1998 died as a result of accidents. In contrast, sixty-one law enforcement officers were feloniously slain in the line of duty in 1998. Of the officers who died in accidents, fifty-two were killed in automobile, motorcycle, or airplane accidents; fourteen were accidentally struck by vehicles; three were accidentally shot; and nine were killed in other types of accidents, such as a fall or drowning. The peak year for accidental officer deaths in the line of duty was 1989, when seventy-nine officers died.

Q **333. What situation causes the most felonious deaths among law enforcement officers?**

A Most of the sixty-one officers who were feloniously killed in the line of duty in 1998 died during arrest situations and while responding to disturbances.

Sixteen officers died while attempting to make an arrest. Of these, seven officers were slain during drug-related situations, three were killed by robbery suspects, and six were killed by assailants suspected of other crimes. Sixteen officers were killed responding to disturbance calls, including nine family quarrels and seven barfights. Of the remaining slain officers, ten were ambushed, nine were killed while enforcing traffic laws, six were slain while investigating suspicious persons or circumstances, and four were slain while handling or transporting prisoners.

Firearms were used in fifty-eight of the sixty-one killings. One officer was struck by a vehicle, one was slain with a hatchet, and one was fatally injured by a bomb.

Of the sixty-one officers, thirty-eight were patrol officers, eighteen were on detective or special-assignment duty, and five were off-duty but acting in an official capacity. Thirty-eight of the officers were employed by city police departments, eight by county police and sheriffs' departments, and four by state agencies. Six deaths were reported by federal agencies, and Puerto Rico reported the remaining five deaths. Fifty-five of the officers were males and six were females. Their average age was thirty-five.

The killings represented fifty-five separate incidents, of which fifty-two have been cleared by arrest or by exceptional means. A total of seventy-five suspects, all but one of whom were male, were identified in the killings.

At least 59,545 officers were the victims of some type of assault in 1998.

Q **334. How has the number of officers who were feloniously killed in the line of duty changed over time?**

A The first American law enforcement officer to be killed in the line of duty was U.S. Marshal Robert Forsyth on January 11, 1794. Forsyth, age forty, was shot through a closed door while attempting to serve court papers to two brothers in connection with a civil suit. The brothers later escaped to Texas and were never recaptured. The National Law Enforcement Officer's Memorial Fund, a Washington, D.C.–based non-profit organization established in 1984 to honor America's law enforcement officers, reports that more than 15,000 law enforcement officers have been killed in the line of duty since Forsyth's death, the first on record. This number includes 828 federal officers, 338 correctional officers, 31 military law enforcement officers, and 139 female officers.

The number of officers feloniously slain in the line of duty has declined notably since the 1970s. A 23 percent decline in such killings took place from 1994 to 1998. Following are statistics from the Federal Bureau of Investigation (FBI) showing the numbers of law enforcement officers feloniously killed in the line of duty each year from 1972 to 1998:

Year	Officers Killed	Year	Officers Killed
1972	117	1986	66
1973	134	1987	74
1974	132	1988	78
1975	129	1989	66
1976	111	1990	66
1977	93	1991	71
1978	93	1992	64
1979	106	1993	70
1980	104	1994	79
1981	91	1995	74
1982	92	1996	61
1983	80	1997	70
1984	72	1998	61
1985	78		

Q 335. Why are fewer law enforcement officers being killed in the line of duty today?

A Officer safety has improved dramatically since 1973, when a record number of 134 law enforcement officers were feloniously killed in the line of duty. Since then the number of police who are feloniously killed in the line of duty each year has been more than halved, despite significant increases in the police population.

In the 1960s concern over police safety prompted many law enforcement agencies to offer improved or additional training in the use of firearms, unarmed self-defense techniques, and use of nonlethal armaments such as batons. Police also began wearing soft body armor beneath outer clothing during routine activities. Departments devised and implemented improved operational procedures or field tactics, such as maximizing the use of cover and waiting for assisting officers to arrive before conducting building or area searches.

As technology developed, more sophisticated, semiautomatic firearms began to replace the police revolver. Modern computer technology allows police to obtain advance information about each call so that they know more about what to expect before reaching the location.

Q **336. How safe are bulletproof vests?**

A According to the National Fraternal Order of Police, the risk of fatality for an officer who is shot is fourteen times higher if that officer is not equipped with soft body armor.

Of the 270 officers who were slain with firearms while wearing body armor from 1989 to 1998, only seventeen died when bullets penetrated the vest. The rest suffered head and neck wounds, wounds below the waist, and wounds to the upper torso. Forty of the ninety-six officers who suffered wounds to the upper torso were killed when bullets entered between the side panels of the vests or the armholes.

A federal study found that 43 percent of police departments required all patrol officers to wear body armor while on duty in 1997.

Q **337. What is suicide by cop?**

A *Suicide by cop* is a term that law enforcement officers use to describe the phenomenon in which suicidal individuals intentionally provoke police to fatally shoot them. Provocations may include engaging in life-threatening and criminal behavior with a lethal weapon or what appears to be a lethal weapon. The police officer involved may experience enormous stress as a result of the killing, causing him or her to leave the department, abuse alcohol or drugs, or get divorced. A study by Los Angeles police determined that suicide by cop accounted for 11 percent of all officer-involved shootings from 1987 to 1997. The suicidal individuals ranged in age from eighteen to fifty-four, and 98 percent were male. Seventy percent of the shootings occurred within thirty minutes of the police arrival at the scene. Thirty-nine percent of the cases involved domestic violence.

Q **338. What is the highest honor that a police officer can receive?**

A Police who perform courageous acts typically are recognized at the state or local level. However, in 1999 both houses of the U.S. Congress gave preliminary approval to a law that would establish a public safety officer medal of valor. This medal would be presented by the president on behalf of Congress to public safety officers who act with extraordinary valor above and beyond the call of duty.

The National Association of Police Organizations, Inc. (NAPO), a coalition of police unions and associations based in Washington, D.C., issues "top cop" awards each year. The NAPO awards recognize valor and honor exceptional service. One of several 1999 award recipients was Poughkeepsie, New York, Detective Karl Mannain, who had responded to a hit-and-run accident in which an unidentified Mexican immigrant was killed. Mannain arrested the driver. He then discovered that the victim had faithfully sent money back to his family in Mexico, and there was not enough money remaining to send his body home for burial. Mannain raised $28,000 in a fundraising drive and accompanied the body back to Mexico, where he presented the money to the family.

Q 339. What is the Public Safety Officers' Benefits Act?

A In 1976 Congress passed the Public Safety Officers' Benefits Act. The act provides financial benefits to the eligible survivors of law enforcement personnel and firefighters who die in the line of duty or who are permanently and totally disabled by a catastrophic personal injury sustained in the line of duty. Adjusted each year for inflation, the one-time benefit was $143,943 in fiscal year 1999.

Q 340. How stressful is police work?

A Police work consistently ranks among the top professions in its association with job-related divorce, substance abuse, and suicide. According to the American Stress Institute, police work is the second most stressful job in America, after that of inner-city high school teacher.

Estimates hold that twice as many police officers commit suicide as are killed in the line of duty each year, and that twice as many officers experience alcohol abuse as commit suicide.

Factors that contribute to these rankings include the reluctance of officers to discuss feelings of depression or rage for fear of putting their career in jeopardy, access to firearms, exposure to and perceived danger from violence, disruptive shift rotations, public scrutiny, negative publicity, lawsuits, and fear of airborne and bloodborne diseases such as AIDS and tuberculosis. Also, the close-knit police culture discourages other officers from reporting colleagues who are experiencing difficulties.

Q 341. How many felons are killed each year by law enforcement officers acting in the line of duty?

A Each year law enforcement authorities kill many more felons than the other way around, but the number is dropping. The Federal Bureau of Investigation reports that law enforcement officers acting in the line of duty killed 365 felons in 1998. These killings—all but three using firearms—were deemed to be justifiable homicides based on a law enforcement investigation. Following are the numbers of justifiable homicides each year from 1994 through 1998:

Year	Justifiable Homicides	Year	Justifiable Homicides
1994	462	1997	366
1995	389	1998	365
1996	358		

One reason for the decline may be advances in nonlethal technologies, such as rubber bullets and stun guns, which allow police to incapacitate a suspect without inflicting mortal damage. Also, until the mid-1980s, state laws allowed police to shoot to stop fleeing suspects in serious crimes. In *Tennessee v. Garner* (1985), the U.S. Supreme Court ruled that police can not kill a fleeing felon unless the officer has probable cause to believe the suspect poses a significant threat of death or serious physical injury to the officer or others.

Private citizens killed an additional 194 felons during the commission of felony crimes in 1998. These, too, were deemed to be justifiable homicides after police investigation.

See 337 What is suicide by cop? 422 When can police use deadly force?

Q 342. How many jurisdictions have 911 service?

A In 1997 about 85 percent of all local police departments employing 97 percent of all officers participated in a 911 emergency telephone system. This percentage represents a significant increase from 1990, when only about half of departments had 911 systems. Most departments used enhanced 911 systems that pinpoint callers' locations.

The 911 system was created after the Presidential Commission on Law Enforcement and Administration of Justice in 1967 called for the establishment of a single telephone number so that police could funnel the most urgent requests for help to a central dispatcher. It also was intended to provide citizens with faster service and encourage them to report serious crimes promptly. Initially, Atlantic Telephone and

Telegraph Company (AT&T)—which then held a monopoly position in the nation's telephone business—resisted the idea. The company finally agreed to launch 911 as a single police and fire emergency telephone number when it became clear that doing so would actually save AT&T money. Until then, many emergency calls were routed through a telephone operator, which meant a costly and personnel-intensive operation for AT&T.

Q 343. What level of government spends the most on police protection?

A Police protection is primarily a local responsibility. Local governments were responsible for 72.7 percent of all police protection expenditures in the country in 1995.

The latest statistics from the U.S. Census Bureau show that local governments spent $35.3 billion on police protection in 1995, compared to $7.5 billion by the federal government and $5.7 billion by state governments.

See 143 How has spending on the justice system changed over time?

FEDERAL

Q 344. How many federal law enforcement officers are there?

A As of June 1998 federal agencies employed about 83,000 full-time personnel authorized to make arrests and carry firearms. Nationwide there were 31 federal officers per 100,000 U.S. residents. State ratios ranged from 50 officers per 100,000 residents in Arizona to 4 officers per 100,000 residents in Iowa. The District of Columbia had 1,384 federal officers per 100,000 residents. Women made up 14.2 percent of all federal officers, and 29.4 percent were members of a racial or ethnic minority.

Q 345. What federal agencies employ the most law enforcement officers?

A Sixty-one percent of all federal law enforcement officers in 1998 were employed by just four federal agencies, as follows:

• Immigration and Naturalization Service (INS), 16,552 officers
• Federal Bureau of Prisons (BOP), 12,587 officers
• Federal Bureau of Investigation (FBI), 11,285 officers
• U.S. Customs Service, 10,539 officers

The INS, BOP, and FBI all are parts of the U.S. Department of Justice, which employs approximately 56 percent of all federal law enforcement officers. The U.S. Customs Service is part of the U.S. Department of the Treasury, which employs about one-quarter of all federal officers with arrest and firearm authority.

Following are numbers of officers employed by other federal agencies that employed at least 500 law enforcement officers as of June 1998:

- U.S. Secret Service, 3,587 officers
- U.S. Postal Service, 3,490 officers
- Internal Revenue Service, 3,361 officers
- Drug Enforcement Administration, 3,305 officers
- U.S. Marshals Service, 2,205 officers
- Bureau of Alcohol, Tobacco, and Firearms, 1,723 officers
- U.S. Capitol Police, 1,055 officers
- General Services Administration's Federal Protective Services, 900 officers
- U.S. Fish and Wildlife Service, 831 officers
- U.S. Forest Service, 601 officers.

Q 346. What federal law enforcement agency refers the most cases to U.S. attorneys for prosecution?

A Federal law enforcement agencies referred a total of 115,670 cases to U.S. attorneys for federal prosecution in 1998. According to a May 2000 report by the U.S. Department of Justice, the agencies that made the most referrals were:

- Federal Bureau of Investigation, 33,388
- Drug Enforcement Administration, 16,610
- Immigration and Naturalization Service, 15,399
- U.S. Customs Service, 8,362
- Bureau of Alcohol, Tobacco, and Firearms, 4,864
- U.S. Secret Service, 4,422
- U.S. Postal Service, 4,191
- Internal Revenue Service, 2,797
- National Park Service, 2,632
- U.S. Marshals Service 1,620
- U.S. Army, 1,288
- U.S. Fish and Wildlife Service, 1,096
- U.S. Air Force, 808
- Bureau of Indian Affairs, 720

Several agencies also contributed to joint task forces with other federal agencies or with state or local law enforcement agencies that resulted in additional referrals. After evaluating these cases, U.S. attorneys agreed to prosecute about 73 percent of the cases and declined to prosecute the rest. Often when the U.S. attorney refuses to prosecute a case the agency will refer the case for prosecution by state and local prosecutors.

Q 347. What is the oldest federal law enforcement agency?

A The U.S. Marshals Service is recognized as the nation's oldest federal law enforcement agency. It was founded in 1789 along with the federal court system to serve as a link between the executive and judicial branches of the government. Then, as now, federal marshals primarily were responsible for providing support and protection to federal courts. However, in 1792 Congress gave marshals the same power as sheriffs to enforce the laws of the United States in the Western territories. A federal marshal was appointed to a four-year term for each territory. Marshals became the chief law enforcement officers on the Western frontier, investigating crimes against the federal government, such as mail or train robberies, and crimes committed on federal lands. As territories became states, local sheriffs and local marshals typically took over policing activities.

See 375 What does the U.S. Marshals Service do?

Q 348. What does the U.S. Department of Justice do?

A Congress created the U.S. Department of Justice (DOJ) on June 22, 1870. The DOJ is led by the U.S. attorney general and employs thousands of lawyers, investigators, and agents who act in the public's interest to enforce federal laws dealing with violent crime, terrorism, white-collar crime, drug smuggling, and many other criminal acts. The DOJ conducts all suits in which the federal government is a party and renders legal advice and opinions, on request, to the president and to the heads of executive-branch departments. The DOJ also supervises federal law enforcement agencies, including the Federal Bureau of Investigation, Drug Enforcement Administration, Immigration and Naturalization Service, the U.S. Marshals Service, and the Federal Bureau of Prisons.

Divisions and departments within the DOJ that handle matters pertaining to the criminal justice system include:

- *The Criminal Division,* which coordinates the enforcement of federal criminal statutes except specialized statutes assigned to other divisions (tax, environmental, antitrust, and civil rights violations). This division oversees criminal matters handled in the field by United States Attorney Offices across the country. It processes requests for immunity clearances for federal witnesses in criminal investigations; oversees the use of electronic surveillance by federal agencies; coordinates federal, state, and local law enforcement activities against organized crime; supervises international extradition proceedings; and provides legal advice and assistance to federal prosecutors and investigative agencies. The largest of the division's numerous sections, the Fraud Section, battles fraud and white-collar crime. This section focuses primarily on complex frauds involving multidistrict and international activities; financial institutions; government programs and procurement procedures; and multi-district schemes that involve consumer victimization schemes, such as telemarketing fraud. Other sections address public integrity, narcotics and dangerous drugs, organized crime and racketeering, computer crime and intellectual property, asset forfeiture and money laundering, child exploitation and obscenity, terrorism and violent crime, special investigations, enforcement operations, internal security, international criminal investigative training, international affairs, and enforcement operations and appeals.

- *The Antitrust Division,* which enforces federal antitrust laws aimed at maintaining competitive markets. Antitrust laws prohibit practices that restrain trade, such as price-fixing conspiracies, corporate mergers likely to reduce the competitive vigor of particular markets, and predatory acts designed to achieve or maintain monopoly power.

- *The Tax Division,* which represents the United States and its officers in criminal litigation arising under the internal revenue laws (other than proceedings in the United States Tax Court). The Division's primary client is the Internal Revenue Service, but it also represents federal officials in actions arising out of the performance of their official duties, as well as other federal departments and agencies in their dealings with state and local tax authorities.

- *The Environment and Natural Resources Division,* which enforces the nation's criminal and civil environmental laws.

- *The Office of the Pardon Attorney,* which assists the president in the exercise of his or her pardon power under Article II, Section 2, of the U.S. Constitution. Generally, all requests for pardon or other forms of executive clemency, including commutation of sentence, are directed to the Pardon Attorney for investigation and review.

- *The Office of Consumer Litigation* (part of the Civil Division), which handles criminal litigation arising under various federal consumer protection and public health statutes.

- *The Criminal Section of the Civil Rights Division,* which prosecutes hate crimes, police misconduct, involuntary servitude matters (including worker exploitation), church arson, and discrimination and violence directed against health care providers.
- *The Special Litigation Section* (part of the Civil Rights Division), which protects the constitutional and statutory rights of persons confined in certain institutions owned or operated by state or local governments, including prisons, jails, and juvenile detention facilities where a pattern or practice of violations exist.

See Figure 4-1 U.S. Department of Justice Organizational Chart.

Q 349. Who is the top law enforcement officer in the United States?

A The U.S. attorney general (AG) is the chief law enforcement officer of the federal government. The AG serves as the head of the U.S. Department of Justice, which enforces more than 900 federal laws and provides support to the ninety-four U.S. Attorneys and U.S. Marshals offices in the various judicial districts around the country. As a member of the president's cabinet, the AG gives advice and opinions to the president and to the heads of the executive departments of the government when so requested. The AG also appears in person to represent the government before the U.S. Supreme Court in cases of exceptional gravity.

The U.S. Congress created the office of the attorney general on September 24, 1789. The AG was a member of the President's Cabinet but not a department head until Congress established the Department of Justice in 1870.

Janet Reno became the first woman and the nation's seventy-eighth attorney general after she was nominated by President Bill Clinton and sworn in on March 12, 1993.

See Table 4-1 U.S. Attorney Generals, 1789–2000.

Q 350. What is the U.S. Customs Service?

A The U.S. Customs Service is an arm of the U.S. Department of the Treasury that is responsible for ensuring that all imports and exports comply with U.S. laws and regulations. Customs agents process the 450 million travelers who cross America's borders annually, as well as their baggage, mail, and an estimated $2.5 trillion in merchandise.

Customs is responsible for seizing any contraband that is being illegally imported or exported. In 1999 the Customs Service inspected about 3 percent of the goods

Figure 4-1 U.S. Department of Justice Organizational Chart

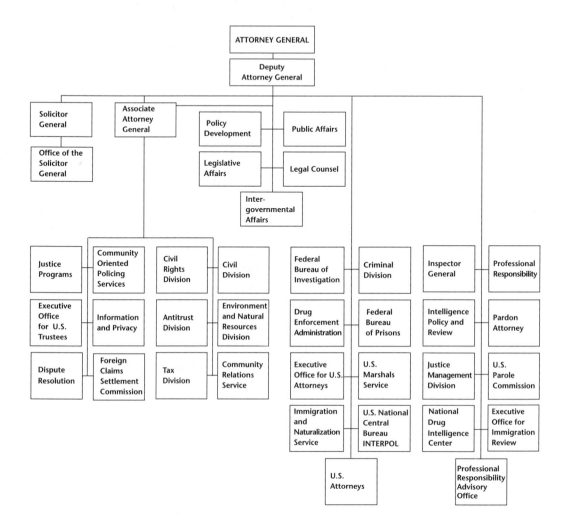

Source: U.S. Department of Justice, http://www.usdoj.gov/dojorg.htm

entering the United States. The service seized 1.3 million pounds of narcotics in fiscal year 1999—more than any other law enforcement agency—and $360 million in cash and other monetary instruments. Drugs seized included 1,900 pounds of heroin, 160,400 pounds of cocaine, and more than 1 million pounds of marijuana.

Table 4-1 U.S. Attorney Generals, 1789–2000

Attorney General	Years Served	Attorney General	Years Served
Edmund Randolph	1789–1794	Richard Olney	1893–1895
William Bradford	1794–1795	Judson Harmon	1895–1897
Charles Lee	1795–1801	Joseph McKenna	1897–1898
Levi Lincoln	1801–1805	John W. Griggs	1898–1901
John Breckinridge	1805–1807	Philander C. Knox	1901–1904
Caesar Rodney	1807–1811	William H. Moody	1904–1906
William Pinkney	1811–1814	Charles J. Bonaparte	1906–1909
Richard Rush	1814–1817	G. W. Wickersham	1909–1913
William Wirt	1817–1829	J. C. McReynolds	1913–1914
John M. Berrien	1829–1831	T. W. Gregory	1914–1919
Roger B. Taney	1831–1833	A. Mitchell Palmer	1919–1921
Benjamin Butler	1833–1838	H. M. Daugherty	1921–1924
Felix Grundy	1838–1840	Harlan F. Stone	1924–1925
Henry D. Gilpin	1840–1841	John G. Sargent	1925–1929
John J. Crittenden	1841	J. D. Mitchell	1929–1933
Hugh S. Legaré	1841–1843	H. S. Cummings	1933–1939
John Nelson	1843–1845	Frank Murphy	1939–1940
John Y. Mason	1845–1846	Robert Jackson	1940–1941
Nathan Clifford	1846–1848	Francis Biddel	1941–1945
Isaac Toucey	1848–1849	Tom C. Clark	1945–1949
Reverdy Johnson	1849–1850	J. H. McGrath	1949–1952
John J. Crittenden	1850–1853	James P. McGranery	1952–1953
Caleb Cushing	1853–1857	H. Brownell Jr.	1953–1957
Jeremiah S. Black	1857–1860	William P. Rogers	1957–1961
Edwin M. Stanton	1860–1861	Robert F. Kennedy	1961–1965
Edward Bates	1861–1864	N. deB. Katzenbach	1965–1967
James Speed	1864–1865	Ramsey Clark	1967–1969
Henry Stanbery	1865–1866	John M. Mitchell	1969–1972
O. H. Browning	1866–1869	Richard G. Kleindienst	1972–1973
Ebenezer R. Hoar	1869–1870	Elliot L. Richardson	1973
Amos T. Akerman	1870–1871	William B. Saxbe	1974–1975
G. H. Williams	1871–1875	Edward H. Levi	1975–1977
Edwards Pierrepont	1875–1876	Griffin Bell	1977–1979
Alphonso Taft	1876–1877	Benjamin R. Civiletti	1979–1981
Charles Devens	1877–1881	William French Smith	1981–1985
Wayne MacVeagh	1881	Edwin Meese	1985–1988
B. H. Brewster	1881–1885	Richard Thornburgh	1988–1989
A. H. Garland	1885–1889	William Barr	1990–1992
W. H. H. Miller	1889–1893	Janet Reno	1993–

Customs also assesses and collects duties, excise taxes, fees, and penalties on imported merchandise; enforces American laws that are intended to prevent illegal trade practices; and works to prevent the export of critical technology used to develop weapons of mass destruction. In addition to enforcing customs laws, the service enforces approximately 400 laws for forty federal agencies involved in international commerce, including laws that pertain to the environment, motor vehicle safety, pesticides, water pollution standards, and endangered wildlife.

The priorities set by the Customs Service's law enforcement unit include narcotics trafficking, money laundering, trade fraud, cybersmuggling, and investigating international criminal activity such as child pornography and child sexual exploitation that is conducted on or facilitated by the Internet.

The Customs Service traces its history to just a few months after the Constitution of the United States went into effect. Facing bankruptcy, the first Congress passed and President George Washington signed the Tariff Act of July 4, 1789, which authorized the collection of duties on imported goods. The act was dubbed "the second Declaration of Independence" by the news media. A month later, Congress established the Customs Service and its ports of entry to collect duties on imported goods. Initially, ten armed revenue cutters patrolled the shores for tariff evaders. Today, the service has a fleet of 96 high-speed boats and 115 aircraft.

For nearly 125 years, Customs funded virtually the entire government and paid for the nation's early growth and infrastructure. Today Customs continues to provide the nation with its second largest source of revenue—after the Internal Revenue Service—returning $22.1 billion to the U.S. Treasury in 1999.

See Table 4-2 U.S. Customs Service Ports of Call.

Q 351. What are *mules*?

A Drug traffickers use the term *mules* to refer to body carriers, or people who attempt to smuggle illegal narcotics into the United States by ingesting rubber pellets containing drugs. The Customs Service in 1998 seized half a ton of narcotics smuggled into the United States in this manner. Pellets are made from the fingers of rubber gloves. They are filled with about 18 grams of drugs. After ingesting a medical relaxant, a smuggler typically swallows about sixty of these pellets, which amounts to roughly 1 kilogram or 2.2 pounds of illegal drugs. When filled with heroin, each pellet is worth about $1,800 on the streets of New York City. A kilogram is worth approximately a quarter of a million dollars. The Customs Service estimates that six persons died from pellet leakage during a six-month period in 1998.

Table 4-2 U.S. Customs Service Ports of Call

State	Ports	State	Ports
Alabama	Mobile	Montana	Great Falls
Alaska	Anchorage	New Jersey	NY / Newark Area
Arizona	Nogales Tucson	New York	Buffalo Champlain New York New York / JFK Area
California	Calexico Otay Mesa San Francisco Los Angeles / Airport Area Los Angeles / Long Beach Seaport Area	North Carolina	Charlotte
		North Dakota	Pembina
		Ohio	Cleveland
Colorado	Denver	Oregon	Portland
District of Columbia	Washington	Pennsylvania	Philadelphia
Florida	Miami Airport Miami Seaport Tampa	Puerto Rico	San Juan
		Rhode Island	Providence
		South Carolina	Charleston
Georgia	Atlanta Savannah	Texas	Dallas / Ft. Worth El Paso Houston / Galveston Laredo / Colombia
Hawaii	Honolulu		
Illinois	Chicago		
Kentucky	Louisville	Vermont	St. Albans
Louisiana	New Orleans	Virgin Islands	Charlotte Amalie Christiansted
Maine	Portland		
Maryland	Baltimore	Virginia	Norfolk
Massachusetts	Boston	Washington	Blaine Seattle Tacoma
Michigan	Detroit		
Minnesota	Duluth Minneapolis	Wisconsin	Milwaukee
Missouri	Kansas City St. Louis		

Source: U.S. Customs Service, http://www.customs.ustreas.gov/location/service1.htm

Faced with criticism that the U.S. Customs Service has engaged in racial profiling and conducted invasive body searches based on an individual's racial profile, the Customs Service has installed noninstrusive body-scan machines, similar to x-ray machines, at its busiest ports of entry. Among other things, these machines disclose whether an individual is a mule who is carrying rubber pellets filled with narcotics.

Q 352. What is the Federal Bureau of Investigation?

A Dating to 1908, the Federal Bureau of Investigation (FBI) is the principal investigative arm of the U.S. Department of Justice. The FBI is charged with investigating all violations of federal law except those assigned by the U.S. Congress to another federal agency. The FBI also is charged with protecting the United States from foreign intelligence and terrorist activities and with providing leadership in the law enforcement field to state, local, and international agencies. The FBI is the closest thing that the United States has to a national police force.

The FBI has jurisdiction over 260 categories of federal crimes. In 1982 the U.S. attorney general assigned concurrent jurisdiction for the enforcement of federal drug laws to the FBI and the Drug Enforcement Administration (DEA). The FBI director is empowered to resolve conflicts involving overlapping jurisdiction between the two agencies.

The FBI's official priorities are organized crime and drugs, counterterrorism, white-collar crime, foreign counterintelligence, and violent crime. A study by Transactional Records Access Clearinghouse (TRAC), a private research group affiliated with Syracuse University, found that 51 percent of all convictions obtained by the FBI in 1997 pertained to drug crimes, fraud against banks, and bank robbery.

The FBI offers cooperative services to other law enforcement agencies, such as fingerprint identification, laboratory examination services, and police training. The FBI also conducts background security checks on nominees to sensitive government positions and, at the request of the president, investigates activities jeopardizing the security of the nation.

Nine divisions operate from the FBI's headquarters in Washington, D.C. In addition to staff serving the director and deputy director, divisions include an Office of the General Counsel, an Office of Public and Congressional Affairs, an Office of Equal Employment Opportunity Affairs, and an Office of Professional Responsibility. The Bureau conducts investigations through fifty-six field offices. Most of its investigative personnel are trained at the FBI Academy in Quantico, Virginia.

Q **353. Has the Federal Bureau of Investigation always been called by that name?**

A No. The Federal Bureau of Investigation (FBI) traces its roots to the Federal Bureau of Identification, which was formed on July 26, 1908, to serve as the investigative arm of the U.S. Department of Justice. U.S. Attorney General Charles J. Bonaparte, a descendant of the former Emperor of France, appointed nine former U.S. Secret Service employees to the bureau. The bureau was authorized to pursue crimes on the high seas, violations of neutrality laws, crimes on Indian reservations, narcotics trafficking, violations of antipeonage (slave labor) laws, and violations of antitrust laws. Congress gradually increased its jurisdiction to include hundreds of crimes. The agency was renamed the Federal Bureau of Investigation on July 1, 1935.

The Federal Bureau of Identification was founded over the objection of many members of Congress, who were wary of increasing President Theodore Roosevelt's investigatory powers. In fact, on Roosevelt's orders, Bonaparte bypassed Congress and created the bureau by executive order after Congress adjourned.

Q **354. Who was the first civil servant to lie in state in the Capitol Rotunda?**

A J. Edgar Hoover, the controversial director of the FBI, was the first civil servant to lie in state in the Capitol Rotunda when he died in 1972.

Hoover was a twenty-nine-year-old former assistant attorney general when he was tapped in 1924 to lead the U.S. Justice Department's Bureau of Investigation, a tiny government agency with 650 employees that was mired in scandal, political cronyism, and corruption. Hoover transformed the agency's image by banning the use of foul language, insisting that agents be clean and wear white shirts, and stressing training and professionalism. On July 30, 1933, Hoover was named director of a new unit that combined the Bureau of Investigation with the Justice Department's Prohibition Bureau and Bureau of Identification. This combined unit was renamed Federal Bureau of Investigation in 1935.

Above all, Hoover was a savvy promoter, both in Congress and in the media. He focused agency resources on high-profile, easy-to-solve crimes, such as bank robberies and kidnappings. Then Hoover made sure the agency got the credit. Hoover crafted an image of FBI agents as incorruptible *G-men* through books, magazine articles, television shows, and movies. He tagged kidnapper Alvin Karpis as Public Enemy Number 1.

In the 1930s Secretary of State Cordell Hull authorized Hoover to investigate fascists and Communists within the United States, opening a door that would eventually lead the FBI astray.

In 1956 Hoover launched a massive secret counterintelligence program to monitor the political activities of Communists. The theft of internal documents from an FBI office in Media, Pennsylvania, in 1971 and Congressional investigations in the mid-1970s showed the FBI had invested a growing part of its budget and staff for political, rather than enforcement, purposes. Hoover's FBI had investigated not only Communists but also President John F. Kennedy and Marilyn Monroe, black political activists such as Martin Luther King Jr., student protestors against the Vietnam War, and even some early leaders in the women's liberation movement. These revelations led President Gerald Ford to issue guidelines governing when the FBI can infiltrate or conduct surveillance on domestic groups.

Congress made sure that no other law enforcement officer would wield the same depth of power as Hoover, who remained in office until his death. In 1968 Congress enacted legislation requiring Senate confirmation of future FBI directors and limiting their tenure to ten years.

After his death, controversial details about Hoover's personal life began to circulate, including allegations of racism and sexism. In fact, the FBI didn't recruit its first African Americans and women agents until after Hoover's death.

Despite the criticisms, in forty-eight years as director of the FBI J. Edgar Hoover transformed the bureau from a small backwater of the U.S. Justice Department into what many consider to be the foremost law enforcement agency in the world. He introduced the FBI Uniform Crime Reporting Program, the leading source of national crime statistics, and developed the FBI Academy at Quantico, Virginia.

Q 355. What is the race and gender breakdown of the FBI's special agent force?

A The Federal Bureau of Investigation reported in 1999 that 83.8 percent of its special agents are men, 16.2 percent are women, and slightly more than 13 percent are minorities, including Hispanics (6.1 percent), Blacks (4.6 percent), Asians (2.2 percent), and American Indians (0.4 percent).

Q 356. How many agents does the FBI employ?

A The Federal Bureau of Investigation (FBI) employed about 11,400 special agents in 1999. In comparison, the FBI employed 6,451 agents at the height of the Cold War.

The FBI also employs more than 16,400 professional, administrative, technical, clerical, craft, trade, and maintenance employees.

About 9,800 employees are assigned to FBI Headquarters in Washington, D.C., while nearly 18,000 employees are assigned to offices around the country. The FBI maintains 56 major field offices, 400 satellite offices (known as resident agencies), 4 information technology centers, and 37 foreign liaison posts.

The FBI maintains a fingerprint facility near Clarksburg, West Virginia, and an academy in Quantico, Virginia, where the FBI trains both its own agents and law enforcement officers from around the country and abroad.

Q 357. How did the Ten Most Wanted Fugitives Program begin?

A In 1949 a reporter from United Press International asked the Federal Bureau of Investigation to name the ten "toughest guys" who were federal fugitives. The resulting feature story in the *Washington Daily News* garnered national attention and prompted FBI Director J. Edgar Hoover to inaugurate the FBI's Ten Most Wanted Fugitives Program on March 14, 1950.

The first fugitive on the list was Thomas Holden, a Chicago man who had murdered his wife and her two brothers after a drinking party. Holden was arrested in 1951 after a citizen recognized his photograph in an Oregon newspaper.

On the fiftieth anniversary of the list, the FBI proudly proclaimed that 429 of the 458 fugitives whose names had appeared on the list had been apprehended or located, and that 137 of the 429 fugitives were located as a direct result of citizen tips. The FBI currently offers a $50,000 reward for information leading directly to the arrest of a top-ten fugitive.

Over time, the list has chronicled the shifting face of crime in American society. In the 1950s bank robbers, burglars, and car thieves were prominent on the list. In the 1960s the list began to include radical criminals charged with crimes like destruction of government property, sabotage, and kidnapping. In the 1970s the list featured fugitives charged with organized crime and terrorism. Today international terrorists, serial murderers, major international drug dealers, and organized crime figures make up the list.

To get on the list, a criminal must be nominated by one of the FBI's fifty-six field offices. The nominees received are reviewed by special agents in the FBI's Criminal Investigation Division (CID) and the Office of Public and Congressional Affairs. A proposed candidate is selected from among the nominees and the name is forwarded to the assistant director of the CID for approval and then to the FBI's deputy director for final approval. Names are removed from the list when fugitives are captured or when federal prosecutors drop the charges against them. In four cases the FBI has removed a fugitive whom the agency no longer considered to be a "particularly dangerous menace to society."

Q **358. Who was the first woman on the FBI's Ten Most Wanted list?**

A In 1968 Ruth Eisemann-Schier became the first woman on the Federal Bureau of Investigation's Ten Most Wanted list. Eisemann-Schier and Gary Steven Krist had kidnapped Barbara Jane Mackle, a college student and the daughter of a wealthy Florida developer. Mackle was buried alive in a pasture for three and a half days, imprisoned in a coffin equipped with an air pump, water, food, a fan, and a battery-powered lamp. Ms. Mackle was freed after her parents doled out $500,000 in ransom money to the kidnappers. Krist was sentenced to life in prison and was released in 1979. Eisemann-Schier, who was apprehended by the FBI on March 5, 1969, served four years in prison before being returned to her native Honduras. She was banned from returning to the United States.

Q **359. What would-be FBI informant wore blue suede shoes?**

A During a tour of the bureau's headquarters in Washington, D.C., in December 1970, entertainer Elvis Presley volunteered to be a confidential informant for the Federal Bureau of Investigation. Presley offered to provide information to the bureau on a confidential basis regarding individuals and groups in and out of the entertainment industry who Presley felt were not acting in the best interests of the country. He was particularly critical of the Beatles and actress Jane Fonda.

Presley had asked to meet in person with Hoover, whom he called the "greatest living American." Just a few days earlier the entertainer had met with President Richard Nixon in the Oval Office. Nixon had awarded Presley an honorary agent's badge from the Bureau of Narcotics and Dangerous Drugs.

Hoover claimed that he would be out of town during Presley's visit but in fact he simply didn't want to meet with Presley. According to an FBI memorandum at the time: "Presley's sincerity and good intentions notwithstanding, he is certainly not the type of person whom the Director would wish to meet . . . it should be noted that at the present time [Presley] is wearing his hair down to his shoulders and indulges in the wearing of all sorts of exotic dress."

In a follow-up letter to Presley about a month later, Hoover wrote: "Your generous comments concerning this Bureau and me are appreciated, and you may be sure that we will keep in mind your offer to be of assistance."

Q 360. What is the mission of the Bureau of Alcohol, Tobacco, and Firearms?

A The Bureau of Alcohol, Tobacco, and Firearms (ATF), a division of the U.S. Department of the Treasury, enforces federal laws relating to alcohol, tobacco, firearms, explosives, and arson, and collects an estimated $12 billion annually in tax revenue. The ATF traces its history to 1862, when Congress formed the Office of Internal Revenue within the Treasury Department to collect taxes on distilled spirits and tobacco products. Two years later, Congress authorized Internal Revenue to hire "three detectives to aid in the prevention, detection, and punishment of tax evaders." The ATF's most daunting battle was during the era of Prohibition (1919–1933), when department *revenuers* were charged with investigating criminal violations of the Internal Revenue law, including illicit manufacture of liquors. In 1972 the ATF separated from the Internal Revenue Service and became an independent bureau.

In 1996 the ATF spearheaded a federal investigation into a rash of church arsons and bombings. The National Church Arson Task Force opened investigations into 670 arsons, bombings, or attempted bombings that occurred at houses of worship and achieved a 34 percent arrest rate, which was more than double the 16 percent rate nationwide. The group concluded that no orchestrated national conspiracy existed.

Congress in 1996 authorized the ATF to establish the first national repository of information on incidents involving arson and suspected criminal use of explosives. Still under development, the system helps investigators identify case-specific similarities regarding explosive devices, types of fuels or explosives used, and methods of operation. The ATF also operates the National Tracing Center, which traces firearms to their owners and assists state and local law enforcement agencies in solving violent crimes. Approximately 210,000 traces were completed in 1999.

The ATF referred a little more than 5,000 cases to the U.S. Attorney's Office for prosecution in 1999. In recent years, more than half of the ATF's criminal enforcement activities have involved firearms, machine guns, and explosives.

Q 361. Who were the Untouchables?

A The Untouchables were a nine-man team of federal agents that battled gangster Al "Scarface" Capone during the Prohibition era. Eliot Ness was a twenty-six-year-old University of Chicago graduate when he was hired in 1929 as a special agent of the U.S. Department of Justice to head the Prohibition Bureau of the U.S. Department of the Treasury in Chicago. After reviewing the files of hundreds of law enforcement officers, Ness carefully selected nine officers with flawless records and expertise in marksmanship, wiretapping, and other crime-fighting techniques. In an era of rampant police corruption, Ness dubbed his group the "untouchables" because they could not be swayed by bribes. Capone finally was brought down, not by Ness and the Untouchables but by the Internal Revenue Service. Capone was tried and convicted on tax evasion charges in 1931 and sentenced to eleven years in prison and $50,000 in fines.

See 106 What is organized crime? 374 Who said, "Income tax law is a lot of bunk"?

🅀 362. How many bombing incidents are linked to the Internet?

🅰 From 1985 to 1995, the Bureau of Alcohol, Tobacco, and Firearms (ATF) reports, bomb-making instructions obtained from computer bulletin boards were implicated in thirty-five known bombing incidents. In 1996 the number of such incidents jumped to twenty, a 600 percent increase in the annual average. In 1999 ATF researchers ran a query of various Internet search engines using the phrase *pipe bomb*. The query produced nearly 3 million "hits" of Web sites containing information on pipe bombs. The top ten matches included articles that described in great detail how to construct pipe bombs using readily available materials.

🅀 363. What ATF arrest helped spark the modern militia movement?

🅰 On February 28, 1993, the Bureau of Alcohol, Tobacco, and Firearms (ATF) secured a warrant to arrest David Koresh, the leader of an apocalyptic cult called the Branch-Davidians in Waco, Texas. Koresh and his followers allegedly had amassed a small arsenal and were selling guns in violation of federal law. Rather than arresting Koresh when he left the cult's compound, ATF agents mounted a show of force that included the use of a military helicopter gunship. Cult members returned fire when agents stormed the compound. Four ATF agents and six Branch-Davidians were killed. Thus began a fifty-one-day siege of the compound.

The Federal Bureau of Investigation (FBI) took over the case, eventually bringing 600 personnel to the scene, and initiated psychological warfare tactics while attempting to negotiate a surrender. The siege ended when Attorney General Janet Reno authorized agents to storm the compound with tanks and tear gas on April 19, 1993. The wooden buildings went up in flames and Koresh and seventy-six men, women, and children were consumed in the inferno.

The Waco fiasco fueled growing concern in the right-wing militia movement that the federal government was conspiring to deprive Americans of civil liberties, including the right to bear arms. Exactly two years later, on April 19, 1995, a massive truck bomb exploded just outside the Alfred P. Murrah Federal Building in Oklahoma City, Oklahoma. The building collapsed, killing 169 people, including 19 children at a daycare center in the building. The FBI captured two men with ties to the militia movement who had been outraged by the way the ATF and the FBI had dealt with the Branch-Davidians. Timothy McVeigh was convicted of murder and conspiracy and sentenced to death for the bombing. Terry Nichols was convicted of conspiracy and involuntary manslaughter and sentenced to life imprisonment without the chance of parole.

Q 364. What is the Drug Enforcement Administration?

A The Drug Enforcement Administration (DEA), a division of the U.S. Department of Justice, enforces U.S. laws and regulations pertaining to narcotics and controlled substances. Created through the merger of four separate drug enforcement agencies in 1973, the DEA enforces chemical diversion and trafficking laws pertaining to federally controlled substances.

The DEA works with other federal and state agencies to dismantle drug syndicates, gangs, and drug traffickers, and coordinates enforcement and intelligence-gathering activities with foreign government agencies. The agency promotes domestic and international programs that are aimed at reducing the availability of and demand for controlled substances. The DEA also investigates the cultivation, production, smuggling, distribution, or diversion of controlled substances appearing in or destined for illegal traffic in the United States. The agency attempts to immobilize drug cartels by arresting their members, confiscating their drugs, and seizing their assets.

The DEA chairs the eleven-agency National Narcotics Intelligence Consumers Committee, which develops an annual report on drug production, trafficking, and abuse trends. The agency also manages the El Paso Intelligence Center (EPIC), a twenty-four-hour tactical drug intelligence center that also uses federal personnel from thirteen other agencies. The DEA maintains a training program for narcotics officers in other federal, state, and local agencies as well as foreign police. The agency maintains liaisons with the United Nations, INTERPOL, and other organizations on matters relating to international narcotics control programs. The DEA has twenty-one domestic field divisions and offices in fifty foreign countries.

Attorney General Janet Reno estimated in 1999 that 6.5 percent of Americans use illegal drugs, compared to 17.5 percent in 1979.

365. What is the U.S. Immigration and Naturalization Service?

A The U.S. Immigration and Naturalization Service (INS), a division of the U.S. Department of Justice, serves as the primary agency charged with enforcing U.S. immigration law. The INS both facilitates legal immigration to the United States and stems illegal immigration by policing the nation's borders. It provides assistance to persons seeking asylum, temporary or permanent resident status, or naturalization and enforces sanctions against persons who act or conspire to subvert the requirements for selective and controlled entry, including employers who knowingly hire illegal aliens.

In fiscal year 1999 the INS effected the removal of more than 178,000 illegal aliens and naturalized more than 1.2 million new American citizens. INS officials estimate that more than 5 million undocumented aliens reside in the United States, reflecting a yearly increase of more than 250,000 aliens. In recent years the INS has emphasized controlling illegal immigration along the Southwest border and removing aliens who entered the United States illegally or who have committed crimes. The INS apprehended 1,537,000 aliens along the Southwest border, of whom nearly 1,497,000 voluntarily agreed to be immediately repatriated to their home countries. Since 1993 the INS has added more than 5,400 new U.S. Border Patrol agents, and the agency plans to add 430 more in 2001.

In 1999 the INS set the following priorities:

- Identify and remove criminal aliens
- Diminish alien smuggling
- Build partnerships with communities
- Minimize benefit fraud
- Block employers' access to undocumented workers

The INS maintains three regional offices, thirty-three district offices, and twenty-one border patrol sectors throughout the United States. The agency also maintains district offices in Bangkok, Thailand; Mexico City, Mexico; and Rome, Italy.

Q **366. How many criminal aliens are deported each year?**

A The Immigration and Naturalization Service (INS) deported nearly 63,000 criminal aliens in fiscal year 1999, more than double the number removed in 1994. The majority of those deported had been convicted on some type of drug charge. Most of the more than 178,000 deportations of illegal aliens in 1999 were noncriminal removals of aliens who were caught living in or trying to enter the country illegally.

Q 367. What is the U.S. Secret Service?

A   The U.S. Secret Service, a division of the U.S. Department of the Treasury, is charged with protecting the president, the vice president, and their families, as well as former presidents and their spouses and widows. As television footage of the 1981 attempted assassination of President Ronald Reagan vividly demonstrated, Secret Service agents literally place their bodies and lives between those whom they protect and would-be assassins.

The Secret Service was created on July 5, 1865, with the original mission of suppressing counterfeit currency. Because the Secret Service was the only general law enforcement agency in existence at the time, it was asked to provide informal, part-time protection for President Grover Cleveland in 1894. The Secret Service assumed full-time responsibility for protecting the president after the assassination of President William McKinley in 1902. At that time, the Secret Service assigned two operatives to the White House. In 1930, after an intruder managed to walk into the White House dining room, the Congress placed the supervision of the White House Police under the direction of the chief of the Secret Service.

In addition to providing security for the White House, the Secret Service provides security at the vice president's residence and for foreign embassies and consulates in the United States. The Secret Service also protects foreign heads of state and heads of government when they visit the United States. In fiscal year 1999 the Secret Service provided protection to 471 foreign dignitaries.

The Intelligence Division of the Secret Service develops threat assessments in support of *protectee* visits to domestic and foreign settings; provides warning indicators for specific and generalized threat environments; maintains liaisons with the mental health, law enforcement, and intelligence communities; and conducts operational studies that are needed to stay at the forefront of the effort to predict the likelihood of danger.

The Secret Service still investigates financial crimes involving the counterfeiting of U.S. currency and securities and also investigates cybercrimes (attacks on critical infrastructures, desktop publishing, and network intrusions), fraud involving access devices such as credit cards, wireless telephone fraud, and identity theft. During fiscal year 1998, the Secret Service completed more than 27,000 criminal cases and intercepted over $110 million in counterfeit currency.

Q 368. What constitutes a threat against the president?

A According to Title 18, Section 871, of the U.S. Code, it is a threat against the president to:

- knowingly and willfully deposit in the mail, at any post office, or by any letter carrier a letter, paper, writing, print, missive, or document containing any threat to take the life of or to inflict bodily harm on the president, vice president, or any other officer in order of succession to the presidency; or
- knowingly and willfully make such threats in any way to the above-named people.

The Secret Service investigates about 3,000 threats against the president annually.

Q 369. Is it legal to photocopy a dollar bill?

A The Counterfeit Detection Act of 1992 permits color illustrations of U.S. currency only if the illustration is one-sided and is either enlarged or reduced. Specifically, the image must be of a size less than three-fourths or more than one-and one-half, in linear dimension, of each part of the item illustrated. Furthermore, the law requires that all negatives, plates, positives, digitized storage media, graphic files, magnetic media, optical storage devices, and any other things used in the making of the illustration that contain an image of the illustration be destroyed or deleted after their final use.

According to the Secret Service, counterfeit U.S. currency produced by advanced reprographic technology accounted for only 0.5 percent of the total amount passed in the United States in 1995. This percentage increased to 44 percent in fiscal 1998. In October 1998 the government initiated a program to find technological solutions to deter reprographically generated counterfeit currency. Approximately 100 representatives from private industry (laser printer manufacturers, computer manufacturers, and desktop software publishers) met representatives of the Secret Service, the Bureau of Engraving and Printing, the Federal Reserve, and the U.S. Department of the Treasury to discuss technological solutions.

Q 370. What is the investigative arm of the Internal Revenue Service?

A The Sixteenth Amendment to the U.S. Constitution gives Congress the power to levy and collect taxes. The Internal Revenue Service (IRS), a division of the U.S. Department of the Treasury, serves as the federal government's tax collector. Congress has granted the IRS a wide variety of legal powers to enforce federal internal revenue laws, including assessing penalties that range from minor fines to lengthy prison sentences.

In the vast majority of cases of noncompliance, the IRS pursues civil remedies, including payment of taxes, fines, and seizure of property, through its Examination and Collection Divisions. The Criminal Investigation Division (CID) of the IRS pursues criminal sanctions in cases of willful and egregious noncompliance with the tax code.

The CID is the only federal law enforcement agency with the authority to investigate criminal tax violations and the only component of the IRS with the authority to conduct searches, make arrests, and carry firearms. Created by the IRS in 1919, CID primarily investigates suspected tax fraud and related violations of the Internal Revenue Code and recommends cases for prosecution by the U.S. Attorney. In recent years because of the war on drugs, Congress has expanded CID's jurisdiction to include investigating money laundering and currency reporting statutes.

In a 1999 report the IRS estimated the tax gap—the annual amount of unpaid taxes nationwide from legal sources of income—at $195 billion. If allocated to individual returns, the IRS says this tax gap would amount to an additional assessment of $1,625 per return.

In fiscal year 1999 the CID initiated 3,952 investigations, including 2,457 fraud-related investigations and 1,495 narcotics-related investigations. In order of priority, areas targeted by the CID were:

- Money laundering
- Tax-gap investigations
- Narcotics
- Organized crime
- Nonfilers
- Questionable refunds
- Bank fraud
- Health care fraud
- Telemarketing fraud
- Public corruption
- Unscrupulous or incompetent return preparation
- Illegal gaming
- Fraudulent trusts
- Bankruptcy fraud
- Employment tax fraud
- Insurance fraud
- Excise tax fraud

Q 371. Are you more likely to be audited if you are rich or if you are poor?

A In 1999, for the first time, the Internal Revenue Service audited more tax returns of poor people than rich people. The IRS audited 1.36 percent of all tax returns filed by people making less than $25,000 per year but only 1.15 percent of returns filed by people making $100,000 or more.

Q 372. How many people simply don't file an income tax return?

A A basic premise of the American tax system is that every citizen will file a tax return. However, many Americans don't file tax returns. By 2004, the Internal Revenue Service predicts, there will be an estimated 8.6 million nonfilers. The IRS obtained 301 criminal indictments of nonfilers in 1999, winning 289 convictions. The average prison sentence meted out was 47 months.

Q 373. What are your chances of being criminally prosecuted by the IRS?

A Transactional Records Clearinghouse, a private research group affiliated with Syracuse University, estimates the chance of being criminally prosecuted by the Internal Revenue Service to be 7 in a million.

Q 374. Who said, "Income tax law is a lot of bunk"?

A Al "Scarface" Capone, one of the most notorious American criminals of the twentieth century, uttered these famous words. Capone, who was number one on the Chicago Crime Commission's Public Enemies List, headed an enormous crime organization that netted huge profits from the illegal liquor trade during Prohibition. Capone managed to elude the Federal Bureau of Investigation's exhaustive investigation of his illegal activities but finally was brought down by the Internal Revenue Service for income tax evasion. Capone had maintained that "[t]he government can't collect legal taxes from illegal money." After less than three hours of deliberation, a jury disagreed. Capone was convicted of three felonies and two misdemeanors relating to his failure to pay income tax from 1925 to 1929. He was sentenced to eleven years of prison and ordered to pay a fine of $80,000.

Q **375. What does the U.S. Marshals Service do?**

A The U.S. Marshals Service, a division of the U.S. Department of Justice, protects the federal courts and the operations of the U.S. judicial system. The oldest federal law enforcement agency, the U.S. Marshals service was created in the first law passed by the first Congress of the United States (the Judiciary Act of 1789), which also established the federal court system. U.S. marshals are appointed by the president in each of the ninety-four federal judicial districts. U.S. marshals supervise roughly 4,300 deputy marshals and administrative personnel in more than 400 office locations. Among other things, the U.S. Marshals Service:

- provides security for 800 judicial facilities and nearly 2,000 judges and magistrates;
- apprehends about 55 percent of all federal fugitives;
- operates the Federal Witness Security program, which ensures the safety of endangered government witnesses;
- maintains custody of 32,000 unsentenced prisoners each day, and transports 200,000 federal prisoners each year;
- executes court orders and all federal arrest warrants;
- assists the Justice Department's Asset Forfeiture Program;
- manages and sells an estimated $1 billion in property forfeited to the government by drug traffickers and other criminals;
- responds to emergency circumstances, including civil disturbances, terrorist incidents, and other crisis situations, through its Special Operations Group; and
- restores order in riot and mob-violence situations.

According to Title 18 of the U.S. Code, "United States marshals and their deputies may carry firearms and may make arrests without warrant for any offense against the United States committed in their presence, or for any felony cognizable under the laws of the United States if they have reasonable grounds to believe that the person to be arrested has committed or is committing such felony."

At the end of 1999 the U.S. Marshals Service had more than 8,000 outstanding fugitive warrants.

See 348 What is the oldest federal law enforcement agency?

Q **376. What does the U.S. Postal Inspection Service do?**

A The U.S. Postal Inspection Service is the law enforcement arm of the U.S. Postal Service. It traces its roots to 1772, when Postmaster General Benjamin Franklin created the position of surveyor because he no longer could single-handedly regulate and audit postal functions. Today about 2,100 postal inspectors are stationed across the country. The postmaster general of the United States appoints the director of the U.S. Postal Inspection Service, who is called the chief postal inspector.

Postal inspectors are responsible for enforcing more than 200 federal statutes that deal with the mails. In the 1800s postal inspectors investigated stagecoach and train robberies. Today they investigate such mail-related schemes as check washing (stolen checks that are "washed" and have new dollar amounts filled in) and identity theft (based on information gleaned from stolen mail), as well as violent crimes such as mail bombs, threats, and assaults on postal employees.

In its annual report the U.S. Postal Inspection Service stated that it arrested 10,388 criminal suspects in fiscal year 1999. Of those arrests, more than 5,000 suspects were arrested on charges related to mail theft. Postal inspectors investigated more than 3,000 mail fraud cases and responded to approximately 70,000 consumer fraud complaints. Mail fraud investigations resulted in more than 1,500 arrests, approximately $606 million in court-ordered and voluntary restitution, and nearly 1,200 civil or administrative actions. Postal inspectors also arrested 163 suspects for mail-related child exploitation offenses and more than 1,500 suspects for drug trafficking and money laundering via the mail.

Under federal law, postal inspectors may:

- serve federal warrants and subpoenas;
- make arrests without warrants for postal-related offenses against the United States committed in their presence or for postal-related felonies if they reasonably believe the person to be arrested has committed or is committing the felony;
- carry firearms; and
- make seizures of property as provided by law.

The U.S. Postal Inspection Service also maintains a security force of about 1,400 uniformed postal police officers who are assigned to major postal facilities, where they provide security and escort high-value mail shipments.

Q 377. Who was the "wood detective"?

A Arthur Koehler (1885–1967), a pioneer arson investigator, worked with the U.S. Forest Service for thirty-six years. Koehler traced the wood used to make the ladder that was used to kidnap Charles Lindbergh's infant son in 1932 to the lumberyard that sold the wood. His investigation yielded information that was critical to the conviction of Bruno Richard Hauptmann. Thereafter, Koehler was known as the "wood detective."

Q **378. What happens when a crime is committed on a cruise ship on the high seas?**

A The Federal Bureau of Investigation (FBI) is responsible for investigating crimes that occur on American cruise ships on the high seas. However, in 1999 it became apparent that many such crimes never are reported to authorities. In a civil lawsuit, a Florida judge ordered Carnival Cruise Lines (the world's largest cruise line, with 2.5 million passengers a year) to disclose the first-ever crime statistics released by a cruise line. Carnival reported that its crewmembers were accused of sexual assault sixty-two times within a five-year period. The International Council of Cruise Lines, which represents the seventeen largest lines in North America, adopted a new standard requiring officials to report all shipboard crimes to the FBI.

STATE AND LOCAL

Q **379. What is a state police department?**

A A state police department is a general-purpose law enforcement agency that is operated by the state. The latest statistics show that in 1997 forty-nine primary state police departments employed more than 82,000 employees, including more than 54,000 full-time sworn and 28,000 nonsworn (civilian) employees. Hawaii is the only state that does not have a state police agency. The Hawaii Department of Public Safety primarily provides court support services.

State police are best known for patrolling state highways, but they provide a wide variety of services to the public and to federal and local law enforcement agencies. State police typically perform statewide criminal investigations, including drug probes and investigations into misconduct or corruption within any agency under the jurisdiction of the governor.

State police also serve as the central repository for criminal history information for the state. They operate statewide criminal intelligence information systems, including computerized fingerprint and DNA databases, a missing children information clearinghouse, firearms registration programs, and sexual predator identification programs. State police also compile and analyze statewide crime statistics and prepare statistical reports for policymakers, planners, program developers, and researchers.

A state police agency also may:

- operate a police training academy;
- provide sophisticated forensic services to local law enforcement agencies;
- provide emergency disaster response, aircraft, and underwater support services;
- apprehend fugitives; and
- maintain K-9 teams for tracking and drug detection.

Q 380. Where are the largest state police agencies?

A The Bureau of Justice Statistics reported in 1999 that the state police agencies with the largest number of full-time sworn officers are:

- California Highway Patrol, 6,532
- Pennsylvania State Police, 4,098
- New York State Police, 3,979
- Texas Department of Public Safety, 2,757
- New Jersey State Police, 2,555
- Massachusetts State Police, 2,270
- Michigan State Police, 2,054
- Illinois State Police, 1,980
- Virginia State Police, 1,658
- Florida Highway Patrol, 1,637

Q 381. Which is the oldest state police agency?

A The Texas Rangers are considered to be the oldest state police agency in the United States. English-speaking settlers in the Mexican territory of Texas received little protection from the Mexican government against hostile Indians. In 1823 they formed small militia companies for self-protection. These militia companies became known as the Rangers. After Texas won independence from Mexico in 1835, the role of the Texas Rangers grew to include policing the border against Mexicans as well as Indians and retrieving runaway slaves and fugitives. The Rangers became part of the Confederate Army during the Civil War and were briefly replaced by a new state police force. However, in 1874 the state police force was dismantled and the Texas Rangers were reinstated. According to the "Ranger's Prayer," by Pierre Bernard Hill, a chaplain for the Texas Rangers, a Ranger's duty was to "Protect when danger threatens, / Sustain when trails are rough; / Help me to keep my standard high / And smile at each rebuff."

The first modern state police department was established in Pennsylvania in 1905. New York followed in 1917; Michigan, Colorado, and West Virginia in 1919; and Massachusetts in 1920. State police agencies traditionally fought rural crime and were used to circumvent corrupt or inefficient local police forces and to control strikes where city police were considered to be sympathetic to the unionists.

Q 382. What are local police departments?

A A local police department is a general-purpose law enforcement agency operated by a municipality, township, county, or tribal government. Local police departments investigate and process the vast majority of all crimes, from petty infractions and misdemeanors to major felonies.

The U.S. Department of Justice reported in 2000 that more than 13,500 general-purpose local police departments were operating in the United States in 1997. These local police departments employed 531,494 full-time employees, including 420,152 sworn personnel, and 60,373 part-time employees. Sworn personnel have arrest authority.

One-third of all full-time local police officers worked in departments with 1,000 or more officers; three-fifths worked in departments with at least 100 officers. Departments with fewer than ten officers employed about 5 percent of all local police officers nationwide.

Municipal governments operated 86 percent of local police departments and township governments operated 13 percent. American Indian tribes operated about 100 local police departments, and county governments operated about 50.

Q 383. How are law enforcement agencies structured?

A American law enforcement agencies always have used a quasi-military model for their organizational structures and administration. This model includes an operational chain of command, officer ranks, general rules, regulations, and uniform attire. Initially, police officers even used army cavalry handguns.

Every police department has two major classifications of personnel: sworn police officers and nonsworn (civilian) personnel. Sworn officers include police officers, troopers, and deputy sheriffs, all of whom have the power to make arrests. Sworn officers take an oath to abide by the U.S. Constitution and state and local laws pertaining to police powers. Nonsworn personnel do not possess traditional police powers and include clerks, secretaries, dispatchers, and operators.

The chain of command of a typical police department is as follows:

- *Chief of police or police commissioner.* The chief is the head of the department and is responsible for all of its operations. The top official within his or her respective jurisdiction, such as the mayor, county executive, or governor, generally appoints the chief.
- *Assistant chief of police.* In large departments, the assistant chief of police may be responsible for administrative control of major police units, such as the patrol or detective unit.
- *Captain.* The captain is responsible for police operations within an assigned geographical area.
- *Lieutenant.* The lieutenant supervises police operations and all of the people working on a shift or tour.
- *Sergeant.* The sergeant is the immediate supervisor of a squad of officers assigned to his or her command and may be called to the scene of a crime to make important decisions.
- *Detective, investigator, or inspector.* This nonuniformed officer investigates serious crimes.
- *Corporal or master patrol officer.* This position holds an intermediate rank between the police officer and the first-line supervisor, the sergeant. The corporal or master patrol officer may perform special training or technical functions.
- *Police officer or patrol officer.* Most police officers are assigned to patrol duties.

Most police departments are governed by a civil service system that consists of regulations designed to eliminate political interference in the operations of the department and to promote merit-based hiring and promotions. With the exception of the chief, police generally are required to take merit-based examinations to progress through the ranks.

Q **384. Which law enforcement agency is the largest in the United States?**

A The largest local law enforcement agency (municipal, county, and state) in the United States is the New York City police department, according to a 1999 report by the U.S. Department of Justice. As of June 30, 1997, the New York City police department had 38,328 full-time sworn law enforcement officers.

Following are the numbers of full-time sworn officers employed in the seven next-largest agencies:

- Chicago police, 13,271
- Los Angeles police, 9,423

- Philadelphia police, 6,782
- Houston police, 5,355
- Detroit police, 4,070
- Washington Metropolitan police (Washington, D.C.), 3,618
- Dallas police, 2,817

Q 385. What is a sheriffs' department?

A States are divided into counties, and every county has a sheriff, who usually is an elected officer. Independent city governments operate some sheriffs' departments. Sheriffs' departments are primarily responsible for performing court-related functions, such as providing courtroom security and serving civil process or notice to people who are being sued in civil court. However, most sheriffs' departments also provide basic law enforcement functions and investigate crimes within their jurisdictions. Most sheriffs' departments respond to calls for service and provide routine patrol services, particularly in unincorporated areas of the county or incorporated areas that are not served by local police.

About 80 percent of sheriffs' departments operate jails. A jail is a locally administered confinement facility that holds inmates beyond arraignment, usually for more than forty-eight hours.

According to a 1999 report by the federal government, 3,088 sheriffs' departments operated in the United States in 1997, employing 174,673 sworn personnel (with arrest powers) and 269,427 total personnel.

Sheriffs were legendary figures in the old West, where they often represented the only real law enforcement presence. Perhaps the best-known sheriff was Patrick Floyd Garrett, the sheriff of Lincoln County, New Mexico, who captured Billy the Kid in 1880. After a trial in which he was found guilty of murder and sentenced to hang, Billy the Kid escaped from jail, killing two deputies. Garrett tracked him down, ambushed him, and shot him to death on July 14, 1881. Garrett was fatally shot himself in 1903 near Las Cruces, New Mexico, when he drew a gun in a dispute with a rancher who had leased his horse ranch.

Q 386. What is the largest sheriffs' department in the country?

A The largest sheriffs' department is the Los Angeles County (California) Sheriffs' Department. As of June 1997, the department employed 8,021 full-time sworn personnel. About half of these officers were assigned to law enforcement field operations, making it at least four times larger than any other law enforcement operation among sheriffs' departments. The agency had about 2,200 officers working in its jails and about 1,400 officers assigned to court-related duties. The agency also employed about 4,500 full-time civilian employees.

Q 387. What is a special police agency?

A A special police agency is a state or local agency that polices a special geographic jurisdiction (such as a park, transit system, public school, college or university, or public housing complex), has special enforcement responsibilities such as those pertaining to natural resource conservation or alcoholic beverage control, or conducts special investigations such as those required by prosecutors' offices. In 1997 there were 1,332 special police agencies in the United States employing 61,220 full-time personnel, including 44,509 sworn officers.

Q 388. What are campus law enforcement agencies?

A Before World War II watchmen patrolled most institutions of higher education. Increasing numbers of students and the growth of campuses prompted many colleges and universities to upgrade their security departments by hiring former military and city police officers. In the 1960s, as a result of campus unrest over the antiwar and civil rights movements, colleges and universities began forming their own full-service law enforcement agencies. In 1995 some 680 campus law enforcement agencies in the United States employed a total of 20,067 employees.

Most campus police officers at public institutions have the same general police powers of arrest as other law enforcement officers in their respective states, either through an act of the legislature or via deputation by state or local police. Almost every state has passed a law authorizing full authority for campus police departments at public institutions. One state, Connecticut, passed a special law granting police authority to campus police at a private institution, Yale University, in New Haven, Connecticut.

Significant distinctions remain between campus and local police, however. Campus police officers generally are appointed by the governing body or chief executive officer of the college or university and may be required to perform regulatory functions, such as enforcing college or university rules, as well as police functions. The jurisdiction of a campus police department may be limited to the campus and its outlying properties. Many local and campus police departments have entered into mutual aid agreements whereby the jurisdiction of campus police is extended beyond the campus under certain circumstances.

A Policing in the United States is undergoing a remarkable transformation from the cops-and-robbers style of policing popular in the past to a new crime-fighting strategy known as community policing. Herman Goldstein, a University of Wisconsin law professor, has been credited with originating the modern concept of community policing in 1979.

It is estimated that law enforcement agencies serving 87 percent of the country's population now have adopted some variant of community policing.

Under community policing, police officers are encouraged to get out of their patrol cruisers and to work in partnership with the local community to identify and solve crime problems. Community policing includes diverse elements such as police foot and bicycle patrols, storefront police stations, and recreational and anticrime programs.

Community policing is proactive. Instead of reacting to isolated reports of crime, police collect data, analyze incidents that may be related to the targeted problem, look beyond the individual incidents, and determine whether the incidents were triggered by a common underlying cause or condition that, if resolved, would prevent many of them from recurring.

In some ways, community policing is reminiscent of the early days of policing, when cops walked a beat and knew everyone in their neighborhood. Officers are encouraged to think creatively about solving problems on their beats. Joint police-community partnerships are thought to promote fairer treatment of all citizens, including minorities who in the past regarded police with suspicion.

By passing the Violent Crime Control and Law Enforcement Act of 1994, the federal government has encouraged community policing. The act provides federal funds to communities to implement community policing concepts. The U.S. Department of Justice created the Office of Community Oriented Policing Services (COPS) to carry out this mission. By 1999 COPS had awarded $5.9 billion dollars to more than 11,300 agencies and had funded 100,000 additional officers to patrol the nation's streets. Under the Twenty-first Century Policing Initiative, known as COPS II, the federal government will provide funding for an additional 50,000 police officers by 2005 and encourage the creation of community-based prosecutors.

Many communities credit community policing with helping lower their crime rates and improving police–community relations. However, some police officers oppose community policing, fearing that the practice will require them to be social workers with guns.

390. What police beating incident exposed the shortcomings of military-style policing?

A The beating of twenty-five-year-old black motorist Rodney G. King by four Los Angeles police officers on March 3, 1991, prompted law enforcement authorities nationwide to reassess modern military-style police techniques.

King was beaten, kicked, and struck by a taser electric stun gun after a high-speed auto chase. Unbeknownst to police, the incident was recorded on tape by a plumbing store manager using a video camera from his apartment balcony. Repeatedly broadcast over national television, a two-minute excerpt of the tape showing the beating made King a national symbol of police brutality. The acquittal of the officers involved in King's beating spurred riots in Los Angeles's black neighborhoods. Later, the officers were tried and convicted in federal court of violating King's civil rights in the beating incident.

When the King beating occurred, the Los Angeles Police Department was a highly militarized department that used a patrol car–based, reactive approach to law enforcement. A commission appointed to investigate King's beating faulted the department for failing to control officers who repeatedly misused force and said "LAPD officers are encouraged to command and to confront, not to communicate." The commission recommended switching to community policing concepts to improve community relations.

A year later a new police chief, Willie L. Williams, who had successfully implemented community policing in Philadelphia, was appointed to head the LAPD. Los Angeles experienced a downturn in crime after Williams implemented community policing.

In a 1999 report to the United States Committee against Torture, the U.S. State Department characterized the King beating as one of eighteen instances of torture committed by American police and correctional officials since 1991. According to the report, "Torture does not occur in the United States except in aberrational circumstances and never as a matter of policy."

See 426 Do a few bad apples spoil the barrel?

Q 391. How do police departments patrol their jurisdictions?

A Most police patrol work remains dominated by automobiles. Virtually every department used automobiles for routine patrols in 1997, the latest year for which statistics are available. Half of all local police departments also used foot patrols on a routine basis, including 94 percent of departments serving a population of a million or more. Other means used by departments included the following:

- Bicycle patrols, 28 percent
- Motorcycle patrols, 9 percent
- Marine patrols, 3 percent
- Horse patrols, 1 percent

Local police departments include those operated by municipal, township, tribal, and county governments.

See 432 What rules of the road must police observe?

Q 392. What is the broken window theory?

A "[I]f a window in a building is broken and is left unrepaired, all the rest of the windows will soon be broken," observed criminologists George L. Kelling and James Q. Wilson in an influential 1982 article in *Atlantic Monthly* magazine titled "Broken Windows."

The criminologists contended that police who aggressively target "disorder" crimes, such as vandalism, aggressive panhandling, and public drunkenness, can prevent a more serious criminal invasion in the area. Disorder left unattended creates fear among area residents, gives the perception that the area is unsafe, and tells criminals that citizens do not care about the area and are unlikely to report crimes. The criminologists said that community preservation, maintaining order, and public safety should be the primary focus of police patrols, and not simply crime fighting.

Crime plummeted when New York City Mayor Rudolph W. Giuliani and Police Commissioner William J. Bratton instituted a campaign against quality-of-life crimes based on the broken window theory. They ordered crackdowns not only on graffiti writers and litterers but also on windshield cleaners, people who urinated in public, and jaywalkers. The New York City Police Department reported that murder dropped 49 percent from 1993 to 1996 and auto theft, 47 percent. Many communities have followed New York's example.

Critics counter that a robust economy, increasing use of imprisonment, and the decline of the crack cocaine market are largely responsible for New York City's crime free-fall. Critics also argue that the broken window theory is responsible for many mentally ill persons being sent through the revolving door of prisons and jails when treatment would be more effective and less costly.

Q **393. What is problem-oriented policing?**

A Problem-oriented policing is a crime-fighting strategy that encourages police to focus on the problems that cause criminal incidents. Like community policing, this strategy arose in the 1980s as an alternative to incident-driven, reactive policing. Problem-oriented policing has four parts, summarized as Scan, Analyze, Response, Assessment (SARA). Groups of officers scan crime data for problems, analyze information from diverse sources to discover the underlying nature of the problem, coordinate a response (with the help of citizens, business owners, and public and private agencies), and assess the effectiveness of the response.

Q **394. What is crime mapping?**

A Since the 1980s many police departments have instituted crime mapping, a form of analysis that uses computer technology to understand the nature and extent of criminal and social problems in a community and to improve the allocation of resources to combat those problems. Computer mapping software enables police to join, or overlay, disparate data sets. For example, one layer of a map display can represent the locations of crimes in the past month. Another layer can represent a possible explanatory variable, such as the unemployment rates of persons living on each city block, the locations of abandoned houses, or citizen reports of drug activity. In addition to crime analysis, crime-mapping technology assists dispatchers in verifying a caller's location and the location of patrol cars.

Q **395. What crime prevention methods work best?**

A In 1996 Congress asked the attorney general to provide a "comprehensive evaluation of the effectiveness" of the more than $3 billion spent annually by the Department of Justice in grants to state and local governments. After evaluating more than 500 state and local programs, authorities reported in 1998 that the following police crime-prevention programs work best:

- Extra police patrols in high-crime hot-spots reduce crime in those places.
- Repeat-offender units reduce the time spent on the streets by known high-risk repeat offenders by monitoring such offenders and returning them to prison more quickly on commission of a repeat offense.
- Domestic abuse arrests reduce the incidence of repeat abuse by certain types of offenders who have a stake in the community (for example, employed suspects).

Other crime-control programs deemed effective include:

- Family therapy and parental training programs regarding delinquent and at-risk pre-adolescents
- Therapeutic drug treatment programs in prisons
- Rehabilitation programs for adult and juvenile offenders that use treatments appropriate to their risk factors
- Ex-offender job training for older males no longer under criminal justice supervision

Less successful programs included gun buyback programs, police counseling visits to homes of couples days after domestic violence incidents, Drug Abuse Resistance Education (D.A.R.E.), neighborhood watch programs organized with police assistance, storefront police offices, scared straight programs in which minor juvenile offenders visit adult prisons, home detention with electronic monitoring, and intensive supervision of offenders on parole or probation.

This study and others have caused experts to reassess traditionally held notions of what constitutes crime prevention. Experts are taking a second look at interventions that are designed primarily to produce other socially desirable results, such as healthier individuals, healthier families, higher educational attainment, and decreased dependence on illegal drugs. If successful, these programs are likely also to reduce crime.

See 109 What causes crime?

Q 396. What are the total annual operating expenditures of local and state police departments?

A According to the U.S. Department of Justice, the total operating expenditures of state and local police departments in fiscal year 1997 were:

- Local police departments, $29.2 billion
- Sheriffs, $13.1 billion
- State police, $5.2 billion

Nationwide, operating expenditures were about $2.16 million per department, ranging from $423 million for departments serving populations of 1 million or more to $128,000 among departments serving populations fewer than 2,500 residents.

Controlling for inflation, the net increase in spending by local police departments was 8 percent over 1993 levels. This increase does not include capital expenditures, such as equipment purchases and construction projects. Local police departments include those operated by municipal, township, tribal, and county governments.

Q 397. How much do residents pay to support their local police departments?

A The overall operating cost for local police departments per resident was $150 in fiscal 1997. Departments in jurisdictions with populations of 1 million or more cost the most to operate, $222 per resident. Departments in jurisdictions with populations of less than 2,500 cost the least to operate, $109 per resident. Local police departments include those operated by municipal, township, tribal, and county governments.

Q 398. What does it cost a local police department to employ a police officer?

A Nationwide, local police departments paid an estimated $67,100 per sworn officer in fiscal 1997. Employee salaries and benefits account for $7 out of every $8 in local police operating expenditures.

LAW ENFORCEMENT OFFICERS

Q 399. How many full-time sworn law enforcement officers are working in the United States?

A About 774,500 full-time sworn law enforcement officers currently work in the United States, including about 74,500 federal officers and almost 700,000 state and local officers. Sworn personnel have arrest powers. Following is the breakdown of state and local officers:

- Local police, 420,152 officers
- Sheriff, 174,673 officers
- Primary state police, 54,206 officers
- Special police, 44,509 officers
- Texas constable offices, 1,838 officers

Q 400. What is the national average of local police officers per 10,000 residents?

A According to the latest figures, an average of nineteen full-time sworn officers per 10,000 residents were employed in all municipal, county, and state law enforcement agencies with 100 or more officers in 1997.

The U.S. Department of Justice estimates that the number of sworn law enforcement officers employed by local police departments increased by 12 percent from 1993 to 1997. Local police departments include those operated by municipal, township, tribal, and county governments.

Q **401. What is the race and gender breakdown among employees of local police departments?**

A The latest statistics (for 1997) show that 11 percent of the full-time sworn personnel employed by all municipal, county, and state law enforcement agencies were female and 18 percent were members of a racial or ethnic minority. About 10 percent were black, 7 percent were Hispanic, and 1 percent were Asian or Pacific Islander.

In local police departments the numbers of female officers and minority officers each increased by about 26 percent between 1993 and 1997.

Q **402. What percentage of police officers work in field operations as opposed to a technical or administrative capacity?**

A About 82 percent of full-time sworn officers in all municipal, county, and state law enforcement agencies with 100 or more sworn personnel work in field operations, according to a 1999 report by the U.S. Department of Justice. Of the remaining sworn employees, 7 percent work in jail operations, 5 percent work in administration, 3 percent work in technical support, 2 percent work in court operations, and 1 percent perform other functions.

Q **403. How much time do police spend on actual law enforcement?**

A There is some truth to the old saying that policing is 99 percent boredom punctuated by 1 percent sheer terror. Some estimates hold that only about 20 percent of police service calls involve reports of criminal activity. The remaining calls involve traffic problems, reports of public nuisance, requests for assistance, and so forth. Various studies show that police officers spend from 10 percent to 30 percent of their time policing and the rest of their time performing myriad other tasks, such as stopping vehicles to check for expired registrations, making house calls to quiet noisy neighbors, or handling other requests.

Q **404. What graphic is displayed on a police officer's badge?**

A Most police officers' badges display the symbol or heraldry of the jurisdiction in which the officer serves, such as the municipality, county, or state. The history of the badge, which is also called an officer's shield or chest piece, can be traced back to the armor worn by knights and warriors to deflect the blows of their enemies.

Q **405. How do police departments screen new recruits?**

A The U.S. Department of Justice reported in 1999 that in 1997 municipal, county, and state law enforcement agencies with 100 or more officers used the following screening methods to select new officer recruits:

- Criminal record check, 99 percent
- Background investigation, 99 percent
- Driving record check, 98 percent
- Medical examination, 98 percent
- Psychological screening, 94 percent
- Drug test, 87 percent
- Written aptitude test, 87 percent
- Physical agility test, 80 percent
- Polygraph examination, 63 percent
- Voice stress analyzer, 6 percent

Q **406. Can an applicant with a criminal record become a police officer?**

A Most—but not all—federal, state, and local police departments refuse to hire an individual with a felony or a misdemeanor recorded within a specified period of time, such as two years. Connecticut's Sheriff's Advisory Board adopted a new policy in 1999 prohibiting the hiring of convicted felons after a newspaper reported that more than a dozen special deputy sheriffs had convictions ranging from disorderly conduct to assault and drug trafficking. One of the special deputy sheriffs, who handled courtroom security, had served almost two years in a Florida prison for attempted cocaine trafficking.

407. What educational and training requirements exist for new officers?

A Until the twentieth century a police officer's job had no prerequisites for training or education. Today virtually every local law enforcement agency requires at least some formal educational and training requirements for new officer recruits.

A presidential commission in 1967 recommended that police educational credentials be raised, with the ultimate goal of requiring a baccalaureate degree. The U.S. Justice Department reported in 1999 that in 1997 78 percent of municipal, state, and county law enforcement agencies with 100 or more officers required a high school diploma, 13 percent required some college, 7 percent required a two-year college degree, and 2 percent required a four-year college degree.

Almost all law enforcement agencies require new officer recruits to complete a training program that is offered by the department or by a state or federal law enforcement agency. In 1997 the combined field and classroom training requirements for new officers averaged more than 1,000 hours. About 3 percent of local police departments, including most departments serving a population of 250,000 or more, operated a training academy.

Q **408. Can you be too smart to be a police officer?**

A In at least one jurisdiction, the answer is yes. The city of New London, Connecticut, chose not to interview Robert Jordan and several other aspiring police officers in 1996 because they scored too high on a required intelligence test. After Jordan sued the city, a federal judge ruled in 1999 that it was not a violation of federal equal protection laws to exclude job candidates for being too intelligent.

The Jordan case fueled a longstanding controversy. Some researchers say that higher education reduces a police officer's quality of service because police work does not provide the kind of stimulation needed by a college-educated person. Officers who are highly educated are deemed more likely to become frustrated with the job and quit. Proponents of more education for police argue that the trend toward neighborhood and community policing has made a complex job infinitely more complex. In addition to enforcing laws within the constraints of the U.S. Constitution, contemporary police officers now must collaborate with diverse community groups and private-sector employers to redress and prevent crime. They say that a highly educated officer is more likely to appreciate the role of police in a democratic society, to be more tolerant of diverse members of the community, and to bring more resources to crime prevention.

A study of police attitudes found that officers with higher educational levels perceive themselves as performing better in several categories, including ethics and honesty.

409. How many police departments have residency requirements for new recruits?

A About two-thirds of municipal, county, and state law enforcement agencies with 100 or more officers have some type of residency requirement. According to a 1999 federal report, in 1997 about 14 percent of agencies required new officers to reside within the state, 28 percent required residency within any city or county in the state, and 22 percent required residency within another specified area. Thirty-seven percent of local law enforcement agencies had no residency requirement. Law enforcement agencies justify residency requirements as promoting an officer's rapport with and understanding of a community.

410. What annual in-service training requirement exists for field or patrol officers?

A Most departments require law enforcement officers to fulfill an annual in-service training requirement. The median number of annual in-service training hours required in 1997 for all municipal, county, and state law enforcement officers with 100 or more officers was twenty-four hours.

411. Which cities have the highest ratios of police to residents?

A According to the Bureau of Justice Statistics, in 1999 the following large cities in the United States had the highest numbers of full-time officers per 10,000 residents:

City	Number of Officers (per 10,000 residents)	City	Number of Officers (per 10,000 residents)
Washington, D.C.	67	St. Louis	46
New York	52	Baltimore	46
Newark, New Jersey	52	Atlanta	40
Chicago	49	Boston	39
Philadelphia	46		

412. What is the average salary paid to local police officers?

A In 1997 the average base starting salary paid to an entry-level officer in a municipal police department with 100 or more officers was $29,859. That salary compares to

$27,901 for a county police officer, $26,877 for a state police officer, and $25,994 for a sheriff.

Salary generally was related to the size of the population served. For example, the base starting salary for an entry-level officer in a department serving a population of 1 million or more was $30,600, while an entry-level officer in a department serving fewer than 2,500 citizens received a starting salary of only $18,000.

Police officers with one year of experience in all municipal, county, and state police departments that employed 100 or more officers earned an average base starting salary of $31,488. That salary compares to $41,876 for a sergeant or first-line supervisor and $76,321 for a chief of police or chief executive.

Q 413. What percentage of local law enforcement agencies authorize collective bargaining?

A It is estimated that almost three-quarters of all police officers are represented by police unions. Nationwide, 63 percent of all municipal, county, and state law enforcement agencies with 100 or more officers authorized sworn personnel to engage in collective bargaining in 1997 and 53 percent allowed civilian employees to engage in collective bargaining. Collective bargaining enables police to negotiate salary, benefits, hours, and working conditions.

Seventy-six percent of local police departments, employing 90 percent of all local police officers, authorized sworn personnel to join a police association. Forty-six percent of local police departments, employing 72 percent of all officers, authorized their sworn personnel to join unions in 1997.

The National Association of Police Organizations, Inc. (NAPO), a coalition of police unions and associations based in Washington, D.C., represents more than 4,000 police unions and associations and 250,000 sworn law enforcement officers (including police officers, deputy sheriffs, state troopers, highway patrol officers, and traffic enforcement personnel).

Q 414. Can police go on strike?

A Law enforcement officers do not have the right to strike under federal or state laws. However, police occasionally do engage in work slowdowns or experience *blue flu* and fail to report for duty when contract negotiations are not going well.

415. What was the Boston Police Strike?

The Boston Police Strike is the most infamous strike in police history. It began on September 9, 1919, when 1,117 of the 1,544 officers on the evening shift stopped working. Police had gone without a raise for about twenty years despite high inflation. The officers formed a group called the Boston Social Club, which was granted a union charter by the American Federation of Labor (AFL). The walkout occurred after city officials forbade participation in the union and attempted to discipline nineteen newly elected union leaders.

The strike prompted forty-eight hours of frenzied looting and rioting in downtown Boston and South Boston. Calvin Coolidge, then governor of Massachusetts, called out the Massachusetts State Guard to restore order. After eight days, the guard was disbanded and the Boston Police Commission hired a new police force from the ranks of young World War I veterans.

Governor Coolidge rebuffed a request by AFL President Samuel Gompers to reinstate the striking police and negotiate their grievances later. Coolidge claimed that the strikers were guilty of desertion of duty, adding, "There is no right to strike against the public safety by anybody, anywhere, any time." President Woodrow Wilson was equally unsympathetic. He said the "strike of the policemen of a great city, leaving that city at the mercy of an army of thugs, is a crime against civilization."

A second campaign to organize police took place in the 1940s. The effort was condemned by the International Association of Chiefs of Police (IACP), which claimed there was little advantage to police unionizing because public sentiment was "so overwhelmingly against strikes by police officers that to exercise this weapon of private employees would bring immediate disaster to the group." The IACP cited the experience of the police in the Boston Police Strike.

Q **416. Are police required to undergo drug tests?**

A Most departments require officers to undergo drug tests under at least some circumstances. Twenty-one percent of municipal, county, and state law enforcement agencies with 100 or more officers required mandatory testing of regular field officers in 1997, compared to 3 percent in 1993. Thirty-two percent of departments had a random drug testing policy and 59 percent performed drug testing when drug use was suspected. Fourteen percent of departments did not do any drug testing of regular field officers.

In *National Treasury Employees Union v. Raab* (1989), the U.S. Supreme Court upheld drug testing of U.S. Customs Service personnel involved in drug interdiction or carrying firearms. Given the national drug crisis, the Court said, the government has a compelling interest in (1) ensuring that front-line drug interdiction personnel are physically fit and have unimpeachable integrity and judgment, and (2) preventing the risk to the citizenry posed by the potential use of deadly force by persons suffering from impaired perception and judgment. The Court said the drug testing program did not intrude on Customs employees' Fourth Amendment right to be free from unreasonable searches and seizures.

Drug tests typically screen for the presence of marijuana, cocaine, opiates, amphetamines, and phencyclidine.

Q 417. What types of weapons do police carry?

A The latest figures show that 94 percent of local police departments, employing 98 percent of all local police officers, authorized the use of semiautomatic sidearms in 1997. Nearly all local police departments also authorized the use of nonlethal weapons by officers. The most common nonlethal weapons were the baton, chemical incapacitators such as pepper spray (oleoresin capsicum), and electronic devices, including stun guns and tasers that temporarily incapacitate a suspect by sending electric current into the suspect's nervous system. Other devices either in use or under development include nets that can be launched with a baton, nonlethal blunt-impact projectiles, and a light dazzler to disorient the suspect. Local police departments include those operated by municipal, township, tribal, and county governments.

Q 418. What is the first thing that a law enforcement officer arriving at a crime scene should do?

A On arriving at a crime scene, the responding officer should first assess the scene and treat the incident as a serious crime, according to a January 2000 report commissioned by the U.S. Department of Justice. The safety and physical well-being of the officer and others must be the officer's first priority. After controlling any dangerous situations or persons, the officer should ensure that medical attention is provided to injured persons while minimizing contamination of any evidence at the scene. The officer should control, identify, and remove persons at the crime scene, limit the number of persons who enter the scene, and limit the movement of persons at the scene. The officer should establish and protect the boundaries of the crime scene and, when investigative personnel arrive, turn over control of the scene to them and brief the investigative officers.

419. When may police officers use force?

A A model policy on the use of force developed by the International Association of Chiefs of Police states that police officers "shall use only that force that is reasonably necessary to effectively bring an incident under control, while protecting the lives of the officer or another." Police officers may use department-approved nondeadly force to protect themselves or others from physical harm, to restrain or subdue a resistant individual, or to bring an unlawful situation safely and effectively under control.

Most law enforcement agencies allow an officer to exercise a degree of discretion regarding the amount of force needed to effect an arrest. The following guidelines represent a use-of-force continuum that is widely taught at police academies:

- *Level I:* Most police-citizen encounters are marked by compliance. Both parties are positive and cooperative.
- *Level II:* The subject passively resists or is unresponsive to police demands but offers no physical threat toward the officer. The officer should gain control by using tactics that are primarily psychologically manipulative, with a minimum of physical contact that does not involve pain.
- *Level III:* The person actively resists the officer and is indifferent to attempts at control. The subject threatens to assault or has assaulted the officer. The officer may use a baton and/or physical contact for leverage and control, and possibly chemical sprays and the deployment of additional officers.
- *Level IV:* The subject shows active, hostile resistance and the officer faces a threat of bodily harm. The officer may use more forceful tactical procedures, including techniques to disarm or counter the subject's attack.
- *Level V:* The subject is assaultive. The officer can draw a reasonable conclusion that the subject intends to kill him or her or inflict great bodily harm. The officer may use deadly force, in which all tactical options are directed toward the officer's survival.

420. What percentage of police encounters are marked by force or threatened force?

A Studies show that police use force infrequently and that it typically occurs at the lower end of the spectrum, involving actions such as grabbing, pushing, or shoving.

According to a 1999 joint report by the National Institute of Justice and the Bureau of Justice Statistics, preliminary research indicates that 1 percent of people who have face-to-face encounters with police say that the officers used or threatened to use force. The study also indicates that most respondents who reported that police had used force against them suggested that they might have provoked the officer by threatening or assaulting the officer, arguing, interfering with the officer's movement, trying to escape, resisting being handcuffed, and resisting being placed in a police vehicle.

The report cites another study of 7,512 arrests in Oregon and Florida in which an adult was taken into police custody. Fewer than one in five arrests involved police use of force. When force was used, 80 percent of the time the type of force used involved pushing, grabbing, or shoving. Half of the time it involved grabbing the suspect. Of suspects who were injured when force was used, about 48 percent suffered a bruise or abrasion, 24 percent suffered a laceration, and 4 percent incurred a gunshot injury. Police officers used chemical agents, including pepper spray, in 1.2 percent of all arrests and used firearms in 0.2 percent of all arrests.

Q 421. What is excessive force?

A *Excessive force* has been defined as the use of more force than is allowable when judged in terms of administrative and professional guidelines or legal standards. Police generally are required to use the least amount of force necessary to accomplish their goals.

In *Graham v. Connor* (1989), the U.S. Supreme Court held that the Fourth Amendment of the U.S. Constitution imposes a requirement that police act with reasonableness in the use of force, whether deadly force or not. An officer's actions must be objectively reasonable in light of the facts and circumstances confronting them, without regard to the officer's underlying intent or motivation. According to the Court, the reasonableness of a particular use of force must be judged from the perspective of a reasonable officer on the scene and must allow for the fact that police often are forced to make split-second decisions about the amount of force necessary in a particular situation.

The term *excessive force* is more expansive than the term *police brutality*, which describes instances of serious physical or psychological harm to civilians that usually involve unlawful savageness. No agreement exists regarding the incidence of wrongful use of force by police, which has received little systematic research.

Q 422. When can police use deadly force?

A Police not only have the power to deprive individuals of liberty by invoking the authority of the state; they also are authorized to use force—even deadly force—in limited circumstances. Deadly force is force that is likely to have lethal consequences for the suspect.

Traditionally, police could use deadly force if a suspect posed a serious threat to an officer or a citizen, or to stop a fleeing felon. The U.S. Supreme Court narrowed that common-law rule in *Tennessee v. Garner* (1985). In *Garner,* a Memphis police officer shot and killed an unarmed young man who fled over a fence at night in the backyard of a house he was suspected of burglarizing. The Court held unconstitutional a Tennessee statute that authorized police to use all necessary means, including deadly force, to effect an arrest of a criminal suspect who flees or forcibly resists. The Court said that police may not use deadly force unless an officer has probable cause to believe the suspect poses a significant threat of death or serious physical injury to the officer or others. In this case the officer could not reasonably have believed that the suspect, who was young, slight, and unarmed, posed any threat.

See 341 How many felons are killed each year by law enforcement officers acting in the line of duty? 435 What is a SWAT team?

Q 423. Who said, "There is more law in the end of a policeman's nightstick than in a decision of the Supreme Court"?

A Alexander S. Williams, a police officer in New York City in the 1870s who became famous for invoking the "gospel of the nightstick," made that statement. Williams's furious clubbing of thugs, sometimes without provocation, resulted in charges being preferred against him some eighteen times. Each time the police commission acquitted Williams.

Q 424. Do Americans think police are honest?

A A 1997 national poll by the Gallup Organization, Inc., determined that Americans rate the honesty and ethical standards of police as follows:

- Very high, 10 percent
- High, 39 percent
- Average, 40 percent
- Low, 8 percent
- Very low, 2 percent

Occupations that Americans rank higher than police for honesty are, in order, pharmacists, clergy, medical doctors, college teachers, and dentists. Sixteen percent of Americans rank pharmacists as very high in terms of ethical behavior and honesty.

Police rank significantly higher than lawyers, members of Congress, newspaper reporters, and car salespeople. In the Gallup poll, only 2 percent of Americans ranked car salespeople as very highly honest.

Q 425. What is police corruption?

A No universal definition exists for police corruption, but most definitions include two important elements: the misuse of the officer's authority or official position and the receipt or expected receipt of material rewards or personal gain. Police corruption exerts a toll on its immediate victims, who pay kickbacks and bribes for police protection and to avoid harassment. More importantly, it undermines society's faith in the police and the criminal justice system.

The Mollen Commission, which investigated police corruption in New York City in 1994, concluded that most police officers who engage in corrupt acts do so for profit. However, the commission said, corrupt officers sometimes want to show that they are in control of crime-ridden streets or feel that vigilante justice is the way to punish criminals who might otherwise go unpunished.

A 1998 General Accounting Office report said that the following practices help prevent police corruption:

- Making a commitment to integrity from the top to the bottom of the police department
- Changing a police culture that supports or ignores corruption
- Requiring command accountability (in other words, requiring a commitment to control corruption throughout the department, especially by field commanders)
- Raising the age and educational requirements and implementing or improving integrity training for recruits in the police academy
- Implementing or improving integrity training and accountability measures for career officers
- Establishing an independent monitor to oversee the police department and its internal affairs unit
- Implementing community policing

Q 426. Do a few bad apples spoil the barrel?

A Research suggests that a small percentage of police officers are responsible for a high percentage of complaints. The behavior of a few officers can besmirch a department's reputation. A commission investigating the Los Angeles Police Department (LAPD) in the wake of the beating of black motorist Rodney G. King found that 10 percent of LAPD officers accounted for 28 percent of the complaints of excessive force or improper tactics from 1986 to 1990. Out of the 8,000-member force, citizen complaints of excessive force were filed against 1,800 officers. More than 1,400 officers had only one or two complaints against them; 183 officers had four or more allegations; and 44 officers, singled out by the commission as problem officers, had six or more complaints against them.

Q 427. What is the blue wall of silence?

A The *blue wall of silence* refers to a value held by some police officers that loyalty to fellow police officers should be the preeminent concern. Under this unofficial code, police do not blow the whistle on officers who make serious mistakes on the job or who violate the law by, for example, accepting bribes or using excessive force. The blue wall of silence may stem from perceptions among police officers that the public is hostile to them, that police are social outsiders, and that police administrators cannot be trusted.

A 1998 General Accounting Office study concluded that one commonly identified factor associated with drug-related corruption is a police culture characterized by a code of silence, unquestioned loyalty to other officers, and cynicism about the criminal justice system. "Such characteristics were found not only to promote police corruption, but [also] to impede efforts to control and detect it," stated the report.

In 1970 Frank Serpico, an undercover officer for the New York City Police Department (NYPD), cracked the NYPD's code of silence and leaked information to the *New York Times* about police divisions being paid off by gamblers and other criminals. Serpico then testified before a police investigatory committee. He was shot in the face during a drug bust in 1971 and resigned about eight months later. Some journalists and police officers suggested that crooked officers had set up Serpico to be shot.

More recently, in 1997 Haitian immigrant Abner Louima was brutally attacked by police officers with a broomstick in the bathroom of the Seventieth Precinct station house. Many officers initially failed to report the incident, though several ended up testifying for the prosecution in a subsequent criminal prosecution that led to the conviction of one officer for assisting in the attack.

See 390 What police beating incident exposed the shortcomings of military-style policing?

Q 428. Who polices the police?

A Every law enforcement agency has an internal mechanism to receive and investigate complaints and to recommend disciplinary action for officers who break the rules. The chief executive of the law enforcement agency typically makes the final decision.

Officers who commit crimes also may be prosecuted in criminal court or sued for civil rights violations in civil court. The employing jurisdiction generally is obligated to indemnify the officer for any money damages awarded in a civil suit, with the exception of punitive damages.

In recent decades concern over persistent patterns of police brutality in major cities has prompted the formation of citizen review boards or agencies to oversee complaints against police. Civilian review is based on the premise that involving citizens in police oversight will result in a more independent and thorough review of complaints. Most large police departments now have some mechanism for civilian oversight of police complaints.

Civilian review boards follow no single model. Some review boards have authority only to review the results of police internal investigations. Other review boards have independent investigatory power, including subpoena power and the authority to hold public hearings.

Increasingly, minority and civil rights groups are pressing jurisdictions to form independent review boards. Police unions and associations generally oppose independent civilian review boards on the grounds that civilians do not understand the pressures of police work and may engage in witch-hunt investigations.

The concept of citizen review arose after racial riots in the 1960s highlighted the need to enhance police accountability to the public. The National Advisory Committee on Civil Disorders in 1968 concluded that police abuse and inadequate complaint procedures were the cause of racial riots throughout the nation in the 1960s. These same factors were deemed to be a cause of the racial riots in Los Angeles following the 1991 beating of Rodney G. King.

When state or local law police departments fail to police themselves, the federal government may intervene. The U.S. Department of Justice's Civil Rights Division can investigate law enforcement agencies that demonstrate a pattern or practice of abuse and brutality. Investigations by the Civil Rights Division in recent years have prompted cities in Pennsylvania and Ohio to agree to implement reforms, such as improved use-of-force training and stronger reporting mechanisms.

Q 429. Aside from a court of law, what authority can overturn a police officer's dismissal?

A Civil service regulations and union contracts restrict the ability of both police chiefs and civilian review boards to impose sanctions against officers for improper conduct. A common model for dispute resolution in police union contracts is the arbitration of grievances by an outside arbitrator. If an officer is dissatisfied with a proposed disciplinary sanction, he or she files a grievance. The employing agency and the police union agree on the appointment of an outside arbitrator who, typically, has the final word on the matter. It is not uncommon for the arbitrator to alter or reverse the disciplinary action. In 1995, for example, two Oregon state police troopers were discharged after an incident in which they had sex with a woman in their police car while on duty. An arbitrator subsequently reversed those disciplinary actions and the officers were reinstated.

Q 430. What percentage of complaints are upheld against police?

A Research indicates that, on average, 10 percent or fewer of complaints of police misconduct are upheld by examination of the facts. One reason frequently cited for this low percentage is that many complainants face criminal charges themselves or have other problems that diminish their credibility. Rarely are independent witnesses available. Also, some jurisdictions require a high standard of proof to uphold a complaint.

Human Rights Watch, an international human rights group based in New York, examined fourteen major U.S. cities from 1995 to 1998 and concluded that police brutality was "persistent in all of these cities; that systems to deal with abuse have had similar failings in all the cities; and that, in each city examined, complainants face enormous barriers in seeking administrative punishment or criminal prosecution of officers who have committed human rights violations." The agency added that police officers who commit human rights violations are "a small minority who taint entire police departments but are protected, routinely, by the silence of their fellow officers and by flawed systems of reporting, oversight, and accountability."

Even a small number of complaints can be very costly. New York City paid out a record $40 million in fiscal 1998 to resolve 739 legal claims and lawsuits that accused its police officers of brutality. In one case, the city paid $2.75 million to an electrician who said that, while walking to work in Greenwich Village on his birthday in 1996, he was beaten by police officers because he fit the profile of a black suspect they were seeking. As with most claims, the electrician's claim was settled by the city without a direct admission of guilt on the part of the police officers.

Q **431. What is the origin of the term *paddy wagon*?**

A In the nineteenth century and up until the 1930s, when use of the automobile became more widespread among police—prisoners were transported in horse-drawn covered wagons called *paddy wagons*. One theory about the origin of the term holds that it refers to the padding that was placed on the walls and floor of the wagons to prevent the prisoners from injuring themselves. Another theory has it that the term was a disparaging reference to the prevalence of Irish police officers in New York City and New England.

Q **432. What rules of the road must police observe?**

A Police who are answering a call to provide assistance as soon as possible in a potential emergency typically are permitted by state statute to disregard traffic laws. However, police are required to use emergency equipment (lights and siren) and to drive with due regard for the safety of all persons.

Q **433. What is a high-speed pursuit?**

A The International Association of Chiefs of Police (IACP) has defined a high-speed pursuit as an active attempt by an officer in an authorized emergency vehicle to apprehend fleeing suspects who are attempting to avoid apprehension through evasive tactics.

Almost every local police department has a written policy on pursuit driving. Most departments restrict pursuits according to specific criteria, such as offense or speed. About one-fourth of departments leave it up to the officers' discretion. Six percent of departments discourage all vehicle pursuits. The IACP issued a model policy in 1990 that said officers should pursue only when the offense would warrant an arrest.

High-speed pursuits increasingly are viewed as a potential form of deadly force. Research shows that more than one-quarter of such pursuits end in accidents and one in every 58.3 such pursuits ends in a fatality. Also, high-speed pursuits are more likely to be triggered by a traffic offense than by a criminal action. Finally, high-speed pursuits tend to generate higher levels of excessive force by police. For example, anxious officers have pulled suspects out of car windows to make an arrest.

Innocent third parties who have been injured in police pursuits have sued, sometimes winning considerable amounts in damages, which has prompted many law enforcement agencies to restrict high-speed pursuits. Some states have passed laws requiring that law enforcement agencies investigate and report on each pursuit.

However, in *County of Sacramento v. Lewis* (1998), the U.S. Supreme Court declined to prohibit high-speed pursuits. That case involved a pursuit by a county sheriff's deputy of an eighteen-year-old motorcycle rider and his sixteen-year-old passenger after they failed to stop as the sheriff requested. The motorcycle rider's bike tipped over and the sheriff slammed on his brakes but was unable to stop. The sheriff's car struck and killed the passenger. The Court rejected claims that the sheriff had acted with deliberate or reckless indifference by engaging in the chase, noting that the police were not to blame for the motorcycle driver's lawless behavior and that the police did not intend to harm the passenger.

Controversy over high-speed pursuits has spurred research into new technologies aimed at slowing down a vehicle while allowing the driver to remain in control. One such device consists of a strip containing hollow metal spikes that puncture and slowly release air from the tires of a fleeing car.

Q 434. What types of specialized units are operated by local police?

A Many local law enforcement agencies—and virtually every large department—have special units that respond to specific community concerns within their jurisdictions. These special units may include the following:

- Animal control units
- Aviation and marine units that assist in search-and-rescue missions
- Bomb disposal units
- Civil defense units
- Drug units
- Emergency services units that offer medical care
- Special tactical units or SWAT teams

A 1997 survey found that more than 75 percent of large police and sheriffs' departments offered drug education programs in schools. Other units, and the percentage of departments that operate them, are:

- Juvenile delinquency, 61 percent
- Gangs, 53 percent
- Child abuse, 49 percent
- Domestic violence, 43 percent
- Missing children, 25 percent
- Youth outreach, about 25 percent

Q **435. What is a SWAT team?**

A Most medium- to large-sized law enforcement agencies as well as most large correctional systems have established Special Weapons and Tactics (SWAT) units to handle potentially dangerous situations, such as barricaded suspects or hostage situations.

Members of SWAT teams, sometimes called special tactics or emergency response teams, receive advanced training in tactics and in the use of sophisticated law enforcement equipment, including semiautomatic machine guns, sniper gear, and even tanks. Some of this equipment is passed down from the military. Instead of the standard police uniform, many SWAT teams wear black, paramilitary-style clothing.

The first SWAT teams were established in Philadelphia and Los Angeles in the 1960s to address riots and incidents of urban unrest. The responsibilities of SWAT teams have broadened in recent years. These units now also serve search warrants in cases of suspected drug sales or possession, sometimes by launching a "home invasion" when the occupants are known to be armed and dangerous.

Instead of using regular agents from the Immigration and Naturalization Service, U.S. Attorney General Janet Reno deployed a SWAT team to seize Cuban boy Elian Gonzalez from the home of his American relatives in Miami's Little Havana district on April 22, 2000. Five months earlier the five-year-old boy had been rescued at sea after his mother and other Cuban refugees drowned while attempting to reach America. Elian's American relatives had sought to keep the boy in the United States, but his Cuban father, asserting parental custody rights, wanted the boy returned to Cuba. After months of legal wrangling and stalled negotiations, the attorney general authorized the early-morning raid. In three minutes, six officers dressed in green military garb and carrying assault rifles broke down the door to the home, snatched Elian from the arms of a man hiding in a closet, and whisked the boy into a waiting van. Reunited with his father, the boy eventually returned to Cuba.

See 422 When can police use deadly force?

V
CORRECTIONS

IN GENERAL

Q 436. What is the United States correctional system?

A The United States correctional system has three major components: prisons, jails, and supervised release (probation, parole, and community corrections). These components have authority over a correctional population of almost 6 million people, an increase of about 35 percent over 1990 levels. The U.S. incarceration rate has more than tripled in twenty-five years to 690 persons per 100,000 Americans, and the number is growing. The population in America's prisons and jails surpassed 2 million in 1999.

As with other areas of criminal justice, state and local governments bear the heaviest burden for corrections. About 90 percent of the total U.S. inmate population falls under the authority of state and local correctional systems, and 10 percent falls under the authority of the federal correctional system. There are 125 federal prisons, 1,373 state prisons, and approximately 3,300 jails operating in the United States.

Defendants who are convicted of serious crimes are sent to state or federal prisons. At the end of 1999, state prisons held 1,231,475 inmates and federal prisons held 135,246 inmates. Overall the nation's prison population grew by 3.4 percent in 1999, compared to an average annual increase of 6.5 percent during the 1990s. This represents the lowest rate of increase since 1979. Drug offenders accounted for about 60 percent of all federal prison inmates.

Defendants who are sentenced to less than one year of incarceration or who are awaiting trial are sent to jail. A jail is a confinement facility, usually run by county or local government, that holds inmates beyond arraignment, usually for more than forty-eight hours. At the end of 1999 local jails held 605,943 offenders, an increase of 2.3 percent from 1998.

Suspects awaiting arraignment typically are held in a police lockup or a temporary holding facility that is operated by a law enforcement agency. Twenty-six percent of police departments in 1993 operated lockups that were separate from their local jails. The average capacity of such lockups was ten inmates.

Through probation or parole, twice as many adults serve sentences in the community as go to prison. Almost 4.5 million adult men and women were being supervised on probation or parole at the end of 1999.

Probation is a criminal sanction in which the offender is allowed to remain in the community under the supervision of a probation officer. The offender typically must abide by certain conditional requirements, such as holding down a job or refraining from drinking. A total of 3,773,600 people were on probation at the end of 1999, up from 3,417,613 in 1999. Probation traditionally was operated by the judicial branch of a jurisdiction, but in recent years some states have formed a centralized statewide administrative body to handle probation services.

Parole is a period of supervision by a parole agency that occurs after a criminal is released from custody but before the expiration of his or her sentence. If the terms of parole are violated, parole is subject to revocation and the offender may be ordered back to prison. At the end of 1999 a total of 712,700 offenders were on parole, up from 704,964 in 1998. Parole has been abolished in the federal system and is being phased out pursuant to the Sentencing Reform Act of 1984. However, parole is still used by many states.

State prison systems typically are run by the executive branch of the state government, whereas jails are operated by the county or municipality. Six states—Alaska, Connecticut, Delaware, Hawaii, Rhode Island, and Vermont—operate a combined prison and jail system.

See 531 What is the most commonly applied criminal sanction? 534 What is parole? Also see Figure 5.1 Corrections and Figure 5.2 Federal Prison Facilities.

Q 437. What are the classic goals of corrections?

A The classic goals of corrections are:

- *Retribution:* The moral culpability of criminals justifies their punishment. Offenders deserve to get their just desserts. Following the maxim, "an eye for an eye, a tooth for a tooth," an offender's punishment is proportional to the harm inflicted on the offender's victims and society.
- *Deterrence:* Punishment is meant to discourage future offenses by the individual who is being punished and to serve as an example, deterring others in the community from committing similar crimes. This theory relies on the premise that a criminal will not commit a criminal act if punishment is certain, swift, and severe.

Figure 5-1 Corrections

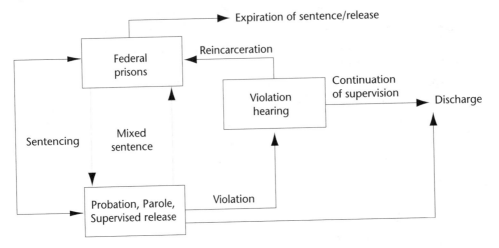

Source: Department of Justice, Bureau of Justice Statistics Publication NCJ180258, *Compendium of Federal Justice Statistics, 1998* (Washington, D.C.: U.S. Government Printing Office, May 2000), 84.

- *Rehabilitation:* Incarceration or supervised probation give society the opportunity to redirect a criminal's conduct. Offenders are cured, or at least treated. A judge may sentence the offender to an indeterminate sentence with a minimum and maximum term, thus encouraging the offender to participate in a treatment program and earn early release. The National Prison Association, the predecessor of the American Correctional Association, embraced the concept of rehabilitation in 1870. The association declared that prisons should be operated on a philosophy of inmate change, with reformation rewarded by release.

- *Incapacitation:* Punishment deprives the criminal of the opportunity to commit another crime. This goal is particularly evident today with respect to repeat violent offenders and career criminals. Three-strikes laws, in particular, reflect the attitude that society should "lock 'em up and throw away the key."

The goals of a correctional institution greatly influence how the institution is managed. For example, Missouri overhauled its approach to prison management in the early 1990s when it adopted the "parallel universe offender management system." This system is based on the notion that life in prison should resemble life outside prison and emphasizes inmate decision-making and accountability. Inmates are

Figure 5-2 Federal Prison Facilities

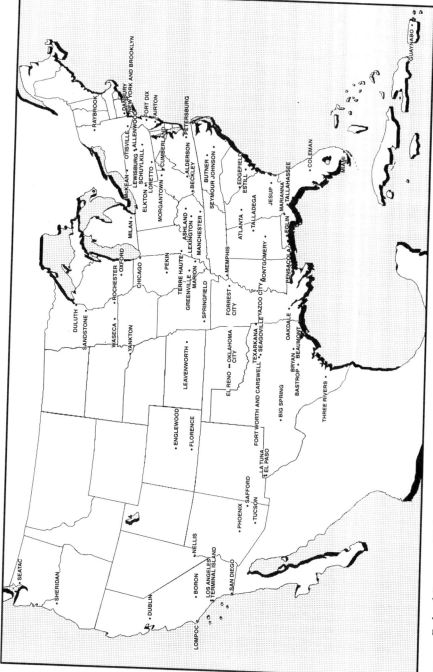

Source: Federal Bureau of Prisons, U.S. Department of Justice, *State of the Bureau, 1998* (Lompoc, Calif.: Federal Prison Industries, Inc., 1999).

Note: The Bureau of Prisoners directory, with addresses and other contact information for each facility, is available at www.bop.gov.

encouraged to engage in work and other activities that parallel productive work in free society, and they are offered the opportunity to improve their status by adhering to the prison's rules and regulations. Missouri corrections officials say that the program, which has won national recognition, reduced recidivism from 33 percent in 1993 to 21 percent in 1999.

Q 438. What are the goals of the American correctional system today?

A In 1999 the mission statement of the Federal Bureau of Prisons read as follows: "The Federal Bureau of Prisons protects society by confining offenders in the controlled environments of prisons and community-based facilities that are safe, humane, cost-efficient, and appropriately secure, and that provide work and other self-improvement opportunities to assist offenders in becoming law-abiding citizens."

This mission reflects the American correctional system's historical emphasis on rehabilitation and incorporates its more recent emphasis on deterrence and incapacitation.

The concept of rehabilitation was embraced in 1870 by the National Prison Association, the predecessor of the American Correctional Association. The association declared that prisons should be operated on a philosophy of inmate change, with reformation rewarded by release.

When crime rates began to spiral upward in the 1970s, public attitudes took a marked shift away from the philosophy of rehabilitation toward the concepts of deterrence, incapacitation, and—with the rise of the victims' rights movement—retribution. One researcher, Robert Martinson, studied the most effective means of rehabilitating prison inmates and concluded in 1974 that "with few and isolated exceptions, rehabilitative efforts have had no appreciable effect on recidivism." Then new research came to light showing a link between incapacitation and less crime. In 1982 a study published by the RAND Corporation projected that doubling imprisonment time for robbery would yield a 20 percent reduction in robberies.

See 448 What entities are responsible for confining persons convicted of federal crimes?

Q 439. What do Americans view as the most important goal of prison?

A The public still considers rehabilitation to be the most important goal of prison, according to a 1996 national opinion survey conducted by the College of Criminal Justice's Survey Research Program at Sam Houston State University. The survey asked, "Once people who commit crimes *are in prison*, which of the following do you think should be *the most important goal of prison?*" Respondents rated the three primary goals of prison as follows:

• Rehabilitation, 48.4 percent
• Crime prevention and deterrence, 33.1 percent
• Punishment, 14.6 percent.

Q 440. Does the United States incarcerate more of its people than other countries do?

A Yes. America's incarceration rate is estimated to be five to ten times the rates of countries in Western Europe and six times the rate in Canada. According to the Sentencing Project, a Washington, D.C.–based advocacy group that supports alternative sentencing and criminal justice reform, only Russia imprisons a larger proportion of its people.

Following are the countries that had the highest rates of prison and jail incarceration per 100,000 population in 1995, as ranked by the Sentencing Project:

Country	Number of Persons Jailed (per 100,000 population)
Russia	690
United States	600
Belarus	505
Ukraine	390
Latvia	375
Lithuania	360
Singapore	287
Moldova	275
Estonia	270
South Africa	265

The rate of incarceration in Japan was 37 prisoners per 100,000 population, and the rate for India was 24 prisoners per 100,000 population.

Q 441. How has the U.S. correctional population changed over time?

A America's correctional population has more than tripled since 1980. About 3.1 percent of the entire adult U.S. population, or one in every thirty-two adults, was either on probation, on parole, or incarcerated in jails or prisons in 1999. Following are the total numbers of people who were under some form of correctional supervision each year between 1980 and 1999:

Year	Correctional Population	Year	Correctional Population
1980	1,840,400	1990	4,348,000
1981	2,006,600	1991	4,535,600
1982	2,192,600	1992	4,762,600
1983	2,475,100	1993	4,944,000
1984	2,689,200	1994	5,141,300
1985	3,011,500	1995	5,335,100
1986	3,239,400	1996	5,523,000
1987	3,459,600	1997	5,726,200
1988	3,714,100	1998	5,890,300
1989	4,055,600	1999	6,458,964

Q 442. What are the chances that an American born in 1999 will be incarcerated at some point in his or her life?

A For any person born in America in 1999, the chance of living some part of his or her life in a correctional facility is one in twenty. For an African American, the chance is one in four. At the end of 1999, 1 in every 137 residents in the United States and its territories were incarcerated in prison or jail.

Q 443. With declining rates of crime, why hasn't America experienced a prison peace dividend?

A The crime rate has been declining since the early 1990s, but America's prison population continues to grow. Almost 60,000 new inmates entered the system in the twelve-month period ending June 1999. This number translates to about 1,122 more inmates every week.

A major reason the prison population has grown during a period of declining crime is the sharp increase in the number of offenders who were returned to prison for parole violations. These offenders either had committed new crimes or violated conditions of their parole, for example by failing to report to a parole officer or by failing a drug test. Of the 565,000 offenders who were admitted to state prisons in 1998, almost 207,000 were returning to prison after violating the conditions of their parole. The number of offenders who were returned to prison for parole violations increased by 54 percent during the 1990s.

Some experts postulate that an inverse relationship exists between the crime rate and the prison population; that is, incarcerating criminals prevents them from committing new crimes. Other experts claim that the growth in the prison population reflects current American policies. For example, unlike many countries, America chooses to incarcerate drug offenders rather than to legalize drugs, offer rehabilitation, or use alternative sanctions. Many jurisdictions have passed mandatory sentencing laws that require judges to put drug offenders in jail.

Another explanation for the anomaly between the rising prison population at a time of declining crime pertains to how the crime rate is measured. The Federal Bureau of Investigation's Crime Index measures eight categories of serious violent and property crimes, the rates of which have fallen in recent years. However, the Crime Index does not measure drug crimes, which have risen in recent years, adding tens of thousands of prisoners to the inmate population.

More than 400,000 people are locked up in the United States for drug-related crimes. A third of these inmates are imprisoned simply for possessing an illicit drug. Drug offenders make up nearly 60 percent of all federal prisoners and 22 percent of state and local inmates.

See 45 How has the rate of serious crime changed over time?

444. How did the colonists punish criminals?

Most colonial American towns were too small to justify the construction of a jail. Colonists relied on capital punishment for serious crimes and a range of quick corporal punishments or prolonged humiliations for lesser crimes.

Calvinist doctrine held that man was naturally sinful and evil, and therefore the focus of criminal punishment was on deterrence rather than rehabilitation. Most defendants convicted of noncapital crimes faced corporal punishments, such as whipping, branding, maiming, or spending time in the pillory or on the ducking stool. According to historian Adam Jay Hirsch, the ducking stool was a chair with restraints that was connected to a pulley and used to repeatedly plunge into a body of water offenders such as slanderers, brawlers, and women of "light carriage."

The most egregious offenders faced branding or mutilation, thus "fixing on [the offenders] an indelible 'mark of infamy' to warn the community of their criminal propensities." In Williamsburg, Virginia, thieves were nailed by the ear to the wooden pillory for a period of time that depended on the seriousness of their offense. When the time was up, authorities ripped the offenders from the pillory without first removing the nails. Offenders were thus *earmarked* as criminals for the rest of their lives.

The public frequently participated in the administration of punishments by throwing old eggs, decomposed vegetables, dead animals, and other objects at the unfortunate offenders.

See 20 What were the first crimes established by the U.S. Congress? 316 How were laws enforced in colonial America? 539 Did the American colonists execute prisoners?

Q **445. Where was America's first prison?**

A Before the Revolutionary War, most states and territories did not have a distinct correctional system. Instead, they relied on local for-profit jails. Housed in one large room, prisoners often were farmed out as convict labor. However, as the prisoner population grew, the need for a more sophisticated correctional system became apparent. One anecdote recounts the extraordinary security measures necessary to hold an inmate mass at a Philadelphia jail. The head jailer instructed his deputy to stand beside the preacher with a lighted torch and a loaded cannon aimed at the convicts. The deputy was to fire should any man move. Eventually reformers adopted a radical solution to increase security: building prisons in which inmates could be incarcerated in private cells.

In 1790 the Quakers were instrumental in passing a law in Pennsylvania that established America's first true prison system. The law required the separation of inmates by gender and by class of offense. Convicts, debtors, and hardened criminals were isolated from each other and from other criminals. The law also specified that "solitary confinement to hard labour and a total abstinence from spirituous liquors will prove the most effectual means of reforming these unhappy creatures."

The plan called for expanding an existing jail in Philadelphia, where male and female prisoners had been locked into a central room with straw on the floor to sleep on. The new jail was bounded by an outer enclosure that included separate exercise areas for convicts and debtors. A second building surrounded by a garden contained sixteen solitary cells. The 8-by-6-foot cells confined the most hardened criminals. Each cell had an outer wooden door, an inner iron door, and one window that was kept blinded and locked. Less-hardened convicts were housed together at night in eight 18-by-20-foot *night rooms* in three buildings. Debtors stayed in a workhouse located off the main enclosure.

Despite its harshness, the Walnut Street Jail marked a major advance for inmates. On entry to the jail each inmate received a uniform and a meal plan. The Walnut Street Jail became the model for all the prisons created in America during the next thirty years. These early American prisons were designed to deter and punish criminals but also to make punishment more humane.

Q **446. How did the development of steel affect the course of penology?**

A Before the nineteenth century most jails in America were built of stone and were designed to hold prisoners temporarily, as they awaited trial or execution. The development of light iron and steel permitted the construction of multi-tiered cells. The expanded capacity offered by multi-tiered cells opened the door to long-term confinement of prisoners.

Q **447. What were the results of early prison experiments with solitary confinement?**

A From 1821 to 1823 New York conducted an infamous experiment on solitary confinement at Auburn Prison. Eighty prisoners were placed in solitary confinement and were not allowed to work like other inmates in common shops. The isolated prisoners became severely depressed, and many suffered more severe mental illness. Five of these prisoners died in a single year, including one who became insane. In 1823 New York's governor pardoned twenty-six of the eighty inmates who had participated in the experiment. The inmates who were not pardoned were permitted to resume leaving their cells during the day to work in common shops.

Auburn prison authorities concluded that solitary confinement without labor causes mental breakdown and insanity. The prison subsequently adopted a new system in which inmates slept alone at night but worked together during the day, subject to a strictly enforced rule of silence. The Auburn system became known as the *congregate system.* Eventually every state adopted the congregate model, in part because the convict labor generated income that helped pay for the prison.

A version of solitary confinement called the *separate system* was first practiced in the United States at Eastern State Penitentiary in Philadelphia. This prison opened in 1829. Under the separate system prisoners remained alone in their cells unless they requested work or a Bible to read. Illiterate prisoners were taught to read. Those who chose work labored alone or in an adjoining yard, weaving, woodworking, or shoemaking. They saw no one except the officers of the institution and an occasional visitor. Overcrowding forced Pennsylvania to abandon the separate system in the 1860s.

Solitary confinement is used today in America's highest security prisons to control the most violent and disruptive prisoners. These prisoners are confined in 8-by-10-foot cells for up to twenty-three hours a day and have little or no contact with other inmates during the remaining time. Despite numerous lawsuits alleging that such confinement causes extreme emotional distress, courts have declined to hold that solitary confinement violates the Eighth Amendment ban on cruel and unusual punishment.

Q **448. What entities are responsible for confining persons convicted of federal crimes?**

A The Federal Bureau of Prisons (BOP), a division of the U.S. Department of Justice, has primary responsibility for confining persons convicted of federal crimes and federal prisoners who are awaiting trial or sentencing.

The BOP operates ninety-four correctional facilities throughout the nation and is responsible for the confinement of federal offenders in contract facilities, including community-based programs, detention centers, juvenile facilities, state prisons, and local jails. The BOP also manages the federal witness protection program.

In January 2000 more than 122,000 of the nation's 135,000 federal prisoners were housed in facilities operated by the BOP. An additional 13,000 prisoners were housed in other prisons under contract with the federal government, including community corrections centers and detention facilities.

The BOP coordinates a wide range of inmate programs, including religious, psychological, counseling, drug treatment, and special-needs programs.

Two other federal agencies—the U.S. Marshals Service (USMS) and the Immigration and Naturalization Service (INS)—confine individuals in special circumstances. In 1998 the USMS maintained custody of about 31,000 prisoners, most of whom were awaiting trial or sentencing in federal courts. These prisoners were housed in about 1,000 state, local, and federal detention facilities nationwide. INS facilities contain bed-space for up to 16,000 aliens who are being detained while awaiting trial, sentencing, immigration hearings, or deportation.

Q **449. What are the security levels of prisons?**

A Facilities operated by the Federal Bureau of Prisons have five security levels, which are determined by whether the facility has such features as fences, gun towers, and dormitory or cell housing. Security levels vary among the states: a maximum-security facility in one state may be a medium-security facility in another. The BOP security levels are:

- *Minimum security.* Also called federal prison camps, these institutions have dormitory housing and no fencing and often are adjacent to larger institutions or military bases, where inmates fulfill labor needs. The staff-to-inmate ratio is lowest in these institutions.
- *Low security.* These institutions have double-fenced perimeters and mostly dormitory housing.

- *Medium security.* These institutions have strengthened perimeters (often double fences with electronic detection systems) and cell-type housing.
- *High security.* Also called U.S. Penitentiaries, these institutions have highly secure perimeters (walls or reinforced fences), multiple- and single-occupant cell housing, and the highest staff-to-inmate ratios.
- *Administrative security.* These institutions have special missions, such as the detention of noncitizen or pretrial offenders, the treatment of inmates with serious or chronic medical problems, or the confinement of extremely dangerous, violent, or escape-prone inmates.

About one-third of all federal prisoners are placed in low-security facilities. Following are the security levels and percentages of the total inmate population held in federal prisons as of November 30, 1999:

- Low, 34 percent
- Minimum, 25.1 percent
- Medium, 22 percent
- High, 11.7 percent
- Security level not assigned, 7.2 percent

Q 450. How do correctional officials decide where to place inmates?

A Classification systems are considered the key to effectively managing a correctional institution and maximizing the use of available resources.

Inmates are placed in a facility according to the security level that is appropriate for the health and safety of the inmate and that protects fellow inmates. Inmates have no right to demand a particular classification. Prison officials determine whether an inmate has special needs that may require special placement (for example, a juvenile who is placed in an adult institution, elderly inmates, or inmates with illnesses like AIDS). Federal law requires that juveniles be separated by sight and sound from adults. The Federal Bureau of Prisons also tries to incarcerate criminals within 500 miles of their homes so that inmates can maintain relationships with their families.

The following types of federal prisoners typically require increased security:

- Inmates who have a history of disruption or affiliation with disruptive groups
- Inmates who have committed extremely severe or violent crimes
- Sex offenders
- Inmates who have threatened a government official
- Deportable aliens

- Inmates sentenced to very long sentences for commission of severe crimes
- Inmates who have a history of escape
- Inmates who have a history of causing or participating in prison disturbances

In many correctional institutions, inmates who begin their term at a high security classification may work toward a lower level within the institution. Conversely, prisoners who consistently misbehave may find their security levels upgraded.

Inmate classification first was implemented at Elmira Reformatory at Elmira, New York, in the late 1800s. Superintendent Zebulon Brockway developed a mark system involving inmate classification, indeterminate sentences, and parole. An inmate could earn marks and be eligible for early release or parole by working hard, completing school assignments, and causing no trouble.

Q 451. How are prisons designed?

A Traditionally prisons were built in a radial design, like the spokes on a bicycle wheel, or in a telephone-pole design, which required inmates to walk down long central corridors crossed by other corridors that led to dining, recreation, and educational facilities. Many prisons today are built in courtyard and campus styles. In the courtyard design, functional units (housing, dining hall, educational facilities, and so forth) are contained in separate buildings on four sides of an open square. In the campus design, which is most often used for low- and medium-security facilities, smaller housing units are located amid other functional units of the prison. Prisons increasingly are being built to reduce the mutual exposure of inmates and staff to reduce the risk to staff and improve security. For example, new maximum-security disciplinary units built in New York state in 1997–1998 included a shower in each cell, which eliminates the need for guards to escort inmates to communal showers.

Q 452. What are supermax prisons?

A Dangerous and disruptive prison inmates historically were either dispersed to various prisons or consolidated at a maximum-security facility. In the early 1990s, when two guards were killed in separate incidents on the same day, prison officials concluded that extreme-problem inmates could not be managed in the same manner as typical penitentiary inmates.

The federal government and thirty-eight states have built supermax prisons to hold the most violent, disruptive, or escape-prone offenders. Between 8 percent and 10 percent of all prisoners currently are housed at supermax prisons. By concentrating the "worst of the worst" in a single location, prison administrators can make more efficient use of resources; increase staff, inmate, and public safety; and allow inmates in other institutions to live with greater freedom of movement and access to educational, vocational, and other correctional programs.

A supermax facility—unlike a segregation unit in a maximum-security penitentiary—is a complete institution, with unique security elements and programs. Handcuffed whenever they come in contact with staff, inmates eat and participate in recreational activities alone or in small, carefully screened and supervised groups. Inmates are confined in their cells for larger portions of the day. Individually based programs include self-study courses and in-cell television viewing.

If inmates demonstrate responsible behavior, they can move incrementally to less restrictive housing units that permit more privileges and more interactions with staff and other inmates. Most inmates return to open-population prisons in about three years. The vast majority of these inmates never return to the supermax facility.

A 1998 study of about 400 inmates in a federal supermax facility in Florence, Colorado, found that 20 percent had murdered or attempted to murder a fellow inmate, 18 percent had assaulted another inmate with a weapon, 16 percent had seriously assaulted a staff member, 10 percent made a serious escape attempt, and 5 percent were involved in rioting. About 6 percent of the inmates were sent to the Florence facility by states because they were involved in the murder of state prison correctional staff or they were too disruptive or dangerous for state officials to house safely. Only about 3 percent of the inmates were sent directly to the facility by a court.

When unrest occurs in other prisons, authorities typically institute a lockdown, confining inmates to their cells and suspending basic services. In some systems difficult prisoners remain confined in a section of a prison, called a *control unit*, that operates in permanent lockdown.

453. What was the deadliest prison riot in U.S. history?

On September 9, 1971, more than 1,200 inmates staged an uprising at the Attica Correctional Facility, a state prison outside Buffalo, New York. Prisoners armed with pipes, razors, and baseball bats took control of a cellblock. Within thirty minutes the inmates controlled most of the prison and were holding forty-one guards and prison employees hostage.

The prisoners demanded coverage under the state minimum-wage laws, an end to censorship of reading materials, no reprisals for the revolt, transfer out of confinement to "a nonimperialist country," and federal takeover of the prison.

Four days of rioting ended when more than 1,400 state troopers, sheriff's deputies, and prison guards, acting on orders from then-Governor Nelson Rockefeller, stormed the facility with tear gas and gunfire, leaving thirty-two inmates and eleven guards dead. It turned out that most of the guards died from friendly fire. Police gunfire killed twenty-nine inmates and ten hostages; inmates killed three fellow prisoners and one hostage.

The inmate revolt subsequently was blamed on prison overcrowding, low morale, and idleness.

Inmates filed a federal lawsuit claiming that they suffered violent reprisals from prison officials following the riots. In 1992 a jury ruled that a deputy warden at Attica during the riot allowed police and guards to beat and torture inmates. In August 2000 a federal judge approved a settlement that awarded 500 inmates a total of $8 million as compensation for the abuse they suffered at the hands of state police. The individual awards ranged from $6,500 to $125,000.

Q **454. What are community corrections?**

A Community corrections programs represent an alternative to full-time incarceration in a prison or jail. Community corrections programs include probation, halfway houses, and drug-treatment programs. Offenders in such programs are allowed to remain in the community but are subject to supervision and limited periods of incarceration. Most inmates serve the last few months of their sentences in a community corrections center, or halfway house.

Community corrections encourages the reintegration of the offender back into the community. The President's Commission on Law Enforcement and Administration of Justice stated in 1967 that the "task of corrections . . . includes building or rebuilding social ties, obtaining employment and education, securing in the larger senses a place for the offender in the routine functioning of society."

States began to provide local communities with funding to create community corrections systems in the 1970s, primarily to reduce reliance on costly state maximum-security prisons. In 1973 Minnesota was the first state to pass a Comprehensive Community Corrections Act that used money saved when offenders were not sentenced to state prisons to provide funding for community corrections systems. More than half of all states now have such laws.

Community corrections programs are far cheaper than incarceration. The Federal Probation and Pretrial Services System estimated that the annual cost of its community corrections system was $2,344 per participant in 1997, compared to $24,783 per inmate for incarceration.

States increasingly are turning to nonprofit organizations and private entities to provide mandated counseling services to probationers. Such services include counseling related to sex offenses, substance abuse, domestic violence, life skills, impulse control, vocational education, and anger management.

Q 455. How has the federal prison population changed over time?

A From 1990 to 1999 the total sentenced inmate population in federal prisons grew by more than 100 percent. The major factor driving the skyrocketing federal prison population is the U.S. Congress's enactment of stricter sentencing laws for drug offenders. The percentage and number of federal prisoners who were drug offenders more than doubled in the 1990s. Other laws that require violent criminals and drug offenders to spend more time behind bars exacerbate this increase. For example, guidelines in the Sentencing Reform Act of 1984, which took effect in November 1987, require offenders convicted of federal offenses to serve a minimum of 85 percent of their actual sentences. Following are the numbers of inmates in federal prisons during select years since 1990:

- 1990, 65,526
- 1995, 100,250
- 1996, 105,544
- 1997, 112,973
- 1998, 123,041
- 1999, 135,246

Q 456. What percentage of federal prisoners are drug offenders?

A More than half of all federal prisoners are drug offenders. In 1998 the percentage of sentenced prisoners who were drug offenders was 58.9 percent, or 56,291 prisoners. That number compares to 16.3 percent, or 3,384 prisoners, in 1970. The number of federal prisoners who were drug offenders doubled from 1990 to 1998. Following are the percentages and numbers of prisoners who were serving time for drug offenses in U.S. Bureau of Prison facilities (not including contract facilities) between 1990 and 1998:

Year	Percentage	Number of Inmates
1990	52.3	25,037
1991	57	30,498

Year	Percentage	Number of Inmates
1992	59.6	36,349
1993	60.9	42,945
1994	61.4	46,743
1995	60.6	48,118
1996	60.8	50,754
1997	60.3	54,099
1998	58.9	56,291

Q 457. How many prisoners are incarcerated in the U.S. territories and commonwealths?

A As of December 31, 1999, almost 18,400 inmates were under the jurisdiction of the prison systems of the U.S. territories and commonwealths (American Samoa, Guam, Northern Mariana Islands, Puerto Rico, and the Virgin Islands). This number represented an increase of 3.2 percent over the prior year. Puerto Rico, the largest of the territories, had the largest sentenced prison population, 15,465. Puerto Rico also had the highest prison incarceration rate, 307 prisoners per 100,000 residents. The Northern Mariana Islands had the smallest sentenced prison population, 71 inmates, and the lowest prison incarceration rate, 61 inmates per 100,000 residents.

Q 458. How many prisoners are incarcerated in military prisons?

A The U.S. Army, Marine Corps, and Navy held 2,279 prisoners in sixty-five facilities as of December 31, 1999. About 45 percent were held in the Army's disciplinary barracks in Fort Leavenworth, Kansas, and in other regional Army facilities. Navy facilities held 30 percent of military prisoners; Marine Corps facilities held 21 percent; and Air Force facilities held 4 percent.

Q 459. How has the state prison population changed over time?

A The number of state prison inmates grew by almost 75 percent between 1990 and 1999. More inmates spent more time in prison as a result of the elimination of parole, increased monitoring of parole, mandatory sentencing, and sentencing enhancement laws. The number of state prison inmates during select years was:

- 1990, 708,393 prisoners
- 1995, 1,025,624 prisoners

- 1996, 1,077,824 prisoners
- 1997, 1,129,180 prisoners
- 1998, 1,177,532 prisoners
- 1999, 1,231,475 prisoners

In the 1990s nine states more than doubled their sentenced inmate populations, led by Texas (173 percent), Idaho (147 percent) and West Virginia (126 percent). The state reporting the lowest percentage inmate population increase was Maine (12 percent).

As of December 31, 1998, twenty-seven states and the District of Columbia had enacted laws that require violent offenders to serve a large percentage (typically 85 percent) of their sentences. Only five states had such laws in 1993.

Violent offenders accounted for about 50 percent of the total growth in state prison inmate populations from 1990 to 1997; drug offenders accounted for 19 percent; property offenders (burglary, larceny, motor vehicle theft, and so forth), 16 percent; and public order offenders (weapons, drunk driving, vice, etc.), 15 percent. Violent offenses include murder, manslaughter, rape, sexual assault, robbery, extortion, intimidation, and other violent offenses.

Q 460. What states have the highest incarceration rates? The lowest?

A Louisiana had the highest incarceration rate in the nation at midyear 1999, with 1,025 prison and jail inmates per 100,000 state residents. Texas (1,014) and Georgia (956) followed Louisiana. The state with the lowest prison incarceration rate was Vermont, with 203 prison and jail inmates per 100,000 state residents. Maine (220), Minnesota (226), North Dakota (239), and Hawaii (291) followed Vermont.

Q 461. How confident are Americans in state prison systems?

A Not very. In a 1996 national survey by the College of Criminal Justice, Sam Houston State University, Americans reported the following degree of confidence in the state prison system:

- A great deal, 7.9 percent
- Quite a lot, 17.6 percent
- Some, 42.2 percent
- Very little, 32.3 percent

462. At what point does a prison become overcrowded?

States apply various measures to determine prison capacity. Typically, these measures take into account the space available to house inmates and the ability of existing staff to effectively manage the prison population and provide all inmates with access to existing programs and services. Another factor is the optimal number of inmates that the architects of the prison intended to be housed in the facility.

Approximately 1,000 new prisons and jails were built in the United States in the 1980s and 1990s. However, the building boom has failed to keep pace with demand, and in 1999 prisons in more than twenty states reported overcrowding. In response to overcrowding, federal and state correctional systems are forced to build new prisons and to expand existing institutions. Other solutions include renting jail space from other jurisdictions to house overflow inmates, releasing certain inmates early to make room for more serious offenders, and incorporating alternative elements into sentencing schemes, including community corrections, boot camps, home confinement, and halfway houses.

In 1998 thirty states sent almost 25,000 inmates—about 2.1 percent of all state prisoners—to local jails, federal facilities, and facilities in other states because of overcrowding. Wisconsin placed the most inmates (3,028) in out-of-state facilities, followed by the District of Columbia (2,660) and Michigan (1,317). Three jurisdictions—the District of Columbia (26.7 percent), Hawaii (23.8 percent), and Arkansas (21.6 percent)—housed more than 20 percent of their prison populations in the facilities of other states or the federal system.

At the end of 1999 federal prisons were operating at 32 percent over capacity, up from 22 percent at the end of 1997. The Federal Bureau of Prisons planned to add new bed space and expand its prison construction program to reduce systemwide overcrowding.

In contrast to state and federal prisons, the U.S. Department of Justice reported that local jails nationwide were operating at 7 percent below their rated capacity as of June 30, 1999.

Research shows that double bunking and prison overcrowding cause higher rates of stress-induced mental disorders, higher rates of aggression, and higher rates of violence. However, the U.S. Supreme Court on two occasions declined to rule that overcrowding violates the constitutional rights of inmates.

Q **463. Who is more likely to be incarcerated—African Americans, whites, or Hispanics?**

A For the year ending June 30, 1999, African Americans were at least seven times more likely than whites and two and one-half times more likely than Hispanics to have been in prison or jail. The federal government estimated that 11 percent of African American males, 4 percent of Hispanic males, and 1.5 percent of white males in their twenties and early thirties were in prison or jail at midyear 1999. Of the almost 1.9 million incarcerated offenders, more than 560,000 were black males ages twenty to thirty-nine.

The U.S. Department of Justice conceded in 1999 that widespread disparities exist in the rates of incarceration of young black men and young men of Hispanic origin compared to young white men. The incarceration rate among black males in their late twenties reached 8,630 prisoners per 100,000 residents in 1997, compared to 2,703 among Hispanic males and 868 among white males.

Following is the racial breakdown of inmates in the custody of the Federal Bureau of Prisons as of November 30, 1999:

- White, 57.8 percent
- African American, 38.9 percent
- Asian, 1.7 percent
- Native American, 1.6 percent

A total of 31.5 percent of inmates identified their ethnic background as being Hispanic.

See 137 Are African Americans disproportionately affected by crime? 299 Who is most likely to be detained by juvenile authorities?

Q **464. What is the juvenile correctional system?**

A A mix of institutional and community correctional facilities and programs serves offenders who are prosecuted through the juvenile court system.

Juvenile corrections programs traditionally have emphasized rehabilitation. Probation is the most widely used sanction. Nevertheless, according to a count undertaken by the Bureau of the Census for the Office of Juvenile Justice and Delinquency Prevention, almost 106,000 juvenile offenders were held in residential placement facilities on October 29, 1997. Three-quarters of these juvenile offenders had been committed to their facilities by the court. The rest were being detained before the adjudication of their offense or before sentencing.

Institutional correctional facilities for juveniles cover a broad spectrum, including small group homes that are intended to substitute for families, halfway houses, or large nonsecure residential centers; detention centers or temporary custodial facilities; and training schools, which are secure facilities with congregate living and strict rules. There are twice as many private facilities as public facilities, although the public facilities collectively hold twice as many juveniles as the private facilities.

The federal government and most states operate *boot camps,* also called *shock incarceration,* for young, first-time, nonviolent offenders. Many boot camps feature military structure and discipline. Juveniles are exposed to a demanding regimen of strict discipline, physical training, drill, inspections, and physical labor. Offenders usually volunteer for the program and must meet physical and mental health requirements. Begun in Oklahoma and Georgia in 1983, boot camps proved popular with the public as a get-tough measure.

Depending on the law in the jurisdiction that determines the maximum age for juvenile court, defendants under age eighteen may be prosecuted in either adult or juvenile courts. Juveniles who are prosecuted in the adult court system and sentenced to a period of incarceration are confined in adult or state prisons.

A federal study estimated that 61 percent of the juvenile offenders under age eighteen who were sent to state prisons in 1997 were incarcerated for violent offenses. An additional 22 percent of juvenile inmates under age eighteen were confined for property crimes.

Q **465. How many juveniles are incarcerated in state prisons?**

A The U.S. Department of Justice reports that the number of juveniles who are sentenced to serve time in state prisons more than doubled from 1985 to 1997. In 1997 about 7,400 youths ages seventeen or younger were sentenced to adult prisons after being convicted of crimes in adult court, compared to 3,400 in 1985. At the end of 1997 about 5 percent of incarcerated offenders under age eighteen were serving time in state prisons, which hold mostly adult felons who are serving sentences of a year or more.

The increase reflects an increasing number of state laws that take away juveniles' legal status as minors in an effort to make them more accountable. Since 1992 thirty states and the District of Columbia have passed laws requiring offenders to be tried in adult criminal court. The crackdown has been fueled in part by drug-related gang violence and high-profile school shootings. The number of young people sent to state prisons rose from 18 per 1,000 violent-crime arrests of persons under age eighteen in 1985 to 33 per 1,000 such arrests in 1997.

Q **466. What is the fastest growing prisoner demographic group?**

A Women are the fastest growing prisoner demographic group. Although women still represent a tiny proportion of all prisoners, the number of women in prison is growing faster than that of any other demographic group.

From 1990 to 1999, the average annual rate of growth of the female inmate population was 8.3 percent, compared to a 6.4 percent average increase in the number of male inmates. The number of female inmates grew by 106 percent, while the number of male prisoners grew by 75 percent. According to one federal study, incarceration of women has increased by 364 percent from 1980 to 1996, compared to an increase of 194 percent for men. Drug offenses accounted for 43 percent of the growth among females in state prisons.

More than 150,000 women were behind bars at the end of 1999, including 90,688 women in state and federal prisons and 68,000 in local jails. There were 59 sentenced female inmates per 100,000 women in the United States serving time in state and federal prisons as of December 31, 1999, compared to 913 sentenced male inmates per 100,000 men. Women constituted 6.6 percent of all state and federal prisoners.

Q **467. Have American prisons always been segregated by gender?**

A During the nineteenth century most women inmates were housed in the same prisons as men. The women stayed in separate cells or in separate quarters attached to the men's prison. The first state prisons specifically for women were built in the 1790s. The first federal correctional institution for women opened in 1927 in Alderson, West Virginia, with 174 inmates, communal cottages instead of cells, and a nursery.

Because they were so few in number, women in men's prisons were lonely, isolated, and vulnerable to exploitation by guards and prisoners. Pregnant inmates were forced to deliver their babies alone in their cells, resulting in a very high infant mortality rate.

A study of Illinois prisoners during the 1800s reveals that at that time about 2 percent of prison inmates were female, and that many women prisoners were foreign-born immigrants. The one or two female inmates in the prison at any one time were housed in cells directly alongside those of the 100 male prisoners. In 1844 penitentiary inspectors demanded separate quarters for the women, stating, "The impropriety of confining them in adjoining cells and working them in the same shops with the male convicts, is too evident to be dwelt on." Not until 1852, however, would a two-story hospital building be converted into a separate female department.

Historically, male prisoners were *punished*, whereas female prisoners were *corrected* as to their proper roles as mothers, wives, and daughters. Female inmates were taught to cook, clean, and wait on tables. On their release, former inmates were sent to work as servants in middle-class homes.

The first Illinois woman sentenced to prison was Sally Jefferson, who was described as "5-feet 4-inches high, black eyes and hair, fair complected [sic], about twenty-four years old. Her left hand and arm considerably seared by a burn when young." Jefferson was convicted of arson and sentenced to twelve months in prison. However, she served only six weeks of her sentence and was pardoned in 1835. No other woman was sentenced to Illinois prisons for five years. -

Q **468. Can male guards serve in female prisons, and vice versa?**

A Yes. Equal employment opportunity laws prohibit discrimination in employment on the basis of gender. As a result, prisons have cross-gender employment policies that allow women to guard male prisoners and men to guard female prisoners. To ensure the privacy of inmates, courts have ruled that staff members of one sex can never supervise inmates of the opposite sex in toilet and shower areas.

Despite precautions, however, a 1998 study by the human rights group Amnesty International found widespread abuse of female inmates by male guards. The group reported that sex between inmates and prison staff "is virtually a fact of life for incarcerated women" in the United States, where about 150,000 women are in jails and prisons.

Some states have passed laws making it a felony punishable by up to five years in prison for correctional officers to have sex with inmates.

In 1997 the Federal Bureau of Prisons launched an employee-training program to prevent the sexual abuse of inmates. The Bureau also set up procedures for inmates to report sexual abuse by staff.

Historically only nursing, teaching, and clerical positions were open to women in institutions with male inmates. A few women worked as correctional officers in these institutions in the early 1970s, but their assignments were limited to peripheral tasks. In the federal system females were prohibited from working in high-security institutions until January 1993.

Q **469. Can a person be jailed for being poor?**

A Debtors were incarcerated alongside criminals in the state prisons until the mid-1800s. However, today's federal bankruptcy laws allow debtors to work out their financial problems in civil proceedings. Still, poor people can be jailed in many jurisdictions if they violate laws that prohibit begging for handouts or if they are considered homeless vagrants. In *Smith v. Fort Lauderdale* (1999) the U.S. Supreme Court let stand the conviction of a group of homeless people in Fort Lauderdale, Florida, who violated a 1993 regulation that prohibited soliciting, begging, or panhandling on a five-mile strip of city beach and on the sidewalks on each side of an adjacent street.

Q 470. What prison system was so bad in the 1970s that it helped spark nation-wide reform?

A Historically, federal judges rarely intervened in civil cases about prison conditions or the institutional rules to which inmates were subjected. However, the abysmal conditions of the Arkansas prison system prompted a federal district judge to order the state to reform its entire penal system.

To be sentenced to an Arkansas prison farm, wrote U.S. District Judge J. Smith Henley in *Holt v. Sarver* (1971), "amounts to a banishment from civilized society to a dark and evil world completely alien to the free world, that is administered by criminals under unwritten rules and customs completely foreign to free world culture." Henley declared the Arkansas prison system to be in violation of the Eighth Amendment ban on cruel and unusual punishment.

Arkansas's self-financing, forced-labor prison farms were heirs to the slave plantation system. They were run essentially by *trusty guards,* or fellow inmates. Housed in barracks, inmates were vulnerable to frequent assaults, including murder and rape. One device used to punish inmates was the Tucker telephone. Powered by a hand crank, the machine generated electricity. Electrodes were attached to a prisoner's extremities, including the genitals. The resulting shocks caused burns, seizures, and even death. The device was prominently placed in a small building called the *telephone booth.* Inmates in Arkansas prisons also were routinely whipped with leather straps. The decision in *Holt v. Sarver* (1971) helped sparked a wave of similar litigation across the country, leading to improvements in inmate housing conditions, security, medical care, sanitation, nutrition, and exercise. In a little more than a decade, the federal courts had enunciated a set of judicially enforceable rules governing the operation of American prisons.

Q 471. Is corporal punishment of prisoners allowed?

A No. Delaware became the last state to abolish corporal punishment of prisoners when its legislature voted in 1972 to ban the use of the whipping post.

Corporal punishment declined in the mid-1800s amid political pressure generated by prison reformers such as Dorothea Dix. Until then, whippings were routinely administered to punish inmates and restore order. Dix wrote that in the year 1844–1845, "the number of lashes in the men's prison [at Sing Sing] has diminished from one thousand one hundred and ninety-five per month, to about two hundred."

In *Weems v. United States* (1910), the U.S. Supreme Court invalidated a particularly severe sentence that involved a form of corporal punishment in the then U.S.-occupied Philippines. The prisoner was ordered to serve a fifteen-year prison sentence in chains, pay a heavy fine, and suffer permanent deprivation of his civil rights. The Court deemed this sentence to be cruel and unusual both because of the bodily torment of the chains and the disproportionality between the punishment and the offense, the falsification of a public record. However, no court has declared corporal punishment per se to be unconstitutional.

Prisoners no longer can be beaten, but corporal punishment of school students remains legal in some states.

Q **472. Have inmates always been able to file lawsuits challenging their imprisonment?**

A The U.S. Constitution provides all prison inmates with the right to file a writ of *habeas corpus* in federal court, a petition challenging a conviction or sentence imposed in state court on constitutional grounds. However, that right was elusive for many prisoners until a landmark ruling by the U.S. Supreme Court in 1941.

In *Ex Parte Hull* (1941) the U.S. Supreme Court invalidated a regulation adopted by the warden of a Michigan prison that required prisoners to file all legal documents and appeals first with prison authorities. The Court said that prisoners have a right to file a writ of *habeas corpus* directly in the federal courts, which would then decide the merits of the allegations.

The *Hull* case involved a convicted sex offender who was unsuccessful in several attempts to mail a petition of *habeas corpus* to the court. The petition asserted that the prisoner was being imprisoned unlawfully. Each time, prison authorities confiscated the petition. The prisoner's father eventually managed to file the petition with the U.S. Supreme Court.

Even after *Hull*, federal courts generally maintained a hands-off policy with respect to prisoners' suits until the 1960s.

The logjam broke when, in *United States v. Muniz* (1963), the U.S. Supreme Court ruled that inmates may sue prison officials for personal injuries sustained during their confinement that resulted from the negligence of a government employee in a federal prison. Then, in *Cooper v. Pate* (1964), the Court said that state and federal prisoners may file civil suits against prison officials under Title 42, United States

Code, Section 1983 (42 U.S.C. 1983), which imposes civil liability on any person who deprives another of his or her constitutional rights.

The number of prisoner lawsuits skyrocketed until 1996, when almost 70,000 suits were filed. Most of these appeals were *in forma pauperis* (the inmate could not afford to pay court costs) and many were prepared by *jailhouse lawyers* (inmates with no formal legal training who specialize in drafting legal documents). Some of the lawsuits asserted serious issues but many were frivolous, with prisoners complaining that they were deprived of deodorant or a second helping of ice cream. One prisoner single-handedly filed 700 lawsuits.

Many prisoners' lawsuits were settled by *consent decrees,* agreements by the parties to settle a case on mutually acceptable terms that the court agrees to enforce as a judgment. These agreements sometimes were more costly than litigation and resulted in ongoing oversight of state courts by federal judges. More than 1,200 state prisons were operating under some form of judicial supervision in 1990.

In 1996 the U.S. Congress began passing laws making it more difficult for prisoners to file *habeas corpus* petitions and civil rights suits.

Article I, Section 9, of the U.S. Constitution forbids the suspension of *habeas corpus* except in cases involving rebellion or invasion that threaten the public safety.

See 259 What is a writ of habeas corpus?

Q 473. Are fewer prisoner lawsuits being filed today?

A Yes. In 1996 the U.S. Congress passed two laws that make it more difficult for prison inmates to file civil rights complaints and appeals.

The Prison Litigation Reform Act (1996) limited the ability of federal judges to interfere in the operations of correctional institutions. The act also restricted the civil complaints that can be filed by inmates in federal court. Congress cited an "alarming expansion in the number of frivolous lawsuits filed by State and Federal prisoners." Among other things, the act requires inmates to show physical injury to receive damages for mental or physical injuries suffered while in custody, imposes filing fees, and includes sanctions against federal inmates who abuse the court system.

The U.S. Department of Justice reports that civil rights–related complaints, including prison condition cases, filed by state and federal prison inmates in federal courts increased from 25,992 in 1990 to 41,679 in 1995. Following the enactment of the Prison Litigation Reform Act, the number of civil rights suits declined to 41,215 in 1996 and 26,462 by 1998.

Congress also passed the Antiterrorism and Effective Death Penalty Act of 1996, which set a one-year statute of limitations for filing *habeas corpus* petitions after state appeals and federal motions to vacate sentence are exhausted. In states that meet the law's standard for providing competent legal counsel to indigent defendants, the limit is only six months. The law also made it more difficult for prisoners to file more than one appeal because it requires federal judges to defer to state court rulings on constitutional and other issues unless those rulings are unreasonable.

Q 474. What types of lawsuits do prisoners file?

A According to the Administrative Office of the U.S. Courts, state and federal prisoners in U.S. District Courts filed almost 55,000 lawsuits in the year ending September 30, 1998. This number represented a decline of about 13 percent from 1997. In descending order of frequency, the number and types of suits filed were:

- *Habeas corpus,* general assertion of denial of federal constitutional rights, 20,897
- Civil rights, 13,756
- Prison conditions, 12,706
- Motion to vacate sentence, 6,287
- Mandamus (a request for an order to command an action) and other, 807
- *Habeas corpus,* death penalty, 262

The vast majority of lawsuits filed by prisoners are dismissed either because the suit does not conform to court rules or because the court has found no evidence of a constitutional rights violation. Most prisoners' lawsuits are filed by inmates acting without counsel.

A 1995 federal study determined that fewer than 2 percent of prisoners' civil rights cases ever get to trial and that the plaintiff prevails in only about half of these cases. The study also found that the largest single issue raised in lawsuits filed by state prisoners in federal court (21 percent) involved the inmates' physical security. Other issues involved medical treatment (17 percent); due process violations (13 percent); challenges to convictions (12 percent); physical conditions (9 percent); access to courts (7 percent); living conditions (4 percent); religious expression (4 percent); assault by an arresting officer (3 percent); and other types of issues (11 percent).

Q 475. How are prisons typically governed?

A Prisons generally fall under the executive branch of government. The state governor appoints a correctional commissioner, who oversees the entire state corrections system. In each prison a warden or superintendent serves as the equivalent of the chief executive officer. Deputy wardens typically assist in administrative duties.

The warden is responsible for the management of both the inmate population and a diverse staff. Perhaps most importantly, the warden is responsible for implementing correctional policies that ensure the safety of staff, inmates, and the general public. A typical medium-security prison houses 1,300 inmates, employs a staff of 400 service and security personnel, and has an annual operating budget of more than $15,000,000.

Employment within the corrections system generally falls into two categories: institutional security and institutional services. The hierarchical ranking among prison security personnel resembles the military in that the warden or superintendent is the highest-ranking officer, followed by captains, lieutenants, sergeants, and correctional or custody officers. Institutional services employees handle all noncustodial programs, including education, medical care, vocational training, drug-treatment programs, self-help programs, and religious services. Institutional services employees are not required to participate in the pre-employment academy training required of guards.

Inmates play a role in the governance of most prisons. Inmate disciplinary councils, which include both prisoners and a small number of correctional officers, serve as neutral third-party arbiters for inmate grievances.

Q 476. What warden was hanged because of his prison's abominable conditions?

A Captain Henry Wirz, the superintendent of Andersonville Prison in Georgia, the military stockade of the Confederate army during the American Civil War, was tried by a U.S. military court, convicted of war crimes, and hanged on November 10, 1865.

Andersonville prison was designed to hold 10,000 Union army enlisted men, but its population quickly swelled to 32,000 because of deteriorating Southern resources and the breakdown of the prisoner exchange system. More than 45,000 captured Union soldiers were sent to the prison between February 1864 and May 1865. Of these, 12,912 prisoners died from disease, malnutrition, overcrowding, or exposure and were buried in shallow trenches.

Some prisoners had crude shelters—huts made out of scrap wood, tent fragments, or simple holes dug in the ground. Many had no shelter at all and were exposed to rain, heat, or cold. A small, slow-moving stream running through the middle of the stockade enclosure supplied water to most of the prison. No clothing was provided, and the daily food ration consisted of one and one-fourth pound of corn meal and either one pound of beef or one-third pound of bacon, occasionally supplemented with beans, peas, rice, or molasses. Exposure, inadequate food, impure water, congestion, and filth led to epidemics of scurvy and dysentery.

Wirz was charged with conspiring to "impair and injure the health and destroy the lives of federal prisoners" and with "murder in violation of the laws of war." At his trial in Washington, D.C., many former prisoners blamed Wirz for their suffering.

The question of whether or not Wirz could have done more to improve prison conditions is the subject of debate today. Some have called Wirz, the only Confederate tried for war crimes during the Civil War, the last casualty of Andersonville.

The prison burial ground now is a national cemetery, and the prison site and surrounding area was designated a national historic site in 1970. The National Prisoner of War Museum, which memorializes the prison experiences of all Americans captured during wartime, opened at the site in 1998.

Q 477. How many correctional officers are employed in the United States?

A The U.S. Department of Labor reports that 383,000 correctional officers were working in 1998. Almost six out of ten correctional officers worked at state correctional institutions, such as prisons, prison camps, and youth correctional facilities. Most of the remainder worked at local jails or correctional institutions run by local governments. About 12,000 correctional officers worked for the Federal Bureau of Prisons and about 10,500 officers worked for private correctional institutions. Most institutions require that a correctional officer be a United States citizen, minimum age eighteen to twenty-one, with a high-school diploma or equivalent and no felony convictions. Most correctional officers are required to undergo a training program. New officers for the Federal Bureau of Prisons must complete 120 hours of training at the BOP's residential training center at Glynco, Georgia, within the first sixty days of employment.

Q 478. What salaries do correctional officers earn?

A The U.S. Department of Labor reports that the nation's correctional officers earned a median annual salary of $28,540 in 1998. The middle 50 percent earned between $22,930 and $37,550.

According to a 1999 survey in *Corrections Compendium,* a national journal for corrections professionals, beginning annual salaries for correctional officers ranged from $14,600 in California to $34,100 in New Jersey.

Civil service systems or merit boards cover most correctional officer positions.

479. How do employees of the Federal Bureau of Prisons break down by race? By gender?

As of July 2000, according to the Federal Bureau of Prisons (BOP), 23,400 of its employees (72.6 percent) were male and 8,731 (27.4 percent) were female.

By race and ethnicity, BOP employees were:

- White (Non-Hispanic), 20,832 (65.5 percent)
- African American, 6,575 (20.5 percent)
- Hispanic, 3,358 (10.5 percent)
- Asian, 599 (1.9 percent)
- Native American, 475 (1.5 percent)
- Other, 16 (0.1 percent)

480. How many correctional officers have been killed in the line of duty in the twentieth century?

According to the National Law Enforcement Officers Memorial Fund, the first law enforcement officer to be killed during the twentieth century was William C. Rooney, a thirty-year-old captain with the Colorado Department of Corrections who died after he was stabbed in the heart during a prison escape on January 22, 1900. Rooney was the first of more than 370 correctional officers to be killed in the line of duty during the twentieth century. The nonprofit National Law Enforcement Officers Memorial Fund formed in 1984 to honor the sacrifices of law enforcement officers.

481. How often do inmates assault correctional officers?

In recent years a steady increase has occurred in the number of inmate assaults against correctional staff. The number of attacks in state and federal prisons jumped by nearly one-third between 1990 and 1995, from 10,731 to 14,165.

482. What is *gassing*?

Correctional officers increasingly are subject to a practice called *gassing*, in which inmates fling bodily fluids at them. The practice is potentially deadly given the high incidence of communicable diseases among inmates.

The California corrections system reports that between 1994 and 1998 gassing incidents in state institutions increased by 40 percent. In 1998, 469 gassing incidents occurred. In one case, an inmate threw a cup of urine, feces, and toilet paper into a correctional officer's face as the officer was retrieving the inmate's dinner tray. The inmate had two communicable and potentially fatal diseases, AIDS and hepatitis C. Initial tests results on the officer were negative, but the officer had to undergo testing for at least two years to determine whether he had been infected.

Q 483. Why are jails and prisons air-conditioned?

A Prisoners are protected from cruel and unusual punishments by the Eighth Amendment to the U.S. Constitution. Courts have interpreted this prohibition to mean that prisons cannot be indifferent to a prisoner's health. When the government incarcerates a prisoner, it cannot endanger the prisoner's health by exposing him or her to excessive heat. A federal court judge in Tennessee assessed compensatory and punitive damages against county officials when an otherwise healthy jail inmate died of died of heat stroke because jail temperatures reached 110 degrees Fahrenheit during the day and 104 degrees at night. Before the incident state inspectors had criticized the jail several times for its poor cooling and ventilation. A nurse's recommendation that a fan be placed in the inmate's cell was ignored. The judge declared that the official policy of the county was one of deliberate indifference.

Q 484. What is *good time*?

A Most state correctional programs allow offenders to earn *good time,* or credit toward early release, if they demonstrate good behavior in prison or participate in vocational, educational, or treatment programs. Correctional authorities consider these back-end discretion policies vital to maintaining order and reducing prison overcrowding. However, the policies often are criticized for undermining public confidence in the sentencing process.

Many states have enacted truth-in-sentencing laws that require offenders to serve specific and substantial portions of their sentences. The U.S. Department of Justice reported in 2000 that inmates released from state prisons in 1996 had served, on average, almost half of their court-imposed sentences, compared to one-third of their court-imposed sentences in 1988.

Depending on the jurisdiction, the amount of good time a prisoner can earn ranges from one day for every three days served to one day for every day served. Federal prisoners who are not sentenced to life in prison but whose sentences are greater than one year receive a flat allocation of fifty-four days of good time per year of sentence served.

Q 485. What percentage of their sentences do prisoners serve?

A On average, prisoners released in 1996 served 45 percent of their sentences. Factors that lead to early prison release include prison crowding, good-time sentence reductions for satisfactory prison behavior, and earned-time credits for participation in work or educational programs. Dissatisfaction over early release of prisoners has prompted many states to enact truth-in-sentencing laws that require offenders to serve a specific percentage of their sentence, usually 85 percent.

See 239 What sentencing models do states use?

Q 486. What is the average sentence served in prison?

A State prison inmates served an average of twenty-eight months in 1998, an increase from twenty-two months in 1990.

Q 487. What is a private prison?

A Generally, a private prison is a correctional facility that is owned and operated by a profit-making corporation, as opposed to a prison that is owned and operated by the government. In a few cases, the prison is owned by the government but is operated by a profit-making corporation under contract.

U.S. Corrections Corporation opened the first private prison for adult felons in 1986 in Kentucky. Since then the number of private facilities for prisoners has skyrocketed.

About 1,345 prisoners, or 0.5 percent of all prisoners, were incarcerated in private prisons in 1985, compared to 106,940 prisoners, or 8.5 percent of all prisoners, in 1997. About 160 private prisons operate in about twenty-five states, Washington, D.C., and Puerto Rico. About three-quarters of all private prisons are in the South or in the West.

The Nashville-based Corrections Corporation of America (CCA) is the largest corporation in the private prison business. It operates seventy-four facilities in the United States and had an estimated $660 million in 1998 revenues.

In recent years an increasing number of jails are privately owned or operated. By midyear 1999, the federal government reported, 47 of the nation's 3,365 local jails were privately owned or operated in seventeen states. These jails held 13,814 inmates, or 2.3 percent of all jail inmates.

Proponents of private prisons claim that they are cheaper to operate and generally have equivalent or better safety standards. In theory, private prisons also are less costly to build because they are not burdened by the red tape associated with public construction projects, including lengthy bidding and financing processes. New prison designs minimize the number of guards needed to watch the maximum number of prisoners. Private prisons also can save on labor costs, which account for about 70 percent of all prison expenses. Private prisons hire more nonunionized employees. Research is inconclusive about whether private prisons cost less to operate, though some studies show that they cost from 1 percent to 30 percent less to operate.

Opponents of private prisons question whether prisons should be privatized at all. They argue that prisons are fundamentally different from other societal institutions in that members of a prison staff exercise considerable discretion in imposing orders, rules, and discipline on prisoners. Critics say that the profit motive of private prisons could cloud their treatment of prisoners. Also, they argue that the lack of state oversight of private prisons compromises public safety. Texas has nineteen private prisons, more than any other state. Most of the prisoners in private prisons in Texas are brought in under contract from other states.

Q 488. Why has the number of private prisons skyrocketed?

A Dramatic increases in inmate populations, fueled in part by public policy changes, have prompted phenomenal growth of private prisons in the past fifteen years. These changes include the adoption of mandatory sentences, elimination by some states of parole and early release, increased penalties for drug offenses, and so-called three-strikes laws that are aimed at locking up repeat offenders. Faced with budget shortfalls, states turned to the private sector to handle the influx of new prisoners.

Some analysts offer a cynical explanation for the increase in private prisons. They say that privatization allowed policymakers the opportunity to appear to be doing something about the country's failed criminal justice system and open up market opportunities for the private business sector. Such critics claim that more promising alternatives to the crime problem, such as early childhood parenting education and school-based violence prevention programs, were ignored in favor of private prisons.

Q 489. Are private prisons accountable to the public?

A Private prisons are as accountable as their contracts or state law requires them to be. This point was vividly illustrated in 1997 when city and state officials discovered that a supposedly medium-security private prison in Youngstown, Ohio, was taking in violent maximum-security inmates from the District of Columbia. A melee resulted in the stabbing of twenty inmates, two fatally. Youngstown and state officials discovered that they had no contractual oversight over the prison. The city joined prison inmates in a suit against Corrections Corporation of America, the prison operator, which resulted in the transfer of hundreds of potentially dangerous inmates. The company also agreed to pay inmates $1.7 million in damages, to adhere to more rigorous standards, and to pay for a Youngstown employee to monitor the prison. Some states are passing laws to limit the number of out-of-state prisoners that can be held in private prisons within their boundaries. Texas passed a law requiring private prisons to meet the same requirements as public prisons after two sex offenders from Oregon escaped from a private prison in Texas in 1996. More than 200 Oregon sex offenders were being housed at the prison, which was supposed to house only illegal immigrants.

Q **490. How many prisons operate a private-sector prison industry?**

A The federal government and more than thirty state correctional agencies operate private-sector prison industries that employ prisoners to provide goods and services to government and private sector buyers. Prisoners do everything from data entry and information processing to telemarketing and making travel reservations. Many major companies, including IBM and Victoria's Secret, use prison-manufactured products.

Federal law requires all sentenced federal inmates to work except those who for security, educational, or medical reasons are unable to do so. In 1934 the U.S. Congress created Federal Prison Industries, Inc. (FPI), to employ federal inmates in making products needed by the government. Inmates receive work and occupational skills and money for personal expenses and family assistance. According to a federal study, inmates who work in prison industries are 24 percent less likely to violate the law again within eight to twelve years after they are released from prison.

In 1998 FPI employed about 20,000 inmates, or about 25 percent of the sentenced federal inmate population. The prisoners made office furniture and uniforms, components of guided missiles, telecommunications equipment, aircraft landing gear, and security systems. FPI's sales reached $534 million in 1998 and were expected to hit almost $600 million in 1999.

American prisons have a long history of using convict labor. Initially, states leased prisoners to private contractors for work off-site. In the 1830s many states—particularly northern states—began to embrace the contract system, in which prisoners worked within prison shops to produce finished goods for private entrepreneurs.

In the 1930s Congress banned the open-market sale of prison-made goods after receiving complaints of unfair competition from organized labor and competing manufacturers. Congress lifted its ban in 1979 for prisons that complied with a specially created program, the Private Sector Prison Industry Enhancement Certification Program. This program requires correctional agencies to certify that inmates are paid not less than the local prevailing wage; that the interests of other parties, which could be adversely affected by the joint venture, are protected; and that local unions were consulted prior to the initiation of a project.

Between 1979 and 1992, the U.S. Department of Justice reports, inmates employed in joint ventures certified by the U.S. Department of Justice earned almost $29 million. Deductions from their wages resulted in contributions of $5 million to offset the cost of their incarceration, $3.2 million in federal and state taxes, $1.7 million in compensation to victims, and $1.8 million toward the support of their families.

Q 491. Are federal prisoners required to work?

A Federal law requires all sentenced inmates to work, with the exception of those who cannot work for security, educational, or medical reasons. This policy is intended to provide inmates with an activity that makes productive use of their time and prepares them for eventual reintegration into society. According to a federal study, inmates who work in prison industries are 24 percent less likely to violate the law again within eight to ten years after they are released from prison.

Inmates earn a small wage, a portion of which some inmates use to make restitution to their victims. About one-fourth of all inmates are employed by Federal Prison Industries, Inc., a government corporation that provides a range of goods and services.

Q 492. How much money does America spend on corrections?

A In 1996, the latest year for which statistics are available, the total direct expenditure on corrections by federal, state, and local governments was a little more than $41 billion. That figure compares to $53 billion for police and $26 billion for courts.

The U.S. Department of Justice reports that states spend far more than either the federal or local governments on corrections. In 1996 the states spent twice as much on corrections as did local governments and about eight times as much as did the federal government.

An analysis by the U.S. Department of Justice showed that, in 1995, 1.7 percent of every dollar went to corrections, compared to 1.8 percent for police protection and 0.9 percent for judicial and legal services.

The federal prison system budget for fiscal year 2000 was $3.7 billion, including about $3.1 billion for salaries and expenses and $557 million for buildings and facilities.

A According to the U.S. Department of Justice, the following amounts represent direct governmental expenditures for corrections from 1982 to 1996:

- 1982, $9 billion
- 1983, $10.4 billion
- 1984, $11.8 billion
- 1985, $13.5 billion
- 1986, $15.8 billion
- 1987, $17.6 billion
- 1988, $20.3 billion
- 1989, $22.6 billion
- 1990, $26.2 billion
- 1991, $29.3 billion
- 1992, $31.5 billion
- 1993, $31.9 billion
- 1994, $34.9 billion
- 1995, $39.8 billion
- 1996, $41 billion

Direct expenditures include salaries, wages, fees, supplies, capital outlays, and all other expenditures except those classified as intergovernmental.

Twenty years ago prison costs represented only about 1 percent or 2 percent of most state budgets. Now prison costs range from 8 percent to 10 percent. In recent years prison costs have represented the fastest-growing budget category, often rising at the expense of higher education, funding for environmental projects, and other discretionary budget categories.

Q **494. Can inmates be charged fees for correctional services and operations?**

A Yes. In recent years virtually every state has passed legislation authorizing that inmates be assessed certain fees for correctional services and operations. Fees are imposed in four major areas:

- Medical services fees, including copayments and other fees for medical care
- Per diems that require inmates to reimburse the jurisdiction for all or a portion of their daily incarceration costs, including housing, food, and basic programs
- Nonprogram services fees, which cover the costs of bonding, telephone use, haircuts, release escorts, and drug testing

- Fees or percentages of any compensation earned by inmates in programs such as work release, weekend incarceration, and electronic monitoring, or charges for participation in rehabilitation programs such as education or substance abuse treatment

Thirty-six states have adopted minimal copayment fees for inmate health care services. These fees, typically $3 per visit, apply to nonemergency medical services and are not required of inmates who are unable to pay. Prison officials say that copayments have sharply reduced unnecessary requests for health services by prisoners seeking to avoid work or to escape the monotony of prison life. They estimate the average reduction in sick-call visits at between 16 percent to 50 percent. Opponents of fees contend that the assessments discourage poor inmates from seeking necessary treatment.

Health care costs for federal prisoners totaled $354 million in 1998, up from $138 million in fiscal year 1990. In 1999 the Federal Bureau of Prisons (BOP) asked Congress to pass a law that would allow the BOP to charge nonindigent federal inmates a minimal copayment for certain self-initiated health care visits. The fee would not be assessed for emergency visits, mental health visits, obstetric care, BOP-scheduled intake physical examinations and initial work-ups, BOP-scheduled follow-up visits, or chronic care clinic visits (such as visits for diabetes, hypertension, or asthma).

Q 495. How much does it cost to incarcerate a prison inmate?

A It costs taxpayers an estimated $20,100 a year to house and feed every new inmate, not including the cost of building new prisons and jails. Building a prison costs, on average, $80,000 per maximum-security cell, $53,000 per medium-security cell, and $43,000 per minimum-security cell.

According to the latest figures from the U.S. Department of Justice, the per-inmate cost to operate a state prison ranged from a low of $8,000 to a high of $37,800 in 1996. This cost includes salaries, wages, and capital expenses. The broad range in costs reflects the wide differences in costs of living and prevailing wage rates among the states.

Following are the five states with the highest annual operating costs per inmate in 1996:

- Minnesota, $37,800
- Rhode Island, $35,700
- Maine, $33,700
- Alaska, $32,400
- Utah, $32,400

Following are the states with the lowest annual operating costs per inmate in 1996:

- Alabama, $8,000
- Oklahoma, $10,600
- Mississippi, $11,200
- Texas, $12,200
- Missouri, $12,800

PRISONERS

 496. For what major types of crimes are state prison inmates incarcerated?

About 545,200 state prison inmates were incarcerated for violent offenses in 1998, compared to 242,900 for property offenses (such as burglary, larceny, or motor vehicle theft), 236,800 for drug offenses, and 113,900 for public order offenses (such as weapons, drunk driving, or vice). The numbers and specific offenses of prisoners who were incarcerated for violent offenses were as follows: for robbery, 159,600; murder, 134,600; assault, 109,500; rape and other sexual assaults, 100,800; manslaughter, 17,600; and other violent offenses, 23,100.

497. Who was the Bird Man of Alcatraz?

Robert Franklin Stroud, a self-taught ornithologist who contributed to the study of birds while serving fifty years in federal prison—including forty-two years in solitary confinement—became known as the Bird Man of Alcatraz.

At age eighteen Stroud was a pimp who was living with a dance-hall girl in Juneau, Alaska. He killed a man in a dispute over the girl and pleaded guilty to manslaughter. After stabbing a fellow prisoner, Stroud was transferred to Leavenworth Federal Penitentiary in Kansas. In 1916 Stroud fatally stabbed a prison guard with a homemade knife after the officer asked Stroud's name and inmate number. Stroud was distraught at the possibility that the guard would file a disciplinary report against him, resulting in the cancellation of a scheduled visit with his brother. Stroud was convicted of murdering the thirty-nine-year-old correctional officer and sentenced to hang. However, President Woodrow Wilson commuted his sentence to life imprisonment eight days before Stroud's scheduled execution.

While incarcerated at Leavenworth, Stroud was permitted to raise canaries and other birds. His research into bird keeping and avian diseases was smuggled out of prison and published in a 1943 book, *Stroud's Digest on the Diseases of Birds.* Stroud was transferred to Alcatraz in 1942, where he was not permitted to keep birds, his research was discouraged, and he was denied the right to further publication.

After Stroud's death in 1963 he was the subject of a popular film, *The Birdman of Alcatraz.*

Q 498. Does a prisoner have a right to privacy?

A A prisoner's right to privacy is strictly limited, even if the prisoner is awaiting trial and has not yet been found guilty of a criminal offense.

Courts have held that guards can conduct strip searches and body-cavity searches of inmates after any contact with the outside world and that guards may, without obtaining a warrant, conduct shakedowns, or random searches, of inmates' cells and seize materials found there. Prisons routinely record all inmate telephone conversations, except those protected by attorney-client privilege. Inmates are observable at all times.

One area of privacy that is retained by prisoners is the right to be supervised in a shower or toilet area by a correctional officer who is of the same gender. Male guards cannot supervise female inmates, for example, in these scenarios.

Intrusions on inmates' constitutional rights are justified as being necessary to maintain a safe and secure prison for guards, other inmates, and the public.

In *Bell v. Wolfish* (1979) the U.S. Supreme Court stated that maintaining institutional security and preserving internal order and discipline may require limitation or retraction of the constitutional rights of convicted prisoners and pretrial detainees. The Court said that because "problems that arise in the day-to-day operation of a corrections facility are not susceptible of easy solutions, prison administrators should be accorded wide-ranging deference in the adoption and execution of policies and practices that in their judgment are needed to preserve internal order and discipline and to maintain institutional security."

Intrusions into inmates' privacy likely will accelerate in the future with the advent of *technocorrections.* This term refers to the use of new technologies to manage inmates, including sophisticated cellular or satellite inmate tracking and location systems, pharmacological treatments to curb violent behavior, and DNA-based risk-assessment methods to identify potential troublemakers. These technologies may prove to be more cost-effective than labor-intensive correctional supervision, and could virtually eliminate any risk of danger from inmates.

Q **499. What Atlanta prison inmate waged a serious campaign for the U.S. presidency in 1920?**

A Labor leader Eugene Victor Debs was founder of the American Railway Union, at one time the country's largest union. Debs ran as a Socialist candidate for president of the United States in 1920, while he was incarcerated at an Atlanta penitentiary. Debs was serving a ten-year prison term for a 1918 conviction under the Espionage Act stemming from his vehement opposition to the U.S. entry into World War I. Debs had previously run as a Socialist candidate for president four times. In the 1920 election, he won 919,802 votes, or 3.6 percent of the total votes.

Debs had served time behind bars before his 1918 conviction. In 1894 the American Railway Union was destroyed during the Pullman strike when federal troops were called out to keep the trains moving and arrest the labor leaders who represented the striking workers. Debs was convicted for contempt of a court injunction during the strike and served six months in jail in 1895. It was during this period that Debs converted to socialism.

President Warren G. Harding commuted Debs's prison sentence in 1921 and Debs was released from prison, although he did not regain his citizenship. Debs devoted his remaining years to writing about prison conditions and serving as editor of the Socialist weekly *Appeal to Reason.* Debs died in Elmhurst, Illinois, on October 20, 1926.

Q **500. What is the educational level of federal prison inmates?**

A According to the Federal Bureau of Prisons (BOP), the educational level of federal inmates as of September 30, 1998, was:

- High school, 34 percent
- Technical school, 4.4 percent
- Some college, 31.5 percent
- Bachelor's degree, 19.3 percent
- Some graduate work, 2.5 percent
- Master's degree, 4.9 percent
- Ph.D., 1.7 percent
- Advanced professional degree, 1.8 percent

The BOP has established a mandatory high school equivalency diploma as a prerequisite for inmates to qualify for preferred jobs and housing.

Q 501. What educational opportunities are available to prisoners?

A Prisons provide inmates with the opportunity to obtain a high school equivalency diploma and, possibly, vocational or occupational training and college credits. In 1998 thirty-four percent of all inmates in federal prisons were enrolled in one or more educational programs.

In the mid-1990s federal Pell Grant money was eliminated for prisoners seeking to take college-level academic courses. At the same time, many states withdrew college tuition assistance for prisoners or instituted requirements that prisoners reimburse the state for tuition costs. According to the American Correctional Association, in most states "the only means for eligible and interested inmates to participate in college classes is by using their own funds."

Research increasingly indicates that education reduces inmate recidivism. According to a 1998 study by the Center on Crime, Communities and Culture, prison-based education programs led to drops in recidivism as high as 15.5 percent.

Some states, such as Indiana, allow an inmate to petition the sentencing court for a reduction of sentence if the inmate successfully completes a substance abuse program, a vocational program, or any of several educational programs, including a general equivalency degree, a high school diploma, an associate's degree, a baccalaureate degree, or another college degree.

Q 502. Do prisoners have a right to read X-rated material?

A No. In March 2000 the U.S. Supreme Court let stand an Arizona county ban on all depictions of frontal nudity from its jails. The Court rejected an appeal by an inmate who wanted to have *Playboy* magazines delivered to his cell. Without comment, the justices turned away arguments that the ban is so sweeping it violates free-speech rights.

The Maricopa County Sheriff's office, which runs one of the nation's largest jail systems, has since 1993 prohibited jail inmates from possessing sexually explicit material, which it defines as anything that shows male or female frontal nudity. The ban covers publications and inmates' own artwork, and is aimed at preventing inmate fights and harassment of female jail employees.

An eleven-judge panel of the Ninth U.S. Circuit Court of Appeals had concluded that the county's policy fell within the guidelines provided by a 1987 Supreme Court decision on jailhouse censorship because the ban is "reasonably related to legitimate penological interests."

Q **503. Do all prisons have law libraries?**

A No. In *Lewis v. Casey* (1996) the U.S. Supreme Court ruled that inmates have a legal right to access to the courts but do not have a "free-standing right to a law library or legal assistance." The Court held that inmates cannot successfully sue a prison simply by proving that the facilities' law libraries or legal assistance programs are inadequate. Inmates must show that the inadequacy of the library hindered their efforts to pursue a legal claim.

The Court's decision represented a clear setback for jailhouse lawyers. In *Bounds v. Smith* (1977) the Court had held that the right of access to the courts requires prisons to provide prisoners not only with adequate law libraries but also with adequate assistance from persons trained in the law.

After *Lewis v. Casey,* the Iowa State Corrections Department proposed shutting down the eight law libraries that it operated in the state's nine-prison system to save money and cut down on frivolous lawsuits by inmates. Iowa's prison law libraries, which serve 7,400 inmates, spent about $500,000 annually to remain current. Iowa officials planned to leave a core of legal volumes in regular prison libraries.

Prison libraries generally have had a much broader role than providing prisoners with access to law books. Prison libraries also support the educational and academic offerings of the institution and—within the limits of the prison's security requirements and regulations—provide cultural and entertainment materials to prisoners.

Q **504. How many prisoners are illegal aliens?**

A The Immigration and Naturalization Service (INS) estimates that, as of December 31, 1998, from 110,000 to 140,000 aliens were incarcerated in federal, state, or local jails. Two-thirds of incarcerated aliens had entered the United States without permission and subsequently committed a crime.

The Federal Bureau of Prisons (BOP) encourages noncitizen inmates to apply for international treaty transfers to their native countries so that they can serve their prison terms in facilities near their families and decrease the U.S. incarceration costs. In 1998 the BOP returned 208 foreign inmates to twelve different countries and 47 American citizens were returned to the United States from foreign prisons.

Because many alien inmates choose to stay in the United States, in 1996 the BOP and the INS began working together to hold deportation hearings in the cases of criminal aliens while they are still serving their federal sentences.

Q 505. What is the breakdown of the citizenship of federal inmates?

A As of November 30, 1999, prisoners in the custody of the Federal Bureau of Prisons had citizenship in the following countries:

- United States, 69.9 percent
- Mexico, 14.6 percent
- Colombia, 3.2 percent
- Cuba, 2.2 percent
- Other or Unknown, 10.1 percent

Q 506. What is the average age of federal prisoners?

A As of November 30, 1999, the average age of inmates in the custody of the Federal Bureau of Prisons was thirty-seven years.

Q 507. What is the gender breakdown of the prisoner population?

A As of December 31, 1999, there were about 90,700 women and 1,276,000 men in state and federal prisons. Women accounted for 6.6 percent of all prisoners nationwide, up from 5.7 percent in 1990.

Q 508. How many prison systems allow conjugal visits?

A Most prisons do not permit inmates to have conjugal visits with their spouses. The U.S. Department of Justice reported that the number of prison systems that allowed conjugal visits dropped from eight in 1994 to six (12 percent) in 1998. States that permitted such visits were California, Connecticut, Mississippi, New Mexico, New York, and Washington.

Q 509. What happens when a prisoner is pregnant?

A In fiscal year 1999 the Federal Bureau of Prisons (BOP) reported sixty-seven pregnancies, twenty-four births, and two abortions in federal prisons. A BOP spokeswoman said that most of the pregnant inmates were released from prison prior to giving birth and for reasons other than pregnancy.

A special residential program, Mothers and Infants Together, allows pregnant women in minimum-security prisons to stay with their newborn babies for three months to allow bonding to occur. The mother must make prior arrangements for the care of her baby at the end of the program, when the mother returns to the prison. Forty-nine mothers participated in the MINT program in 1997.

A pregnant inmate must pay for an abortion out of her own funds unless her life would be endangered by carrying the fetus to term or in the case of rape. In the latter case, the BOP provides the inmate with an elective abortion.

In the 1800s, when a female convict had a baby, she was forced to deliver it alone in her cell—a practice that led to high rates of infant mortality. In 1927 the first separate federal institution for female offenders was built in Alderson, West Virginia. The new prison included a nursery. Babies were delivered in the prison hospital and remained in the nursery until age two. By the 1970s prisons sent female convicts to maternity wards at community hospitals to give birth. The babies did not return to the institutions because social service agencies regarded the presence of children in prisons to be unhealthy.

Today most correctional institutions provide pregnancy testing on request. Less than half of correctional systems provide routine pregnancy testing of incoming female inmates.

Q 510. What percentage of prisoners have AIDS or are HIV-positive?

A According to the latest statistics, 5,874 inmates—0.5 percent of all inmates in U.S. prisons—had confirmed acquired immune deficiency syndrome (AIDS) at the end of 1996. This number included 5,521 state inmates and 353 federal inmates. An additional 15,697 inmates had tested positive for human immunodeficiency virus (HIV), the virus that causes AIDS, but showed no symptoms of acute illness.

The rate of confirmed AIDS cases in state and federal prisons was six times higher than in the total U.S. population. More than half of all confirmed AIDS cases in state prisons were in New York, Florida, Texas, and California facilities.

Beginning in 1991 AIDS-related causes were the second-leading natural cause of death in state prisons. In 1996 AIDS deaths accounted for 29 percent of all deaths among state prisoners, down from 34 percent in 1995.

All state and federal prisons conduct some level of inmate testing for AIDS. A 1997 survey found that almost 60 percent of state and federal prisons and 41 percent of jails offered intensive counseling programs to help inmates make behavioral changes to reduce their risk of acquiring or transmitting HIV and other sexually transmittable diseases. Pre- and post-HIV counseling are offered in virtually all prisons and jails.

Only three state prison systems—Alabama, Mississippi, and California—segregate inmates with confirmed AIDS from the rest of the prison population. In most prisons inmates with HIV and AIDS face no restrictions on work assignments, with the exception of food preparation in some prisons.

Most prisons do not routinely notify correctional officers of an inmate's HIV status. Many institutions require guards to practice universal precautions and to treat all persons as if they are HIV-infected, avoiding contact with potentially infective bodily fluids, especially blood and semen.

Q 511. What is the extent of the problem of rape and coercive sex in correctional facilities?

A Few statistics exist with which to track the incidence of rape or coercive sex in prisons. However, a 1999 report issued by the U.S. Department of Justice states that "rape and coercive sex are serious and possibly widespread problems in correctional facilities."

Human immunodeficiency virus (HIV, the virus that causes AIDS) and many other communicable diseases can be transmitted sexually, which compounds the obvious problems of prison rape and sexual abuse. According to a 1999 report by U.S. Department of Justice, only six correctional systems make condoms available to inmates for use in their facilities. These systems are in Vermont, Mississippi, New York City, San Francisco, Philadelphia, and Washington, D.C.

Q 512. What happens when prisoners become elderly and infirm?

A The number of elderly prison inmates rose from about 9,000 in 1986 to 35,000 in 1997, primarily as a result of longer sentences. In most prison systems prisoners who become elderly and infirm are transferred to a hospital unit. Increasingly, states are building special nursing-home prison facilities for elderly and infirm prisoners.

A 1999 study by the National Center on Institutions and Alternatives, a nonprofit prison reform group in Alexandria, Virginia, reports that nearly 50,000 inmates age fifty-five or older are incarcerated in state and federal prisons. This number represents a 750 percent increase over the past twenty years. More than half of these prisoners were convicted of nonviolent offenses.

Older inmates tend to have more chronic health problems that require continuing care, including pharmacy care, physical therapy, dietary provisions, skilled nursing care, and related services. The cost of incarcerating an elderly inmate averages $69,000 per year—two to three times the average cost to incarcerate other prisoners. The average cost to the state to care for one person in a nonsecure nursing home is $32,000 per year. Virginia alone spends more than $61 million annually on 891 elderly inmates, who represent 3 percent of the state's inmate population.

Q 513. What are the leading causes of prisoner deaths?

A More than 3,200 prisoners die each year in state and federal correctional facilities, and this number is expected to grow. More than half of prisoners die of natural causes other than AIDS. Following are the causes and rates of death per 100,000 inmates in 1997, as reported by the U.S. Department of Justice:

Cause of Death	Rate of Death (per 100,000 Inmates)
Natural causes other than AIDS	170
AIDS	90
Suicide	15
By another person	6
Accident	4
Execution	4
Other or unspecified	16

In the 1980s prisons began establishing hospice programs to meet the spiritual, psychological, and medical needs of patients with six months or less to live. Interdisciplinary care teams include physicians, nurses, social workers, clergy, dietary professionals, pharmacists, psychologists, administrators, and security officials. Inmate volunteers occupy key care-giving roles. The National Prison Hospice Association was founded in 1991 to promote prison hospice care.

Almost two-thirds of state and federal prison systems and almost half of city and county jail systems permit compassionate release of dying prisoners. These prisoners are allowed to die at home or somewhere other than prison.

Q 514. How many prisoners were abused as children?

A Studies report that the rate of childhood abuse suffered by prison and jail inmates is roughly double that of the overall population.

A 1996–1997 survey by the U.S. Department of Justice found that more than 36 percent of women in state prisons and jails reported sexual or physical abuse at age seventeen or younger, whereas 14 percent of male inmates reported suffering abuse as children. The survey also found that rates of alcohol and drug abuse were higher among inmates who had suffered physical and sexual abuse at age seventeen or younger than among those who had not. Counting sexual or physical abuse at any age before imprisonment, nearly 50 percent of the women and 10 percent of the men in prison, in jail, or on probation had been attacked.

A 1998 federal study of 301 convicted male felons incarcerated in a New York State medium-security prison found that 68 percent reported some victimization—either neglect or physical or sexual abuse—before age twelve. About 35 percent reported suffering very severe violence as children.

Q 515. How many prisoners are mentally ill?

A The emptying of mental hospitals in the 1960s inundated the U.S. correctional system with mentally ill inmates. The proportion of mentally ill prisoners has been estimated at five times that of the general population. The Los Angeles County jail system, where 16 percent of the inmates require daily mental health services, has been called the largest mental institution in the United States.

The U.S. Department of Justice (DOJ) reports that at midyear 1998 about 283,800 mentally ill offenders were incarcerated in the nation's prisons and jails. Sixteen percent of all state prison inmates, 7 percent of federal prison inmates, and 16 percent of inmates in local jails were mentally ill. Offenders were identified as mentally ill if they reported a current emotional or mental condition or an overnight stay in a mental hospital or treatment program. The study also indicated that, overall, nearly one-third of all inmates "reported they had a current mental condition or had received mental health services at some time."

The DOJ study found that about 20 percent of mentally ill state prisoners were homeless, compared to 0.9 percent of other inmates. Mentally ill prisoners were twice as likely to have been physically or sexually abused in childhood and were far more likely than other prisoners to be regular users of alcohol and drugs.

The percentages of mentally ill inmates who had committed violent crimes were:

• State prisons, 53 percent (compared to 46 percent of other inmates)
• Federal prisons, 33 percent (compared to 13 percent of other inmates)
• Local jails, 30 percent (compared to 26 percent of other inmates)

Until 1825 prison officials were not authorized to transfer even obviously mentally ill convicts to mental institutions.

See 117 Does a link exist between mental illness and crime?

Q 516. Does the Americans With Disabilities Act protect disabled prisoners?

A In *Pennsylvania Dept. of Corrections v. Yeskey* (1998) the U.S. Supreme Court ruled that the Americans With Disabilities Act of 1990 (ADA) applies to inmates in state correctional institutions. Ronald Yeskey was sentenced to eighteen to thirty-six months in a Pennsylvania correctional facility. The sentencing judge recommended that Yeskey be placed at Pennsylvania's motivational boot-camp program for first-time offenders, successful completion of which would have led to his parole in just six months. Yeskey was refused admission to the program because he had a history of hypertension. The Court ruled that state prisons are public entities and as such are prohibited by the ADA from discriminating against a qualified individual with a disability on account of that disability.

The *Yeskey* ruling requires state prisons to make reasonable accommodations for inmates with disabilities to enable them to participate in prison recreational activities, medical services, and educational and vocational programs. Under the ADA, individuals are disabled if they have a physical or mental impairment that substantially limits a major life activity. This group includes hearing-impaired, blind, and physically disabled prisoners as well as prisoners who test positive for the human immunodeficiency virus or have acquired immune deficiency syndrome (AIDS).

Q 517. Can inmates smoke cigarettes?

A A 1998 national survey sponsored by the Robert Wood Johnson Foundation, a philanthropic group devoted to health care, found that about 55 percent of jails ban smoking by staff and inmates throughout the facility. Nine percent of jails ban smoking by inmates but not by staff. Two percent ban smoking by staff but not by inmates. A third of all jails allow smoking by both inmates and staff. Of the institutions that allow smoking, more than two-thirds prohibit smoking in some areas of the jail, and the rest have no smoking policy.

Q 518. How many prisoners have drug or alcohol problems?

A Research by the National Center on Addiction and Substance Abuse at Columbia University in 1998 indicates that 80 percent of prison and jail inmates have drug problems. Other research shows that at least three-quarters of prisoners abused alcohol or drugs in the time leading up to their arrest.

According to the U.S. Department of Justice, 57 percent of state prisoners and 45 percent of federal prisoners surveyed in 1997 said they had used drugs in the month before their current offenses, up from 50 percent and 32 percent, respectively, in 1991. Twenty-five percent of state prisoners and a little more than 16 percent of federal prisoners reported histories of abusing alcohol. Thirty percent of federal prisoners and 39 percent of state prisoners reported using marijuana. Twenty percent of federal prisoners and 25 percent of state prisoners reported using cocaine or crack.

Q 519. Can inmates obtain treatment for drug or alcohol problems in prison?

A The National Center on Addiction and Substance Abuse at Columbia University issued a report in 1998 stating that the gap between substance abuse treatment programs available in prisons and the need for such treatment is enormous and widening. The center estimated that 70 percent to 85 percent of inmates need treatment but that only 13 percent received treatment in 1996. The center reported that, on average, states spend only 5 percent of their prison budgets on drug treatment and that the Federal Bureau of Prisons (BOP) spent only 0.9 percent of its 1997 budget on drug treatment.

According to the BOP, forty-two federal prisons operate six-month residential drug-treatment programs. In 1998 these programs served about 10,000 inmates. In 1999 the programs had a waiting list of about 4,500 inmates. One reason for the popularity of prison drug-treatment programs is that, under federal law, inmates may reduce their prison sentences by a year if they successfully complete such a program.

The BOP also offers transitional services for inmates who are about to be released into the community, either to halfway houses or to the supervision of the U.S. Probation Service. These inmates are required to participate in community-based treatment programs to prevent relapse. In 1998 almost 7,000 inmates participated in such programs.

The BOP says it has made it a priority to provide residential drug-abuse treatment to all inmates with a substance abuse problem who volunteer for treatment. Experts say that reducing alcohol and drug abuse and addiction is important to reducing crime.

Q 520. Do substance abuse treatment programs cut recidivism among inmates?

A Yes. According to the U.S. Department of Justice's Office of National Drug Control Policy, providing treatment to inmates during and after incarceration can cut recidivism by half. Drug treatment costs an estimated $6,500 above usual incarceration costs but produces $68,800 in cost savings and benefits in the first year after release for each successful inmate. A 1998 study by the Federal Bureau of Prisons (BOP) and the National Institute on Drug Abuse shows that after six months out of custody, former inmates who had completed the BOP's residential drug abuse treatment program were 73 percent less likely to be rearrested and 44 percent less likely to use drugs than former inmates who had not participated in residential treatment.

See 527 What is the recidivism rate for prisoners?

A In 1998 the Federal Bureau of Prisons installed twenty-eight ion spectrometry drug-detection systems in various federal prisons to test visitors for trace amounts of drugs. Visitors who tested positive for drugs were not permitted to visit inmates. During a ninety-day pilot program at two institutions, about 4,000 visitors were tested. Of these visitors, about 200 tested positive for drugs. An additional 450 potential visitors refused to be tested and voluntarily left the prisons on learning that the device was in use.

Q 522. **Must prisons accommodate an inmate's special religious requirements?**

A Yes, but only up to a point. In *Cruz v. Beto* (1972) the U.S. Supreme Court ruled that inmates must have a reasonable opportunity to pursue their faith comparable to that offered other prisoners adhering to conventional religious precepts. However, in evaluating inmate religious complaints, the Court has accorded great deference to the needs of prison administrators to maintain institutional order and security. For example, the Court refused to force New Jersey prison authorities to allow Muslim prisoners assigned to an outside work detail to attend Jumu'ah, a Muslim congregational service held at the prison on Friday afternoons. In *O'Lone v. Estate of Shabazz* (1987) the Court noted that extra supervision would be required for inmates to attend the service, other inmates would complain that Muslims had escaped a work detail, and prison authorities feared that the gathering could reinforce an affinity group that would challenge institutional authority. The justices ruled that the New Jersey prison policies were reasonably related to a legitimate penological interest.

Prisons typically make some attempt to provide at least Jewish and Muslim inmates with a diet consistent with their religious beliefs and allow special ceremonies to observe major religious holidays.

Q 523. **How many faith groups are represented in federal prisons?**

A The Federal Bureau of Prisons estimates that thirty-one faith groups are represented in the federal prison population. Regular religious activities include Protestant services, Catholic Mass, Islamic and Nation of Islam Jumu'ah prayer services, Native American sweat lodge ceremonies, Jewish Sabbath services, and various other services and rituals prescribed for other religious groups.

Q 524. What "religion" did the U.S. Supreme Court refuse to recognize?

A The Court refused on at least three occasions to consider appeals filed by two prison inmates who founded the Church of the New Song, also called the Eclatarian faith.

Harry W. Theriault and Jerry M. Dorrough founded the faith in 1971 when they were inmates at the federal penitentiary at Atlanta, Georgia. Theriault said he received prophetic messages from an entity named Eclat informing him that he was the Eclatarian Nazarite and directing him to establish the Church of the New Song.

Theriault, who had obtained a doctor of divinity certificate through the mail, filed numerous federal lawsuits against various prison chaplains and prisons, including a class action lawsuit on behalf of 164 inmates seeking recognition of the religion. Among other things, the suits demanded the Church of the New Song be given the right to use the prison chapel and that Theriault be extended all of the privileges of a prison chaplain. When all of the cases were consolidated, they filled two legal-size cabinet drawers and approximately twenty-one volumes.

At one point in 1973, a federal court judge in Georgia agreed that the faith was a religion. However, in 1978 and 1980, two U.S. courts of appeals concluded that the Church of the New Song was a sham that was not entitled to First Amendment protection.

Prison officials charged that Theriault, who had been convicted of theft, assault and escape, began the religion as a game but became more serious as he gained converts. They also charged that the so-called religion fostered a do-as-you-please philosophy that encouraged the disruption of prison discipline.

Undaunted, in the mid-1980s Theriault founded another new religion, which he called the Holy Mizanic faith.

Q 525. How many prisoners escape from federal prisons each year?

A In 1997 and 1998 no federal prisoners escaped from secure Bureau of Prison institutions, including low, medium, high, and administrative security facilities. The rate of escapes from secure federal prisons has fallen dramatically since 1982, when 16.2 inmates per 5,000 inmates escaped. The decrease has been attributed to various causes, including improved lighting patterns, fortified fences, enhanced escape detection systems, modified patrol patterns, improved key and tool control, and increased staff training.

Q 526. What is the most notorious prison break in history?

A The most notorious prison break in history may be the 1962 escape of three bank robbers from Alcatraz prison. Alcatraz was located on a small island off the coast of San Francisco and was considered by many authorities to be inescapable. From 1934 to 1963, Alcatraz housed many of the most notorious and dangerous offenders in the federal prison system.

On June 12, 1962, during a 7:15 A.M. bed-check, prison guards discovered dummy faces in the bunks of Frank Lee Morris and brothers John William and Clarence Anglin. The three prisoners had escaped the island prison using a makeshift raft fashioned from the olive-colored rubberized raincoats that were supplied to prisoners. The escapees had used hot steam pipes to vulcanize the seams to make them airtight. Frank Lee Morris had bought a concertina, which the prisoners used as a bellows to blow up the raft. To get to the roof of the cellblock, the prisoners had crawled through a ventilator shaft. They even had stolen a motor from a vacuum cleaner to make a drill so they could open bolts on a lid covering the ventilator shaft. The prisoners had worked on their escape plan for approximately one year.

The Federal Bureau of Investigation (FBI) conducted an intensive air and sea search but concluded that the prisoners never reached the shore. A homemade life jacket and a packet made of the same type of rubberized material as the escape raft were found. The packet contained personal effects of the Anglin brothers, pictures, and names and addresses. Shortly thereafter, the FBI pronounced that the men were presumed to be dead.

One bit of evidence suggested that the prisoners might have succeeded. A homemade paddle, one of four made by the prisoners, was found in about twelve feet of water less than 200 yards off Angel Island, which was their apparent destination. Also, the warden of Alcatraz received a postcard postmarked June 16, 1962, containing the hand-printed message, "Ha Ha We Made It."

After the escape, prison officials found a variety of hacksaws, metal files and various tools in the inmates' cells. Lee's cell also contained a copy of *Sports Illustrated* magazine that described the making of a rubberized boat.

Built in 1909, Alcatraz was used as a military installation until 1933, when it was turned over to the Federal Bureau of Prisons for use as a penitentiary. The bureau added tool-proof iron bars to the cells that required a minimum of six hours of sawing to cut through. FBI Director J. Edgar Hoover reportedly said that anyone who successfully escaped from Alcatraz deserved a pardon. Alcatraz closed in 1963 because the facility had become too expensive to operate.

527. What is the recidivism rate for prisoners?

A Nationally at least half of the inmates released from prison return to prison for subsequent criminal infractions. An analysis of the criminal records of more than 16,000 men and women representing the almost 109,000 offenders who were released from prisons in eleven states in 1983 found that 62.4 percent were rearrested for a felony or serious misdemeanor within three years. About 47 percent of the former prisoners were convicted of new crimes and 41 percent were sent back to prison or jail. By the end of 1986 those prisoners who were rearrested averaged an additional 4.8 new charges.

Among other things, the analysis found:

- The more extensive a prisoner's prior arrest record, the higher the rate of recidivism. More than 74 percent of those with eleven or more prior arrests were rearrested, compared to 38 percent of first-time offenders.
- The older the prisoner, the lower the rate of recidivism.
- Released rapists were 10.5 times more likely than nonrapist offenders to be rearrested for rape.
- An estimated 6.6 percent of released murderers were rearrested for homicide, and released murderers were about 5 times more likely than other types of offenders to be rearrested for homicide.

One study found that in 1996 the average recidivism rate after four years following release from prison was 32.5 percent.

See 520 Do substance abuse treatment programs cut recidivism among inmates?

Q **528. How many prisoners are released each year?**

A The national release rate for state prisoners declined from 37 per 100 prisoners in 1990 to 31 per 100 prisoners in 1998. In 1998, an estimated 520,000 offenders were released from state prisons, up from 405,400 in 1990.

See 248 Do tougher prison sentences deter crime? 538 How many inmates are released from prison with no post-release supervision?

Q **529. What is the *civil death* doctrine?**

A In medieval Europe, infamous offenders suffered the equivalent of a *civil death* that entailed "the deprivation of all rights, confiscation of property, exposure to injury, and even to death, since the outlaw could be killed with impunity by anyone." Prisoners who suffered a civil death lost the right to vote, contract, marry, sue, or be sued. Colonists brought this doctrine with them to America, and remnants of it persist even today.

Today civil disabilities continue to attach to a felony conviction, including limitations on the right to vote and to hold public office, to serve on juries, to parental rights, to own firearms, and to hold public employment.

Most states have disenfranchisement laws that deprive convicted felons of the right to vote while they are in prison. Most states also bar convicted offenders from voting while they are on parole or probation. Three states—Maine, Massachusetts, and Vermont—do not disenfranchise convicted felons.

Felons in ten states permanently forfeit the right to vote unless the inmates receive pardons from the governor or dispensations from a board of pardons or parole. These states are: Alabama, Delaware, Florida, Iowa, Kentucky, Mississippi, Nevada, New Mexico, Virginia, and Wyoming. In addition, Arizona and Maryland permanently disenfranchise offenders who are convicted of a second felony.

According to the Sentencing Project, a Washington, D.C., advocacy group that promotes sentencing reform, 2 percent of the adult population of the United States cannot vote because they are felons or ex-felons. Many of these disenfranchised individuals are members of minority groups.

Loss, suspension, or restriction of a professional or occupational license may result from a felony conviction, and felons may be disqualified from obtaining a license in the future. For example, sex offenders commonly are prohibited from working in such fields as teaching and childcare.

The federal government, forty-three states, the District of Columbia, and the U.S. Virgin Islands have passed laws making it a crime (usually a felony) for a person who was previously convicted of a felony to own, possess, or carry a firearm. Persons—including law enforcement personnel—who are convicted of misdemeanor crimes involving domestic violence also are barred from possessing a firearm.

Felons also may lose their right to be left alone. Felons may be required to register with a local law enforcement agency. Every state now has a law requiring the registration of convicted sex offenders on their release from custody, and virtually every state has a law that permits law enforcement agencies to share information from the state sex offender registry with local communities.

In *Richardson v. Ramirez* (1974), the U.S. Supreme Court held that states have broad constitutional authority to disenfranchise persons convicted of crimes under the Fourteenth Amendment, which allows states to deny citizens the right to vote as part of the punishment "for participation in rebellion, or other crime." The Court found this authority to be so broad as to justify permanent disenfranchisement of convicted persons.

Q 530. Do all prisoners have the right to go free after completing their prison terms?

A No. In *Kansas v. Hendricks* (1997) the U.S. Supreme Court ruled that the state can initiate civil commitment proceedings to detain dangerous sex offenders in mental institutions after completion of their criminal sentences. The Court said it has "consistently upheld involuntary commitment statutes that detain people who are unable to control their behavior and thereby pose a danger to the public health and safety, provided the confinement takes place pursuant to proper procedures and evidentiary standards."

According to the Court, involuntary commitment of individuals who are suffering from a mental abnormality or mental illness is not punishment, and its purpose is not retributive. Therefore, involuntary commitment does not violate the double jeopardy clause in the Fifth Amendment to the U.S. Constitution, which prevents the government from prosecuting a defendant twice for the same conduct. Theoretically, dangerous sex offenders can be detained indefinitely, until they show that they no longer pose a danger to others.

The Court upheld Kansas's Sexually Violent Predator Act, which defines a *sexually violent predator* as "any person who has been convicted of or charged with a sexually violent offense and who suffers from a mental abnormality or personality disorder which makes the person likely to engage in the predatory acts of sexual violence." The defendant in this case was a pedophile with a long history of arrests and incarcerations for child molestation. After serving nearly ten years of his sentence the offender was slated for release to a halfway house when a court ordered his civil commitment. The prisoner had refused to participate in a sexual offender treatment program during his incarceration and testified that he still harbored urges to molest children.

In the 1990s many states passed registration and notification laws that require most sex offenders to register with police and require authorities to notify neighbors of the names and addresses of known sex offenders.

See 5 What is the significance of the Bill of Rights to criminal law? 11 What rights are afforded defendants under the Fifth Amendment to the U.S. Constitution?

Q **531. What is the most commonly applied criminal sanction?**

A Under a sentence of probation the offender typically is released into the community under the supervision of a probation officer in lieu of incarceration. Probation is the most commonly applied criminal sanction. Almost 60 percent of adults under correctional supervision are on probation. Slightly more than 3.7 million people were on probation as of December 31, 1999, an increase since 1998 of more than 350,000 people. Nearly three out of five probationers were convicted of felony offenses.

An offender may be sentenced to both probation and incarceration. For example, an offender may be required to spend weekends or nights in jails. With *shock probation* an offender—typically a young, first-time offender—is sentenced to a period of incarceration, often at a boot camp, after which the defendant is released and re-sentenced to probation. Shock probation reflects the hope that a relatively brief imprisonment will sufficiently impress the inmate to avoid future criminal activity.

Traditionally probation was considered an act of clemency that offers eligible offenders the chance to reform and rehabilitate themselves. Since the 1970s probation has come to be considered a form of risk management.

All probationers must comply with standard conditions of probation, such as reporting to a probation office, remaining in the jurisdiction, staying employed, and informing the probation office of changes of address. Many probationers also are required to comply with special conditions, such as mandatory drug testing, drug treatment, employment training, community service, and payment of fines or restitution. Special conditions of probation are designed to protect the community by minimizing the possibility the probationer will re-offend, and they also sometimes seek to repair some of the damage the offender has caused to the community.

Failure to comply with probation requirements or a new arrest and conviction can result in revocation of probation and possible jail. A violation of a rule that results in revocation of probation is called a *technical violation*. According to most studies, from one-fifth to one-third of probationers fail to abide by the terms of their probation.

Q **532. What does a probation officer do?**

A Probation officers have two major tasks: they help the court determine an appropriate sentence in a case, and they supervise offenders who are granted probation.

The probation officer conducts a pre-sentence investigation (PSI) of the convicted offender and prepares a report that typically includes a recommended sentence. The PSI contains the police version of the event, the defendant's version of the event, and a statement from the victim. It includes the offender's prior record, including arrests that did not result in convictions and an account of how the offender performed if previously sentenced to prison, parole, or probation. Finally, the PSI includes details of the offender's personal history, including family, educational, employment, military, and medical history.

Probation officers also are responsible for supervising offenders who are placed on probation to ensure that they adhere to the conditions of probation. Probation officers may supervise more than 100 offenders at any one time. Probation offices generally use a case management system to help probation officers focus their efforts and determine which cases require intensive supervision or special services.

The administration of probation services varies widely among the states. A probation office may be under the authority of either the judiciary or the executive branch. It may be part of a highly centralized statewide administrative body or be a localized county-based agency.

Q 533. Who was the first probation officer in the United States?

A A Boston bootmaker and philanthropist, John Augustus, is considered to have been the first probation officer in the United States. In 1841 Augustus convinced a Boston Police Court judge to defer sentencing and release into Augustus's custody a man charged with being a common drunkard. Three weeks later, the judge agreed that the drunkard had reformed himself and issued him a nominal fine in lieu of incarceration. Augustus is credited with devising the concepts of the pre-sentence investigation, supervision conditions, social casework, reports to the court, and revocation of probation.

Q 534. What is parole?

A Parole is the conditional release from incarceration of a prisoner who has served part of his or her sentence. Generally an offender is granted parole by an executive authority, such as a parole board, or enters parole pursuant to a sentencing statute or a "good time" provision. An offender who is on parole must fulfill conditional requirements, such as keeping a job, not using drugs, and reporting regularly to a parole officer. Successful completion of parole results in termination of the sentence.

Outrage over criminals who commit crimes while on parole has led to a dramatic decline in the number of offenders who are released each year by state parole boards. Parole boards released 29 percent of offenders in 1997, compared to 41 percent in 1990. In addition, the number of inmates returned to prison because of parole violations grew almost 40 percent from 1990 to 1997. The U.S. Department of Justice estimates that nearly half of parolees successfully complete their terms of parole and the majority of the balance are returned to incarceration. Nearly 712,700 adults were on parole as of December 31, 1999, up from about 705,000 in 1998.

The Sentencing Reform Act of 1984 abolished parole eligibility for federal offenders who commit offenses on or after November 1, 1987. The U.S. Parole Commission still exists to consider paroles for prisoners who were eligible before that date, to supervise parolees, and to fulfill other duties, such as determining whether or not persons convicted of certain crimes may serve as officials in the field of organized labor. Since 1998 the commission also has been responsible for making parole decisions for District of Columbia offenders.

As of 1998 fourteen states had abolished parole board release for virtually all offenders, and six other states had abolished parole board release for certain types of violent offenders. Following are the states that have effectively abolished parole:

- Arizona
- Delaware
- Florida
- Illinois
- Indiana
- Kansas
- Maine
- Minnesota
- Mississippi
- North Carolina
- Ohio
- Oregon
- Washington
- Wisconsin

The states that abolished parole board release for certain violent or felony offenders were Alaska, New York, Tennessee, and Virginia. Louisiana has abolished parole for certain crimes against a person, and California allows discretionary release by a parole board only for offenders with indeterminate life sentences.

Q 535. What inmate's weekend furlough swayed a presidential election?

A The criminal record of Willie Horton became a focal point in the 1988 presidential contest between Democrat Michael Dukakis, the former governor of Massachusetts, and Republican George Bush. Horton had been convicted of a grisly first-degree murder in Massachusetts and sentenced to life in prison without parole. When he was given a weekend pass, Horton escaped, and he later kidnapped and brutally assaulted a white couple in their home, raping the woman and stabbing the man. A group that was technically not affiliated with Bush's campaign released a television commercial focusing on Horton, who was an African American, and criticizing the law-and-order record of Dukakis. As governor, Dukakis had refused to meet with crime victims seeking to discontinue the prison furlough program. Some analysts said the flap was more about exploiting racial stereotypes than fear of crime. Nevertheless, the controversy helped Bush defeat Dukakis.

Q 536. Do parolees have the same rights as criminal defendants?

A No. The U.S. Supreme Court has ruled that a parolee is not entitled to "the full panoply" of due process rights to which a criminal defendant is entitled. In *Morrissey v. Brewer* (1972) the Court said a parolee generally has no right to counsel at parole revocation proceedings. The Court subsequently ruled in *Pennsylvania Bd. of Probation and Parole v. Scott* (1998) that evidence seized in violation of a parolee's Fourth Amendment rights may be introduced in federal parole revocation hearings. The Court said that the exclusionary rule is a judicially created means of deterring illegal searches and seizures. It applies only where the deterrence benefits of excluding evidence outweigh the substantial social costs inherent in precluding consideration of reliable, probative evidence. According to the Court, "The social costs of allowing convicted criminals who violate their parole to remain at large are particularly high . . . and are compounded by the fact that parolees (particularly those who have already committed parole violations) are more likely to commit future crimes than are average citizens." In *Scott* the Court upheld parole officers' seizure without a warrant of firearms and a bow and arrows from the home of a parolee who was barred, as a condition of his parole, from owning or possessing weapons.

See 15 What is due process?

Q 537. What is *Buck Rogers time?*

A *Buck Rogers time* is prison slang for a parole date that is so far into the future that the inmate has trouble imagining ever being released. *Buck Rogers in the Twenty-Fifth Century* was a popular science-fiction comic strip that began in the 1930s. Movies and a short-lived television series (1979–1981) extended familiarity with Buck Rogers to later generations.

Q **538. How many inmates are released from prison with no post-release supervision?**

A In 1999 about 100,000 of the inmates released from state prisons had no post-release supervision. They had maxed out and served their full sentences. No criminal justice agency was responsible for them as they moved from a prison cell to the outside world. Critics say the abolition of parole and the enactment of truth-in-sentencing laws have decreased the likelihood that inmates will receive post-release supervision. They say the lack of such supervision increases the risk of recidivism and the danger these prisoners pose to society. The federal government is working with eight states to develop reentry courts, a program in which state correctional officials, local police agencies, and community groups will work with returning prisoners to create support networks and accountability systems to enhance the chances of successful reintegration of the offender into the community.

See 310 What is a reentry court? 528 How many prisoners are released each year?

CAPITAL PUNISHMENT

Q **539. Did the American colonists execute prisoners?**

A Colonists in America brought with them the practice of capital punishment. In 1636 the Massachusetts Bay Colony listed the following thirteen crimes as punishable by death:

- Adultery
- Assault in sudden anger
- Blasphemy
- Buggery
- Idolatry
- Manstealing (stealing a slave or indentured servant)
- Murder
- Perjury in a capital trial
- Rape
- Rebellion
- Sodomy
- Statutory rape
- Witchcraft

In 1682 Pennsylvania passed a law limiting the death penalty to murder and treason. There were 162 executions in the colonies during the 1600s. The first recorded execution was that of Captain George Kendall, a councilor of Jamestown Colony, who was executed in 1608 after he was accused of being a spy for Spain. Persons who were convicted of capital crimes often faced public hanging.

See 20 What were the first crimes established by the U.S. Congress? 316 How were laws enforced in colonial America?

Q 540. What does the U.S. Constitution say about capital punishment?

A The Framers of the U.S. Constitution recognized the existence of capital punishment. The Fifth Amendment provides that "[n]o persons shall be held to answer for a capital crime unless on presentment or indictment of a grand jury . . . nor be deprived of life . . . without the due process of law." This provision establishes that the death penalty was not considered one of the "cruel and unusual punishments" prohibited by the Eighth Amendment.

The Fourteenth Amendment to the U.S. Constitution, adopted after the Civil War, similarly says that no state shall "deprive any person of life, liberty, or property without the due process of law."

In 1972 the U.S. Supreme Court concluded that the death penalty violated the Eighth Amendment because it was arbitrarily applied. In *Furman v. Georgia* (1972) the Court voided the death penalty laws of thirty-two states, removing 629 persons across the country from death row. "These death sentences are cruel and unusual in the same way that being struck by lightning is cruel and unusual," wrote Justice Potter Stewart.

Four years later, the Court in a 7–2 decision said that the death penalty is not cruel and unusual punishment if it is applied in accordance with carefully drafted statutes that ensure the sentencing authority is given adequate information and guidance. In *Gregg v. Georgia* (1976), the Court approved two-stage trials that allowed juries to consider "aggravating or mitigating circumstances" before sentencing. "No longer can a jury wantonly and freakishly impose the death sentence," Justice Stewart wrote.

Q **541. What states have a death penalty?**

A As of midyear 2000 thirty-eight states and the federal government authorized the death penalty. Following are the states that authorize the death penalty:

- Alabama
- Arizona
- Arkansas
- California
- Colorado
- Connecticut
- Delaware
- Florida
- Georgia
- Idaho
- Illinois
- Indiana
- Kansas
- Kentucky
- Louisiana
- Maryland
- Mississippi
- Missouri
- Montana
- Nebraska
- Nevada
- New Hampshire
- New Jersey
- New Mexico
- New York
- North Carolina
- Ohio
- Oklahoma
- Oregon
- Pennsylvania
- South Carolina
- South Dakota
- Tennessee
- Texas
- Utah
- Virginia
- Washington
- Wyoming

Following are the jurisdictions that do not authorize the death penalty:

- Alaska
- District of Columbia
- Hawaii
- Iowa
- Maine
- Massachusetts
- Michigan
- Minnesota
- North Dakota
- Rhode Island
- Vermont
- West Virginia
- Wisconsin

New Hampshire's legislature voted to repeal the state's death penalty statute in May 2000, but the governor vetoed the bill.

A moratorium was placed on the death penalty in Illinois in January 2000 when the state's Republican governor, George Ryan, said he would approve no more executions until a review of the state's administration of the death penalty. Ryan said that the Illinois system was fraught with error. Since 1977, when the death penalty was reinstated in Illinois, the state had executed twelve inmates and rescinded the death penalty in thirteen cases. A local newspaper determined that in at least thirty-three death-penalty cases lawyers who were later disbarred or suspended had represented defendants.

Concern about the fairness of the death penalty has prompted several other states to initiate a review of the administration of their death penalty statutes.

See Figure 5-3 Prisoners on Death Row, 1953–1998.

Q 542. How do Americans feel about the death penalty?

A A national survey of attitudes about the death penalty shows a dramatic shift from 1965 to 1999. More Americans support capital punishment today. The poll, conducted by Louis Harris and Associates, Inc., asked, "Do you believe in capital punishment, that is, the death penalty, or are you opposed to it?" In 1999, 71 percent of respondents said they believed in the death penalty, 21 percent were opposed, and 8 percent were not sure. Following is a sampling of years and the percentage of respondents who replied affirmatively:

Year	*People Who Say They Believe in the Death Penalty*
1965	38 percent
1970	48 percent
1976	67 percent
1983	68 percent
1997	75 percent
1999	71 percent

Support for the death penalty softens when respondents are given other alternatives, such as the choice between the death penalty and a sentence of life in prison without parole. Also, even death penalty proponents express concerns about the fairness of the death penalty.

Figure 5-3 Prisoners on Death Row, 1953–1998

Number of prisoners on death row

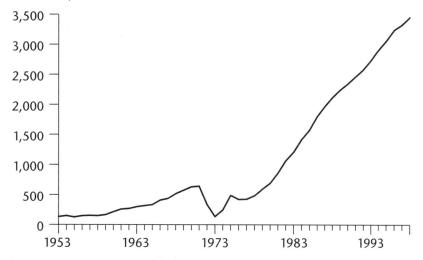

Source: Department of Justice, Bureau of Justice Statistics Publication NCJ179012, *Capital Punishment, 1998* (Washington, D.C.: Government Printing Office, 1999).

Q 543. What is a Simmons instruction?

A A Simmons instruction is an instruction given to a jury before the jury starts its deliberations in a death penalty case where the defendant is ineligible for parole under state law. The judge informs the jury that the defendant is parole ineligible. That fact influences how a jury perceives the defendant's future dangerousness and the amount of time the defendant will actually serve in prison.

In *Simmons v. South Carolina* (1994) the U.S. Supreme Court ruled that failing to inform the jury that a defendant is parole ineligible is a violation of the due process clause of the U.S. Constitution. According to the Court, "The State may not create a false dilemma by advancing generalized arguments regarding the defendant's future dangerousness while, at the same time, preventing the jury from learning that the defendant never will be released on parole."

Q **544. Is the death penalty a deterrent?**

A This question has generated one of the great continuing debates of our time. Proponents of the death penalty say that no one knows the number of people who would have become murderers—and consequently the number of lives saved—if they did not fear the death penalty. Opponents of the death penalty cite research that shows that the death penalty has no greater deterrent effect than other punishments. A Columbia University study in June 2000 found no apparent reduction in homicide in states with the death penalty. According to the study, the murder rate from 1973 to 1995 was 9 murders per 100,000 population for the nation as a whole and 9.3 per 100,000 for states with the death penalty.

Q **545. What Supreme Court Justice had second thoughts about the death penalty?**

A Justice Harry A. Blackmun in 1994 wrote a dissent from a U.S. Supreme Court decision denying review in a Texas death penalty case in which he said: "From this day forward, I no longer shall tinker with the machinery of death. For more than 20 years I have endeavored . . . to develop . . . rules that would lend more than the mere appearance of fairness to the death penalty endeavor. . . . Rather than continue to coddle the Court's delusion that the desired level of fairness has been achieved . . . I feel . . . obligated simply to concede that the death penalty experiment has failed."

Q **546. Has a defendant ever been executed twice?**

A In 1947 Willie Francis, age sixteen, was convicted of murder in Louisiana and sentenced to death by electrocution. When the executioner threw the switch, the chair malfunctioned. The electric current that passed through the prisoner's body was insufficient to kill him. In *Louisiana ex rel v. Resweber* (1947) the U.S. Supreme Court ruled that Francis could be executed again because the failure of the first attempt related to an unforseeable accident that did not involve intentional cruelty. The Court said that the Constitution protects an offender from cruelty inherent in the method of punishment, not necessary suffering involved in any method employed to extinguish life humanely.

Q **547. What crimes are punishable by death?**

A The states reserve the death penalty for the most serious crime, murder, especially when it is accompanied by aggravating circumstances, such as a murder committed in furtherance of drug trafficking or a kidnapping. Historically rape had been a capital offense, but it is no longer. In *Coker v. Georgia* (1977) the U.S. Supreme Court struck down a Georgia law permitting executions in rape cases, calling the punishment excessive in its severity and revocability.

Dozens of federal crimes carry the death penalty, including espionage, treason, and genocide. Federal law spells out numerous aggravating situations that convert a murder into a capital offense. These include murder for hire, murder of a law enforcement or correctional officer, murder by an escaped federal prisoner already sentenced to life imprisonment, murder related to the smuggling of aliens, drive-by drug shootings, a retaliatory murder of a member of the immediate family of law enforcement officials, and murder of a member of Congress, an important executive official, or a Supreme Court justice.

Q 548. How many defendants are executed annually?

A Ninety-eight prisoners were executed in the United States in 1999, the highest number since the U.S. Supreme Court reinstated the death penalty in 1976. A total of 598 persons were executed from 1976 to 1999. Following are the years and numbers of executions for selected years from 1930 through 1999:

Year	Number of Executions	Year	Number of Executions
1930	155	1986	18
1940	124	1987	25
1950	82	1988	11
1960	56	1989	16
1976	0	1990	23
(death penalty reinstated)		1991	14
1977	1	1992	31
1978	0	1993	38
1979	2	1994	31
1980	0	1995	56
1981	1	1996	45
1982	2	1997	74
1983	5	1998	68
1984	21	1999	98
1985	18		

See Figure 5-4 Executions, 1930–1999.

Figure 5-4 Executions, 1930–1999

Number of prisoners executed

Source: Department of Justice, Bureau of Justice Statistics Publication NCJ179012, *Capital Punishment, 1998* (Washington, D.C.: Government Printing Office, 1999).

Q 549. What state executes the most inmates?

A In 1999, for the third straight year, Texas—at 35 inmates—led the nation in number of executions. Since the death penalty was reinstated, Texas has executed 199 inmates. Texas is followed by Virginia, with 73 executions, and Florida, with 44 executions. One study showed that from January 1, 1977, to December 31, 1998, nearly two-thirds of the 500 executions that had taken place in eighteen states occurred in Texas (164), Virginia (59), Florida (43), Missouri (32), and Louisiana (24).

See 544 Is the death penalty a deterrent?

Q 550. What methods are used to execute inmates?

A The federal government and thirty-four states authorized death by lethal injection in 1998. Eleven states authorized death by electrocution, and five states authorized death by lethal gas. Death by hanging was permitted in three states, as was death by firing squad.

Lethal injection is by far the most common method of execution. Of the 500 prisoners executed between 1977 and 1998, 344 were executed by lethal injection, 141 by electrocution, 10 by lethal gas, 3 by hanging, and 2 by firing squad. Lethal injection typically involves three drugs. The first drug is sodium thiopental, a barbiturate that renders the prisoner unconscious. The second drug, pancuronium bromide, a muscle relaxant, paralyzes the diaphragm and lungs. The third, potassium chloride, causes cardiac arrest.

See 562 How did "Old Sparky" get its name? Also see Table 5-1 Method of Execution by State, 1998.

Q 551. Has an innocent person ever been executed?

A This question is hotly contested. There is no generally acknowledged modern-day example of an innocent person who was executed. However, there also is no dispute that mistakes occur in the application of the death penalty.

Since the death penalty was reinstated in 1976, approximately seventy-five people who were sentenced to death have been later released from prison after being declared innocent or after charges against them were dropped because of overwhelming evidence of innocence.

A Columbia University study reported in June 2000 that two out of three death penalty convictions were overturned on appeal from 1976 to 1995, mostly because of serious errors by incompetent defense lawyers or overzealous police officers and prosecutors who withheld evidence. Seventy-five percent of the people whose death sentences were set aside were later given lesser sentences after retrials, in plea bargains, or by order of a judge; 7 percent were found not guilty of the capital offense on retrial, and 18 percent were given the death penalty on retrial—but many of these defendants had their convictions overturned again in the appeals process.

In January 2000 Illinois Gov. George H. Ryan imposed a moratorium on executions after concluding that thirteen people in his state had been unjustly sentenced to death (though not executed) since 1977.

No government official has acknowledged that an innocent person has been executed since 1887, when four defendants were hanged in Illinois after a bomb exploded at a workers' rally at Haymarket Square in Chicago, killing a police officer. Six years later, Illinois Governor John Altgeld pardoned three surviving codefendants because all eight "had been wrongfully convicted and were innocent of the crime."

The human rights group Amnesty International contends that at least twenty-three innocent prisoners were executed between 1900 and 1987.

Table 5-1 Method of Execution by State, 1998

Lethal Injection		Electrocution	Lethal Gas	Hanging	Firing Squad
Arizona[a,b]	New Hampshire[a]	Alabama	Arizona[a,b]	Delaware[a,c]	Idaho[a]
Arkansas[a,d]	New Jersey	Arkansas[a,d]	California[a]	New Hampshire[a,e]	Oklahoma[f]
California[a]	New Mexico	Florida	Missouri[a]	Washington[a]	Utah[a]
Colorado	New York	Georgia	North Carolina[a]		
Connecticut	North Carolina[a]	Kentucky[a,g]	Wyoming[a,h]		
Delaware[a,c]	Ohio[a]	Nebraska			
Idaho[a]	Oklahoma[a]	Ohio[a]			
Illinois	Oregon	Oklahoma[f]			
Indiana	Pennsylvania	South Carolina[a]			
Kansas	South Carolina[a]	Tennessee[a,i]			
Kentucky[a,g]	South Dakota	Virginia[a]			
Louisiana	Tennessee[a,i]				
Maryland	Texas				
Mississippi	Utah[a]				
Missouri[a]	Virginia[a]				
Montana	Washington[a]				
Nevada	Wyoming[a]				

Note: The method of execution of federal prisoners is lethal injection, pursuant to 28 CFR, Part 26. For offenses under the Violent Crime Control and Law Enforcement Act of 1994, the method is that of the state in which the conviction took place, pursuant to 18 U.S.C. 3586.

[a]Authorizes two methods of execution.

[b]Arizona authorizes lethal injection for persons whose capital sentence was received after November 15, 1992; for those sentenced before that date, the condemned may select lethal injection or lethal gas.

[c]Delaware authorizes lethal injection for those whose capital offense occurred after June 13, 1986; for those whose offense occurred before that date, the comdemned may select lethal injection or hanging.

[d]Arkansas authorizes lethal injection for those whose capital offense occurred on or after July 4, 1983; for those whose offense occurred before that date, the comdemned may select lethal injection or electrocution.

[e]New Hampshire authorizes hanging only if lethal injection cannot be given.

[f]Oklahoma authorizes electrocution if lethal injection is ever held to be unconstitutional, and firing squad if both lethal injection and electrocution are held unconstitutional.

[g]Kentucky authorizes lethal injection for persons whose capital sentence was received on or after May 31, 1998; for those sentenced before that date, the condemned may select lethal injection or electrocution.

[h]Wyoming authorizes lethal gas if lethal injection is ever held to be unconstitutional.

[i]Tennessee authorizes lethal injection for those whose capital offense occurred after December 31, 1998; those whose offense occurred before that date may select lethal injection or electrocution.

Source: Department of Justice, Bureau of Justice Statistics Publication NCJ179012, *Capital Punishment, 1998* (Washington, D.C.: Government Printing Office, 1999).

Q 552. Can an inmate who becomes insane be executed?

A No. In *Ford v. Wainwright* (1986) the U.S. Supreme Court ruled that executing an inmate who becomes insane violates the Eighth Amendment's ban on cruel and unusual punishment. To be eligible for execution, the Court said, a prisoner must have the mental capacity to understand the nature of the death penalty and why it was imposed. The inmate may still be executed in the future if an impartial officer or board determines that the prisoner has regained his or her sanity.

Q 553. Can a mentally retarded inmate be executed?

A Yes. The U.S. Supreme Court has ruled that mentally retarded people can be executed if, at the time of the offense, they possessed the cognitive, volitional, and moral capacity to act with the degree of culpability associated with the death penalty. In *Penry v. Lynaugh* (1989) the Court said that a blanket rule pertaining to mental retardation was inappropriate, given the varying capabilities of retarded people. A sentencing authority can consider mitigating evidence of mental retardation when imposing a sentence, after making an individualized determination as to whether death is an appropriate punishment. About a dozen mentally retarded inmates have been executed since the death penalty was reinstated in 1976. A dozen states prohibit the death penalty for mentally retarded inmates.

Q 554. Can a person be too young to get the death penalty?

A To be eligible for the death penalty, a juvenile must have attained a minimum age at the time of the crime. The U.S. Supreme Court has declared that it is unconstitutional to execute offenders who were age fifteen or younger when they committed their crimes. Thus, the minimum execution age is sixteen, though most states have established higher minimum ages.

Since the death penalty was reinstated in 1976, more than two dozen persons have been executed for crimes they committed when they were under age eighteen. About 70 of the estimated 3,630 prisoners on U.S. death rows as of January 2000 had committed a murder before age eighteen.

Following are the effective minimum ages for the death penalty in those jurisdictions that allow the death penalty:

• Federal government, age eighteen
• Alabama, age sixteen

- Arkansas, age sixteen
- California, age eighteen
- Colorado, age eighteen
- Connecticut, age eighteen
- Delaware, age sixteen
- Florida, age sixteen
- Georgia, age seventeen
- Illinois, age eighteen
- Indiana, age sixteen
- Kansas, age eighteen
- Kentucky, age sixteen
- Maryland, age eighteen
- Mississippi, age sixteen
- Missouri, age sixteen
- Nebraska, age eighteen
- Nevada, age sixteen
- New Hampshire, age seventeen
- New Jersey, age eighteen
- New Mexico, age eighteen
- New York, age eighteen
- North Carolina, age seventeen
- Ohio, age eighteen
- Oklahoma, age sixteen
- Oregon, age eighteen
- Tennessee, age eighteen
- Texas, age seventeen
- Virginia, age sixteen
- Washington, age eighteen
- Wyoming, age sixteen

No minimum age for the death penalty is specified in Arizona, Idaho, Louisiana, Montana, Pennsylvania, South Carolina, South Dakota, or Utah.

Technically, the minimum age is fourteen in Alabama and Virginia. However, in *Thompson v. Oklahoma* (1988) the U.S. Supreme Court said that executing a person under age sixteen would violate the Eighth Amendment's ban on cruel and unusual punishments. A year later, in *Stanford v. Kentucky* (1989), the Court upheld capital punishment in the case of offenders who are ages sixteen or seventeen. Citing a lack of consensus among the states, the Court ruled that such executions would not violate society's evolving decency standards.

Q **555. Do other countries execute juveniles?**

A According to the United Nations, only the United States and the following five non-democracies permit capital punishment against offenders who commit their crimes before age eighteen: Nigeria, Yemen, Pakistan, Saudi Arabia, and Iran.

The International Covenant on Civil and Political Rights, adopted by the UN General Assembly in 1996, bans the death penalty for persons who committed their crimes when they were under age eighteen. The U.S. Senate ratified the covenant in 1992 but reserved the right to execute persons convicted of capital crimes who were under age eighteen when their murders were committed.

Q **556. What was the largest mass execution in the country's history?**

A The largest mass execution in the nation's history was the hanging of thirty-eight members of the Sioux Nation on December 26, 1862, in Mankato, Minnesota. Herded onto reservations along the Minnesota River, the Sioux became disturbed when their government annuity payments failed to arrive and they were threatened with starvation. Chief Little Crow took angry braves on the warpath and massacred at least 500 Minnesotans. An army unit quelled the uprising and a military court sentenced 303 Sioux to death. President Abraham Lincoln intervened and reduced the number of executions to thirty-eight—which was the largest act of executive clemency in American history.

Q **557. Where are federal prisoners executed?**

A The first federal execution in thirty-seven years was scheduled to take place at the U.S. Penitentiary at Terre Haute, Indiana, in the summer of 2000. In 1993 the Federal Bureau of Prisons designated the Terre Haute facility as the site for federal executions. The prison opened a special confinement unit in 1999 to provide what it described as humane, safe, and secure confinement of male offenders who were sentenced to death. The unit is a two-story facility with fifty single-cells, an industrial workshop, indoor and outdoor recreation areas, a property room, a food preparation area, attorney and family visiting rooms, and a video-teleconferencing area that is used to facilitate inmate access to the courts and their attorneys.

The Court approved the reinstatement of state death-penalty statutes in 1976 but did not approve a new federal death penalty statute until 1988. Because of appeals, there were no executions for federal cases until 2000.

Q 558. Is the death penalty discriminatory?

A More white offenders are executed than are black offenders, but African Americans are executed in disproportionate numbers. About 35 percent of inmates who have been executed were black, even though blacks constitute only about 11 percent of the U.S. population. Among those who are awaiting execution on death row, a disproportionate number are African Americans. Following are the numbers of prisoners under a sentence of death in 1998, by race:

- Whites, 1,906
- African Americans, 1,486
- American Indians, 29
- Asian, 18
- Other, 13

Statistics show that a murderer is more likely to get the death penalty if the victim is white. One study of 500 prisoners executed between 1977 and 1998 found that almost 82 percent were convicted of murdering a white person, even though African Americans and whites are the victims of homicide in almost equal numbers.

Amnesty International, a human rights group, charged in 1999 that race discrimination "pervades the U.S. death penalty at every stage of the process," beginning with the discretion exercised by predominately white district attorneys in deciding whether or not to seek the death penalty in a particular case.

In 1999 the American Bar Association called for a moratorium on the use of the death penalty until all jurisdictions strive to "eliminate discrimination in capital sentencing on the basis of the race of either the victim or the defendants."

The death penalty also discriminates along economic and social class lines. Many if not most defendants in death-penalty cases are indigent and cannot afford to hire experienced attorneys. Women seldom are executed, partly because they commit fewer murders. Only five female offenders have been executed since 1976. Of the 3,600 inmates on death row in the United States as of April 1, 2000, only 55 were women.

See 137 Are African Americans disproportionately affected by crime? 463 Who is more likely to be incarcerated—African Americans, whites, or Hispanics?

Q **559. How often are reprieves granted in death-penalty cases?**

A After all appeals are exhausted through the courts, the final decision as to whether a person will be executed rests with the governor of the state, a state clemency board, or—in the case of the federal government—the president of the United States.

According to the Death Penalty Information Center in Washington, D.C., a non-profit group that is often critical of the death penalty, forty-two death-row inmates have been granted clemency for humanitarian reasons since the U.S. Supreme Court reinstated the death penalty in 1976. Humanitarian reasons include doubts about the defendant's guilt, questions about the defendant's mental capacity, rehabilitation of the defendant, or the personal convictions of the governor.

Five state governors granted clemency in five cases in 1999, when ninety eight people were executed. This number represents the highest number of reprieves since 1976.

The last president to grant a death penalty reprieve was President Abraham Lincoln.

Q **560. Can the public watch an execution?**

A No. The last public execution was the 1936 hanging of a nineteen-year-old African American in Owensboro, Kentucky. The event reportedly attracted a festive crowd, estimated at from 10,000 to 20,000 people.

A federal judge ruled in 1991 that prison authorities could prevent a San Francisco television station from televising an execution at San Quentin prison. The judge termed reasonable prison officials' concern that a televised execution might be seen by other death-row inmates and cause a severe reaction.

A frequent argument for televising the death penalty is that capital punishment would be far more effective as a deterrent if people knew of its use. However, an unintended consequence of televising executions could be public outrage, particularly if there were mistakes in the procedure.

Q **561. What is the most frequent cause of death on death row?**

A Natural causes are the most frequent cause of death on death row. Lethal injection and electrocution are runners-up.

In the past, at least, prisoners spent years on death row while their appeals worked their way through the legal system. A study of the prisoners who were executed between 1977 and 1998 found that the average time spent between the imposition of the most recent sentence and the execution was more than nine years. The sixty-eight prisoners executed in 1998 were under sentence of death for an average of ten years and ten months.

Q 562. How did "Old Sparky" get its name?

A Florida's electric chair was dubbed "Old Sparky" after several botched executions led to public outrage. Controversy over the chair prompted the Florida legislature in January 2000 to adopt lethal injection as the state's primary means of execution.

The most recent incident involving Florida's electric chair occurred when Allen Lee "Tiny" Davis suffered a nosebleed at his July 1999 execution for the 1982 murders of a pregnant woman and her two young daughters. Blood dripped from the prisoner's face mask.

In a 4–3 decision in September 1999, the Florida Supreme Court upheld the use of the electric chair. Florida Supreme Court Justice Leander Shaw, one of the dissenters, attached to his dissent three post-electrocution photographs of Davis's bloody, purple face. In an apparent first, the photographs were posted on the court's Internet site, where they were viewed by tens of thousands of people.

Florida's electric chair had malfunctioned before, causing flames to erupt from the headpiece worn by a condemned killer.

Three states—Alabama, Georgia, and Nebraska—still require the use of the electric chair for executions. Most of the thirty-eight states where capital punishment is used have switched to lethal injection, a process that some say is less objectionable. A few states still allow death by firing squad or hanging.

In February 2000 the U.S. Supreme Court declined to hear an appeal by an Alabama death-row inmate who challenged the use of the electric chair as cruel and unusual punishment.

See 550 What methods are used to execute inmates?

Q 563. How many other countries sanction the use of the death penalty?

A The United States is one of about ninety countries to have the death penalty and is, by no means, the most enthusiastic proponent of its use. Since China launched its Strike Hard anticrime campaign in 1996, more than 6,000 people have been sentenced to die in China. At least 1,876 Chinese were executed in 1997 alone, according to the human rights group Amnesty International.

REFERENCE MATERIALS

CONSTITUTION OF THE UNITED STATES

We the People of the United States, in Order to form a more perfect Union, establish Justice, insure domestic Tranquility, provide for the common defence, promote the general Welfare, and secure the Blessings of Liberty to ourselves and our Posterity, do ordain and establish this Constitution for the United States of America.

ARTICLE I

SECTION 1. All legislative Powers herein granted shall be vested in a Congress of the United States, which shall consist of a Senate and House of Representatives.

SECTION 2. The House of Representatives shall be composed of Members chosen every second Year by the People of the several States, and the Electors in each State shall have the Qualifications requisite for Electors of the most numerous Branch of the State Legislature.

No Person shall be a Representative who shall not have attained to the age of twenty five Years, and been seven Years a Citizen of the United States, and who shall not, when elected, be an Inhabitant of that State in which he shall be chosen.

[Representatives and direct Taxes shall be apportioned among the several States which may be included within this Union, according to their respective Numbers, which shall be determined by adding to the whole Number of free Persons, including those bound to Service for a Term of Years, and excluding Indians not taxed, three fifths of all other Persons.][1] The actual Enumeration shall be made within three Years after the first Meeting of the Congress of the United States, and within every subsequent Term of ten Years, in such Manner as they shall by Law direct. The Number of Representatives shall not exceed one for every thirty Thousand, but each State shall have at Least one Representative; and until such enumeration shall be made, the State of New Hampshire shall be entitled to chuse three, Massachusetts eight, Rhode-Island and Providence Plantations one, Connecticut five, New-York six, New Jersey four, Pennsylvania eight, Delaware one, Maryland six, Virginia ten, North Carolina five, South Carolina five, and Georgia three.

When vacancies happen in the Representation from any State, the Executive Authority thereof shall issue Writs of Election to fill such Vacancies.

The House of Representatives shall chuse their Speaker and other Officers; and shall have the sole Power of Impeachment.

SECTION 3. The Senate of the United States shall be composed of two Senators from each State, [chosen by the Legislature thereof,][2] for six Years; and each Senator shall have one Vote.

Immediately after they shall be assembled in Consequence of the first Election, they shall be divided as equally as may be into three Classes. The Seats of the Senators of the first Class shall be vacated at the Expiration of the second Year, of the second Class at the Expiration of the fourth Year, and of the third Class at the Expiration of the sixth Year, so that one third may be chosen every second Year; [and if Vacancies happen by Resignation, or otherwise, during the Recess of the

Legislature of any State, the Executive thereof may make temporary Appointments until the next Meeting of the Legislature, which shall then fill such Vacancies.][3]

No Person shall be a Senator who shall not have attained to the Age of thirty Years, and been nine Years a Citizen of the United States, and who shall not, when elected, be an Inhabitant of that State for which he shall be chosen.

The Vice President of the United States shall be President of the Senate, but shall have no Vote, unless they be equally divided.

The Senate shall chuse their other Officers, and also a President pro tempore, in the Absence of the Vice President, or when he shall exercise the Office of President of the United States.

The Senate shall have the sole Power to try all Impeachments. When sitting for that Purpose, they shall be on Oath or Affirmation. When the President of the United States is tried, the Chief Justice shall preside: And no Person shall be convicted without the Concurrence of two thirds of the Members present.

Judgment in Cases of Impeachment shall not extend further than to removal from Office, and disqualification to hold and enjoy any Office of honor, Trust or Profit under the United States: but the Party convicted shall nevertheless be liable and subject to Indictment, Trial, Judgment and Punishment, according to Law.

SECTION 4. The Times, Places and Manner of holding Elections for Senators and Representatives, shall be prescribed in each State by the Legislature thereof; but the Congress may at any time by Law make or alter such Regulations, except as to the Places of chusing Senators.

The Congress shall assemble at least once in every Year, and such Meeting shall [be on the first Monday in December],[4] unless they shall by Law appoint a different Day.

SECTION 5. Each House shall be the Judge of the Elections, Returns and Qualifications of its own Members, and a Majority of each shall constitute a Quorum to do Business; but a smaller Number may adjourn from day to day, and may be authorized to compel the Attendance of absent Members, in such Manner, and under such Penalties as each House may provide.

Each House may determine the Rules of its Proceedings, punish its Members for disorderly Behaviour, and, with the Concurrence of two thirds, expel a Member.

Each House shall keep a Journal of its Proceedings, and from time to time publish the same, excepting such Parts as may in their Judgment require Secrecy; and the Yeas and Nays of the Members of either House on any question shall, at the Desire of one fifth of those Present, be entered on the Journal.

Neither House, during the Session of Congress, shall, without the Consent of the other, adjourn for more than three days, nor to any other Place than that in which the two Houses shall be sitting.

SECTION 6. The Senators and Representatives shall receive a Compensation for their Services, to be ascertained by Law, and paid out of the Treasury of the United States. They shall in all Cases, except Treason, Felony and Breach of the Peace, be privileged from Arrest during their Attendance at the Session of their respective Houses, and in going to and returning from the same; and for any Speech or Debate in either House, they shall not be questioned in any other Place.

No Senator or Representative shall, during the Time for which he was elected, be appointed to any civil Office under the Authority of the United States, which shall have been created, or the Emoluments whereof shall have been encreased during such time; and no Person holding any Office under the United States, shall be a Member of either House during his Continuance in Office.

SECTION 7. All Bills for raising Revenue shall originate in the House of Representatives; but the Senate may propose or concur with Amendments as on other Bills.

Every Bill which shall have passed the House of Representatives and the Senate, shall, before it become a Law, be presented to the President of the United States; If he approve he shall sign it, but if not he shall return it, with his Objections to that House in which it shall have originated, who shall enter the Objections at large on their Journal, and proceed to reconsider it. If after such Reconsideration two thirds of that House shall agree to pass the Bill, it shall be sent, together with the Objections, to the other House, by which it shall likewise be reconsidered, and if approved by two thirds of that House, it shall become a Law. But in all such Cases the Votes of both Houses shall be determined by yeas and Nays, and the Names of the Persons voting for and against the Bill shall be entered on the Journal of each House respectively. If any Bill shall not be returned by the President within ten Days (Sundays excepted) after it shall have been presented to him, the Same shall be a Law, in like Manner as if he had signed it, unless the Congress by their Adjournment prevent its Return, in which Case it shall not be a Law.

Every Order, Resolution, or Vote to which the Concurrence of the Senate and House of Representatives may be necessary (except on a question of Adjournment) shall be presented to the President of the United States; and before the Same shall take Effect, shall be approved by him, or being disapproved by him, shall be repassed by two thirds of the Senate and House of Representatives, according to the Rules and Limitations prescribed in the Case of a Bill.

SECTION 8. The Congress shall have Power To lay and collect Taxes, Duties, Imposts and Excises, to pay the Debts and provide for the common Defence and general Welfare of the United States; but all Duties, Imposts and Excises shall be uniform throughout the United States;

To borrow Money on the credit of the United States;

To regulate Commerce with foreign Nations, and among the several States, and with the Indian Tribes;

To establish an uniform Rule of Naturalization, and uniform Laws on the subject of Bankruptcies throughout the United States;

To coin Money, regulate the Value thereof, and of foreign Coin, and fix the Standard of Weights and Measures;

To provide for the Punishment of counterfeiting the Securities and current Coin of the United States;

To establish Post Offices and post Roads;

To promote the Progress of Science and useful Arts, by securing for limited Times to Authors and Inventors the exclusive Right to their respective Writings and Discoveries;

To constitute Tribunals inferior to the supreme Court;

To define and punish Piracies and Felonies committed on the high Seas, and Offences against the Law of Nations;

To declare War, grant Letters of Marque and Reprisal, and make Rules concerning Captures on Land and Water;

To raise and support Armies, but no Appropriation of Money to that Use shall be for a longer Term than two Years;

To provide and maintain a Navy;

To make Rules for the Government and Regulation of the land and naval Forces;

To provide for calling forth the Militia to execute the Laws of the Union, suppress Insurrections and repel Invasions;

To provide for organizing, arming, and disciplining, the Militia, and for governing such Part of them as may be employed in the Service of the United States, reserving to the States respectively, the Appointment of the Officers, and the Authority of training the Militia according to the discipline prescribed by Congress;

To exercise exclusive Legislation in all Cases whatso-ever, over such District (not exceeding ten Miles square) as may, by Cession of particular States, and the Acceptance of Congress, become the Seat of the Government of the United States, and to exercise like Authority over all Places purchased by the Consent of the Legislature of the State in which the Same shall be, for the Erection of Forts, Magazines, Arsenals, dock-Yards, and other needful Buildings;—And

To make all Laws which shall be necessary and proper for carrying into Execution the foregoing Powers, and all other Powers vested by this Constitution in the Government of the United States, or in any Department or Officer thereof.

SECTION 9. The Migration or Importation of such Persons as any of the States now existing shall think proper to admit, shall not be prohibited by the Congress prior to the Year one thousand eight hundred and eight, but a Tax or duty may be imposed on such Importation, not exceeding ten dollars for each Person.

The Privilege of the Writ of Habeas Corpus shall not be suspended, unless when in Cases of Rebellion or Invasion the public Safety may require it.

No Bill of Attainder or ex post facto Law shall be passed.

No Capitation, or other direct, Tax shall be laid, unless in Proportion to the Census or Enumeration herein before directed to be taken.[5]

No Tax or Duty shall be laid on Articles exported from any State.

No Preference shall be given by any Regulation of Commerce or Revenue to the Ports of one State over those of another; nor shall Vessels bound to, or from, one State, be obliged to enter, clear, or pay Duties in another.

No Money shall be drawn from the Treasury, but in Consequence of Appropriations made by Law; and a regular Statement and Account of the Receipts and Expenditures of all public Money shall be published from time to time.

No Title of Nobility shall be granted by the United States: And no Person holding any Office of Profit or Trust under them, shall, without the Consent of the Congress, accept of any present, Emolument, Office, or Title, of any kind whatever, from any King, Prince, or foreign State.

SECTION 10. No State shall enter into any Treaty, Alliance, or Confederation; grant Letters of Marque and Reprisal; coin Money; emit Bills of Credit; make any Thing but gold and silver Coin a Tender in Payment of Debts; pass any Bill of Attainder, ex post facto Law, or Law impairing the Obligation of Contracts, or grant any Title of Nobility.

No State shall, without the Consent of the Congress, lay any Imposts or Duties on Imports or Exports, except what may be absolutely necessary for executing it's inspection Laws: and the net Produce of all Duties and Imposts, laid by any State on Imports or Exports, shall be for the Use of the Treasury of the United States; and all such Laws shall be subject to the Revision and Controul of the Congress.

No State shall, without the Consent of Congress, lay any Duty of Tonnage, keep Troops, or Ships of War in time of Peace, enter into any Agreement or Compact with another State, or with a foreign Power, or engage in War, unless actually invaded, or in such imminent Danger as will not admit of delay.

ARTICLE II

SECTION 1. The executive Power shall be vested in a President of the United States of America. He shall hold his Office during the Term of four Years, and, together with the Vice President, chosen for the same Term, be elected, as follows

Each State shall appoint, in such Manner as the Legislature thereof may direct, a Number of Electors, equal to the whole Number of Senators and Representatives to which the State may be entitled in the Congress: but no Senator or Representative, or Person holding an Office of Trust or Profit under the United States, shall be appointed an Elector.

[The Electors shall meet in their respective States, and vote by Ballot for two Persons, of whom one at least shall not be an Inhabitant of the same State with themselves. And they shall make a List of all the Persons voted for, and of the Number of Votes for each; which List they shall sign and certify, and transmit sealed to the Seat of the Government of the United States, directed to the President of the Senate. The President of the Senate shall, in the Presence of the Senate and House of Representatives, open all the Certificates, and the Votes shall then be counted. The Person having the greatest Number of Votes shall be the President, if such Number be a Majority of the whole Number of Electors appointed; and if there be more than one who have such Majority, and have an equal Number of Votes, then the House of Representatives shall immediately chuse by Ballot one of them for President; and if no Person have a Majority, then from the five highest on the list the said House shall in like Manner chuse the President. But in chusing the President, the Votes shall be taken by States, the Representation from each State having one Vote; A quorum for this Purpose shall consist of a Member or Members from two thirds of the States, and a Majority of all the States shall be necessary to a Choice. In every Case, after the Choice of the President, the Person having the greatest Number of Votes of the Electors shall be the Vice President. But if there should remain two or more who have equal Votes, the Senate shall chuse from them by Ballot the Vice President.][6]

The Congress may determine the Time of chusing the Electors, and the Day on which they shall give their Votes; which Day shall be the same throughout the United States.

No Person except a natural born Citizen, or a Citizen of the United States, at the time of the Adoption of this Constitution, shall be eligible to the Office of President; neither shall any Person be eligible to that Office who shall not have attained to the Age of thirty five Years, and been fourteen Years a Resident within the United States.

In Case of the Removal of the President from Office, or of his Death, Resignation, or Inability to discharge the Powers and Duties of the said Office,[7] the Same shall devolve on the Vice President, and the Congress may by Law provide for the Case of Removal, Death, Resignation or Inability, both of the President and Vice President, declaring what Officer shall then act as President, and such Officer shall act accordingly, until the Disability be removed, or a President shall be elected.

The President shall, at stated Times, receive for his Services, a Compensation, which shall neither be encreased nor diminished during the Period for which he shall have been elected, and he shall not receive within that Period any other Emolument from the United States, or any of them.

Before he enter on the Execution of his Office, he shall take the following Oath or Affirmation:—"I do solemnly swear (or affirm) that I will faithfully execute the Office of President of the United States, and will to the best of my Ability, preserve, protect and defend the Constitution of the United States."

SECTION 2. The President shall be Commander in Chief of the Army and Navy of the United States, and of the Militia of the several States, when called into the actual Service of the United States; he may require the Opinion, in writing, of the principal Officer in each of the executive Departments, upon any Subject relating to the Duties of their respective Offices, and he shall have Power to grant Reprieves and Pardons for Offences against the United States, except in Cases of Impeachment.

He shall have Power, by and with the Advice and Consent of the Senate, to make Treaties, provided two thirds of the Senators present concur; and he shall nominate, and by and with the Advice and Consent of the Senate, shall appoint Ambassadors, other public Ministers and Consuls, Judges of the supreme Court, and all other Officers of the United States, whose Appointments are not herein otherwise provided for, and which shall be established by Law: but the Congress may by Law vest the Appointment of such inferior Officers, as they think proper, in the President alone, in the Courts of Law, or in the Heads of Departments.

The President shall have Power to fill up all Vacancies that may happen during the Recess of the Senate, by granting Commissions which shall expire at the End of their next Session.

SECTION 3. He shall from time to time give to the Congress Information of the State of the Union, and recommend to their Consideration such Measures as he shall judge necessary and expedient; he may, on extraordinary Occasions, convene both Houses, or either of them, and in Case of Disagreement between them, with Respect to the Time of Adjournment, he may adjourn them to such Time as he shall think proper; he shall receive Ambassadors and other public Ministers; he shall take Care that the Laws be faithfully executed, and shall Commission all the Officers of the United States.

SECTION 4. The President, Vice President and all civil Officers of the United States, shall be removed from Office on Impeachment for, and Conviction of, Treason, Bribery, or other high Crimes and Misdemeanors.

ARTICLE III

SECTION 1. The judicial Power of the United States, shall be vested in one supreme Court, and in such inferior Courts as the Congress may from time to time ordain and establish. The Judges, both of the supreme and inferior Courts, shall hold their Offices during good Behaviour, and shall, at stated Times, receive for their Services, a Compensation, which shall not be diminished during their Continuance in Office.

SECTION 2. The judicial Power shall extend to all Cases, in Law and Equity, arising under this Constitution, the Laws of the United States, and Treaties made, or which shall be made, under their Authority; — to all Cases affecting Ambassadors, other public Ministers and Consuls; —to all Cases of admiralty and maritime Jurisdiction; —to Controversies to which the United States shall be a Party; —to Controversies between two or more States; —between a State and Citizens of another State;[8] —between Citizens of different States; —between Citizens of the same State claiming Lands under Grants of different States, and between a State, or the Citizens thereof, and foreign States, Citizens or Subjects.[8]

In all Cases affecting Ambassadors, other public Ministers and Consuls, and those in which a State shall be Party, the supreme Court shall have original Jurisdiction. In all the other Cases before mentioned, the supreme Court shall have appellate Jurisdiction, both as to Law and Fact, with such Exceptions, and under such Regulations as the Congress shall make.

The Trial of all Crimes, except in Cases of Impeachment, shall be by Jury; and such Trial shall be held in the State where the said Crimes shall have been committed; but when not committed within any State, the Trial shall be at such Place or Places as the Congress may by Law have directed.

SECTION 3. Treason against the United States, shall consist only in levying War against them, or in adhering to their Enemies, giving them Aid and Comfort. No Person shall be convicted of Treason unless on the Testimony of two Witnesses to the same overt Act, or on Confession in open Court.

The Congress shall have Power to declare the Punishment of Treason, but no Attainder of Treason shall work Corruption of Blood, or Forfeiture except during the Life of the Person attainted.

ARTICLE IV

SECTION 1. Full Faith and Credit shall be given in each State to the public Acts, Records, and judicial Proceedings of every other State. And the Congress may by general Laws prescribe the Manner in which such Acts, Records and Proceedings shall be proved, and the Effect thereof.

SECTION 2. The Citizens of each State shall be entitled to all Privileges and Immunities of Citizens in the several States.

A Person charged in any State with Treason, Felony, or other Crime, who shall flee from Justice, and be found in another State, shall on Demand of the executive Authority of the State from which he fled, be delivered up, to be removed to the State having Jurisdiction of the Crime.

[No Person held to Service or Labour in one State, under the Laws thereof, escaping into another, shall, in Consequence of any Law or Regulation therein, be discharged from such Service or Labour, but shall be delivered up on Claim of the Party to whom such Service or Labour may be due.][9]

SECTION 3. New States may be admitted by the Congress into this Union; but no new State shall be formed or erected within the Jurisdiction of any other State; nor any State be formed by the Junction of two or more States, or Parts of States, without the Consent of the Legislatures of the States concerned as well as of the Congress.

The Congress shall have Power to dispose of and make all needful Rules and Regulations respecting the Territory or other Property belonging to the United States; and nothing in this Constitution shall be so construed as to Prejudice any Claims of the United States, or of any particular State.

SECTION 4. The United States shall guarantee to every State in this Union a Republican Form of Government, and shall protect each of them against Invasion; and on Application of the Legislature, or of the Executive (when the Legislature cannot be convened) against domestic Violence.

ARTICLE V

The Congress, whenever two thirds of both Houses shall deem it necessary, shall propose Amendments to this Constitution, or, on the Application of the Legislatures of two thirds of the several States, shall call a Convention for proposing Amendments, which, in either Case, shall be valid to all Intents and Purposes, as Part of this Constitution, when ratified by the Legislatures of three fourths of the several States, or by Conventions in three fourths thereof, as the one or the other Mode of Ratification may be proposed by the Congress; Provided [that no Amendment which may be made prior to the Year One thousand eight hundred and eight shall in any Manner affect the first and fourth Clauses in the Ninth section of the first Article; and][10] that no State, without its Consent, shall be deprived of its equal Suffrage in the Senate.

ARTICLE VI

All Debts contracted and Engagements entered into, before the Adoption of this Constitution, shall be as valid against the United States under this Constitution, as under the Confederation.

This Constitution, and the Laws of the United States which shall be made in Pursuance thereof; and all Treaties made, or which shall be made, under the Authority of the United States, shall be the supreme Law of the Land; and the Judges in every State shall be bound thereby, any Thing in the Constitution or Laws of any State to the Contrary notwithstanding.

The Senators and Representatives before mentioned, and the Members of the several State Legislatures, and all executive and judicial Officers, both of the United States and of the several States, shall be bound by Oath or Affirmation, to support this Constitution; but no religious Test shall ever be required as a Qualification to any Office or public Trust under the United States.

ARTICLE VII

The Ratification of the Conventions of nine States, shall be sufficient for the Establishment of this Constitution between the States so ratifying the Same.

Done in Convention by the Unanimous Consent of the States present the Seventeenth Day of September in the Year of our Lord one thousand seven hundred and Eighty seven and of the Independence of the United States of America the Twelfth. IN WITNESS whereof We have hereunto subscribed our Names,

George Washington,
President and deputy from Virginia.

New Hampshire:

John Langdon,
Nicholas Gilman.

Massachusetts:

Nathaniel Gorham,
Rufus King.

Connecticut:

William Samuel Johnson,
Roger Sherman.

New York:

Alexander Hamilton.

New Jersey:

William Livingston,
David Brearley,
William Paterson,
Jonathan Dayton.

Pennsylvania:

Benjamin Franklin,
Thomas Mifflin,
Robert Morris,
George Clymer,
Thomas FitzSimons,
Jared Ingersoll,
James Wilson,
Gouverneur Morris.

Delaware:

George Read,
Gunning Bedford Jr.,
John Dickinson,
Richard Bassett,
Jacob Broom.

Maryland:	James McHenry,
	Daniel of St. Thomas Jenifer,
	Daniel Carroll.

| Virginia: | John Blair, |
| | James Madison Jr. |

North Carolina:	William Blount,
	Richard Dobbs Spaight,
	Hugh Williamson.

South Carolina:	John Rutledge,
	Charles Cotesworth Pinckney,
	Charles Pinckney,
	Pierce Butler.

| Georgia: | William Few, |
| | Abraham Baldwin. |

[The language of the original Constitution, not including the Amendments, was adopted by a convention of the states on September 17, 1787, and was subsequently ratified by the states on the following dates: Delaware, December 7, 1787; Pennsylvania, December 12, 1787; New Jersey, December 18, 1787; Georgia, January 2, 1788; Connecticut, January 9, 1788; Massachusetts, February 6, 1788; Maryland, April 28, 1788; South Carolina, May 23, 1788; New Hampshire, June 21, 1788.

Ratification was completed on June 21, 1788.

The Constitution subsequently was ratified by Virginia, June 25, 1788; New York, July 26, 1788; North Carolina, November 21, 1789; Rhode Island, May 29, 1790; and Vermont, January 10, 1791.]

AMENDMENTS

Amendment I

(First ten amendments ratified December 15, 1791.)

Congress shall make no law respecting an establishment of religion, or prohibiting the free exercise thereof; or abridging the freedom of speech, or of the press; or the right of the people peaceably to assemble, and to petition the Government for a redress of grievances.

Amendment II

A well regulated Militia, being necessary to the security of a free State, the right of the people to keep and bear Arms, shall not be infringed.

Amendment III

No Soldier shall, in time of peace be quartered in any house, without the consent of the Owner, nor in time of war, but in a manner to be prescribed by law.

Amendment IV

The right of the people to be secure in their persons, houses, papers, and effects, against unreasonable searches and seizures, shall not be violated, and no Warrants shall issue, but upon probable cause, supported by Oath or affirmation, and particularly describing the place to be searched, and the persons or things to be seized.

Amendment V

No person shall be held to answer for a capital, or otherwise infamous crime, unless on a presentment or indictment of a Grand Jury, except in cases arising in the land or naval forces, or in the Militia, when in actual service in time of War or public danger; nor shall any person be subject for the same offence to be twice put in jeopardy of life or limb; nor shall be compelled in any criminal case to be a witness against himself, nor be deprived of life, liberty, or property, without due process of law; nor shall private property be taken for public use, without just compensation.

Amendment VI

In all criminal prosecutions, the accused shall enjoy the right to a speedy and public trial, by an impartial jury of the State and district wherein the crime shall have been committed, which district shall have been previously ascertained by law, and to be informed of the nature and cause of the accusation; to be confronted with the witnesses against him; to have compulsory process for obtaining witnesses in his favor, and to have the Assistance of Counsel for his defence.

Amendment VII

In Suits at common law, where the value in controversy shall exceed twenty dollars, the right of trial by jury shall be preserved, and no fact tried by a jury, shall be otherwise re-examined in any Court of the United States, than according to the rules of the common law.

Amendment VIII

Excessive bail shall not be required, nor excessive fines imposed, nor cruel and unusual punishments inflicted.

Amendment IX

The enumeration in the Constitution, of certain rights, shall not be construed to deny or disparage others retained by the people.

Amendment X

The powers not delegated to the United States by the Constitution, nor prohibited by it to the States, are reserved to the States respectively, or to the people.

Amendment XI (Ratified February 7, 1795)

The Judicial power of the United States shall not be construed to extend to any suit in law or equity, commenced or prosecuted against one of the United States by Citizens of another State, or by Citizens or Subjects of any Foreign State.

Amendment XII (Ratified June 15, 1804)

The Electors shall meet in their respective states and vote by ballot for President and Vice-President, one of whom, at least, shall not be an inhabitant of the same state with themselves; they shall name in their ballots the person voted for as President, and in distinct ballots the person voted for as Vice-President, and they shall make distinct lists of all persons voted for as President, and of all persons voted for as Vice-President, and of the number of votes for each, which lists they shall sign and certify, and transmit sealed to the seat of the government of the United States, directed to the President of the Senate; — The President of the Senate shall, in the presence of the Senate and House of Representatives, open all the certificates and the votes shall then be counted; — The person having the greatest number of votes for President, shall be the President, if such number be a majority of the whole number of Electors appointed; and if no person have such majority, then from the persons having the highest numbers not exceeding three on the list of those voted for as President, the House of Representatives shall choose immediately, by ballot, the President. But in choosing the President, the votes shall be taken by states, the representation from each state having one vote; a quorum for this purpose shall consist of a member or members from two-thirds of the states, and a majority of all the states shall be necessary to a choice. [And if the House of Representatives shall not choose a President whenever the right of choice shall devolve upon them, before the fourth day of March next following, then the Vice-President shall act as President, as in the case of the death or other constitutional disability of the President. —][11] The person having the greatest number of votes as Vice-President, shall be the Vice-President, if such number be a majority of the whole number of Electors appointed, and if no person have a majority, then from the two highest numbers on the list, the Senate shall choose the Vice-President; a quorum for the purpose shall consist of two-thirds of the whole number of Senators, and a majority of the whole number shall be necessary to a choice. But no person constitutionally ineligible to the office of President shall be eligible to that of Vice-President of the United States.

Amendment XIII (Ratified December 6, 1865)

SECTION 1. Neither slavery nor involuntary servitude, except as a punishment for crime whereof the party shall have been duly convicted, shall exist within the United States, or any place subject to their jurisdiction.

SECTION 2. Congress shall have power to enforce this article by appropriate legislation.

Amendment XIV (Ratified July 9, 1868)

SECTION 1. All persons born or naturalized in the United States, and subject to the jurisdiction thereof, are citizens of the United States and of the State wherein they reside. No State shall make or enforce any law which shall abridge the privileges or immunities of citizens of the United States; nor shall any State deprive any person of life, liberty, or property, without due process of law; nor deny to any person within its jurisdiction the equal protection of the laws.

SECTION 2. Representatives shall be apportioned among the several States according to their respective numbers, counting the whole number of persons in each State, excluding Indians not taxed. But when the right to vote at any election for the choice of electors for President and Vice President of the United States, Representatives in Congress, the Executive and Judicial officers of a State, or the members of the Legislature thereof, is denied to any of the male inhabitants of such State, being twenty-one years of age,[12] and citizens of the United States, or in any way abridged, except for participation in rebellion, or other crime, the basis of representation therein shall be reduced in the proportion which the number of such male citizens shall bear to the whole number of male citizens twenty-one years of age in such State.

SECTION 3. No person shall be a Senator or Representative in Congress, or elector of President and Vice President, or hold any office, civil or military, under the United States, or under any State, who, having previously taken an oath, as a member of Congress, or as an officer of the United States, or as a member of any State legislature, or as an executive or judicial officer of any State, to support the Constitution of the United States, shall have engaged in insurrection or rebellion against the same, or given aid or comfort to the enemies thereof. But Congress may by a vote of two-thirds of each House, remove such disability.

SECTION 4. The validity of the public debt of the United States, authorized by law, including debts incurred for payment of pensions and bounties for services in suppressing insurrection or rebellion, shall not be questioned. But neither the United States nor any State shall assume or pay any debt or obligation incurred in aid of insurrection or rebellion against the United States, or any claim for the loss or emancipation of any slave; but all such debts, obligations and claims shall be held illegal and void.

SECTION 5. The Congress shall have power to enforce, by appropriate legislation, the provisions of this article.

Amendment XV (Ratified February 3, 1870)

SECTION 1. The right of citizens of the United States to vote shall not be denied or abridged by the United States or by any State on account of race, color, or previous condition of servitude.

SECTION 2. The Congress shall have power to enforce this article by appropriate legislation.

Amendment XVI (Ratified February 3, 1913)

The Congress shall have power to lay and collect taxes on incomes, from whatever source derived, without apportionment among the several States, and without regard to any census or enumeration.

Amendment XVII (Ratified April 8, 1913)

The Senate of the United States shall be composed of two Senators from each State, elected by the people thereof, for six years; and each Senator shall have one vote. The electors in each State shall have the qualifications requisite for electors of the most numerous branch of the State legislatures.

When vacancies happen in the representation of any State in the Senate, the executive authority of such State shall issue writs of election to fill such vacancies: Provided, That the legislature of any State may empower the executive thereof to make temporary appointments until the people fill the vacancies by election as the legislature may direct.

This amendment shall not be so construed as to affect the election or term of any Senator chosen before it becomes valid as part of the Constitution.

Amendment XVIII (Ratified January 16, 1919)[13]

SECTION 1. After one year from the ratification of this article the manufacture, sale, or transportation of intoxicating liquors within, the importation thereof into, or the exportation thereof from the United States and all territory subject to the jurisdiction thereof for beverage purposes is hereby prohibited.

SECTION 2. The Congress and the several States shall have concurrent power to enforce this article by appropriate legislation.

SECTION 3. This article shall be inoperative unless it shall have been ratified as an amendment to the Constitution by the legislatures of the several States, as provided in the Constitution, within seven years from the date of the submission hereof to the States by the Congress.

Amendment XIX (Ratified August 18, 1920)

The right of citizens of the United States to vote shall not be denied or abridged by the United States or by any State on account of sex.

Congress shall have power to enforce this article by appropriate legislation.

Amendment XX (Ratified January 23, 1933)

SECTION 1. The terms of the President and Vice President shall end at noon on the 20th day of January, and the terms of Senators and Representatives at noon on the 3d day of January, of the years in which such terms would have ended if this article had not been ratified; and the terms of their successors shall then begin.

SECTION 2. The Congress shall assemble at least once in every year, and such meeting shall begin at noon on the 3d day of January, unless they shall by law appoint a different day.

SECTION 3.[14] If, at the time fixed for the beginning of the term of the President, the President elect shall have died, the Vice President elect shall become President. If a President shall not have been chosen before the time fixed for the beginning of his term, or if the President elect shall have failed to qualify, then the Vice President elect shall act as President until a President shall have qualified; and the Congress may by law provide for the case wherein neither a President elect nor a Vice President elect shall have qualified, declaring who shall then act as President, or the manner in which one who is to act shall be selected, and such person shall act accordingly until a President or Vice President shall have qualified.

SECTION 4. The Congress may by law provide for the case of the death of any of the persons from whom the House of Representatives may choose a President whenever the right of choice shall have devolved upon them, and for the case of the death of any of the persons from whom the Senate may choose a Vice President whenever the right of choice shall have devolved upon them.

SECTION 5. Sections 1 and 2 shall take effect on the 15th day of October following the ratification of this article.

SECTION 6. This article shall be inoperative unless it shall have been ratified as an amendment to the Constitution by the legislatures of three-fourths of the several States within seven years from the date of its submission.

Amendment XXI (Ratified December 5, 1933)

SECTION 1. The eighteenth article of amendment to the Constitution of the United States is hereby repealed.

SECTION 2. The transportation or importation into any State, Territory, or possession of the United States for delivery or use therein of intoxicating liquors, in violation of the laws thereof, is hereby prohibited.

SECTION 3. This article shall be inoperative unless it shall have been ratified as an amendment to the Constitution by conventions in the several States, as provided in the Constitution, within seven years from the date of the submission hereof to the States by the Congress.

Amendment XXII (Ratified February 27, 1951)

SECTION 1. No person shall be elected to the office of the President more than twice, and no person who has held the office of President, or acted as President, for more than two years of a term to which some other person was elected President shall be elected to the office of the President more than once. But this Article shall not apply to any person holding the office of President when this Article was proposed by the Congress, and shall not prevent any person who may be holding the office of President, or acting as President, during the term within which this Article becomes operative from holding the office of President or acting as President during the remainder of such term.

SECTION 2. This article shall be inoperative unless it shall have been ratified as an amendment to the Constitution by the legislatures of three-fourths of the several States within seven years from the date of its submission to the States by the Congress.

Amendment XXIII (Ratified March 29, 1961)

SECTION 1. The District constituting the seat of Government of the United States shall appoint in such manner as the Congress may direct:

A number of electors of President and Vice President equal to the whole number of Senators and Representatives in Congress to which the District would be entitled if it were a State, but in no event more than the least populous State; they shall be in addition to those appointed by the States, but they shall be considered, for the purposes of the election of President and Vice President, to be electors appointed by a State; and they shall meet in the District and perform such duties as provided by the twelfth article of amendment.

SECTION 2. The Congress shall have power to enforce this article by appropriate legislation.

Amendment XXIV (Ratified January 23, 1964)

SECTION 1. The right of citizens of the United States to vote in any primary or other election for President or Vice President, for electors for President or Vice President, or for Senator or Representative in Congress, shall not be denied or abridged by the United States or any State by reason of failure to pay any poll tax or other tax.

SECTION 2. The Congress shall have power to enforce this article by appropriate legislation.

Amendment XXV (Ratified February 10, 1967)

SECTION 1. In case of the removal of the President from office or of his death or resignation, the Vice President shall become President.

SECTION 2. Whenever there is a vacancy in the office of the Vice President, the President shall nominate a Vice President who shall take office upon confirmation by a majority vote of both Houses of Congress.

SECTION 3. Whenever the President transmits to the President pro tempore of the Senate and the Speaker of the House of Representatives his written declaration that he is unable to discharge the powers and duties of his office, and until he transmits to them a written declaration to the contrary, such powers and duties shall be discharged by the Vice President as Acting President.

SECTION 4. Whenever the Vice President and a majority of either the principal officers of the executive departments or of such other body as Congress may by law provide, transmit to the President pro tempore of the Senate and the Speaker of the House of Representatives their written declaration that the President is unable to discharge the powers and duties of his office, the Vice President shall immediately assume the powers and duties of the office as Acting President.

Thereafter, when the President transmits to the President pro tempore of the Senate and the Speaker of the House of Representatives his written declaration that no inability exists, he shall resume the powers and duties of his office unless the Vice President and a majority of either the principal officers of the executive departments or of such other body as Congress may by law provide, transmit within four days to the President pro tempore of the Senate and the Speaker of the House of Representatives their written declaration that the President is unable to discharge the powers and duties of his office. Thereupon Congress shall decide the issue, assembling within forty-eight hours for that purpose if not in session. If the Congress, within twenty-one days after receipt of the latter written declaration, or, if Congress is not in session, within twenty-one days after Congress is required to assemble, determines by two-thirds vote of both Houses that the President is unable to discharge the powers and duties of his office, the Vice President shall continue to discharge the same as Acting President; otherwise, the President shall resume the powers and duties of his office.

Amendment XXVI (Ratified July 1, 1971)

SECTION 1. The right of citizens of the United States, who are eighteen years of age or older, to vote shall not be denied or abridged by the United States or by any State on account of age.

SECTION 2. The Congress shall have power to enforce this article by appropriate legislation.

Amendment XXVII (Ratified May 7, 1992)

No law varying the compensation for the services of the Senators and Representatives shall take effect, until an election of Representatives shall have intervened.

Notes

1. The part in brackets was changed by section 2 of the Fourteenth Amendment.
2. The part in brackets was changed by the first paragraph of the Seventeenth Amendment.
3. The part in brackets was changed by the second paragraph of the Seventeenth Amendment.
4. The part in brackets was changed by section 2 of the Twentieth Amendment.
5. The Sixteenth Amendment gave Congress the power to tax incomes.
6. The material in brackets was superseded by the Twelfth Amendment.
7. This provision was affected by the Twenty-fifth Amendment.
8. These clauses were affected by the Eleventh Amendment.
9. This paragraph was superseded by the Thirteenth Amendment.

10. Obsolete.
11. The part in brackets was superseded by section 3 of the Twentieth Amendment.
12. See the Nineteenth and Twenty-sixth Amendments.
13. This amendment was repealed by section 1 of the Twenty-first Amendment.
14. See the Twenty-fifth Amendment.

Source: U.S. Congress, House, Committee on the Judiciary, *The Constitution of the United States of America, as Amended,* 100th Cong., 1st sess., 1987, H Doc 100-94.

SIGNIFICANT LAWS AND COURT DECISIONS

CHAPTER 1

Juvenile Justice and Delinquency Prevention Act of 1974 Pub. L. No. 93–415, 88 Stat. 1109 (Title 42 § 5601 et seq., 1974)
National Narcotics Leadership Act of 1988 Pub. L. No. 100–690, 102 Stat. 4181–4189 (1988)
Payne v. Tennessee, 501 U.S. 808 (1991)
Robinson v. California, 370 U.S. 660 (1962)
Strauder v. West Virginia, 100 U.S. 303 (1879)
United States v. Cruikshank, 92 U.S. 542 (1875)
United States v. Miller, 307 U.S. 174 (1939)
Violent Crime Control and Law Enforcement Act of 1994 Pub. L. No. 103–322, 108 Stat. 176 (1994)
Wisconsin v. Mitchell, 508 U.S. 476 (1993)

CHAPTER 2

Argersinger v. Hamlin, 407 U.S. 25 (1972)
Brady v. Maryland, 373 U.S. 83 (1963)
Brady v. United States, 397 U.S. 742 (1970)
Brinegar v. United States, 338 U.S. 839 (1949)
Chandler v. Fretag, 348 U.S. 3 (1954)
Chapman et al. v. California, 386 U.S. 18 (1967)
Davis v. United States, 512 U.S. 452 (1994)
Draper v. United States, 358 U.S. 307 (1959)
Duncan v. Louisiana, 391 U.S. 145 (1968)
Dusky v. United States, 362 U.S. 402 (1960)
Faretta v. California, 422 U.S. 806, (1975)
Florida v. J. L. No. 98–1993 (March 28, 2000)
Florida v. Royer, 460 U.S. 491 (1983)
Gideon v. Wainwright, 372 U.S. 335 (1963)
Green v. United States, 355 U.S. 184, 188 (1957)
Griffin v. California, 380 U.S. 609 (1956)

Griffin v. Illinois, 351 U.S. 12 (1956)
Illinois v. Gates, 462 U.S. 213 (1983)
Illinois v. Wardlow, No. 98–1036 (January 12, 2000)
In re. Winship, 397 U.S. 358 (1970)
Jacobson v. United States, 503 U.S. 540 (1992)
Jencks v. United States, 353 U.S. 657 (1957)
Kastigar v. United States, 406 U.S. 441 (1972)
Katz v. United States, 389 U.S. 347 (1967)
Malloy v. Hogan, 378 U.S. 1 (1964)
Mapp v. Ohio, 367 U.S. 643 (1961)
McNeil v. Wisconsin, 501 U.S. 171 (1991)
Miranda v. Arizona, 384 U.S. 436 (1966)
New York v. Quarles, 467 U.S. 649 (1984)
Nix v. Williams, 467 U.S. 431 (1984)
North Carolina v. Alford, 400 U.S. 25 (1970)
Payton v. New York, 445 U.S. 573 (1980)
Riverside County, California v. McLaughlin, 500 U.S. 44 (1991)
Schmerber v. California, 384 U.S. 757 (1966)
Scott v. Illinois, 440 U.S.367 (1979)
South Dakota v. Neville, 459 U.S. 553 (1983)
Speedy Trial Act of 1974, Pub. L. No. 93–619, 88 Stat. 2076 (Title 18 § 3161 et seq., 1975)
Strickland v. Washington, 466 U.S. 668 (1984)
Taylor v. Taintor, 83 U.S. 366 (1872)
Terry v. Ohio, 392 U.S. 1 (1968)
United States v. Salerno, 481 U.S, 739 (1987)
United States v. Scott, 437 U.S. 82 (1978)
United States v. Leon et al., 468 U.S. 897 (1984)
Weeks v. United States, 232 U.S. 383 (1914)
Williams v. United States, 504 U.S. 36 (1972)

CHAPTER 3

Gideon v. Wainwright, 372 U.S. 335 (1963)
In re Gault, 387 U.S. 1 (1967)
McKeiver v. Pennsylvania, 403 U.S. 528 (1971)
Oliphant v. Suquamish Indian Tribe, 435 U.S. 191 (1978)
Schall v. Martin, 467 U.S. 253 (1984)
Uniform Code of Military Justice, 10 U.S.C.A. § 801 et seq.

CHAPTER 4

County of Sacramento v. Lewis, 523 U.S. 833 (1998)
Graham v. Connor, 490 U.S. 386 (1989)
Lopez v. United States, 514 U.S. 549 (1995)
National Treasury Employees Union v. Raab, 489 U.S. 656 (1989)
Tennessee v. Garner, 471 U.S. 1 (1985)

CHAPTER 5

Bell v. Wolfish, 441 U.S. 520 (1979)
Bounds v. Smith, 430 U.S. 817 (1977)
Coker v. Georgia, 433 U.S. 584 (1977)
Cooper v. Pate, 378 U.S. 546, (1964)
Cruz v. Beto, 405 U.S. 319 (1972)
Estelle v. Gamble, 429 U.S. 97 (1976)
Ex Parte Hull, 312 U.S. 546 (1941)
Ford v. Wainwright, 477 U.S. 399 (1986)
Furman v. Georgia, 408 U.S. 238 (1972)
Gregg v. Georgia, 428 U.S. 153 (1976)
Harmelin v. Michigan, 501 U.S. 957 (1991)
Holt v. Sarver, 443 F.2d 308 (8th Cir. 1971)
Kansas v. Hendricks, 521 U.S. 346 1997)
Lewis v. Casey, 518 U.S. 343 (1996)
Louisiana ex rel Francis v. Resweber, 329 U.S. 459 (1947)
Morrissey v. Brewer, 408 U.S. 471 (1972)
O'Lone v. Estate of Shabazz, 482 U.S. 342 (1987)
Pennsylvania Bd. of Probation and Parole v. Scott, 524 U.S. 357 (1998)
Pennsylvania Dept. of Corrections v. Yeskey, 524 U.S. 206 (1998)
Penry v. Lynaugh, 492 U.S. 302 (1989)
Prison Litigation Reform Act, Pub. L. No. 104-134, 110 Stat. 1321 (1996)
Richardson v. Ramirez, 418 U.S. 24 (1974)
Simmons v. South Carolina, 512 U.S. 154 (1994)
Smith vs. Fort Lauderdale, No. 99–377 (November 1, 1999)
Stanford v. Kentucky, 492 U.S. 361 (1989)
Thompson v. Oklahoma, 487 U.S. 815 (1988)
United States. v. Muniz, 374 U.S. 150 (1963)
Weems v. United States, 217 U.S. 349 (1910)

HOW TO READ
A COURT CITATION

The official version of each Supreme Court decision and opinion is contained in a series of volumes entitled *United States Reports*, published by the U.S. Government Printing Office.

While there are several unofficial compilations of Court opinions, including *United States Law Week*, published by the Bureau of National Affairs; *Supreme Court Reporter*, published by West Publishing Company; and *United States Supreme Court Reports, Lawyers' Edition*, published by Lawyers Cooperative Publishing Company, it is the official record that is generally cited. An unofficial version or the official slip opinion might be cited if a decision has not yet been officially reported.

A citation to a case includes, in order, the name of the parties to the case, the volume of *United States Reports* in which the decision appears, the page in the volume on which the opinion begins, the page from which any quoted material is taken, and the year of the decision.

For example, *Colegrove v. Green*, 328 U.S. 549, 553 (1946) means that the Supreme Court decision in the case of Colegrove against Green can be found in volume 328 of *United States Reports* beginning on page 549. The specific quotation in question will be found on page 553. The case was decided in 1946.

Until 1875 the official reports of the Court were published under the names of the Court reporters, and it is their names, or abbreviated versions, that appear in cites for those years, although U.S. volume numbers have been assigned retroactively to them. A citation such as *Marbury v. Madison*, 1 Cranch 137 (1803) means that the opinion in the case of Marbury against Madison is in the first volume of reporter Cranch beginning on page 137. (Between 1875 and 1883 a Court reporter named William T. Otto compiled the decisions and opinions; his name appears on the volumes for those years as well as the *United States Reports* volume number, but Otto is seldom cited.)

The titles of the volumes to 1875, the full names of the reporters, and the corresponding *United States Reports* volumes are:

1–4 Dall.	Dallas	1–4 U.S.
1–9 Cranch or Cr.	Cranch	5–13 U.S.
1–12 Wheat.	Wheaton	14–25 U.S.
1–16 Pet.	Peters	26–41 U.S.
1–24 How.	Howard	42–65 U.S.
1–2 Black	Black	66–67 U.S.
1–23 Wall.	Wallace	68–90 U.S.

CRIMINAL JUSTICE CONTACT INFORMATION

Bureau of Alcohol, Tobacco, and Firearms

650 Massachusetts Avenue N.W.
Washington, DC 20226
Phone: (202) 927-8500
Internet: www.atf.treas.gov/

Bureau of Prisons

320 First Street N.W.
Washington, DC 20534
Phone: (202) 307-3198
Internet: www.bop.gov/

Department of Justice

950 Pennsylvania Avenue NW.
Washington, DC 20530
Phone: (202) 514-2000
Internet: www.usdoj.gov/

Department of Justice

Office for Victims of Crime
810 7th Street N.W.
Washington, DC 20531
Phone: 1-800-627-6872
Internet: www.usdoj.gov/ovc/

Drug Enforcement Administration

600-700 Army Navy Drive
Arlington, VA 22202
Phone: (202) 307-1000
Internet: www.usdoj.gov/dea/

Federal Bureau of Investigation

J. Edgar Hoover F.B.I. Building
935 Pennsylvania Avenue N.W.
Washington, DC 20535
Phone: (202) 324-3000
Internet: www.fbi.gov/

Immigration and Naturalization Service

425 I Street N.W.
Washington, DC 20536
Phone: 1-800-375-5823
Internet: www.ins.usdoj.gov/

Internal Revenue Service

Criminal Investigation Division
1111 Constitution Avenue N.W.
Washington, DC 20224
Phone: 1-800-829-0433
Internet: www.treas.gov/irs/ci/

Mothers Against Drunk Driving (MADD)

P.O. Box 541688
Dallas, TX 75354-1688
Phone: 1-800-GET-MADD
Internet: www.madd.org/

Office of Juvenile Justice and Delinquency Prevention

810 Seventh Street, N.W.
Washington, DC 20531
Phone: (202) 307-5929
Internet: www.ojjdp.ncjrs.org

U.S. Customs Service

1300 Pennsylvania Avenue, N.W.
Washington, DC 20229
Phone: (202) 927-1000
Internet: www.customs.ustreas.gov/

U.S. Marshals Service

600 Army Navy Drive
Arlington, VA 22202-4210
Phone: (202) 307-9000
Internet: www.usdoj.gov/marshals

U.S. Postal Inspection Service

475 L'Enfant Plaza S.W.
Washington, DC 20260
Phone: (202) 268-2999
Internet: www.usps.gov/postalinspectors/

U.S. Secret Service

950 H Street N.W.
Washington, DC 20001
Phone: (202) 406-5708
Internet: www.ustreas.gov/

Violence Against Women Office

810 7th Street, N.W.
Washington, DC 20531
Phone: (202) 616-8894
Internet: www.usdoj.gov/vawo/

GLOSSARY OF COMMON LEGAL TERMS

Accessory. In criminal law, a person not present at the commission of an offense who commands, advises, instigates, or conceals the offense.

Acquittal. Discharge of a person from a charge of guilt. A person is acquitted when a jury returns a verdict of not guilty. A person may also be acquitted when a judge determines that there is insufficient evidence to convict him or that a violation of due process precludes a fair trial.

Adjudicate. To determine finally by the exercise of judicial authority to decide a case.

Affidavit. A voluntary written statement of facts or charges affirmed under oath.

A fortiori. With stronger force, with more reason.

Amicus curiae. A friend of the court, a person not a party to litigation, who volunteers or is invited by the court to give his views on a case.

Appeal. To take a case to a higher court for review. Generally, a party losing in a trial court may appeal once to an appellate court as a matter of right. If he loses in the appellate court, appeal to a higher court is within the discretion of the higher court. Most appeals to the U.S. Supreme Court are within the Court's discretion. However, when the highest court in a state rules that a U.S. statute is unconstitutional or upholds a state statute against the claim that it is unconstitutional, appeal to the Supreme Court is a matter of right.

Appellant. The party that appeals a lower court decision to a higher court.

Appellee. One who has an interest in upholding the decision of a lower court and is compelled to respond when the case is appealed to a higher court by the appellant.

Arraignment. The formal process of charging a person with a crime, reading him the charge, asking whether he pleads guilty or not guilty, and entering his plea.

Attainder, Bill of. A legislative act pronouncing a particular individual guilty of a crime without trial or conviction and imposing a sentence upon him.

Bail. The security, usually money, given as assurance of a prisoner's due appearance at a designated time and place (as in court) in order to procure in the interim his release from jail.

Bailiff. A minor officer of a court usually serving as an usher or a messenger.

Brief. A document prepared by counsel to serve as the basis for an argument in court, setting out the facts of and the legal arguments in support of his case.

Burden of proof. The need or duty of affirmatively proving a fact or facts that are disputed.

Case law. The law as defined by previously decided cases, distinct from statutes and other sources of law.

Cause. A case, suit, litigation, or action, civil or criminal.

Certiorari, Writ of. A writ issued from the Supreme Court, at its discretion, to order a lower court to prepare the record of a case and send it to the Supreme Court for review.

Civil law. Body of law dealing with the private rights of individuals, as distinguished from criminal law.

Class action. A lawsuit brought by one person or group on behalf of all persons similarly situated.

Code. A collection of laws, arranged systematically.

Comity. Courtesy, respect; usually used in the legal sense to refer to the proper relationship between state and federal courts.

Common law. Collection of principles and rules of action, particularly from unwritten English law, which derive their authority from longstanding usage and custom or from courts recognizing and enforcing these customs. Sometimes used synonymously with case law.

Consent decree. A court-sanctioned agreement settling a legal dispute and entered into by the consent of the parties.

Contempt (civil and criminal). Civil contempt consists in the failure to do something that the party is ordered by the court to do for the benefit of another party. Criminal contempt occurs when a person willfully exhibits disrespect for the court or obstructs the administration of justice.

Conviction. Final judgment or sentence that the defendant is guilty as charged.

Criminal law. That branch of law which deals with the enforcement of laws and the punishment of persons who, by breaking laws, commit crimes.

Declaratory judgment. A court pronouncement declaring a legal right or interpretation but not ordering a specific action.

De facto. In fact, in reality.

Defendant. In a civil action, the party denying or defending itself against charges brought by a plaintiff. In a criminal action, the person indicted for commission of an offense.

De jure. As a result of law, as a result of official action.

Deposition. Oral testimony from a witness taken out of court in response to written or oral questions, committed to writing, and intended to be used in the preparation of a case.

Dicta. See Obiter dictum.

Dismissal. Order disposing of a case without a trial.

Docket. See Trial docket.

Due process. Fair and regular procedure. The Fifth and Fourteenth Amendments guarantee persons that they will not be deprived of life, liberty, or property by the government until fair and usual procedures have been followed.

Error, Writ of. A writ issued from an appeals court to a lower court requiring it to send to the appeals court the record of a case in which it has entered a final judgment and which the appeals court will now review for error.

Ex parte. Only from, or on, one side. Application to a court for some ruling or action on behalf of only one party.

Ex post facto. After the fact; an ex post facto law makes an action a crime after it has already been committed, or otherwise changes the legal consequences of some past action.

Ex rel. Upon information from; usually used to describe legal proceedings begun by an official in the name of the state, but at the instigation of, and with information from, a private individual interested in the matter.

Grand jury. Group of twelve to twenty-three persons impaneled to hear in private evidence presented by the state against persons accused of crime and to issue indictments when a majority of the jurors find probable cause to believe that the accused has committed a crime. Called a "grand" jury because it comprises a greater number of persons than a "petit" jury.

Grand jury report. A public report released by a grand jury after an investigation into activities of public officials that fall short of criminal actions. Grand jury reports are often called "presentments."

Guilty. A word used by a defendant in entering a plea or by a jury in returning a verdict, indicating that the defendant is legally responsible as charged for a crime or other wrongdoing.

Habeas corpus. Literally, "you have the body"; a writ issued to inquire whether a person is lawfully imprisoned or detained. The writ demands that the persons holding the prisoner justify his detention or release him.

Immunity. A grant of exemption from prosecution in return for evidence or testimony.

In camera. "In chambers." Refers to court hearings in private without spectators.

In forma pauperis. In the manner of a pauper, without liability for court costs.

In personam. Done or directed against a particular person.

In re. In the affair of, concerning. Frequent title of judicial proceedings in which there are no adversaries, but rather where the matter itself—as a bankrupt's estate—requires judicial action.

In rem. Done or directed against the thing, not the person.

Indictment. A formal written statement based on evidence presented by the prosecutor from a grand jury decided by a majority vote, charging one or more persons with specified offenses.

Information. A written set of accusations, similar to an indictment, but filed directly by a prosecutor.

Injunction. A court order prohibiting the person to whom it is directed from performing a particular act.

Interlocutory decree. A provisional decision of the court that temporarily settles an intervening matter before completion of a legal action.

Judgment. Official decision of a court based on the rights and claims of the parties to a case that was submitted for determination.

Jurisdiction. The power of a court to hear a case in question, which exists when the proper parties are present, and when the point to be decided is within the issues authorized to be handled by the particular court.

Juries. See Grand jury and Petit jury.

Magistrate. A judicial officer having jurisdiction to try minor criminal cases and conduct preliminary examinations of persons charged with serious crimes.

Mandamus. "We command." An order issued from a superior court directing a lower court or other authority to perform a particular act.

Moot. Unsettled, undecided. A moot question is also one that is no longer material; a moot case is one that has become hypothetical.

Motion. Written or oral application to a court or a judge to obtain a rule or an order.

Nolo contendere. "I will not contest it." A plea entered by a defendant at the discretion of the judge with the same legal effect as a plea of guilty, but it may not be cited in other proceedings as an admission of guilt.

Obiter dictum. Statement by a judge or justice expressing an opinion and included with, but not essential to, an opinion resolving a case before the court. Dicta are not necessarily binding in future cases.

Parole. A conditional release from imprisonment under conditions that if the prisoner abides by the law and other restrictions that may be placed upon him, he will not have to serve the remainder of his sentence. But if he does not abide by specified rules, he will be returned to prison.

Per curiam. "By the court." An unsigned opinion of the court or an opinion written by the whole court.

Petit jury. A trial jury, originally a panel of twelve persons who tried to reach a unanimous verdict on questions of fact in criminal and civil proceedings. Since 1970 the Supreme Court has upheld the legality of state juries with fewer than twelve persons. Because it comprises fewer persons than a "grand" jury, it is called a "petit" jury.

Petitioner. One who files a petition with a court seeking action or relief, including a plaintiff or an appellant. But a petitioner is also a person who files for other court action where charges are not necessarily made; for example, a party may petition the court for an order requiring another person or party to produce documents. The opposite party is called the respondent.

When a writ of certiorari is granted by the Supreme Court, the parties to the case are called petitioner and respondent in contrast to the appellant and appellee terms used in an appeal.

Plaintiff. A party who brings a civil action or sues to obtain a remedy for injury to his rights. The party against whom action is brought is termed the defendant.

Plea bargaining. Negotiations between prosecutors and the defendant aimed at exchanging a plea of guilty from the defendant for concessions by the prosecutors, such as reduction of charges or a request for leniency.

Pleas. See Guilty and Nolo contendere.

Presentment. See Grand jury report.

Prima facie. At first sight; referring to a fact or other evidence presumably sufficient to establish a defense or a claim unless otherwise contradicted.

Probation. Process under which a person convicted of an offense, usually a first offense, receives a suspended sentence and is given his freedom, usually under the guardianship of a probation officer.

Quash. To overthrow, annul, or vacate; as to quash a subpoena.

Recognizance. An obligation entered into before a court or magistrate requiring the performance of a specified act—usually to appear in court at a later date. It is an alternative to bail for pretrial release.

Remand. To send back. In the event of a decision being remanded, it is sent back by a higher court to the court from which it came for further action.

Respondent. One who is compelled to answer the claims or questions posed in court by a petitioner. A defendant and an appellee may be called respondents, but the term also includes those parties who answer in court during actions where charges are not necessarily brought or where the Supreme Court has granted a writ of certiorari.

Seriatim. Separately, individually, one by one.

Stare decisis. "Let the decision stand." The principle of adherence to settled cases, the doctrine that principles of law established in earlier judicial decisions should be accepted as authoritative in similar subsequent cases.

Statute. A written law enacted by a legislature. A collection of statutes for a particular governmental division is called a code.

Stay. To halt or suspend further judicial proceedings.

Subpoena. An order to present one's self before a grand jury, court, or legislative hearing.

Subpoena duces tecum. An order to produce specified documents or papers.

Tort. An injury or wrong to the person or property of another.

Transactional immunity. Protects a witness from prosecution for any offense mentioned in or related to his testimony, regardless of independent evidence against him.

Trial docket. A calendar prepared by the clerks of the court listing the cases set to be tried.

Use immunity. Protects a witness against the use of his own testimony against him in prosecution.

Vacate. To make void, annul, or rescind.

Writ. A written court order commanding the designated recipient to perform or not perform acts specified in the order.

SELECTED BIBLIOGRAPHY

Barnes, Patricia G. *Desk Reference on American Courts: Over 500 Answers to Frequently Asked Questions about Our State and Federal Courts.* Washington, D.C.: CQ Press, 2000.

Beck, Alan J. *Prisoners in 1999.* Washington, D.C.: U.S. Department of Justice, Bureau of Justice Statistics, 2000.

Bilchik, Shay. *Minorities in the Juvenile Justice System,* 1999 National Report Series, Juvenile Justice Bulletin. Washington, D.C.: Office of Juvenile Justice and Delinquency Prevention, U.S. Department of Justice (December, 1999).

Bonczar, Thomas P., and Lauren E. Glaze. *Probation and Parole in the United States, 1998.* Washington, D.C.: U.S. Department of Justice, Bureau of Justice Statistics, 1999.

Bureau of Justice Statistics. *Compendium of Federal Justice Statistics, 1998.* Washington, D.C.: U.S. Department of Justice, 2000.

Bureau of Justice Statistics. *Sourcebook of Criminal Justice Statistics, 1998.* Washington, D.C.: U.S. Department of Justice, 1999.

Clear, Todd R., and George F. Cole. *American Corrections,* 5th ed. Belmont, Calif.: Wadsworth Publishing Co., 2000.

Cooter, Robert, and Thomas Ulen. *Law and Economics,* 2d ed. Reading, Mass.: Addison-Wesley Educational Publishers, Inc. 1997.

Dempsey, John S. *An Introduction to Policing,* 2d ed. Belmont, Calif.: Wadsworth Publishing Co., 1999.

Durham, Jennifer L. *Crime in America: A Reference Handbook.* Contemporary World Issues Series, Santa Barbara, Calif.: ABC-CLIO, 1996.

Federal Bureau of Investigation. *Crime in the United States, 1998.* Washington, D.C.: U.S. Government Printing Office, 1999.

Friedman, Lawrence M. *A History of American Law,* 2d ed. New York: Simon and Schuster, 1985.

Gaines, Larry K., et al. *Criminal Justice in Action.* Belmont, Calif.: Wadsworth / Thomson Learning, 1999.

Gifford, Lea S., et al. *Justice Expenditure and Employment in the United States, 1995.* Washington, D.C.: Bureau of Justice Statistics, U.S. Department of Justice, 1999.

Goldberg, Andrew, and Brian A. Reaves. *Sheriff's Department, 1997.* Washington, D.C.: Bureau of Justice Statistics, U.S. Department of Justice, 2000.

Henderson, Dwight F. *Congress, Courts, and Criminals: The Development of Federal Criminal Law 1801–1829.* Westport, Conn.: Greenwood Press, 1985.

Hirsh, Adam J., "From Pillory to Penitentiary: The Rise of Criminal Incarceration in Early Massachusetts." 80 *Michigan Law Review* 1179 (1982).

Kelling, George L. "Broken Windows and Police Discretion," National Institute of Justice Research Report. Washington, D.C.: U.S. Department of Justice, October 1999.

Kaufman, Philip, et al. *Indicators of School Crime and Safety, 1999.* Washington, D.C.: U.S. Department of Education and U.S. Department of Justice, 1999.

Levinson, Laurie L. *Criminal Law.* New York: Aspen Law and Business, 1997.

Mecham, Ralph L. *Judicial Business of the United States Courts, 1999.* Washington, D.C.: Administrative Office of the United States Courts, 2000.

Meskell, Matthew W. "An American Resolution: The History of Prisons in the United States from 1777 to 1877." 51 *Stanford Law Review* 839 (1999).

Ostrom, Brian J., and Neal B. Kauder. *Examining the Work of State Courts, 1998: A National Perspective from the Court Statistics Project.* Williamsburg, Va.: National Center for State Courts, 1999.

Reaves, Brian A., and Andrew L. Goldberg. *Law Enforcement Management and Administrative Statistics, 1997: Data for Individual State and Local Agencies with 100 or More Officers.* Washington, D.C.: Bureau of Justice Statistics, U.S. Department of Justice, 1999.

Reaves, Brian A., and Andrew L. Goldberg. *Local Police Departments, 1997.* Washington, D.C.: Bureau of Justice Statistics, U.S. Department of Justice, 2000.

Rennison, Callie Marie. *Criminal Victmization 1998: Changes 1997–98 with Trends 1993–98.* Washington, D.C.: Bureau of Justice Statistics, National Crime Victimization Survey, U.S. Department of Justice, 1999.

Rossiter, Clinton. *1787: The Grand Convention: The Creation of the United States.* New York: Mentor Books, 1968.

Rothman, David J. *The Discovery of the Asylum.* Boston, Mass.: Little Brown, 1971.

Rottman, David B., et al. *State Court Organization, 1998.* Washington, D.C.: Bureau of Justice Statistics, U.S. Department of Justice, 2000.

Samaha, Joel. *Criminal Justice,* 5th ed. Belmont, Calif.: Wadsworth / Thomson Learning, 2000.

Smith, Patricia, ed. *The Nature and Process of Law.* New York: Oxford University Press, 1993.

Snell, Tracy L. *Capital Punishment, 1998.* Washington, D.C.: Bureau of Justice Statistics, U.S. Department of Justice, 1999.

Snyder, Howard N., and Melissa Sickmund. *Juvenile Offenders and Victims: 1999 National Report* Washington, D.C.: Office of Juvenile Justice and Delinquency Prevention, 1999.

U.S. Department of Justice and National Institute of Justice. *Use of Force by Police: Overview of National and Local Data.* Washington, D.C.: U.S. Government Printing Office, 1999.

Vila, Bryan, and Cynthia Morris. *The Role of Police in American Society: A Documentary History.* Westport, Conn.: Greenwood Press, 1999.

Witt, Elder. *The Supreme Court A to Z: A Ready Reference Encyclopedia,* rev. ed. Washington, D.C.: Congressional Quarterly, 1994.

INDEX

NOTE: Numbers refer to question numbers, not to page numbers. Italics indicate figures or tables related to a question.

Beatles, 19, 359
Bell v. Wolfish (1979), 498
Bench trial, 215
Bench warrant, 161
Benefit of clergy forbidden in capital executions, 20
Berkman, Alexander, 325
Bertillon, Alfonse, 329
Beyond a reasonable doubt, 215
  insanity and, 231
Bias crimes. *See* Hate crimes
Bicycle patrols, 318, 389, 391
Bill of Rights, 5, 120
  applied to states, 153, 174, 179
  due process and, 15, 153
Billy club, 317
Billy the Kid, 385
Bin Laden, Usama, 17
Bird Man of Alcatraz, 497
Black, Hugo L., 237, 284
Blackboard Jungle (film), 114
Blacks. *See* African Americans
Blood alcohol concentration (BAC), 98, 174
Blood samples, required, 174
Blue flu, 414
Blue wall of silence, 427
Blumstein, Alfred, 118
Bobbies, 317
Body armor. *See* Soft body armor
Body searches, 351, 498
Bomb disposal units, 434
Bombing incidents and Internet, 362
Bonaparte, Charles J., 352
Booking, 184
Boomer, Timothy, 105
Boot camps, 242, 464, 516, 531
Booth, John Wilkes, 330
Bootleggers, 35
Border crossing and search and seizure, 178
Border Patrol agents, 365
Boston Police Strike, 415
Bounds v. Smith (1977), 503
Bounty hunters, 164
Brady, James, 121, 229
Brady Handgun Violence Prevention Act (1993), 121
Brady v. Maryland (1863), 214
Brady v. United States (1970), 200
Branch-Davidians, 363
Branding, as a criminal punishment, 444

Bratton, William J., 392
Bribery of judge, 20
Brinegar v. United States (1949), 157
British criminal justice system, 2
Brockway, Zebulon, 450
Broken window theory, 392
Brönnimann, Roland, 108
Buck Rogers time, 537
Bullet and gun identification, 209
Bulletproof vests. *See* Soft body armor
Bundy, Ted, 19
Burden of production, 226
Burden of proof, 151, 226, 231, 255
Bureau of Alcohol, Tobacco, and Firearms (ATF), 121, 209, 346, 360
Bureau of Indian Affairs (BIA), 276, 346
Bureau of Justice Statistics, 37
Bureau of Prisons, 1, 345, 448, 504
Burger, Warren E., 153
Burglary, 40, 88, 89
Bush, George H. W., 61, 253, 323, 535

California Supreme Court, 19
Campus police, 388
Capital punishment. *See* Death penalty
Capitol Police, 345
Capone, Al "Scarface," 361, 374
Carnegie, Andrew, 325
Carnival Cruise Lines, and crime reporting, 378
Case disposition, methods of, 195
CCC Information Service, 96
Centers for Disease Control and Prevention, 71, 72
Chain of custody, 206
Chandler v. Fretag (1954), 170
Chapman et al. v. California (1967), 257
Charge bargaining, 196
Charges, statement of to defendant, 184
Checks and balances, federal government, 2
Chief law enforcement officer of U.S., 349
Chief of police/police commissioner, 383
Chief postal inspector, 376

Child abuse, 109, 133, 276, 283, 514
Child abuse units, 434
Child molesters, 246, 530
Child pornography, 176
Child victimizers, 135
Child welfare standards, 294
Children, missing, 86
Children's Bureau, 294
Church of the New Song, 524
Citation, 33
Cities, safe vs. dangerous, 53
Citizen's arrest, 164
City courts, 277
City Crime Rankings, 53
Civil commitment, 530
Civil death doctrine, 529
Civil defense units, 434
Civil law, 7
Civil protection orders, 74
Civil Rights Act (1967), 250
Civil rights and prisoners, 472, 473, 474
Civil Rights Division, Department of Justice, 348
Civilian review boards, 428
Clanton, Ike, 326
Cleared or solved crimes, 47
Clemency, presidential, 252, 253, 348
Clemency powers, 251
Clergy, benefit of, forbidden in capital executions, 20
Cleveland, Grover, 367
Clinton, Bill, 98, 124, 160, 254, 349
Clinton, Hillary Rodham, 254
Clothing, model in lineup, 174
Cocaine, 32, 50
Code of silence, 427
Code of the West, 326
Codes of law, model, 28
Coerced confessions, 151, 167, 257
Coercion or duress as defense, 227
Coker v. Georgia (1977), 547
Columbine High School (Littleton, Col.), 132
Common law of England, 6, 8
Commonwealth attorney, 282
Community corrections, vs. incarceration, 454
Community Oriented Policing Services (COPS), 389
Community policing, 50, 389, 393

NOTE: Numbers refer to question numbers, not to page numbers. Italics indicate figures or tables related to a question.

Community preservation, vs. crime fighting, 392
Community risk, bail and, 191
Community service, 242
Commutations, vs. pardons, 251
Compelled testimony, 225
Competent to stand trial, 181, 228
Comprehensive Community Corrections Act (1973), 454
Computerization, criminal records, 207
Concurrent jurisdiction statute, juveniles in adult courts, 306
Condoms, availability in prisons, 511
Confederate prison, Andersonville, 476
Confessions, forced, 151, 167, 257
Confront witnesses, right to, 5
Congregate system, 447
Conjugal visits in prisons, 508
Consent, age of, 73
Consent decrees of prisoners, 472
Conspiracy, 24
Constable-and-watch system, 316
Constitutional rights, 21, 472
Consumer Litigation Office, Department of Justice, 348
Contempt of court, 174
Controlled substances, 32. *See also* Illegal drugs
Convict labor, 490
Conviction override, 251
Cook County (Ill.) Juvenile Court, 294
Coolidge, Calvin, 34, 415
Cooper v. Pate (1964), 472
Corporal punishment, 444, 471
Corporate Crime Reporter, 108
Corporate criminals, 108
Correctional officers, 468, 475, 477, 478, 480
    assaults by inmates, 481, 482
Correctional systems, 1, 436
    Americans with Disabilities Act (1990) and, 516
    boot camps, 242, 464, 531
    classification of prisoners for placement, 450
    colonial America, 444
    conjugal visits, 508
    conjugate system, 447
    cost of, 142, 492, 493
    crime rates effect on, 443

drug and alcohol treatment programs, 519
    employees and employment, 475, 479
    gender segregation, 445, 467
    goals, 437, 438
    hospice care, 513
    incarceration rates, 440, 460
    inmate educational opportunities, 501
    inmate grievances, 475
    inmate law libraries, 503
    inmate lawsuits against, 453
    mental illness and, 515
    military prisons, 458
    mission statement, 438
    prison governance, 475
    prison overcrowding, 193, 239, 453, 462, 484
    probation, 531
    rape and coercive sex, 511
    reform of, 470
    security levels, 449
    separate system and solitary confinement, 447
    sexually transmitted diseases, 510, 511
    smoking policies, 517
    supermax prisons, 452
    tracking and location systems, 498
    visitor drug testing, 521
    wardens, 475
    See also Prison inmates
Corrections Corporation of America, 487, 489
Corruption of politicians and police, 35, 425
Counsel, right to assistance of. *See* Right to counsel
Count bargaining, 196
Counterfeiting, 2, 3, 20, 367, 369
Counter-Terrorism Rewards Program, 17
County attorney, 282
County of Sacramento v. Lewis (1998), 433
Court appointed attorney, 284. *See also* Right to counsel
Court martial, 275
Court of Appeals, 1, 260
Court of Appeals for the Armed Forces, 1

Court of Appeals for the Federal Circuit, 1
Court of common pleas, 261, 277
Court of International Trade, 260
Court of last resort, 1, 261
Courtroom security, 384
Courts
    appellate, 1, 260, 261
    common pleas, 261, 277
    cost of, 142, 264, 265
    federal appeal, 260
    Federal Claims, 260
    International Trade, 260
    of last resort, 1, 261
    of limited jurisdiction, 261
    local, 277
    municipal/magistrates, 261, 277
    patents and trades, 1
    public trust and, 292
    state general jurisdiction, 261, 280
    states appeals, 291
    system of, 1
    trial, 297
Crime, 6
    Bill of Rights and, 5
    congressional power to define and punish, 4
    elements of, 23
    fighting, vs. community preservation, 392, 403
    mapping, 394
    policy, 37
    reporting, vs. arrests, 315
Crime Index, 23, 41, 443. *See also* Uniform Crime Reporting Program (UCR)
Crime in the United States, 38
Crime prevention, 128, 145, 395, 488
Crime rates, 43, 50, 112, 113, 314, 443
Crime scene procedures, 418
Crime victim. *See* Victims of crime
Crime Victims Fund, 136
Crimes
    age not responsible for, 80
    arrests, 54
    causes of, 109
    classification of, 25
    cleared or solved rates, 47
    cost to insurance industry, 149
    cost to society, 146
    drug addiction and, 115

NOTE: Numbers refer to question numbers, not to page numbers. Italics indicate figures or tables related to a question.

NOTE: *Numbers refer to question numbers, not to page numbers. Italics indicate figures or tables related to a question.*

federal courts and, 263, 268
juveniles, 465
Drug units, 434
Drugs
  addiction to, 62
  crime and, 56, 57, 115
  driving and, 98
  handguns and, 118
  high school students and, 116
  illegal, 350
  possession of, 56
  prisoners and, 518
  smuggling, 351
  testing for, 416, 521, 531
  trafficking, 351, 364
  "war" metaphor, vs. disease
    control, 61
Drummond, Edward, 232
Drunk driving, 64, 98, 99, 101, 174
Due process of law, 15. *See also*
  Right to due process of law
DUI, 98
Dukakis, Michael, 535
Duncan v. Louisiana (1968), 153
Duress or coercion as defense, 227
Durham Rule, 229
Dusky v. United States (1960), 228
Duty-related causes of death,
  police, 332
DWI, 98

Earmarking, as criminal
  punishment, 444
Earp, Wyatt, 326
Eastern State Penitentiary of
  Pennsylvania, 447
Eclatarian faith, 524
Economic status and equal justice,
  258, 285
Economy and crime rates, 113
Education and recidivism, 501
Educational level of prison
  inmates, statistics, 500
Effective assistance of counsel, 224
Eighth Amendment, 191
  Coker v. Georgia (1977), 547
  electric chair, 562
  Ford v. Wainright (1986), 552
  Furman v. Georgia (1972), 540
  Gregg v. Georgia (1976), 540
  Holt v. Sarver (1971), 470
  Louisiana v. Resweber (1947),
    546
  solitary confinement and, 447

Stanford v. Kentucky (1989), 554
Thompson v. Oklahoma (1988),
  554
Weems v. United States (1910),
  471
Eiseman-Scheir, Ruth, 358
El Paso Intelligence Center (EPIC),
  364
Elderly citizens, fear and, 139
Elderly prisoners, 512
Electrocution, 550, 562. *See also*
  Cruel and unusual punishment
Electronic monitoring, 242
Elmira Reformatory, 450
English common law, 6, 8
Entrapment, 176, 227
Environment and Natural
  Resources Division, Department
  of Justice, 348
Equal justice and economic status,
  258, 285
Equal protection, 13, 151. *See also*
  Sixth Amendment
Error, harmless, 257
Escapes from prison, 525, 526
Evidence, 203
  admissible, 204
  biological, 181
  chain of custody, 206
  circumstantial, 203
  defendants' right to disclosure
    of, 214
  DNA, 211, 212
  hearsay, 204
  illegally obtained, 153
  impression, 203
  inadmissible, 180, 256
  indirect, 203
  physical, 174, 203, 206
  polygraph results, 210
  preponderance of, 7
  stale, 164
Ex Parte Hull (1941), 472
Ex post facto (after-the-fact) laws, 9
Excessive bail, 191
Excessive fines, 5, 14
Excessive force, 421
Exclusionary rule, 179, 536
Executions, 546
  of federal prisoners, 557
  of innocent persons, 551
  insanity and, 552
  juveniles, foreign countries, 555
  mentally retarded and, 553

methods of, *550*
mistakes in procedure, 560, 562
public present, 560
of Sioux Nation, 556
statistics, 548, *548,* 549
Executive clemency, 251
Exhibits of physical evidence at
  trial, 203
Extradition, 2, 21, 22
Eyewitness testimony, 213

Failure to act, 23
Falsifying a record or process, 20
Family, as defined by FBI, 75
Family violence. *See* Domestic
  violence
Family Violence, Attorney
  General's Task Force on, 136
Faretta v. California (1975), 223
FBI. *See* Federal Bureau of
  Investigation (FBI)
Fear for safety, 131, 139
Federal Bureau of Investigation
  (FBI), 1, 17, 269, 345, 352
  agents, number of, 356
  agents, race and gender statistics,
    355
  Branch-Davidians and, 363
  case statistics, 346
  crime statistics responsibility, 38
  Drug Enforcement
    Administration and, 352
  fingerprint identification system,
    207, 329, 352
  Roosevelt, Theodore, and, 327
  Ten Most Wanted Fugitives, 357
Federal Claims Court, 260
Federal court system, 1, 260, 266,
  267, 268
Federal criminal laws vs. state
  criminal laws, 21
Federal government and crime, 1,
  312
Federal judges, 260
Federal judicial system and
  Constitution, 2
Federal Jury Selection and Service
  Act (1968), 220
Federal Prison Industries, Inc., 490
Federal prison facilities, locations
  of (map), *436*
Federal prisons, 1, *436,* 455, 456
Federal prosecutors, 269
Federal Rules of Evidence, 205

NOTE: Numbers refer to question numbers, not to page numbers. Italics indicate figures or tables related to a question.

NOTE: *Numbers refer to question numbers, not to page numbers. Italics indicate figures or tables related to a question.*

NOTE: *Numbers refer to question numbers, not to page numbers. Italics indicate figures or tables related to a question.*

Justice of the peace courts, 277
Justifiable homicides, 341
Juvenile correctional systems, 1, 464
Juvenile crimes
  court filings vs. arrest rates, 302
  demographics and, 111
  drugs and, 115, 118
  handguns and, 118, 119
  murder statistics, 83
  prosecuted in adult courts, 304, 305
  statistics, change in, 82
Juvenile Justice and Delinquency Prevention, Office of (OJJDP), 86, 110, 298
Juvenile justice systems, 1, 293, 294, 304
  adult criminal justice systems, compared to, 78, 306
  probation and, 303
  statistics, 295, 296, 297
  structure (flow chart), *297*
Juvenile units in adult prisons, 434
Juveniles
  in adult criminal justice system, 78, 297, 304, 305, 306, 307
  in adult prisons, 450
  age definitions, 293, 306, 554
  arrest statistics by age, 81
  case statistics by disposition of case, 303
  crimes against underreported, 134
  criminal records, confidentiality of, 85
  death penalty and, 554
  detention, statistics by race, 299
  detention and, 300
  disposition of cases, statistics, 84
  executions and foreign countries, 555
  in federal courts, 306
  as murder victims, 133
  rehabilitation vs. incarceration, 464
  sentence lengths in adult courts, 308
  state prison population statistics, 465

Kaczynski, Theodore, 19
Kanka, Megan, 246
Kansas v. Hendricks (1997), 530

Karpis, Alvin, 353
Kastigar v. United States (1972), 225
Katz v. United States (1967), 177
Kelling, George L., 392
Kendall, George, 539
Kennedy, John F., 19, 353
Kennedy, Robert F., 121
Kentucky, 560
Kenya, bombing of U.S. embassy in, 17
Key, Francis Scott, 233
Key, Philip Barton, 233
Kinetic interviewing, 210
King, Martin Luther, Jr., 19, 121, 353
King, Rodney G., 390, 428
"Knowing" action, 29
Koehler, Arthur, 377
Koresh, David, 363
Krist, Gary Steven, 358

La Cosa Nostra, 106
Lack-of-respect crimes, 104. *See also* Hate crimes
Larceny-thefts, 90, 91, 92, 97
  juvenile arrests, 81
  women and, 93
Lathrop, Julia, 294
Laundering, money, 370
Law enforcement agencies, 1, 313, 345, 383, 384
  depoliticizing, 327
  officer training, 407
  oldest, 347
  See also Police departments
Law Enforcement and Administration of Justice, President's Commission on (1967), 454
Law Enforcement Assistance Administration (LEAA), 207
Law enforcement in colonial America, 315
Law enforcement officers, 33, 312, 314, 327, 343
  crime scenes procedures, 418
  duty-related death statistics, 332, 333, 334, 335
  federal agencies and, 345
  statistics, 344, 399
  See also Police officers
Law libraries in prison, 503
Law of Nations, 2

Laws, interpretation of, 6
Lesser of two evils, as defense, 235
Lethal injection, 550, 562
Lewis v. Casey (1996), 503
Liability, 23, 27, 31, 73
Lie detectors. *See* Polygraphs
Limited jurisdiction courts, statistics, 281
Lincoln, Abraham, 254, 330, 556, 559
Lindbergh, Charles, Jr., 19, 377
Lindsey, Ben B., 294
Lineups, 173, 174
Little Crow, Chief, 556
Local courts, 277
Lockdowns, 452
Locking doors for protection, 128
Lombroso, Cesare, 109
Lopez v. United States (1995), 312
Los Angeles Police Department, 390
Louima, Abner, 427
Low security in prisons, 449
Lynch, Charles, 250
Lynching, 250

Mackle, Barbara Jane, 358
MADD (Mothers Against Drunk Driving), 100
Mafia, 106
Magistrates, 261, 277
Magna Carta, 13, 15
Mail fraud, 376
Mail-related crimes, 376
Maiming on U.S. property, 20
Mala in se crimes (immoral or dangerous), 6
Mala prohibita crimes (prohibited by law), 6
Malloy v. Hogan (1964), 153
Mandatory sentencing laws, 241
Mannain, Karl, 338
Manslaughter, 20, 63, 64, 65
Manson, Charles, 19
Mapp, Dollree, 179
Mapp v. Ohio (1961), 153, 179
Marine patrols, 391
Marital rape, 71, 72
Marks for good behavior, 450
Marshals Service, 345, 346, 347, 375, 448
Marston, William, 210
Mass execution, Sioux Nation, 556
Material elements of crime, 32

NOTE: Numbers refer to question numbers, not to page numbers. Italics indicate figures or tables related to a question.

NOTE: Numbers refer to question numbers, not to page numbers. Italics indicate figures or tables related to a question.

NOTE: Numbers refer to question numbers, not to page numbers. Italics indicate figures or tables related to a question.

NOTE: Numbers refer to question numbers, not to page numbers. Italics indicate figures or tables related to a question.

NOTE: Numbers refer to question numbers, not to page numbers. Italics indicate figures or tables related to a question.

NOTE: *Numbers refer to question numbers, not to page numbers. Italics indicate figures or tables related to a question.*

NOTE: Numbers refer to question numbers, not to page numbers. Italics indicate figures or tables related to a question.